A
DICTIONARY
OF
ECONOMICS
AND
COMMERCE

A
DICTIONARY
OF
ECONOMICS
AND
COMMERCE

T. E. Daniel-Kagbare

authorHOUSE®

AuthorHouse™ LLC
1663 Liberty Drive
Bloomington, IN 47403
www.authorhouse.com
Phone: 1-800-839-8640

Published by AuthorHouse   03/13/2014

ISBN: 978-1-4918-6253-7 (sc)
ISBN: 978-1-4918-6254-4 (e)

Library of Congress Control Number: 2014902987

Contents

Preface

This book is designed as a standard text as well as reference book of basic economics and commerce. It covers the requirements of those preparing for Ordinary level examinations, in a way that should stimulate further interest in its subject. It is also a handy resource material for the curious, intelligent reader—student, professional, executive, businessman etc.—and indeed anyone intent on making sense of the economic environment.

A

Absolute Advantage: a measure of efficiency of resource use. Given two economic units, e.g. two individuals, firms or countries, one is said to have an absolute advantage over the other, if it can produce more with the same amount of resources. However, whether or not there is a basis for specialization depends on the respective opportunity costs of engaging in the activities by the two economic units. For, while a Managing Director might be a better cook than his paid chef, he might find it more profitable to pay for the services of the chef, because his time will be more valuably spent on his directorial activities than on cooking. That is, what the director will gain in one hour spent cooking is not up to what he will have to pay the chef, and the same amount of time will produce much more if he were to concentrate or specialize on his directorial responsibilities. This means that, though he has an absolute advantage in management and cooking over the chef, he has a comparative disadvantage, in terms of opportunity cost, in cooking.

In international trade theory, a country which has an absolute advantage in producing a good is able to produce that good more efficiently (more output per unit of input) than any other country. In the table below, country A can produce good X and good Y more efficiently than Country B, because it produces more of both from the same amount of input; it therefore has absolute advantage over Country B.

	Country A	Country B
Good X	100	20
Good Y	20	10

However, though Country A has absolute advantage over B, it has to forgo more units of X in order to produce an additional unit of Y; it incurs greater opportunity cost than B, as shown below:

	Country A	Country B
Good X	20/100 = 0.2B	10/20 = 0.5B
Good Y	100/20 = 5.0A	20/10 =2.0A

Country A has to give up 5 units of Y in order to produce an additional unit of X; country B has to give up only 2units. Therefore, though Country A has absolute advantage over country B, it has a *comparative disadvantage* in the production of good Y. It will therefore be better off specializing in the production of good X, and import good Y from country B.

Also see Comparative Advantage.

Abandonment: insured goods may be abandoned when i) they are completely destroyed, such that actual loss is unavoidable; or ii) the cost of repairing them exceeds their value.

Absolute Monopoly: a situation where the total output of a good or service, for which there is no substitute, is supplied by a single producer or supplier. However, this is theoretical, as there is hardly a good or service without a substitute.

Absorption: in a merger with a much larger company, a small company completely loses its identity, and becomes part of the larger one. The small company is said to have been absorbed by the larger one.

Acceptance: a bill of exchange may be referred to an acceptance once the debtor (drawee) accepts it by signing it.

Accident Insurance: see under Insurance, Types of.

Account Payee only: a cheque crossed in this way can only be paid into account of the payee written on it; it cannot be transferred to another by endorsement, as in the case with simple crossing. See Cheque Crossings

'Acid-test' Ratio: in Balance Sheet Analysis; current assets divided by current liabilities; it measures the extent to which a firm can meets its maturing short-term obligations. If ratio is less than 1, it could be an indicator of overtrading.

Act of God: an event outside of the human control, and which could not be foreseen and provided against—e.g. earthquake, lightening, storms, floods, etc. An 'Act of God' can activate a Force Majeure clause in a contract.

Actuarial Science: branch of statistics concerned with the calculation of risks, premiums, life expectancy, annuities as well as pension issues.

Actuary: an actuarial science practitioner.

Adam Smith (1723-90). Generally regarded as the founder of modern economics, Adam Smith was born in 1723 in Kirkaldy, Scotland. Educated at Glasgow College and at Oxford, he eventually gained the chair of moral philosophy at the University of Edinburgh. His great work, *An Inquiry into the Nature and Causes of the Wealth of Nations* was published in 1776, and its influence is still felt today in that in it Adam Smith advanced the argument that continue to be the basis for capitalism or free market economies. This is the notion that individuals are motivated not by altruism, but by self-interest. In pursing their own interests, however, they inadvertently advance the interest of society as a whole, led by "an invisible hand," in addressing the basic economic problems of resource allocation (*what to produce*), method of production (*how to produce*) and distribution (*for whom to produce*). This proposition was later to be challenged by Karl Marx who contended that these questions can best be addressed through a central planning authority. Thus Adam Smith became the ideological father of capitalism while Karl Marx that of communism.

Ad *valorem* tax: a tax based on a percentage of the value of the item taxed. For example, 10% as import duty of the value of an imported item; the amount paid as tax depends on the value of the item taxed. Compare *specific tax*.

Value of item taxed	Tax rate	Tax paid
10, 000.00	10%	1,000.00
50,000.00	10%	5,000.00

Advertising: the art of informing or persuading consumers about a product or service. Advertising may be informative or persuasive. *Informative advertising* seeks to make consumers aware of a product, its sources of supply, price, features, uses, etc. *Persuasive advertising* aims at convincing consumers to buy a product instead of others by suggesting its superiority in one form or another. Advertising is a part of selling, which itself is a part of marketing, and can make the difference in terms of profitability between products in a competitive market. Ultimately, persuasive advertising seeks to create brand loyalty and thereby secure a measure of monopoly power which may be seen in the degree of elasticity of demand of the product concerned. Successful advertising campaigns create strong lasting impressions of lifestyle, status, reliability, etc., in the mind of consumers to bias buying decisions in favour of the particular product. Where advertising is successful, loyalty to a particular brand may be strong enough to make demand relatively inelastic even for a product in competitive demand. However, for advertising to be successful in making a difference in the market share, it must be backed up with an adequate distribution system to ensure availability of the product upon demand.

Advertising is mostly overt, utilizing electronic media (Television, radio, the internet), print media (newspapers, magazines, newsletters, journals, catalogues, handbills/fliers), and bill boards. It may sometimes take on subtle forms as when messages are embedded in films, sponsorship of public events and infomercials.

Methods of Advertising
Direct Advertising: this method is used to target a particular segment of the market e.g. a demographic segment e.g. students, women, parents; or industry or institutions e.g. schools. An advertisement of baking flour, for example, will target bakers and bakeries to ensure effectiveness.

Indirect Advertising: this is used to advertise goods such as bread, soap, salt, water etc., that relate to the general public.

Advertising Media
1. Electronic Media: Television, Radio, Cinemas, Internet. Advantages: Electronic media can be used to target literate and illiterate audience. Television appeals to both visual and hearing senses. Disadvantages: copies cannot be stored for reference; electronic adverts lasts for brief minutes or even seconds and audience can miss parts of the message.

2. Print Media: Newspapers and Magazines, Catalogues, Billboards, Handbills and flyers
Advantages: copies of the advert can be stored for further reference; Copies of printed material can be dispersed over wide areas; products advertised can be seen and visually appreciated. Disadvantages: only literate persons can be targeted through printed advertisement.

Consumer Protection in Advertising
In Nigeria, advertising is regulated by the Advertising Practitioners Council of Nigeria (APCON), through its Advertising Standards Panel (APS), which ensures that advertisements comply with the laws of the Federation as well as the Code of the Advertising Practice and Sales Promotions.

The mandate of the APS is to (a) Ensure that only decent, honest, and truthful advertisements are exposed to the Nigerian public; (b) Ensure that advertisements exposed to the public reflect a high sense of social responsibility; (c) Ensure that advertisements conform to the principle of fair competition; (d) Enhance public confidence in advertising and espouse the values of good advertising.

APCON works with other government agencies such as:
- Consumer Protection Council (CPC).
- National Broadcasting Commission, (NBC).
- National Food and Drug Administration and Control (NAFDAC),
- Standards Organization of Nigeria (SON),
- Nigeria Communications Commission, (NCC)

Certain categories of advertisement must get clearance from the ASP.

The following associations also assist to ensure professional conduct in advertising in Nigeria:
1. Advertiser's Association of Nigeria (ADVAN)
2. Association of Advert Agencies of Nigeria, (AAAN)
3. Outdoor Advertising Association of Nigeria (OAAN)

Advice Note: see under Commercial Documents.

African Development Bank (AfDB): is a multilateral development finance institution, based in Abidjan, Ivory Coast, established in 1963 by 23 independent African countries, to finance economic development and social projects, programmes in its African member countries. The other two organizations in the AfDB Group are the African Development Fund (ADF) and the Nigerian Trust Fund (NTF). AfDB funds come from member subscriptions, borrowings from international money and capital markets as well as income generated from investments, loan repayments and donors. The AfDB provides non-concessional loans with financial charges that reflect the direct market cost of funds. Its loan maturity generally ranges from 12 to 20 years, including a five-year grace period.

AfDB member countries are of two categories, regional (i. e. African) member countries and non-regional (i.e. non-African) member countries. Regional member countries are Algeria, Angola, Benin, Botswana, Burkina-Faso, Burundi, Cameroon, Cape-Verde, Central African Republic, Chad, Comoros, Congo, D.R. Congo, Côte d'Ivoire, Djibouti, Egypt, Eritrea, Equatorial Guinea, Ethiopia, Gabon, The Gambia, Ghana, Guinea, Guinea-Bissau, Kenya, Lesotho, Liberia, Libya, Madagascar, Malawi, Mali, Mauritania, Mauritius, Morocco, Mozambique, Namibia, Niger, Nigeria, Rwanda, Sao Tome and Principe, Senegal, Seychelles, Sierra Leone, Somalia, South Africa, Sudan, Swaziland, Tanzania, Togo, Tunisia, Uganda, Zambia and Zimbabwe.

Non-regional member countries: Argentina, Austria, Belgium, Brazil, Canada, China, Denmark, Finland, France, Germany, India, Italy, Japan, Korea, Kuwait, Netherlands, Norway, Portugal, Saudi Arabia, Spain, Sweden, Switzerland, the United Kingdom and the United States of America. AfDB is the NEPAD lead agency for infrastructure development.

See African Development Fund (ADF) and Nigeria Trust Fund (NTF).

African Finance Corporation (AFC): a Nigerian-pioneered multilateral financial institution, set up in 2007, with the mission to finance infrastructure, industrial and financial assets in Africa. Since inception AFC has invested in heavy industries and infrastructure across Africa, including $4m in Kenyan cement factory, co-financing of US$160million construction of cross-country highways in South Africa, US$240million co-financing of fibre optic cable project from Portugal to South Africa, and wind farm project in Cape Verde among others. The Nigerian government through the Central Bank of Nigeria holds the majority of the shares (42.5 per cent). Other members are Chad, Ghana, Guinea-Bissau, The Gambia, Sierra Leone, Liberia, and Guinea. The AFC is based in Lagos.

After-Sale Service: see under Customer Service.

Age Distribution: refers to the way in which the population is spread among the different age groups or brackets:

Under 20	Dependent Population
20-64	Working population/ labour force
65 and above	Dependent population

The age distribution is of economic, political and social importance. It determines, for example, what types of goods will be in demand, and thus what will be produced; the size of the labour force, dependency ratio and migration policy.

Agency: the legal relationship that exist between a principal and his agent wherein the agent has the principal's authority to bring the principal into legal relationship with third parties.

Agent: a person given authority by another, the principal, to enter into a contract on the principal's behalf. Any person or legal entity with contractual capacity may appoint an agent.

Duties of an Agent
1. Loyalty and good faith to the principal
2. Reasonable care, skill and diligence
3. Accountability
4. Personal responsibility
5. Inform and update the principal

Duties an Agent Cannot Perform
1. Vote for the principal
2. Execute an affidavit for the principal
3. Testify in court on behalf of the principal
4. Make a will for the principal

Types of Agents
a. Universal Agent: He can act on behalf of the principal in any business or transaction. They are usually appointed expressly by a **power of attorney.**
b. General Agent: one authorized to act in all matters of a particular business on behalf of the principal. For example, an agent may be empowered to do everything pertaining to the importation and sale of good on behalf of an offshore manufacturer.
c. Special Agent: authorized to act for a particular purpose.
d. Commission Agent: this is a trader who buys and sells on commission.
e. Broker: an agent with expert knowledge, for which he are employed by a principal to act on his behalf. Examples are insurance broker, stock broker, etc.
f. Del Credere Agent: this type of agent guarantees payment to his principal

whether he makes a loss or not. His remuneration—the del credere commission—is therefore higher than that received by other agents.

Appointment of Agents
a. By Expressly: when an agent is appointed verbally (word of mouth) or in writing, i.e. by a letter of appointment, by the principal.
b. By Implication: where a person by conduct implies another person has authority to act on his behalf. A landlord, may be said to have implicitly appointed one of tenants as a caretaker-agent, where the landlord, overtime, has not objected to the tenant's actions and functions as a caretaker-agent.
c. By Necessity: Where someone is forced, due to an emergency or unforeseen circumstance, to act, for example, to preserve the asset of another, agency by necessity arises.

Aggregate Demand: the total demand of households, businesses, government and net exports in the economy.

AD = C + I + G + (X-M)

Where,
C = Households expenditure
I = Business investment expenditure
G = Government expenditure
X-M = Net Exports (Exports minus Imports)

The level of business activity is dependent on the level of aggregate demand. Weak aggregate demand would mean firms are not selling and inventories are piling up. This could lead to deflation and unemployment. In such instances, aggregate supply is higher than aggregate demand. According to Keynesian theory, this could persist unless the government intervenes to increase disposable income. This may be by reducing taxes or investment in, say, infrastructure. These would be injection into the circular flow of income, which would be amplified by the multiplier effect. Level of impact on national income would depend on the marginal propensity to consume (MPC), the higher the MPC, the higher the multiplier effect. Leakages such as taxation and savings reduce the multiplier by reducing consumption.

National Income is at equilibrium where aggregate demand is equal to aggregate supply.

Thus, macroeconomic management aims to avoid inflationary or deflationary gaps by ensuring aggregate demand is neither above nor below aggregate supply i.e. the sum of goods and services available in the market.

Agriculture: the production of animals, fishes, forestry and farming. As a form of primary production, its percentage of national output declines as the economic develops.

The importance of agriculture in laying the foundation for self-sustaining economic development can be seen historically in the following instances:

Britain: Agricultural reform foreran the industrial revolution in Britain with the 'enclosures' which reorganized rural land; brought thousands of previously untended acres into cultivation and made mechanized agriculture widespread.

China: Agricultural reforms were among the first reforms in 1978 that set China on the path of high economic growth. According to Prof. Gregory Chow of Princeton, 'the success of agricultural reforms in China provided the economic foundation for reforms in other sectors."

Types of Agriculture
1. Crop farming: this is the cultivation of cash (cotton, cocoa, rubber, coffee, kola, etc.) and food (cassava, maize, rice, yam, etc.) crops.
2. Livestock farming: the rearing of animals.
3. Fishing: the rearing and catching of fish.
4. Forestry: the growing of trees and the tapping of forestry resources.

7.2 Systems of Agriculture
1. Peasant Farming: This is farming carried out by rural farmers on communal land, using rudimentary tools like hoes, cutlass, etc. It is mainly subsistence agriculture that is, for the provision of food for the household, with the surplus, if any, sold. The work is done by members of the family with occasional hiring of labour.
2. Plantation Farming: This is highly capitalistic or capital-intensive farming covering several acres of land, using machines, improved seedlings and fertilizers for large scale production. A plantation is often a small community unto itself with living quarters, water and power supply, etc. Crops planted include cocoa, oil palm, coffee, cotton, rice, etc. They are usually by large corporations or government agencies e.g. Nigerian Institute for Oil Palm Research (NIFOR), Edo State, the various Agricultural Development Authorities in various states of the federation, etc.
3. Mechanized Farming: this is also capital-intensive farming with extensive use of machines such as tractors, planters, harvesters, irrigators, herbicide and insecticide spraying machines, etc. to produce food or cash crops on a large or commercial scale. Mechanized farming has gained popularity among with the elite as many public officers have retired into mechanized farming.
4. Co-operative Farming: This where individuals pool their resources together in order to go into mechanized farming, obtain loans, effective marketing, etc. This enables them to produce on a large scale by deriving economies of large scale production.

Importance of Agriculture
1. Source of food: food crops from agriculture provide food for the teeming population.
2. Source of Raw Materials: inputs in the form of cocoa, rubber, cotton, etc. provide much needed raw material for industry to transform into finished products.
3. Source of Employment: in countries where the industrial sector is developed, agriculture provides over 60 per cent of employment for the populace.
4. Source of Foreign Exchange: export of cash crops such as cocoa, rubber, etc., provide much needed foreign exchange for the government of developing countries.
5. Source of Government Revenue: taxes and duties paid by farmers

provide the government with revenue required for development.

6. Market for industrial goods: agriculture provides market for industrial goods like cutlasses, hoes, tractors, fertilizers, herbicides etc.

7. Contribution to National Income: where the industrial sector is still under-developed, agriculture contributes the greater percentage to national income.

Problems of Agriculture in West Africa

1. The Use of Crude Implements: the use of sophisticated implements is highly limited. Instead simple implements like cutlass, hoes, etc. are used. As a result productivity is low.

2. Conservatism: many farmers are not exposed to modern methods and have a negative attitude to new approaches and techniques. They refuse to learn new, more efficient ways and techniques to enhance their crop yield and output.

3. Land Tenure System: Land is communally owned and cannot be sold to outsiders. This means that farmers do not have long-term claim to land, and this discourages long-term land improvement. This makes it hard for people to acquire large enough land for commercial farming purposes. Communal ownership also means that they cannot use the land as collateral security.

4. Illiteracy: Knowledge of modern techniques and methods of farming is highly limited because many farmers cannot read the pamphlets prepared by Ministries of Agriculture and other agricultural extension services.

5. Small farms: Due to land fragmentation size of farms is small,

useful only for subsistent farming. This means that farming is mostly done on small scale, and therefore economies of scale are not enjoyed.

7. Poor transportation System: Much farm produce perish before they reach the market because of bad roads.

8. Lack of Storage Facilities: Large scale production is limited by inadequate storage facilities like silos and cold rooms. For this reason many produce perish due to lack of preservation.

9. Lack of Credit Facilities: Large scale is limited as it hard for farmers to obtain loans from banks. Shortage of capital makes it impossible to acquire the machinery and equipment required for large scale farming.

10. Pest attacks: Poor yield results from persistent pest attacks on crops and farm produce.

11. Poor Marketing System: There is no organized marketing system for food crops to enable farmers effectively market their produce. This is discourages farmers who lack the resources to undertake their own marketing.

12. Unfavourable Climate: In some parts of West Africa, there are long dry seasons making the area arid and unsuitable for agriculture whereas in some other areas there is heavy rainfall leading to flooding and erosion, also unsuitable for sustained farming.

Marketing of Agricultural Commodities

The marketing of agricultural commodities involve the purchasing, grading and distribution of farm produce. This is carried out in two major ways.

1. The informal system of marketing of agricultural commodities involving many individual middlemen who buy and aggregate relatively small quantities from farmers in diverse areas and sell to wholesalers in urban centres.

2. There is also the formal marketing system involving commodity boards, and agents. Historically, the formal marketing system dates back to the colonial days when the marketing boards were established by the colonial government during the Second Word War. The marketing boards were abolished in 1976, and replaced in 1977 by the following 7 commodity boards: Cocoa Board (for cocoa, coffee and tea), Groundnut Board (groundnut, ginger and soyabeans among others), Cotton Board, Rubber Board, Palm Produce Board, Grains Board, and Root Crops Board (tubers and root crops). These boards performed the following functions with respect to their commodities:

   a. Marketing of produce: This entailed the buying, grading, transportation and sale of farm produce. They buy from farmers or from farmers' co-operative societies. Grading is the process of ensuring that produce are of the right standard and quality and this role is carried out by licensed agents appointed by the boards. The boards also ensured ready market for the sale of farm produce locally and for export. It was also the responsibility of the boards to move these goods from the farm to the market.

   b. Fixing and Stabilization of prices: Prices at which produce were to be bought were set by the commodity boards at the beginning of the season. Prices were set moderately so that the board below the prevailing world market prices, enabling it to accumulate a surplus during periods of high world prices. Such reserves enabled the board to pay farmers a fair price for their output during periods of unusually low world prices. In this way, the board ensured price stability by minimizing fluctuation in commodity prices.

   c. Financing Research: commodity boards funded research into improved crop yields and seeds, better farming techniques, etc.

   d. Implementation of Governments' Agricultural Policy: The commodity boards serve to ensure that government's intention for the development and growth of agriculture was carried out.

3. 5. Middlemen: The commodity boards performed the functions of middlemen like buying in bulk, storage, transportation, credit facilities, etc.

Agricultural Policies in Nigeria

The aim of government agricultural policies in Nigeria can be summarized in thus:

1. Self-sufficiency in food production.
2. Supply of agricultural inputs or raw materials for industry.
3. Export of agricultural produce for foreign exchange.

4. To provide as source of employment opportunities.

To achieve these objectives the government has implemented several programs at various times. Some of these programs are discussed below:

Extension services: trained personnel are sent out to teach, train inform and farmers of new farming methods, application of fertilizer and insecticides, as well as farm management practices. Many State governments and the Federal government, through their ministries of agriculture and sometimes in conjunction with the World Bank, carry out extension services whereby farmers are trained on new farming techniques, improved seeds and fertilizers and insecticides are distributed.

The objective is to improve productivity of the farmers.

Commercial Agriculture Credit Scheme: N200billion fund for medium and large scale farmers set up in 2009.

River Basin Development Authorities: by 1985 there was a total of 19 river basin development authorities were set up. The objective behind this program was to commercialize or bring development to the rural areas where they were established to encourage the use of machinery in farming.

Operation Feed the Nation: This program was started by the Obasanjo military administration in 1976; the objective was to bring about self-sufficiency in food production by encouraging subsistent farming. Simple farm implements were supplied at subsidized rates.

Green Revolution: this was the successor to the Operation Feed the Nation (OFN); under this program, more River Basin Development Authorities were established. The scope was expanded beyond individual to include corporate organizations; corporate organizations were encouraged to invest in agriculture by incentives such as tax relief and duty-free importation of farm machinery. Agricultural infrastructure such as processing and storage facilities was built.

Like the OFN, it failed to achieve its objective.

Agricultural Development Projects: these projects are jointly financed by the World Bank across the federation. Agricultural inputs such as insecticides, fertilizers, improved seedlings are distributed alongside with improvement in rural infrastructure.

Encouragement of Foreign Investment: the government has amended the Nigerian Enterprises Promotion Decree to enable 100% foreign ownership of enterprises. This has made it possible for Zimbabwean farmers, for example, to be re-settled in Kwara State.

Prospects for Agriculture in West Africa

The realization that minerals deposits are finite has made West African countries to appreciate the need to focus on agriculture. More attention and resources are allocated to the development of agriculture at all government levels. This is shown clearly in the various government programs discussed above.

Aids to Trade: this refers to services such as advertising, communication, transportation, banking, insurance, and warehousing that facilitate or enable trading. They are also referred to as ancillaries to trade.

Amalgamation: the coming together of two or more businesses. This is one of the ways in which a business enterprise grows, the other being by organic growth. The reasons for amalgamation include taking advantages of economies of large scale production and to command a larger share of the market. The new company secures a stronger footing in the industry. Merging or amalgamating companies may integrate vertically or horizontally. A new corporate identity may or may not result depending on the relative sizes of the merging companies. An amalgamation may be described as an *absorption* where a small or distressed company completely loses its corporate identity to a larger one. A new corporate identity may result where the merging companies compare in size. For example, Stanbic IBTC Bank emerged from the amalgamation of Stanbic Bank and IBTC Chartered Bank, while the Oceanic Bank was absorbed by Ecobank.

In order to bring about an amalgamation, the shareholders of the merging business exchange their shares for shares in the new company in an agreed ratio.

Amortization: the process of gradually paying off a debt (principal plus interest) over a period of time by setting aside a certain sum at regular intervals e.g. monthly. Instead of amortization, a debtor may decide to pay the interest during the period and then pay the principal at the end of the tenor.

Annual General Meeting (AGM): mandatory meeting of shareholders of a limited liability company (private or public)

held once a year at which the financial statements of the company (including the Balance Sheet and Profit and Loss Account) and report of the directors are presented by the directors to shareholders. Agenda of an AGM typically include the election of directors, approval of remuneration of the auditors; election of auditors; approval of dividend proposed by the directors.

Arbitrage: the act of buying at lower prices in one market and selling in another where prices are higher. It is common on foreign exchange markets and quoted shares, where a differential exist in rates between trading centres or exchanges. If a broker in Lagos observes a difference in the price of a share which is quoted on the Lagos Stock Exchange and Johannesburg Stock Exchange, he may buy in one and sell in the other where the price is higher. Arbitrage is facilitated by technology which makes instantaneous communication possible, and serves to equalize prices in different markets. Convergence of international markets, due to globalization, has greatly reduced opportunities for arbitrage.

Arbitration: the process of settling a dispute by referring the matter to competent person instead of going to court. Parties to the dispute must approve of the arbitrator, who may be a person with legal education e.g. a barrister or a judge. Industrial disputes involving employers and trade unions are often settled through arbitration.

Arithmetic Mean: an average, along with the median and mode that measures the central tendency of a set of data.

Calculation: given a set of data, comprising of 5 numbers, e.g., 43, 48, 50, 45, 49, the mean is calculated thus:

$$\frac{43+48+50+45+49}{5} = \frac{235}{5} = 47$$

The calculated figure, 47, is a summary figure around which the 5 numbers in the distribution tend towards. It is therefore representative of the distribution.

Advantages
a. It is representative of the distribution because every value in the distribution is used to calculate it.
b. It is useful for further statistical analysis. For, example, in the calculation of the standard deviation.
c. Easy to understand

Disadvantages
a. It may be unduly affected by extreme values. Take the following distribution, for example, 50, 45, 55, 50, 51, 500. The mean of the distribution, (751/6), 125.17, does not truly reflect the distribution, because it is unduly affected by the extreme value of 500.
b. It may sometimes give a ridiculous figure. For example, the mean number of employees per department may be 3.7 employees.

Articles of Association: document of limited liability or joint-stock company which contains the internal rules of the company e.g. the rights of shareholders, borrowing powers, procedures for meetings, audits, etc. See Memorandum of Association.

Articles of Partnership: see Deed of Partnership

Assurance, Life: see **Life Assurance:** insurance policy taken as a protection against loss caused by death. Life assurance is used instead of life insurance as there is no uncertainty involved as it is certain a person will die and a claim made, the only question being a matter of when. The principle of *Utmost Good Faith (uberrimae fides)* requires that the assured's health condition be truthfully stated, otherwise the insurer may disclaim liability. Life assurance is an effective savings which provides a cushion of protection to dependants. The main types of life assurance are:

1. *Term Assurance*: this policy is for an agreed period: the policy lapses if the assured survives the term specified, and no claim is payable. There are variations of term assurance including Decreasing Term, whereby the sum assured decreases annually; Convertible Term, which may be converted to a Whole Life policy or Endowment assurance.
2. *Whole Life Assurance:* the premium is payable throughout the life of the assured and the sum assured is payable at death.
3. *Endowment Policy*: under this policy, if the assured survives a specified period, he is paid the sum assured, if not it is paid to his dependants.

Auction: a process of sale whereby buyers bid competitively until a final, highest bid is reached, and the item is sold to the highest bidder. Prior to the bid, the goods are put on *show*, and interested parties would inspect the items and make assessment to inform their bids. This method is used in organized commodity or produce exchanges, and specialist agents/brokers, with good knowledge of the items on offer, are commissioned by interested buyers, in assess and bid on their behalf.

Audit: the examination of a company's books of accounts, by a qualified person i.e. a certified accountant, to see if the accounts have been properly kept and if they give 'true and fair view' of the affairs of the company. Audit reports give a seal of authenticity to any set of accounts, and are required by third parties, e.g., investors or prospective creditors, to inform their decisions. Public companies are required by the Companies and Allied Matters Act to annually carry out an audit and to publish the report along with their annual financial statements.

Austerity Measures: deflationary belt-tightening, cost reduction policies in order to bring its expenditure within its means or revenue. This cost reduction drive is carried out alongside measures to increase the revenue i.e. tax increases. It entails rationalization of government expenditures, cuts on social services—including health, education, reduction and removal of subsidies and subventions to public corporations.

Below is sample of austerity measures:

a. Elimination or reduction of subsidies including petroleum products.

b. Increase in utility tariffs such as electricity, water rates

c. Increase in or introduction of tuition fees in schools.

d. Reduction in the minimum wage; wage bill cuts/caps, including the salaries of education, health and other public sector workers;

e. Recruitment freeze or embargo of employment the civil service;

f. Retrenchment of civil servants;

g. Rationalizing and cuts in social benefits and safety nets;

h. Pension reform e.g. increase in retirement age; equalizing of retirement age for men and women;

i. Healthcare reform e.g. payment for medicines in public hospitals;

j. Liberalization of labour laws: making it easy to hire and fire; reduction in notice periods, rise in the lawful redundancy rate, softening of unfair dismissal rules and cuts in severance pay entitlements;

k. Closure and merger of public corporations;

l. Commercialization and privatization of some public corporations;

m. Introduction of, or increase in the rate of value added tax;

n. Increase in income tax rates for all income categories.

These measures may be the last recourse to stem chronic or persistent budget deficit, dwindling revenue and mounting government debt which has combined to undermine the confidence of trading partners, creditors and investors in the economy.

Austerity measures may be self-imposed by the government in order to pre-empt the inevitable in view of its dwindling revenue or it may be forced to do so by international finance institutions like the International Monetary Fund as a pre-condition for financial assistance.

The result of these measures is mass retrenchment, shortage of essential commodities, and high unemployment.

The economy invariably goes into a severe recession in the midst of credit crunch, low aggregate demand and low investment.

THEORETICAL BASIS: Two prominent economists, John Maynard Keynes and Friedrich Hayek, held opposing views about what to do about the combination of chronic budget and balance of payment deficits that can put an economy in a state of coma. While Keynes and Keynesians (like Nobel laureates like Paul Krugman and Joseph Stiglitz) are of the opinion that at such times what is required is a stimulus package to revive aggregate demand; spending cuts, tax hikes, and higher interest rates is counter-productive in the face of mass unemployment; austerity should wait until a strong recovery is well under way. In his words, "The boom, not the slump, is the right time for austerity . . ." The government should not bother about balancing the budget while the economy is in recession; to do so would prolong the recession; it should spend, e.g. in public works, tax less and induce low interest rates, to stimulate the economy out of the recession so as to inspire the confidence of households, firms and investors.

In contrast to the Keynesian stimulus, Hayek, Joseph Schumpeter and others of the Austrian School advocated austerity, to "purge the economic system of its excesses". According to them, unemployment and general depression result from a previous unsustainable episode of 'easy money' due to misallocation of capital.

The merits of both views can only be considered in the context of the particular economies concerned and the underlying factors leading to the economic slump. And it is a germane question whether both views are necessarily mutually exclusive.

It is debatable whether the circumstances of African economies in the 1980s were the same as European economies, such as Ireland, Spain, and Greece, in 2012. There is hardly any question that the circumstances that put many countries in Africa in a position for austerity measures to be pushed down their throats arose out of systemic misuse and waste of capital resources and an unsustainable pattern of consumption. And that those issues needed to be addressed, if the boom-bust cycle was to be broken. And, if that was the case, the question arises whether it makes any sense for the patient to be bled to death—by way of austerity measures—in order to cure the disease. The real problem is the grandstanding by ideologues on both sides.

Keynes' view was the theoretical foundation for the New Deal program that rescued United States of America's economy from the Great Depression in the 1930s. Also aggressive public spending got the German economy back on its feet from the ravages of high unemployment and hyperinflation in the same decade. In more recent times the American administration revived the economy from the near-depression precipitated by the financial crisis of 2008, by a stimulus package of historic proportions.

In contrast, Hayek's view, which was forced down the throats of African and Latin American countries in the 1980s and some Eurozone countries in 2010s, cannot claim the same results. Perhaps this was more of a reflection of a lack of a forceful, visionary political leadership in these countries at these critical times in their history when a sense of belief was generally lacking and despair was prevalent.

The argument for austerity is that it is brought about by a set of factors and circumstances and a mode of thinking and outlook that must be corrected if the boom-bust cycle is to be avoided, as a prelude to reforms that will put the economy on the path of self-sustaining growth and development. In that sense, the fiscal difficulties and crises that necessitates austerity measures are an indication of a culture of waste of scarce resources typified by the misuse and embezzlement of national borrowing/debt; an unsustainable import bill, predominantly made up of consumer goods subsidized by an over-valued exchange rate; over-staffed, wasteful public corporations; an over-regulated business terrain that does not reward competitive use of scarce resources and that generally over-powers bureaucrats and connected individuals over investors and entrepreneurs; an economic system characterized by structural rigidities that render market forces ineffective, etc. The net effect of these factors is an unsustainable level of national debt; an un-dynamic business environment that barely creates value and does not generate jobs, a bloated public service; high import bills; dependence on the export of a primary product for foreign exchange and low government tax revenue. This mixture is triggered ultimately by a shock that precipitates the road to austerity: a significant fall in the price of exports, resulting in drastic fall in foreign exchange revenue (the case of most Africa countries) or financial crisis that impact the country's banking system (the case of some European countries).

Austerity Measures in Nigeria

Austerity measures were first imposed in Nigeria in 1978 following the fall in crude oil prices, and the attendant near-fiscal crises that ensued.

However, when crude oil prices revived in 1979, the successor civilian government abandoned these policies but instead went on an external borrowing frenzy and (import) consumption pattern that soon proved unsustainable. Crude oil collapsed in 1980, and the country was practically grounded. Fiscal crisis soon followed as the government could not pay its workers for months, schools were shut as teachers went on strike, hospitals ran out of essential drugs, contractors could not be paid; it was hard pressed to meet its obligations to trading partners and service its debts.

The resulting balance of payments deficit, budget deficit, and shortage of foreign exchange forced the government to approach the IMF. The government rejected the stringent IMF conditions for assistance, but decided to initiate the austerity measures under the Economic Stabilization Act in 1982, in its bid for credibility in the international finance community. The government lacked the political will to implement the measures which remained no more than a statement of intentions. The intended improvement in finances was not achieved and the succeeding government further tightened these measures and took steps to implement them, to no avail; government finances continued their slide along with confidence of creditors and trading partners.

The economic situation was worsening by the day with high unemployment, shortage of essential commodities and low investment and business activities: the economy was in severe recession.

Against this backdrop, the government acquiesced to the long-spurned IMF-inspired Structural Adjustment Program in 1986.

Autarky (Autarchy): Economic self-sufficiency; the concept of a country depending on itself to produce its needs as much as possible as opposed to interdependence with other countries by participation in international trade. Experience has shown that national output and standard of living are highly reduced in countries which followed this path compared to those that engaged in international trade.

Authorized Capital: the maximum amount of ordinary share capital a company can raise as stated in its Memorandum of Association. The shareholders may resolve to increase the authorized capital.

Automatic Stabilizers: income taxes and social security payments adjust without deliberate action (i.e. automatically) to moderate the level of the trade or business cycle i.e. the extent of recession/depression or boom. Taxes rise as business booms and unemployment benefits falls. During times of recession taxes fall, and unemployment benefits rise. These adjustments help to moderate the effects of the phases of the business cycle.

Autonomous Consumption: amount of consumption expenditure incurred for essential feeding, clothing, and shelter whether or not an individual is earning income or not. The amount required for basic needs may come from savings or from family and friends. Determinants of autonomous consumption include past savings/wealth, expectations of future income, credit availability, taxes, and social standards. It is mathematically indicated by the intercept of the consumption function. Given the consumption function, C = a + bY; a refers to autonomous consumption.

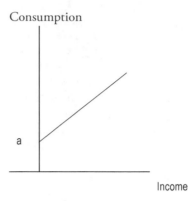

Consumption

a

Income

Average: measures of central tendency of a group of data. The three statistical averages are the mean, the median and the mode. Each of these can be used to summarize a set of data, for example, prices of a commodity, stock prices, with varying degrees of accuracy.

Average Cost: the cost per unit of output produced. It is mathematically expressed as Total Cost (TC) divided by Output (Q). AC=TC/Q.

Average Fixed Cost: Average fixed costs are total fixed costs divided by the number of units of output, that is, fixed cost per unit of output.

Average Revenue Product: In the theory of factor pricing, average revenue product is total revenue divided by the number of units of the factor employed.

Average Variable Cost: In the theory of the firm, the variable cost per unit of output; Total Variable Cost divided by the number of units of output

Average Propensity to Consume (APC): the proportion of income spent on goods and services. It indicates the amount of consumption expected at different levels of income. Mathematically expressed as the ratio of total consumption (C) to income (Y), i.e., C/Y

Average Propensity to Save (APS): the proportion of income not consumed. It indicates the expected amount of savings at different levels of income. Mathematically expressed as the ratio of total savings (S) to income (Y), i.e. S/Y

B

Backward Integration: businesses may grow from within i.e. organically or by integration with other businesses. Integration may be in the form of merger with or acquisition of other business firms. Backward integration is business expansion by acquisition of firms supplying it with raw materials or inputs e.g. when a business in a secondary production acquires a business in primary stage of production. Instance of this is where a tyre manufacturing company, for example, acquires controlling interest in a rubber plantation or shoe making firm buys over a tannery. Backward integration is a form of vertical integration. Compare forward integration and horizontal integration.

Bad Debt: a debt that is almost impossible to collect e.g. due to the circumstances of the debtor being unemployed or a company is facing liquidation. Prudent book keeping dictates the need to make provisions to cover possible occurrence of bad debts in the Profit and Loss Account so that the amount of bad debt is accommodated in the net profit. If bad debt is successfully collected, the provision is 'written back'.

Balance of Payments: The total of all inflows of money into a country from abroad less outflows during the same period. It is usually in the form of a statement showing the sum of payments and receipts of individuals, businesses, and government agencies located in a country, against those of all other countries. It has three main sections—the Current Account, the Capital Account and the Monetary Movement Account. Payments and receipts are of three kinds—i) the visible balance of trade of goods or merchandise ii) the invisible items consisting of services and iii) capital transfers. The visible balance of trade, i.e. payments and receipts for goods, e.g. machinery, raw materials, etc *plus* the invisible items comprising payments and receipts for services such as shipping and aviation, banking and insurance, tourism, etc. make up the Current Account of the balance of payments.

BALANCE OF PAYMENTS

1. **Current Account—(a)** *Balance of trade*
   Visible trade

Visible Imports
Vehicles..xxx
Industrial machinery...............................xxx
Industrial raw materials xxx
Consumer products.................................xxx
Total _____N3m
Visible Exports
Crude oil...xxx
Natural Gas xxx
Cocoa xxx
Groundnuts xxx
Total _____ N5.6m

Balance of Trade= **5.6m – 3.0m = 2. 6m**
(favourable)

Current Account—(b) Invisible Items
Invisible Imports___
Interests, dividends, profits paid.............xxx

Tourism xxx
Shipping & Aviation xxx
Banking & Insurance xxx
Total _____ N3.4m
Invisible Exports
Interests, dividends, etc. received xxx
Tourism xxx
Shipping & Aviation xxx
Banking & Insurance xxx
Total _____ N2.0m

Invisible trade balance
= N2.0 – 3.4m
= – N1.4m (unfavourable; deficit)

The Capital Account is made up of foreign direct investment (FDI), foreign portfolio investment (FPI), loans, dividends, remittances, etc. between the country and other countries.

2. Capital Account
—Capital Payments
a. Direct Investment in other countries...xxx
b. Loans to foreigners...............................xxx
c. Loan repayments to foreigners.............xxx
Total _____ N6.8m

—Capital Receipts
a. Foreign Direct Investment (FDI) xxx
b. Loans from foreigners xxx
d. External Borrowing xxx
Total _____ N3.0m

Balance of Payment
= balance of Current and Capital Accounts
= Total Exports – Total Imports
= 10.6 – 13.2 = – 2. 6m (unfavourable)

The Monetary Movement Account shows how the balance in the Current and Capital Accounts is settled. A deficit in the balance of payments may be settled or financed in the following ways:
  a) decrease in foreign reserves;

b) imports on credit;
c) selling or disposing foreign investments;
d) External borrowing e.g. from trading partners, banks or International Monetary Fund (IMF).
e) Grants and aid
f) Recalling loans

A surplus in the balance of payments may be used up in the following ways:
  a) Increasing foreign reserves;
  b) Increase in foreign investments;
  c) Lending to other countries;
  d) Paying off foreign debt;

Balance of Payments disequilibrium and adjustments:
In any given year, the balance of payment may be favourable (surplus) or unfavourable (deficit). Where a country records a persistent, year-on-year, deficit or surplus in its balance of payments position, it is facing a *fundamental or chronic disequilibrium*. A persistent surplus shows that the country is financially strong, and is not a serious cause for concern. A persistent deficit, however, implies that the country is facing a worsening financial position with its trading partners, and it must make urgent adjustments to remedy the situation.
Adjustments: The aim of these adjustments is to reduce imports and encourage exports.

Fiscal Policy:
Use of tariffs to restrict imports
  - Imposing or Increasing import duties;
  - Reduction or removal of export duties;
  - Subsidizing exports to make them cheaper in the international market;
  - *Deflationary policy*: in order to reduce aggregate demand, the government may take any of the following measures:
    a. Increase taxes;
    b. Reduce government expenditure.

Monetary Policy: deflationary monetary policy aimed at reducing aggregate demand involves the following measures:
1. Increase interest rates
2. Reduce bank lending

Import controls
3. Import quotas
4. Import licensing
5. Embargo on certain imports.

Exchange Controls: reduce the amount of foreign exchange available and thereby reducing the propensity to import.

Devaluation: where a combination of the above measures fails to bring about the desired outcome, the government may resort to the ultimate step of devaluation of its currency in relation to other currencies. This may be the case where the exchange value of the currency is thought to be overvalued relative to the productive capacity of the underlying economy of which it is supposed to be an index.

The success of the above measures depends on the elasticity of demand for imports; how quickly exports can be significantly increased and the absence of unintended undesirable effects e.g. unemployment and inflation that may result from deflationary measures and devaluation.

Balance of Trade: sub-section of a country's balance of payments dealing with exports and imports, that is, trade in goods (i.e., visible), over a given period.

Balance Sheet: a statement of the financial position of a business as at a date. It 'balances' the assets of a company against how the assets are financed in terms of equity or shareholders' funds, and long-term liabilities such as debentures, if any. It reflects the accounting equation:

Assets = Liabilities + Owners' Equity

Along with the Profit and Loss Account— which shows the results of business operations during a period—are the two principal financial statements of a company. They are connected by the balance of the Profit & Loss Account which is brought to the Balance Sheet.

Bank: primarily a bank is a financial institution which takes in (monetary) deposits for safekeeping. From this pool of deposits, a bank gives out loans. A bank, therefore, stands between savers and borrowers. This is the process of financial intermediation i.e. pooling savings from those with monetary surpluses (lenders) and making funds available to those in monetary deficit (borrowers), i.e., people in need of money or credit. By lending, banks create credit, which effectively is money, and thereby expand the money supply or contract it when their ability to create credit is constrained or restricted by monetary policy. Banks also facilitate commerce and exchange by enabling payments and settlement by means of cheques or transfers.

A bank's profit comes from the difference between the interest it pays to depositors and the interest it receives from borrowers. This difference between received and interest paid is called *spread*. Additional income comes from fees and from interest on investments.

Regulation: banks are highly regulated by the Central Bank and by special laws because the functions and activities of banks directly impact on the economy as a whole; also because government wants to ensure that depositors' funds are safe and properly managed at all times. Regulation is in the form of specification of minimum capital requirement, licensing and withdrawal of license, inspection, reporting, specified way of rendering accounts and returns, directives, moral suasion, etc. In Nigeria, all banks must comply with the provisions of the Banking and Other Financial Institutions Act (BOFIA), Anti-Money Laundry Act (AML) among others.

Economic Role Banks are a key feature of modern economy and society as distinct from a rudimentary barter economy. Commercial production will not be possible without credit and a means of payments and settlement between parties provided by banks. The functions of money are complemented by banks to enable commerce and exchange. Investment funds necessary for production and economic development are also made possible by the pooling of savings by banks.

The Structural Adjustment Programme greatly impacted the development of modern banking in Nigeria. The removal of exchange controls in 1986 and deregulation of interest rates in 1991 as well as the emphasis on indirect tools of monetary controls such as liquidity requirement, cash reserves, open market operations greatly boosted activities in the banking industry. The regulatory and supervisory framework was strengthened with a new Central Bank legislation which practically granted it autonomy.

Types: commercial banks: these take in deposits, give out loans and provide short-term loans. They deal in the money market. *Merchant/ investment banks* deal with corporate organizations enabling them raise funds from the money and capital markets.

They facilitate the issue of securities by underwriting new issues and provide advise on mergers and acquisitions (M&A).

Mortgage banks provide long-term loans at low rates of interest to finance real estate projects; these are the primary mortgage banks and the Federal Mortgage Bank of Nigeria

Microfinance banks cater to the finance needs of very small-scale traders and artisans.

Development banks or development finance institutions: these do not take in deposits but provide long-term capital from resources made available by government. Examples are the Nigeria Export-Import Bank (NEXIM), Bank of Industry, Federal Mortgage Bank of Nigeria (FMBN), Urban Development Bank of Nigeria and the Bank of Agriculture (formerly, the Nigeria Agricultural Co-operative and Rural Development Bank).

A universal bank is one that services of commercial and merchant banking services.

Banks, Assets and Liabilities of:
Assets of banks are usually listed in order of liquidity in the balance sheet, in the following order
1. Cash: coins and notes and balances with the Central Bank
2. Money at call or short notice
3. Treasury Bills and Commercial Bills
4. Stocks and Bonds
5. Advances: Loans and Overdrafts to customers
6. Investments
7. Fixed assets such as buildings, equipment, etc.

A typical balance sheet:

ACORN TRADING CO. LTD		**FSB BANK LTD**	
Balance Sheet		Balance Sheet	
As at December 31, 2010		As at December 31, 2010	

Assets	N'million	Assets	N'million
Fixed Assets		Cash and short-term funds	250
- Land	100	Due from other financial institutions	150
- Building	120	Deposit with central bank	25
- Motor Vehicles	50	Loans and Advances	100
- Furniture	100	Long-term investment	150
Current Assets		Fixed Assets	170
- Cash	75		
- Trade Debtors	250		
Total Assets	845		845
Financed By		Financed By	
Ordinary Shares		Ordinary Shares	
- Authorized	1,000.00	Authorized and paid	150.00
- Issued	500		
- Called-up	400		
- Paid-up	300		
5% Preference Shares	120	5% Preference Shares	20
10% Debentures	100	10% Debentures	5
Reserves	50	Reserves	50
Profit and Loss Account	25	Profit and Loss Account	5
	595		**230**
Liabilities		Liabilities	
Trade Creditors	80	Depositors funds	600
Creditors	70	Due to other banks	10
Tax payable	100	Tax payable	5
	845		**845**

The balance sheet of a bank is laid out in a way that emphasizes its liquidity.

Liabilities

1. Capital: shareholders' funds and reserves i.e. the total amount subscribed by shareholders as well as accumulated reserves or profits.
2. Depositors' funds: total of all customers' deposits with the bank.

Banks, Functions of

1. Acceptance of deposits: Customers do not have to keep their keep their cash at home and risk attendant theft and burglary. Instead moneys can be deposited in savings, current or fixed deposit account in a bank from which payment can be made to others.
2. Lending: banks grant credit facilities such as loans and overdrafts to their customers for which they charge fees and interest.
3. Agents of Payments: Banks offer a platform through which customers can pay third parties through cheques, money transfers, direct debits and standing orders.
4. Safe keeping of valuables: valuable items such documents, certificates, jewelries, etc.
5. Discounting of Bills: a bank may agree to pay the holder of a bill of exchange a discounted amount e.g. 95 percent or 85 per cent of the face value of the bill before maturity.

Bank Account, Types of

- Current Account: these are accounts on which withdrawals may be made at any time by means of cheques. Current account holders can draw cheques in favour of third parties, who may present the cheques for payment across the counter or into their own current account. The bank charges a commission-on-turnover (c.o.t) on withdrawals. Unlike a savings account, interest is not paid on the balance of a current account. The bank may allow a current account holder to overdraw on her balance i.e. an overdraft facility at an agreed rate of interest.
- Savings Account: interest is paid on the balance of a savings account but the holders cannot usually make withdrawals through third parties. Savings account holders are issued passbooks instead of cheques.
- Fixed Deposit Account: these are accounts in which a quantum sum may be placed for a fixed time or tenure such as 30, 60 or 90 days at an agreed rate of interest. At maturity, the money may be withdrawn or renewed or 'rolled over'. Withdrawals before the end of the tenure may attract a charge.
- Domiciliary Account: this is an account in which foreign currencies are deposited.

Banks: Credit Creation: banks create money by their lending activities. Banks are required to maintain only fraction of their deposits and lend out the remainder. This is specified by the Cash Ratio. A cash ratio of 10% means that a bank keeps N100.00 as cash and can give out N900.00 as loan out of every N1,000.00 deposit. The N900.00 may not be withdrawn as cash but may be used as deposit for another account from which a further N810.00 loan or credit may be created, and so on. Thus, from an initial N1, 000.00 deposit, given a cash ratio of 10%, the money supply may be expanded by a total credit of N10, 000.00.

Bank Consortium: a group of banks, formed for the purpose of availing credit, beyond the capacity of the individual banks. Where the funding requirement of a project is too large for a bank to single-handedly undertake, a consortium of banks may be formed to pool the required amount of funds between them.

Bank Draft: a cheque drawn on a bank. A debtor may pay a bank the cheque amount plus fee to draw on the bank to a pay a third party, where the third party is unwilling to accept a cheque in payment.

Banker's Acceptance: an order drawn on (and accepted by) a bank by a customer to pay a certain sum of money at a specified future date. Before the order is accepted, it is like a post-dated cheque. Once the bank accepts the order by endorsing or signing it, it assumes responsibility for payment, and it becomes a negotiable instrument which can be traded—by discounting—in the money market. BAs are short-term financial instruments or assets, usually with a maximum tenor of 365 days, used often in international trade. An importer may arrange and agree with his bank to write or draw on the bank, for example, to pay an exporter. In effect, the bank is extending the customer a short-term facility (loan), by keeping the acceptance and paying the exporter or guaranteeing the customer to borrow from the money market, by selling or re-discounting it.

Banker's Lien: the right of a bank to retain property deposited as collateral or security for a loan until the loan is repaid.

Bank of Agriculture: a development finance institution, under the Federal Ministry of Agriculture, targeted at providing finance for agricultural and rural development. The bank also works with cooperative societies to provide micro-credit at the local community level. The BOA, like the Bank of Industry, is intended as a key driver of the overall economic development strategy. Leadership and vision are however essential for the necessary impetus to deliver on its promises. The BOA evolved from the merger of the Peoples Bank of Nigeria and the Family Economic Advancement Program (FEAP) with the Nigerian Agricultural and Cooperative Bank (NACB). The new institution was called the Nigerian Agricultural Cooperative and Rural Development Bank in year 2000; the name was changed to Bank of Agriculture in 2010.

Bank of Industry (BOI): a Development Finance Institution (DFI), owned and funded by the Federal Government of Nigeria, established to provide long-term loans to large, medium, and small industries. It is result of the reconstruction of the Nigerian Industrial Development Bank and Nigerian Bank for Commerce and Industry (NBCI) in 2001. The bank has been instrumental in government's efforts to stimulate the development of the real economy through the administration of approved funds for certain industries such Power and Aviation Fund, Rice Processing Fund, Manufacturers Refinance Fund, Textile, Cotton and Garment Revival Fund among others, under which funds were advanced to qualifying enterprises at single-digit interest rate in the respective sectors. The bank also works with state governments in the disbursement and administration of funds, averaging N1billion per state, for the training and finance for micro, small and medium scale enterprises.

Between being administrator of government's intervention funds to being an enterprise incubator, the BOI's mandate is far from clearly defined. The BOI is also not adequately capitalized.

South Korea and China have shown how development banks can be successfully used to drive a country's industrial policy – supporting private enterprises which have already achieved a level of success on their own to make them world-class brands. The BOI's support to privately successful Nigerian brands like the Doyin Group, Omatek Computers, Honeywell, Zinox Computers, etc., e.g. to enable them become world players or lynchpin the country's industrialization, is not known.

See Development Finance Institutions.

Bank Note: paper money or currency issued by the central bank. Notes are, in effect, a promise to pay the bearer on demand the amount stated on the face of the note.

Bank Rate: the rate at which the Central Bank lends money to commercial banks; also the rate at which it discounts or re-discounts bills to financial institutions. The bank rate is central tool of monetary policy as it determines other interest rates in the economy. The Central Bank may increase or reduce the bank rate in order to encourage or discourage the creation of credit by banks, thereby directly affecting the money supply and the general price level.

Bank Run (bank panic): a series of unexpected cash withdrawals (i.e. many depositors withdraw cash almost simultaneously) caused by a sudden decline in depositor confidence or fear that the bank may go out of business. Since the cash reserve a bank keeps on hand is only a small fraction of its deposits, a large number of withdrawals in a short period of time can

deplete available cash and force the bank to close and possibly go out of business.

Bank for International Settlements (BIS): is the central bank of the world's leading central banks. BIS fosters co-operation between central banks in its mission to maintain international monetary and financial stability. The BIS was established in 1930 with headquarters in Basel, Switzerland. The Basel Accords—Basel I, Basel II, and Basel III—have become the benchmark for banking law, and regulation are issued under the auspices of the Basel Committee on Banking Supervision of the BIS.

Barter: a system whereby commodities are exchanged for other commodities. Barter is necessary when there is no article or commodity that is generally acceptable as a means of exchange. Before money came into use, for example, the farmer exchanged his produce e.g. maize, for the meat of the hunter. This was burdensome and difficult and therefore limited exchange. Due to the problems associated with barter, people tend to be self-reliant as much as possible in a barter economy; as a result specialization is practically non-existent and this greatly limited production and the standard of living that could be achieved in a barter economy.

Problems of Barter
1. *Double coincidence of wants:* for A and B to trade by barter, A must have to have what B want and B must have to want what A have. The farmer who wants some meat has to find someone who has meat and who also needs what the farmer has, e.g. maize. Until he finds such a person, exchange is not possible.

2. *No Rate of exchange*: there is no standard of value. For every transaction, there will be a long discussion and haggling to determine how many units of a commodity should be exchanged for another. For example, when the farmer finally finds a hunter who wants maize, they still have to determine how many cobs of maize should be exchanged for what quantity of meat. This problem is worse for services.

3. *Problem of movement or transportation:* this is the problem of moving what you have about in search of what you need. If what you have is bulky or heavy, you might not be able to move it around in search of something to exchange it for.

4. *Impossible to save:* saving is almost impossible with barter. Small perishable items cannot be stored while large, durable items would be difficult and costly to store.

5. *No standard of deferred payment*: credit transactions (borrowing and lending) are almost impossible in the barter economy. How can the creditor be assured that what he will be paid back, in the future, will be of the right quality?

6. *Limited Exchange/Production*: Under the barter system only subsistent production is possible. People will have to produce all their needs by themselves. There is no specialization which is necessary in order to produce on a large scale. Modern economic system of mass production is only made possible because of the surplus of output brought about by specialization/division of labour. The barter economy limits specialization and division of labour and thereby limits the total output. This is because people must produce as much of their own needs as possible. This makes it impossible to generate a surplus, thereby limiting the standard of living.

7. *Indivisibility*: if someone has a large commodity like a cow and he is in need of cooking salt, he faces a problem of how to go about exchanging what he has for what he wants.

Basic Economic Problem of Society: While human wants are unlimited, the means or resources to satisfy them are unlimited. There is therefore a problem of scarcity of resources relative to wants. This is a basic economic problem faced by all societies. In order to ensure that resources are efficiently allocated and used, the economic system must address the following questions:

- *What to Produce,*
- *How to Produce.*
- *For Whom to Produce.*

What to Produce addresses the problem of *resource allocation.* Given that resources are limited, producers and the government must decide which of our wants they must allocate resources to produce. Should we produce for export or for local consumption? Should more resources be allocated for defense or for education? If resources are not allocated efficiently, i.e. to produce what is required, wastage of resources will result, and the economic welfare of the citizens will be worse off. For example, if resources are allocated to produce what is not required, i.e. for which there is no demand, goods so produced will be unsold, and resources used in producing them wasted.

How to Produce addresses the problem of *technique or method of production*. Once we have decided what to produce, the next question is how do we produce? That is, how should the factors of production be combined in order to ensure that the best use is made of them? A method or technique of production is either *capital-intensive* or *labour-intensive*. A capital-intensive method uses more machines in production. A labour-intensive method uses mainly labour in the production process. The method used, at any point in time, will depend on which resource (labour or capital) is relatively cheaper.

For Whom to Produce addresses the problem of *distribution*. How do we distribute what we have produced? How should the various groups (owners of factors of production) in the society be rewarded? Should output be distributed equally or should it be based on individual contribution to production?

The way the basic questions are answered depends on the economic system in the society. In a capitalist or free-market economic system, the questions are resolved by the market or price mechanism. The interaction of demand and supply for goods and services as well as factors of production will determine what is produced; the greater the demand for a good or service, the more profitable it is to produce it; the more resources will be allocated to produce it. The method of production used depends on the relative prices of factors of production. If it is cheaper to use labour in production, a labour-intensive method of production will be used. Also, for distribution, i.e. person's share of what is produced, in a free market economy, is based on one's purchasing power or income.

In a socialist economic system, the state decides what to produce, the method or technique of production and who gets what in the society.

Bear: a speculator, especially in the stock market, who sells in anticipation of increase in prices.

Bilateral Trade: trade exclusively between two countries not involving hard currency. It is usually based on agreements or deals between the countries concerned. It may take the form of direct exchange of goods (barter) or countertrade.

Bill of Exchange: a written order in which a party agrees to pay another party a certain amount of money at a specified future date. It is written (or drawn) by the creditor and "accepted" by the debtor. It may be referred to as an 'Acceptance' once the debtor accepts. The creditor may i) hold the bill until it is due for payment; ii) take it to a bank and 'discount' it, i.e. receive immediately payment less interest and bank fees or iii) endorse it and use it make payment, if the creditor accepts this mode of payment.

Bills of exchange are mainly used in international trade and may be drawn by banks as well as individuals.

A bill of exchange in defined by the Bill of Exchange Act 1990 as "an unconditional order in writing, addressed by one person to another, signed by the person giving it, requiring the person to whom it is addressed to pay on demand or at a fixed or determinable future time a sum certain in money to or to the order of a specified person, or to bearer."

Bill of Lading: a document of title used in foreign trade which shows particulars of the goods e.g. quantity, type, etc as well as ports of departure and destination.

Birth Rate: the number of births per thousand of the population in a year. The birth rate is one of the determinants of the growth rate of population. Other determinants are death rate, and emigration and immigration. Factors that affect birth rate include fertility or number of females in the population, availability of medical facilities, early/late marriage, practice of birth control, average family size, etc.

Black Market: illegal market that arises where prices do not reflect actual demand and supply conditions, due to physical/administrative controls as opposed to market-determined prices. For example, where the exchange rate is administratively set and overvalued, smuggling activities will tend to be lucrative and pervasive. Also a parallel foreign exchange market will thrive.

Blue Chip: a reputable company capable of withstanding temporary changes in the market and the economy.

Board of Directors: group of individuals chosen by shareholders of a limited liability company to direct and provide strategic leadership for the company. A director may or may not be a shareholder.

Bond: a long-term financial security usually with a maturity of three years and above. Bonds are used to borrow long-term funds to finance capital projects. They may be issued by the Federal Government, State or Local Government or corporate bodies on the strength of their balance sheets and credit rating. In advanced capital markets

utility companies and other big industrial organizations issue bonds to finance their long-term capital projects.

Bonds issuance is regulated by the Securities and Exchange Commission (SEC), the capital market regulator. Bonds may be listed on the Stock Exchange for secondary trading.

Federal Government of Nigeria (FBN) Bonds are issued by the Central Bank of Nigeria with authority of the Debt Management Office (DMO) on behalf of the Federal Government. In recent years, the State governments have successfully approached the Nigerian capital market to raise long-term funds by issuing their own sub-national bonds. These states include Bayelsa, Delta, Ebonyi, Imo, Kaduna, and Lagos for amounts ranging from N16billion and N50billion. These issues are secured against the states allocations from the Federation Account, and are thus considered risk-free.

Investors in bonds include high net worth individuals, insurance companies, pension fund managers, banks, etc.

Bonded Warehouse: a warehouse where goods are stored until Customs Duty is paid.

Bonus Share: shares issued free of charge by a limited liability company out of its undistributed profits or reserves to shareholders in direct proportion to their original shareholding e.g. one for every two originally held. This exercise is necessary where the company wants to bring its issued capital in line with capital employed.

Boom: a period of high economic activity; characterized by rising employment, investment and production. The high point of the business cycle.

Bourse: alternative term for the stock exchange

Branding: the marketing art of building a distinct identity for a product or company so as to differentiate or distinguish it from others. This is usually done by a manufacturer by registering an exclusive trade mark or trade name which may be accompanied by intense advertisement campaign to associate the good with certain qualities and attributes in the minds of consumers. The purpose is to develop a niche market by generating a degree of loyalty among consumers. Successful branding gives the manufacturer a certain level of monopoly power as loyal consumers may not be ready to use competing goods choosing rather to pay a higher price, if need be. Thus successful branding increases the degree of inelasticity of demand.

Branding, along with advertisement, is a feature of imperfect competition by bringing about product differentiation.

Bretton Woods Agreement/System: outcome of the United Nations Monetary and Financial Conference held in July, 1944 at Bretton Woods, New Hampshire, in the United States after the Second World War. The agreement set up the International Bank for Reconstruction and Development (IBRD) and the International Monetary Fund (IMF).

The conference was held against the backdrop of the failed return to the gold standard after World War 1 and the global depression of the 1930s, which ultimately brought about the collapse of international economic and financial relations with countries engaged in unsustainable devaluation of their currencies in a bid to shore up their competitiveness and balance of payment position in the face of depressed economic conditions.

The conference agreed to peg or fix the exchange rate of IMF member countries to the United States dollar, with a maximum variation of 1% either side of the agreed rate; rates could only be adjusted beyond this set band if a country's balance of payments was in fundamental disequilibrium. The United States dollar itself was linked to gold at a fixed rate of 35 ounce. This meant that the one US dollar was worth 35 ounce of gold and that the United States Treasury stands ready to exchange 35 ounce of gold for a dollar with anybody who turn up at the "window".

The IMF was established to oversee and administer the Bretton Woods agreement whose overall objective was to ensure stability in international economic and financial relations. It succeeded in returning confidence and boosted trade between nations during the post-WWII economic boom.

However, being based on a set of fixed (theoretically adjustable) exchange rates, it lacked the flexibility to adjust when conditions so required, without undermining confidence. Basically, with the US dollar as the international reserve currency, the US was the bulwark of the system. In the post-WWII boom, the US was the market for the resurgent economies of Europe and Japan, even as the US gave out aid to those and other countries. This ultimately resulted in chronic US trade deficits between 1958 and 1971 and declining reserves while its' trading partners were amassing trade surpluses and reserves, which strengthened their currencies against the dollar. Against this backdrop, the United States' dollar became overvalued against other currencies like the German mark. Mounting liabilities and decreasing reserves meant that the US Treasury could not back the dollar with reserves. Confidence in the dollar as the international reserve currency was gradually overridden.

In 1971, the US President Richard Nixon accepted the reality by announcing that the US government was closing the "gold window" i.e. it was no longer obliged to convert dollar to gold at the fixed rate, and imposing measures to restrict imports. The Bretton Woods system of fixed exchange rate thus collapsed. Its collapse meant the end of money with intrinsic value as it marked the end of the promise to exchange a bank note with a real commodity i.e. gold. Henceforth money became fiduciary issue or legal tender i.e. backed by the force of law to be accepted as a means of exchange. Appropriately, necessary amendments were made in the Agreement, allowing members countries to adopt exchange rate arrangements of their choice.

After a failed attempt to patch things up under the Smithsonian Agreement, a regime of floating exchange rates, where the forces of demand and supply reflect the dynamic conditions of the underlying economies, became the norm among countries.

Broad Money (M2): the total volume of money in circulation. Money in circulation plus all deposit in banks i.e. savings and current account balances as well as time and foreign denominated deposits. See Narrow Money.

Broker: an agent, usually one dealing in specialist or professional, e.g. a stockbroker, insurance broker, etc.

Brokerage: broker's commission.

Bubble: excessive speculation especially on shares of companies with no proven track record of earnings such that the share prices ultimately bears no relation to the real value of the assets of the company.

Budget: A budget is a financial statement which sets out government's *estimated* revenue and *proposed* expenditure for the coming fiscal year. The budget contains the government's programmes, policy direction and intentions for the economy during the period concerned. It is prepared by the Ministry of Finance on behalf of the executive arm of government and sent to the legislature (National Assembly) for passage into law, upon signing by the President. No money can be spent unless it is contained in *the budget*.

The Budget as an Instrument of Economic Policy: The budget is the central fiscal policy instrument used by the government to manage the economy so as to bring about its desired outcomes in terms of *employment*, the *general price level* and *international competitiveness* of the economy. Depending on the state of the economy and the government's priorities, the government may propose and administer a *deficit, surplus* or *balanced* budget. A balanced budget is desirable when the economy is at equilibrium. Deficit or surplus budgets are respectively used to bring the economy to equilibrium position by closing a deflationary gap or inflationary gap.

Surplus Budget: this refers to situation where estimated government revenue is more than proposed expenditure. For example, where the government proposes to spend N250billion against estimated revenue of N300billion, there is a surplus of N50billion for the fiscal year concerned.

Uses of surplus budget:
Check or control inflation (by increasing taxes and/or reducing government expenditure). A surplus budget reduces the amount of money in circulation. It therefore reduces aggregate demand by reducing purchasing power. A budget surplus is therefore used to bring down an upward trend in the general price level (inflationary pressures) to tolerable levels. Government's reduced spending and investment may, however, lead to increased unemployment. Thus the reduced inflation may be achieved at the cost of increased unemployment.
Deficit Budget: this describes a budget where estimated receipts or revenue is less than proposed expenditure. For example, if the government proposes to spend N200billion, whereas its estimated revenue amounts to N180billion, there is a deficit of N20billion. The shortfall or deficit of N20billion in revenue will be met from reserves accumulated from previous years or by borrowing.

Uses of deficit budget:
1. *Revive or stimulate the economy from recession or depression* (by reducing taxes)**:** During a period of recession or depression characterized by widespread unemployment because aggregate demand is not enough to purchase national output of goods and services. Weak aggregate demand causes downward pressure on the general price level (deflation).

By implementing a deficit budget, government increases aggregate demand by boosting the purchasing power of the public. People are thereby enabled to buy the output of firms, who are thereby in turn enabled to continue production and to invest and employ. In this way, a deficit budget may be used to close a *deflationary gap* and bring the economy to equilibrium.

2. *Economic development* (by embarking capital intensive projects e.g. construction new infrastructure) : a deficit budget is used not just to manage the economy at its present level but to develop it to the next level; to take the economy from one level of development (e.g. under developed) to another (e.g. developing). The government will need to embark on massive development of its infrastructure and investment in basic industries. This might necessitate deficit budgeting.

3. *Balanced budget*: This budget where estimated revenue is equal to proposed expenditure. A balanced budget has a neutral effect on the economy in terms of the employment, general price level, and international competitiveness. It is used where the economy is in equilibrium i.e. there is neither inflationary nor deflationary gap.

The Role of the Budget in a Modern Economy
The government's fiscal policies are set out in the budget. The budget contains the government's revenue and expenditure proposals, and the government uses its spending and income pattern to control the economy and in order to achieve certain

objectives. Some of these ways are identified below:

1. *Revenue*: how much revenue the government intends to raise as revenue and from what sectors of the economy are revealed in the budget.

2. *Economic Development*: what the government intends to do with the revenue in terms of development of the economy is set out in the budget.

3. *Economic Management:* the budget reveals the direction the government intends to take the economy during the year. The budget is the government's economic road map for the period. It shows the targets of the government in terms of employment, the general price level, and major sectors of the economy e.g. agriculture, manufacturing, social services, infant industries, international trade, foreign investment, etc.

4. *Control of deflation and inflation:* deflationary or inflationary pressures in the economy can be managed through deficit or surplus budgeting as may be necessary. If there is a *downward trend* in the general price level the government can implement a deficit budget. What kind of budget is called for to control an upward trend in the general price level?

5. *Redistribution of Income:* inequality in the distribution of income can be addressed through the budget by increasing taxes on the upper class and increasing expenditure on essential public services like transportation, health and education.

6. *Commercial Policy (international trade):* the budget is used to manage how a country is faring in trade with other countries, so as ensure that the country is competitive. This means the budget is used to ensure that imports does not exceed exports. When imports are more than exports, necessary measures to control imports are taken through the budget to bring about a favourable balance of payments.

Budget Space, The: in the theory of consumer behaviour; the budget space refers to the space between the budget line and the origin. The budget space represents all sets of combinations that the consumer may spend his income on. Any point outside the budget space is unattainable at the present level of income.

Bureau de Change: a licensed trader in foreign exchange first authorized in Nigeria in 1989. These came into existence as part of efforts to deregulate the foreign exchange market and reduce the differential between the formal market and the parallel market exchange rates by increasing access to foreign exchange for small users.

Business cycle: fluctuation in the level economic activity over time. Phases in the business cycle are boom i.e. period of high business activity, indicated by expansion in economic activity, high employment; recession i.e. slowdown in business activity, low output of goods and services, job cuts, retrenchment and high unemployment level. see Trade Cycle

C

Cabotage: the carriage of goods and passengers between shipping ports in the same country.

Called-up Capital: that part of a company's share capital which its shareholders have been asked to pay.

Call Money: money at call or short notice. Liquid assets, mostly money market instruments, such as Treasury Bills and Treasury Certificates, which can be easily converted to cash.

Canons of Taxation: principles which must be followed in the administration of a tax system if it is to be successful. As enunciated by Adam Smith, they are:

Equity or Equality: a tax system should be fair; people should pay the same proportion of their income. Progressive tax is an example as it takes into account a person's income. Poll tax, on the other hand lack this principle.

Convenience: the time and method of payment should suit or be convenient for the tax payer.

Certainty: the tax payer should be clear and know the rate of tax and its calculation. Economy: cost of collecting the tax should not be excessive relative to receipts.

Modern tax principles include Flexibility: a tax system should be amenable to change so that it can be adapted to suit changing circumstances of the economy, if need be. Neutrality: a tax should not interfere with the supply and demand for goods and services. It should have neutral effect on people's willingness to work, save and invest.

Capital: material resources used in production; it includes long-term funds and assets such as equipment and machinery, factory, etc. See under Factors of Production.

Capital Account: That part of the balance of payments which records a country's long-term financial dealings (investments, borrowing and lending) with the rest of the world. See Balance of Payments

Capital Accumulation: see Capital Formation.

Capital Budget: part of the budget concerned with major items of revenue and expenditure that do not occur yearly. Capital Expenditure relates to cost incurred in developmental projects e.g. construction of roads, schools, hospitals, airports etc.

Capital Consumption Allowance: Depreciation or wear and tear of fixed capital. In national income accounting, the amount by which the capital stock has been used up or depreciated during the accounting period. It must be subtracted from Gross National Product or Gross Domestic Product to arrive at Net National Product or Net Domestic Product.

Capital Controls: restrictions or regulations on movement of capital in and out of a country. It includes limits on foreign investment in financial markets like the stock market and on foreign direct investment in businesses and property.

This may be in the form of exchange controls under which residents of a country can only obtain foreign currencies upon approval of an application by the Central Bank.

Capital controls were part of the gold standard in the 1930s and the Bretton Woods System which succeeded it after World War II, both underpinning regimes of fixed exchange rates.

Market-determined (i.e. flexible) exchange rates systems increasingly became the norm in the 1980s, and capital controls became dated against the backdrop of accelerated globalization and increasing bias for pro-trade policies. Among developing countries, the need to attract foreign investment to drive economic development played a key role in the removal of capital controls as this enabled the flow of capital from capital surplus countries to countries with rich natural resources but lacking in material and human capital necessary for their exploitation to power economic development.

Where, however, attracted foreign capital consist of a disproportionate amount of portfolio investment, relative to direct investment, a country's economy may become prone to the excesses of speculators on the international capital market with their tendency to induce capital flight.

This was brought to the fore in the Mexican and Asian Financial Crises of 1994 and 1997 respectively, which tested the limits of economic liberalism vis-à-vis capital controls. The crisis forced a rethink especially as these controls shielded countries like India and China, which retained them, from the crisis. Also, Malaysia was able to limit the damage to its economy by reacting fast to impose controls as the crisis spread. Against this experience, even the International Monetary Fund and the World Bank among other influential voices have come to acknowledge a limited role for capital controls.

Capital controls were among the many controls that prevailed in the Nigerian economy prior to the implementation of the Structural Adjustment Programme in 1986. The amendment of the Nigerian Enterprises Promotion Decree in 1989, to allow foreign ownership in all businesses except banking, insurance and mining, repeal of the import licensing system, and the adoption of market-driven mechanism to determine the exchange rate of the naira, marked the new trend.

Capital Duty: stamp duty paid by a company on its issued shares.

Capital Flight: mass outflow of capital out of country within a short period of time. This may be due to investors panic arising of financial difficulties which investors perceive may lead to default on international obligations, devaluation, or unpredictable political situation which they fear may lead to nationalization or expropriation in extreme cases resulting in a crisis of confidence. This often compounds the situation for the country concerned. Foreign Portfolio Investment are far more prone flight at short notice than Foreign Direct Investment, and the greater the amount of portfolio investment there is in the economy, the greater the harm to the economy from capital flight. See Foreign Capital.

Capital Formation: the process of growth in capital i.e. productive assets which is necessary for the creation of wealth. A country's—and for that matter a person's – economic status is a function of the amount of capital at its disposal. Capital in this sense includes money capital, technology, knowledge and training, physical assets, etc. required to produce and sustain production. The total level and the quality of these, accumulated over time, determine the wealth of the country. At the initial stages of development, capital may be borrowed. This will necessitate the need to save i.e. to defer consumption, in the immediate term. It may also mean that production will be biased in favour of capital goods instead of consumer goods. This implies sacrifices that may be considered part of the bootstrapping stages of development that a country must overcome in order to attain the minimum threshold or foothold in the journey to emergence.

Given that the physical stock of factors of production is fixed, increase in productive capacity will be in the form of increase in the rate of production or increase in value creation. How well and how fast a country is able to do this determines its rate of economic development.

Capital formation may be indicated by:
1. Quantitative increase in productive assets. The rate of production may be increased through increase/enhancement in (physical) substructure such as transport, electric power and telecommunication systems, etc., which reduces the cost of investment and reduces the costs of business transactions.
2. Qualitative changes e.g. technologies enabling greater productive efficiencies. Technological development increases the capacity to create value, i.e. whether wood is used mainly as firewood or more in the production of paper or whether hides and skins are used as food or processed into leather.
3. Level of human capital development; reflected in the level of literacy, quality of training and manpower institutions. All these impact on the quality of the labour force. Where these are low the odd situation arises where companies find it hard to fill vacant positions in the face of unemployment as many of those available lack requisite training.
4. The total level investible funds that can be sourced within the country, or the level of dependence on foreign capital or aid. Savings is only possible by a financial system that can pool and avail them as investible funds. Where the financial system is rudimentary or non-existent savings may find their way abroad.
5. The ratio of internal to national debt.

The rate of capital mobilization is key determinant of the rate of industrialization. Japan, South Korea and Russia are example of countries which were able to transform into industrial societies within a relatively short time by focused programmes of aggressive capital formation.

Capital Gain: the increase in the amount at which a capital asset—a house or other real estate; a financial security such as shares or stock—is bought and the amount at which it is sold. This is subject to capital gains tax.

Capital Gain Tax: tax levied on the increase in the value of a capital asset at the point of sale over its purchase price.

Capital Goods: goods used to produce other goods. The demand for capital goods is therefore *derived*. Examples are machinery, trucks, factories, etc. Compare *consumer goods*.

Capital Intensive: capital and labour are combined in the process of production. A method of production is described as capital intensive if a large amount of capital e.g. machinery, is used, relative to labour. In mechanized farming, for example, tractors, harvesters, etc. are used instead of labour.

Capitalization Issue: same as Bonus or Scrip Issue, whereby Revenue Reserves of a company are converted to issued shares by offering existing shareholders new shares in proportion to their existing shareholding. The shares are issued free to the shareholders as the money is already theirs as undistributed dividend. The process merely formalizes the shareholder's individual right to what was collectively theirs.

Capitalism: A system of economic organization characterized by the private ownership of the means of production and market determination of prices through the interaction of forces of demand and supply. The basic economic question of *what to produce* (allocation of resources) is left to the market to determine through the interaction of private participants. It is also referred to as Private or Free Enterprise System. In reality, the government plays a role in the economy and finds it necessary to intervene in the market in cases of market failure or externalities. Capitalism contrasts with the central planning system of communism where the private ownership of property and means of production was not allowed and resource allocation or what to produce was the preserve of the government.

Capital Market: The market for medium and long-term funds; the capital market is a financial intermediary that brings together those with surplus funds with those in need of funds to finance businesses and projects. It offers long-term investment/financial securities with financial returns in exchange for funds to finance businesses and projects.

It facilitates economic development by providing a mechanism for the pooling of savings for investment. Savings are converted into investment/financial securities such as corporate equity e.g. *ordinary shares* and long-term debt securities e.g. *debentures and bonds* which are issued and traded on the capital market.

Capital markets are necessary for capital formation and mobilization necessary for economic development. Capital markets drive capital mobilization and allocation of funds to businesses, in the push for economic growth. The capital market is a mechanism whereby companies and governments mobilize long-term funds for investment, while offering reliable platforms and investment vehicles for profitable investment of funds to investors. It is a very organized market with laid down rules and regulations, designed to ensure trust, confidence, viability, sustainability, and transparency, etc. due to the complex financial processes, large sums of money involved.

This market is divided into primary capital market for new issues being introduced into the market and the secondary capital market where old or existing issues are traded.

Governments and companies raise fresh funds through the primary market. This may be through Initial Public Offering (IPO), Offer for Sale or Offer for Subscription. Although fresh funds are not raised in the secondary market, by making it possible for investors to trade in securities, it facilitates liquidity.

The Capital Market comprise of the following:

The Market: the framework, arrangements and mechanism through which issued securities are bought and sold. Basically, this may be categorized into the organized market, such as the stock market, a physical place where securities are bought and sold by registered members, and the 'unorganized' market comprising over-the-counter (OTC) market made up of dealers in diverse locations connected via a network of computers who trade on securities that may not necessarily be listed.

Products: financial instruments or securities such as ordinary and preference Shares, Bonds, Debentures, Treasury-bills and Options. These are issued by companies and governments to raise long-term funds.

Investors: The investments are done by the institutional investors such as banks, insurance companies, mutual funds, pension funds and individual investors. They hope to earn capital gains, when the prices of securities appreciate or dividends, when declared and paid out by companies they invest in.

Operators:
- The stock exchange, which provides a platform for the listing and trading of shares;
- Issuing houses, who mid-wife the listing of shares by inter-facing between the listing company and the investing public, sometimes underwriting the shares;
- Stockbrokers, through whom shares are bought and sold for a fee;
- Registrars who prepare and provide new share certificates, update and maintain shareholders' registers;
- Clearing and Settlement to facilitate the transfer process so that deals are finalized within the shortest possible time. In Nigeria this function is performed by the Central Securities Clearing System, a subsidiary of the Nigeria Stock Exchange.
- Investment and Securities Tribunal (IST): in Nigeria, the Investment and Securities Act establishes the IST to fast track resolution of disputes arising from investments and securities transactions in a cost effective manner.

Regulators: The Security and Exchange Commission and the Stock Exchange.

CAPITAL MARKET IN NIGERIA
The Nigerian capital market comprises of the Nigerian Stock Exchange, the Abuja Securities and Commodities Exchange which are regulated by the Securities and Exchange Commission. Contrast *Money Market*.

Capital Market Development in Nigeria
The development of the capital market in Nigeria can be viewed in terms of the development of the institutions and

products. The equities market has witnessed growth in market capitalization. The following developments have marked the evolution of the capital market in Nigeria.

- The Nigerian Stock Exchange commenced trading as the Lagos Stock Exchange in 1961.
- The Nigerian Enterprises Promotion (Indigenization) Decrees of 1972 and 1977, which made it mandatory for Nigerians to be shareholders in certain industries, positively impacted the growth of the capital market as it provided the platform to carry out the requirement of the law.
- During the SAP, the capital market was impacted by reforms aimed at deregulating securities pricing, and the Securities and Exchange Commission relinquished its securities pricing function to issuing houses, for new issues and old issues to stockbrokers through the market. elimination of double taxation e.g. for unit trust schemes among others, with reduction in withholding taxes and capital gains taxes on securities.
- The Second-tier Securities Market was introduced by the NSE in 1985. It has now been replaced by the Alternative Securities Market.
- In order to encourage foreign investment, the Federal Government abrogated the Nigerian Enterprises Promotion Decree and the Exchange Control Act of 1962, and introduced the Nigerian Investment Promotion Commission Decree 16 and the Foreign Exchange (Monitoring and Miscellaneous Provisions) Decree 17 in 1995 enabling foreign ownership of Nigerian businesses through the capital market.

- Privatization of state-owned enterprises: the first phase of the exercise increased the market capitalization from under N10billion, in 1987, to over N65billion in 1994; and created about 800,000 new shareholders.
- The Central Securities Clearing System: a subsidiary of the NSE, responsible for clearing and settlement and Nigerian Stock Exchange's central depository. It also provides custodian services. From a T+5 settlement cycle on commencement in 1997, transactions are now settled after three days (i.e. T+3).
- In 2005/2007, Banking and Insurance Consolidation: most of the affected concerns raised the balance required to meet, and in certain cases surpassed the revised minimum through the capital market.

Capital Movement: movement of capital funds between and across international borders. Capital movements are of two types 1. Those for investment in businesses i.e. *foreign direct investment.* 2. Those for speculative purposes i.e. portfolio investment. Foreign direct investments are often long-term in nature and highly coveted to boost the economic development. Portfolio investment is usually opportunistic, short-term and volatile, capable of magnifying and aggravating any perceived challenges in the government's finances e.g. in balance of payment or debt servicing obligations. This can occasion a panic leading to massive sale and withdrawal of portfolio investment which can negatively impact exchange rates, a country's financial system and overall financial stability. Control over portfolio investment is therefore a concern to a country's economic managers.

Capital Transfers: see Capital Movement

Cartel: Association or combination of sellers or producers formed for the purpose of pursuing common interests, for example, by controlling output and price. A cartel often constitutes an oligopoly. OPEC (Organization of Petroleum Exporting Countries) is an example of an international cartel sponsored by sovereign states.

Cash Discount: a reduction from the price charged offered to encourage prompt payment. See Discount.

Cash on Delivery (C.O.D): a term of delivery. Where goods are to be delivered on these terms, the buyer will not be able to take possession of the goods until he has made payment for them. Thus the seller may be able to repossess the goods if the goods are already in the possession of the buyer. Related terms: Carriage insurance and freight (c.i.f); carriage forward; free on board (f.o.b); free on rail (f.o.r); ex-ship;

Cash Ratio: The fraction of a bank's reserve or assets held in cash to meet customers' demand at any point in time. This ratio is stipulated by the Central Bank, and is one of the ways the apex bank regulates the money supply by restricting the ability of banks to create credit. The Central Bank may increase or decrease the amount of cash with banks through open market operations. In order to meet the required cash ratio banks may be forced to reduce or increase lending, in case of excess cash. The higher the level of cash transactions in the economy, the higher the cash ratio required; as more payment are effected by means of cheques or electronically, the less cash banks have to keep, and the less the importance of the cash ratio as an instrument of monetary policy.

Caveat Emptor: Latin legal term meaning "let the buyer beware". Warning to prospective buyers to exercise due diligence before making a purchase

Cedi: Ghanaian currency, subdivided into 100 pasewa.

Ceiling prices: the maximum price chargeable under a price control regime

Census: an official headcount of the people in a country or geographical area. A census is carried out to inform planning purposes, political representation, geographical and age distribution of the population, determination of population policies e.g. whether to encourage or discourage immigration, estimation of available manpower. Conduct of census in Nigeria, and indeed other West African countries has been hampered by cost, political factors as revenue sharing is based on census figures, ignorance and shortage of qualified personnel, etc.

Importance of Population Census
Economic Planning: Census provides statistical information required for good planning. Such statistics include the number of children, sex distribution, number of people living in different geographical areas, etc. This information is required to enable the government plan the provision of schools, hospitals, roads, electricity, etc. Government is able to know, and thus plan for job opportunities, infrastructural needs, etc.

Political Representation: Number of constituencies is based on the population of the area. Census helps us to determine the number of representatives in the House of Representatives. Also, whether an area has enough people to make a state or local government depends on the population figures.

Available Manpower: Census figures provide information about the number of persons that are available to exploit available resources.

Population Growth Rate: the birth, death rate and migration can be deduced from the census figures. These can used to know the population growth rate of the country.

Estimation of Government Revenue: on the basis of the census figures, government can estimate the amount expected from taxation.

Number of Unemployed: With the census figures we can determine the number of unemployed.

Number of Dependants: The number of people who are below working age (below 18 years old) and those retired (above 60 years old) can be gotten from the census figures.

Per Capita Income: per capita income is the income per head of country. It is result of dividing national income by the population of the country. This information is provided by census.

Government Policies: government policies are better informed because of the information that census provide. For example, government attention is drawn to particular geographical areas and groups and addressed in policies.

Diplomatic Status: in the comity of nations, special status is accorded nations with high populations. A high population also implies a huge market for goods and services, which is necessary to attract foreign investment.

Problems of Census in West Africa
1. *High Cost:* to conduct a successful census a lot of staff, trucks and equipment have to be acquired. The total cost of procuring and the necessary and conduction the census is high especially to the undeveloped economies of West African countries.
2. *Shortage of qualified personnel:* qualified specialist personnel like statisticians and demographers are needed to conduct and analyze the results of census. These personnel are short in supply in West African countries.
3. Illiteracy: self-enumeration cannot be sued in West African countries because of the high level of illiteracy.
4. *Politics:* Census figures are often falsified and manipulated as political representation and revenue allocation depends on it.
5. *Poor town planning:* most towns are not planned at all. This makes the process of enumeration difficult as houses are built in haphazard manner.
6. *Poor transportation system:* poor transportation makes it impossible to access some remote areas to conduct the process of enumeration.
7. *Religious and Superstitious beliefs:* Some people are of the belief that it is wrong to count their children. In some Muslim communities, a woman may not appear in public when she is in purdah. Thus, people

may not cooperate fully with census enumerators.

8. *Ignorance:* Many people do not understand the purpose of enumeration. They often think it is for tax purposes and thus avoid being counted.

Central Bank: The principal monetary authority of a country, primarily in charge of monetary policy; the government's bank as well as the bank of last resort. Its functions include banker to the government, management of monetary policy, issuance of currency, management of the country's external reserves, management of the rate of exchange, and regulation of banks in general.

Functions of the Central Bank

1. *Issue and management of currency:* only the central bank can issue bank notes (paper money) and coins. It manages the currency by withdrawing old and defaced notes from circulation and replacing it with new ones.

2. *Banker to the government:* government receipts comprising of aids, grants and loans from abroad, tax and other revenues are deposited with the central bank; it keeps and manages the accounts of the government, public corporations (also known as parastatals).

3. *Bankers' bank:* all financial institutions (banks, discount and acceptance houses, etc.) are required to maintain accounts with the central bank. The central bank enables banks to settle debts between them through the clearing house.

4. *Lender of Last Resort:* as the bankers' bank, central bank is the last hope of other banks when they are in urgent need of financial assistance e.g. due to huge withdrawals by customers. The bank rate is the rate of interest at which the central bank lends to the other banks.

5. *Provision of Economic Statistics:* the central bank monitors and gathers statistics on economic activities in the economy, which enables it to know the rate of economic growth, the performance of the different sectors of the economy (agriculture, manufacturing, services, exports, imports, etc.), and to design policies and advise the government on what it needs to do in its overall economic development strategy.

6. *Adviser to the government:* the central bank advises the government on finance for development projects, financial planning and budgeting.

7. *Management of the exchange rate:* the Central bank ensures the availability of foreign exchange in the foreign exchange market. and that the exchange rate, as determined in the foreign exchange market, is within certain limits that ensures overall economic stability, and often reserves the right to intervene in the market.

8. *Management of assets and liabilities:* The country's gold and foreign exchange reserves as well as international investments are also managed by the central bank. The National Debt is managed by the central bank, hand in hand with the Debt Management Office.

9. *External financial transactions:* the country's relations with international financial organizations like the African Development Bank, International Monetary

Fund, International Bank for Reconstruction and Development (IBRD), Bank for International Settlements (BIS), etc. are managed by the Central Bank. It also plays a major role in the country's dealings and relations with economic organizations like the Economic Organization of West African States (ECOWAS), Economic Commission for Africa (ECA), etc.

10. *Money Supply/ management of monetary policy*: the central bank ensures stability in the general price level by managing the amount of money in circulation through the regulation of the level of credit available in the economy.

Central Bank: control of commercial banks

The central bank is the bankers' bank and the bank of last resort. It exercises control over commercial banks and other banks in the economy through the use of monetary policy instruments.

1. *Bank Rate*: the bank rate is the rate at which the central bank lends/ discounts or rediscounts bills to the commercial banks. If the central bank lends at a high bank rate to the commercial banks, the commercial banks will lend at a high interest rate to their customers. Thereby bringing about desired changes in the economy.

2. *Open market operations*: this refers to the buying and selling of government securities from and to the public and business organizations. The central bank may increase or reduce the amount of money in circulation and the ability of banks to give loans by selling or buying government securities to the public.

3. *Cash-deposit ratio:* cash-deposit ratio is the legally required amount of deposit the commercial banks are required to maintain with the central bank for every Naira of deposit with it. The lower the cash-deposit ratio, the higher the amount of money available to the banks for lending to the public. The central bank can increase or decrease the reserve ratio as it deems necessary, and accordingly control the policies of the commercial banks. Where the central bank wants the commercial banks to reduce their lending to the public it may increase the cash-deposit ratio; when it wants the commercial banks to increase the amount of money in circulation, it may reduce it.

4. *Special deposits*: Apart from the legally required minimum, the central bank may ask the commercial banks for special deposits. This further reduces the amount the commercial banks have to lend to the public.

Central Bank Intervention: Actions by the central bank to influence market conditions e.g. in the management of the money supply, interest rate, exchange rate, etc. Examples of such activity include the buying or selling of currency, in order to influence the exchange rate.

Central Bank of Nigeria: The history of central bank of Nigeria dates back to the *West African Currency Board*, established in 1912 with headquarters in London. It issued the West African Pound for British West Africa (the Gambia, Ghana, Nigeria and Sierra-Leone), which replaced the commodity money (cowries, iron bars, etc) that were in use before then. The WACB was not a central bank in the modern sense as it played a limited role in the economy, serving mainly to exchange West African pound for the British sterling (pound). It had no control over commercial banks in the respective countries. With independence these countries withdrew from the WACB. The Central Bank of Nigeria Act was passed in 1958, and it began operations in 1959.

The emergence of more banks and other financial intermediaries following the Structural Adjustment Program in 1986, saw the enactment of the Banking and Other Financial Institutions Decree in 1991. This law strengthened and extended the powers of the CBN to cover the new institutions in order to enhance the effectiveness of monetary policy, regulation and supervision of banks as well as non-banking financial institutions. The rollback of the reform drive and the amendments to the BOFI Decree in 1997 brought the CBN under the Ministry of Finance; completely removed the limited autonomy of the CBN, leaving it little room to exercise any discretionary powers. Autonomy was fully restored with the CBN Act of 2007, with powers to discharge its functions under the Act and the Banks and Other Financial Institutions Act, and widened its objects to include ensuring monetary and price stability as well as rendering economic advice to the Federal Government.

Central Planning: economic development through resource allocation by the State. The government takes the central role to grow the economy in a particular direction. This strategy of economic development proved particularly effective in mobilizing and accumulating capital in the course of the industrialization of the former Soviet Union. The Russian economy was transformed from a backward, rural economy into a modern, industrial economy under the First Five-Year Plan starting from 1929, albeit at under an extreme totalitarian political regime. The South Korean economy was equally transformed between 1962 and 1982, using a combination of central planning and market-based development strategies.

Central planning contrasts with a free enterprise system where market forces are the determinants of what, how and for whom to produce.

Certificate of Incorporation: document issued by the Corporate Affairs Commission to a limited liability company upon registration, certifying its legal entity status.

Certificate of Origin: document issued by an exporting country showing from which country the goods are exported from. This document is very important where discriminating tariffs are applied depending on the country of origin.

Ceteris paribus: Latin phrase, translating to "other things being equal".

Chamber of Commerce: association of business people across diverse industries based in a town established to pursue and protect their common interests. Unlike a trade association, a Chamber of Commerce is not limited to a particular trade. Among the functions of Chambers of Commerce is the organization of Trade Fairs and Exhibitions, collection and dissemination of information to members, promotion of co-operation between members, dispute resolution. They are also platform through which international business connections can be made by members. They can also lobby government to pass legislation in favour of members. Examples are the Lagos

Chamber of Commerce and Industry (LCCI), Kano Chamber of Commerce, Kaduna Chamber of Commerce, Port Harcourt Chamber of Commerce.

The Nigerian Association of Chambers of Commerce, Industries, Mines and Agriculture (NACCIMA) is the umbrella body Chambers of Commerce in Nigeria.

Chancellor of the Exchequer: the head of the Bank of England, the United Kingdom's central bank.

Change in Demand: Shifts (outward or inward) of the demand curve (a new demand schedule) so that more or less is now being demanded without any change in price. It may be brought about by change in other *conditions of demand* other than price of the good such as weather, income, taste and preferences/fashion, price of other goods, etc.

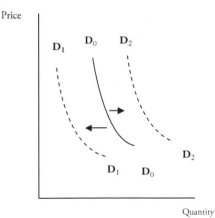

In the harmattan season, for example, the demand for sweater may increase causing the demand curve to shift outward from D_0D_0 to D_2D_2. More is now being demanded without a change in price.

Similarly, the demand for raincoats, during this season will fall, causing the demand curve to shift inwards to D_1D_1.

Change in Quantity Demanded: movement along the same demand curve brought about by a change in the price of the commodity. Quantity demanded increases as price reduces or quantity demanded reduces as price increases. This the law of demand in operation.

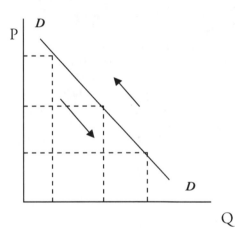

Change in Quantity Supplied: movement along the same supply curve in response to a change in price of the commodity.

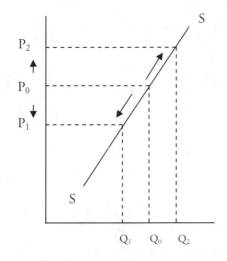

Change in Supply: shifts (outward or inward) of the supply curve (a new supply schedule) so that a different quantity (more or less) is now being supplied at the same price. It may be brought about by change in other conditions of supply other than price of the commodity such as change in technology, number of firms in the industry, cost of production, price of other goods, weather, etc.

Charter Party: a written agreement or contract by which a ship or aircraft is temporarily leased or hired by the owners to another person or firm. The ship or aircraft is said to be chartered, and the owners are paid a "chartered freight".

Cheque: a written order by a current account holder (drawer) on a bank (drawee), to pay on demand a specified amount of money to the bearer or person named on it (payee). It is a bill of exchange.

Types of Cheques
i. Order Cheque: a cheque that can only be cashed by the person or entity indicated on it i.e. the payee.

The payee may endorse it to another person to whom it may be paid.
ii. Open Cheque: a cheque that may be presented for payment across the counter. There are no crossings.
iii. Crossed Cheque: Payment of a cheque may be restricted to guard against paying the wrong person by crossing.
iv. General Crossing: where two transverse parallel lines, marked across the cheque face with the words *"& Co."*, or *"Non Negotiable"* or *""A/c. Payee"* between the two parallel lines. Such cheques cannot be paid across the counter but must pass through clearing and be paid into a current account.

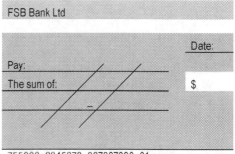

v. Special Crossing: This is when, in addition to the words a particular bank's name is written in between the two parallel lines across the face of the cheque. In addition, the words *"A/c. Payee Only"*, *"Not Negotiable"* may also be written.

Payment can only be made to the bank indicated on a special crossing

Choice: the need by economic units (individuals/households, firms and government) to decide on which want(s) to satisfy given that unlimited wants must be satisfied out of limited or scarce resources. Choice is necessary because resources are limited in supply or scarce. Because of the need to make a choice a scale of preference need to make a choice a scale of preference has to be made, and an opportunity cost incurred.

Individual	Firm	Government
Car or House?	Use machines or labour?	New hospitals or bridge?
Problem of choice		

Chose in Action: the right to a thing as distinct from the thing itself. The term includes all rights arising out of contracts—debts, negotiable instruments, policies of insurance and the property of intangible nature e.g. copyrights. Compare *Chose in Possession*.

Chose in Possession: legal term, it refers to the ownership of physical goods and chattels actually in one's possession. Compare *Chose in Action*.

Circular Flow of Income: A diagram showing the flow of payments for the use of factor services (wages/salaries, rent, interest, and profit) and the flow of payments for goods and services between households and business sectors. The circular flow of income is a simplified model of the economy showing only two sectors (households and businesses), leaving out the other two sectors (government and international trade).

Circular flow of income

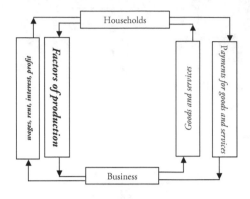

It is based on certain assumptions:
1.   The economy consists of two sectors; households and business.
2.   The economy is a close economy: this means there is no trade with foreign countries; there are no exports and imports.
3.   All output is purchased by households
4.   There are no savings: Households and businesses spend or consume all their incomes.
5.   There is no government sector; taxes and subsidies are disregarded.
6.   There is no financial sector i.e. no banks, insurance companies, etc.

Classical School of Economics: The economics of Adam Smith, David Ricardo, Thomas Malthus, and later followers such as John Stuart Mill. The theory concentrated on the functioning of a market economy, spelling out a rudimentary explanation of consumer and producer behaviour in particular markets and postulating that in the long term the economy would tend to operate at full employment because increases in supply would create corresponding increases in demand.

Classical (or **Real Wage**) **Unemployment**: unemployment due to wage rate being too high i.e. above the equilibrium wage rate or market clearing rate. Wage rate often do not adjust downwards even when the economy slows down, for example, during a recession/depression. This may be due to minimum wage legislation and/or activities of industrial unions. In effect, employers will hold back from employing people, and this will lead to surplus of labour i.e. (classical) unemployment

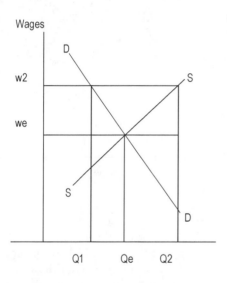

Demand for labour is the same as supply of labour at Q_e and the wage rate is W_e. However, employers have to pay W to workers due to rigidity in the labour market which prevent the wage rate from adjusting downward to W_e. As a result, quantity supplied is more than quantity demanded in the labour market leading to a surplus ($Q_2 - Q_e$) of workers.

This explanation of the cause of unemployment was put forward by Classical economists, and was the dominant view until the Great Depression in the 1930s and the advent of Keynesian economics. Keynes argued that cutting wages during a recession or depression would be counter-productive as this would lead to even lower aggregate demand. Instead, there is a need during such times to stimulate economic activity by boosting aggregate demand.

Close Company: a private limited liability company. It is so-called because sale of its shares is restricted to members (shareholders) only i.e. it is closed to members of the public.

Collateral Security: Property that is offered to secure a loan or other credit and that becomes subject to seizure on default.

Collective Bargaining: negotiations undertaken by trade unions with the employers of their members (employees). Collectively employees stand a chance of securing favourable terms than they would individually. Collective bargaining makes it possible for employers to save time and resources than if they have to deal with employees individually.

Collective Goods: goods owned by the community such as parks, libraries, roads, markets, etc; alternatively referred to as social wealth or capital. Collective goods impact on the quality of life and marginal productivity of labour.

Collectivism: an economic system, such as Communism, where the state owns most means of production and production is coordinated by a central body.

Command Economy: an economy where the government makes all economic decision e.g. determining what to produce (allocation of resources), how to produce (method of production) and who gets what (distribution). It is typified by a communist system. While the system succeeded mobilizing capital on a massive scale to transform backward economy to catch-up with the industrialized West, it failed as a self-sustaining system. See Communism.

Commerce: term used to describe all trading activities, which involve distribution of goods i.e. wholesale and retail, import and export as well as services which facilitates or enables the business of trading, namely, advertising, banking, communications, insurance, transportation, and warehousing.

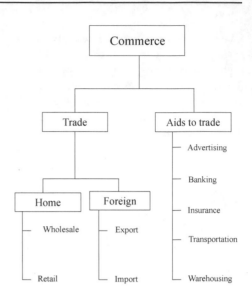

Commercial Documents:

1. Advice Note: a document sent by post by supplier, e.g. a producer or wholesaler, to a purchaser, e.g., a retailer, giving details of the goods, mode of transportation and the date of dispatch. The term is sometimes used to describe a note informing a person that a transaction has been completed.

2. Consignment Note: a document accompanying goods dispatched showing details of the goods such as quantity, name and address of sender and consignee. It is signed by the consignee upon receipt of the goods to acknowledge delivery of the consignment.

3. Credit Note: a commercial document sent by a supplier to a buyer showing buyer has credit due to him from the supplier. This is usually when such credit arises out of: 1. Returned goods e.g. due to damage. 2. upon discovery that the customer was overcharged or overpaid. 3. Goods do not meet the buyer's specifications or are otherwise unsuitable.

4. Debit Note: a commercial document issued by a seller to a buyer showing amount due from the buyer arising from a mistake in an invoice resulting in an undercharge.

5. Delivery Note: a document containing details of the consignment it accompanies, and against which the consignment may be checked.

6. Invoice: a document that records a transaction involving the sale of goods. It is issued by the seller to the buyer. It shows the name of the buyer, date, description of items, quantity, prices, and terms of payment among others. It is generally taken as a request for payment.

7. Pro-Forma Invoice: a commercial document sent in the following circumstances: 1. when the document serves as a quotation 2. When no charge is being made for the goods, for example, after servicing or repairs of goods under warranty. 3. When the goods are sent subject to approval; the document then serves as an invoice, if the goods are retained. 4. As an advice to an agent on the prices he is expected to sell. Upon completion of a transaction, the pro forma invoice will either serve as a normal invoice or a fresh invoice will be made out and sent.

8. Quotation: a statement of current prices and terms of sale of a product. It usually a reply to an inquiry made by a prospective buyer. It relates to a particular transaction.

9. Receipt: a written acknowledgement of payment.

10. Statement of Account: a statement issued by a seller to his customers showing details of transaction within a period and the balance due to or from the customer.

Commercial Economies: see under Economies of Scale.

Commercial Paper (CP): a short-term promissory note issued by a reputable company to raise short-term finance, for example, for working capital. It is a money market financial security. Tenure is typically 9 months maximum.

Commodity: a tangible product or good that is a subject of trade. The term connotes a standardized commercial or mass produced good as opposed to customized products or works of art. Commodities may be classified into Consumers' Goods, which are demanded for direct satisfaction, and Producers' Goods which are required for the production of other goods.

Commodity Boards: agricultural produce marketing boards which were responsible for setting prices for and purchase of Nigeria's cash crops between 1947, when they were established, and 1986 when they were scrapped under the Structural Adjustment Programme. The seven boards were: the Nigerian Cocoa Board (cocoa, coffee, and tea); Groundnut Board (groundnut, soya beans, benniseed, and ginger); Cotton Board; Nigerian Palm Produce Board; Nigerian Rubber Board; Nigerian Grains Board (corn, millet, maize, wheat, rice and beans). The boards were monopsonists (sole buyers) of farmer's produce and provided a mechanism for ensuring quality by standard bagging and grading of produce as well as organization through Licensed Buying Agents (LBAs). However, overtime they became a major disincentive to production, and oversaw a steady decline in the export of cash crops through the 1970s. This was because they offered increasingly lower prices relative to international commodity prices, to farmers, becoming an excessive implicit tax on farmers' incomes.

Commodity Boards were one of the many examples of direct controls and regulations which were perceived to stifle competition and lead to inefficient allocation of scarce resources which were targeted by economic reforms. Deregulation of economic activities brought about the scrapping of the boards in under the Structural Adjustment Programme in 1986. As a result, farmers could directly export their produce. The scrapping of the boards, coupled with devaluation of the naira, brought about an increase in export of major agricultural crops, reaching over 85% of the 1970s peak level by 1989.

Commodity Money: commodities accepted as a means of payment or medium of exchange. In order to overcome the many challenges of barter, different commodities where used by different communities at different times. These include tobacco, salt, rice, cowries, etc. Cigarettes were used as money in Germany for a period after the devastation of WWII, due to hyperinflation, which rendered the currency worthless as a store of value.

Common Market: a customs *and* economic union having a unified market of all the member countries with free movement of goods, capital and labour i.e. without visa restrictions. It is a stage in the process of economic integration of countries the essence of which is bigger markets for goods, services and labour. The Economic Community of West African States (ECOWAS) is an example.

Commonwealth of Nations: an international organization comprising of Great Britain and its former colonies.

Communication: the dissemination or transmission of information—news and ideas—from one person to another and to the general public; modes include post and telephone, radio and television, the press, as well as the internet. Communication extends the reach of producers and consumers alike, increasing the volume of trade and enhancing living standards. It is one of the auxiliaries of trade.

Today the world is one big market—the global village—thanks to communication systems. Advances in information technology has revolutionized communication so much so that instantaneous communication is now common place and available through individual handheld devices. Before this time, however, communication was based on transportation systems—the coach, the steam boat, railway, etc.

Communism: a political and economic system founded on socialist ideological principles in which the State owns all resources and determines the allocation of resources, production and distribution of output/income. This contrast with Capitalism where private ownership of capital is allowed and the economic decisions are determined by the market. Communism derives from the writings of German economists Karl Marx and Frederich Engels (Marxism) as interpreted by Bolshevik leadership of the Union of Soviet Socialist Republics (USSR) after the 1917 Revolution from where it was exported to its satellite states. Communism succeeded in turning Russia into modern economy under two decades and put that country in a position to contend with the United States as the leading economy after the Second World War. But perhaps it was destined to fail as a self-sustaining mechanism for efficient running of the economy being dependent on subjective discretionary powers of State officials as opposed to Capitalism which depended on interactive, self-regulatory, objective market forces. Between the end of the WWII and the 1990s, the world was divided between countries practicing capitalism and communism. Widespread shortages and other economic problems in the Soviet Union assumed a chronic dimension and prompted reforms from 1985 under the leadership of Mikhail Gorbachev. These political (*glasnost* in Russian) and economic (*perestroika*) reforms ultimately set in motion—within and outside the USSR—forces that were end Soviet hegemony over its Eastern European satellites States and end the Cold War between the capitalist West and the Communist East. The fall of the Berlin Wall in 1989 precipitated the fall of communist governments in Eastern European countries. China, a bastion of communism, has succeeded in combining State ownership of factors of production with private production. Today only North Korea and Cuba can be described as countries where communist economic systems are in place.

Company: a group of persons united e.g. in a business enterprise, in pursuit of a common goal. Generally, the term is used to refer to joint stock companies, duly registered with the Corporate Affairs Commission, which have separate legal entities different from the owners, whose liabilities are limited to the amount invested.

Comparative Advantage: measure of relative efficiency of resource use when the opportunity cost of production is taken into consideration. It is the basis of specialization or division of labour and international trade. A country/producer/individual has a comparative advantage relative to another if it has a lower opportunity cost of production. Given two countries A and B, for example, Country A may be able to produce more of good X and good Y with the same amount of resource, compared to country B. This means that country A has an *absolute advantage* over country B.

	Good X	Good Y
Country A	100	20
Country B	60	80
Total Output	**160**	**100**

But when we consider the opportunity cost involved, we see that for every 20 units of good Y country A produces, it forgoes the production of 100 units good X; i.e. 5 units of X for every 1 unit of Y. Country B, on the other hand, only gives up 60 units of X for 80 units of Y.

	Country A	Country B
Opportunity Cost of Good X	1/5 of Y	4/3 of Y
Opportunity Cost of Good Y	5 of X	¾ of X

Thus, though country A has an absolute advantage over country B in the production of both goods, it has only a comparative advantage in the production of good Y; country B has a comparative advantage over country A in the production of good X.

If country A specializes in the production of Y and country B specializes in production of X:

	Good X	Good Y
Country A	200	
Country B		160
Total Output	**200**	**160**

Thus, if countries, firms or individuals specialize in producing only that in which they have a comparative advantage, greater output or surplus would result, and a better standard of living would be achieved. See absolute advantage, opportunity cost.

Comparative Cost Advantage, Principle of: comparative cost advantage is the theoretical basis for international trade. A country is said to have a comparative cost advantage in the production of a good if its opportunity cost incurred in the production of that good is the lowest compared to others. According to David Ricardo, the 19th century English economist who advanced the theory, total output and economic welfare will be increased if countries specialize in the production of goods in which they have comparative advantage and import goods in which they have a relative comparative disadvantage.

According to the theory, even where a country can produce all commodities cheaper than other countries, (**absolute advantage**), it is better for that country to specialize in the production of that commodity in which it has comparative cost advantage, and then trade with other countries for its other needs.

Country A has *absolute advantage* over country B in the production of both goods (it produces more of each product with the same amount of resources). But what are the *opportunity costs*? What is the best possible use to which country A's resources can be put?

	Good X	Good Y	Ratio
Country A	100	20	5:1
Country B	20	10	2:1
Total Output	**120**	**30**	

Note that for each unit of X, it gives up 5 units of Y. On the other hand, country B gives up only 1 unit of Y for each unit of X produced.

Comparative Cost Advantage: Assumptions
The theory of Comparative Cost Advantage is based on certain assumptions, as follows:

1. No transport cost: there are no transport involved in the movement of goods and people.
2. Factors of production are perfectly mobile between occupations.
3. The cost of production in both countries is the same; also labour cost is the same in terms of skill and efficiency.
4. There is perfect and full employment in the countries involved.
5. Diminishing returns do not occur in production.
6. There are no trade restrictions of any kind—artificial or natural.
7. There are two countries involved.
8. There are only two commodities.
9. Constant Returns to Scale: doubling of input results in doubling of output.

Comparative Cost Advantage, Criticism of: if a model is only as good to the extent it reflects what it purports to represent or the assumptions upon which it is based, then the theory of comparative advantage is weak in view of the assumptions listed above.

The theory relate more to advantages based on natural resource endowment which are relatively fixed, and become more dynamic and changeable in the secondary stages of production i.e. manufacturing, where technological and managerial efficiency/capacity is of greater importance in production possibilities and cost.

Comparative advantage is therefore a dynamic concept, for example, countries like South Korea and China have gained an advantage in the production of clothing and consumer electronics over countries of Europe in the course of their industrialization. Critically, these countries would not have gained the advantage if their economic managers/leaders have based their production and commercial policy on comparative cost advantage.

Competitive Demand: where two goods are considered substitutes, changes in the price or supply of one directly the demand for the other. Butter and margarine and, tea and coffee are examples. Different brands of the same product are in competitive demand, and producers do all they can to differentiate their brand through advertising.

Complementary Demand/Goods: also known as Joint Demand; this refers to demand for goods which are used together, to give total satisfaction. An increase in the price of one brings about an increase in demand for the other good. Where the demand for two goods (A and B) are complementary, an increase in quantity demanded for A, due to a fall in price, for example, leads to an increase in demand for B and vice versa. Tea and milk are examples: a decrease in the price of milk will lead to an increase in the demand for tea.

Composite Demand: demand for a good that is used multiple purposes. This is the case with most raw materials. Palm oil is an example of a good with composite demand because it is demanded for several purposes, e.g. for cooking and for industrial purposes. If there is an increase in the demand for palm oil for industrial purposes, the price of the commodity will increase, affecting all users alike.

Concealed Unemployment: Numbers of unemployed people who are eligible for work but who are not reflected in unemployment statistics.

Concentration of Industry: the localization of an industry in a particular area. This may be due the presence of vital production requirement e.g. a bulky raw material which is cumbersome and expensive to transport.

Conditions/determinants of demand: factors such as consumer incomes, tastes and fashion, price of other goods, weather condition, etc. which influences the quantity demanded of a good at any given price.

Conditions/determinants of supply: factors such as cost of production, weather, number of producers in the industry, price of other commodities, taxation and subsidies, etc that affect the quantity supplied of a commodity at any given price.

Consideration: the benefit derived by a party to a contract in return for his obligations. The gain derived by a party to a contract must be balanced by the benefit (consideration) derived by the other party.
For a contract to be valid, there must a consideration.

Consignment Note: see under Commercial Documents.

Constant Returns to Scale: a situation where a change in inputs brings about a proportionate change in output; there is constant returns to scale where, by increasing inputs by, say 10% , output increase by the same factor.

Consumer Price Index: a price index that measures changes in the price level of consumer goods and services over a period of time or regions. It is a measure of change in the purchasing power of money i.e. inflation/deflation. The CPI is calculated by taking a representative collection or basket of goods and services, which are assigned weights to reflect the degree of importance to the consumer. The representative basket of goods and services consist of items in common use e.g. food and drink, clothing, transportation, entertainment, etc. to which weights are attached to reflect relative importance. A base year is chosen against which comparison can be made to determine changes. The base year is assigned the price index number 100, to enable changes to be expressed as percentage.

Illustration: Given the following prices for the respective items of expenditure for year 2000 and 2004 with the assigned weights, calculate the price index.

Solution

Item	2000 Price =N=	2004 Price =N=	Weight
Food	125	150	9
Kerosene	85	130	6
Clothing	95	105	8
Housing	90	125	9
Transport	99	135	5

Item	Base year Price (P_0)	Latter year Price (P_1)	P_0/P_1	P_0/P_1 x 100	Weight	Weighted Index
Food	125	150	1.2	120	9	1080
Kerosene	85	130	1.529412	152.9412	6	917.6471
Clothing	95	105	1.105263	110.5263	8	884.2105
Housing	90	125	1.388889	138.8889	9	1250
Transport	99	135	1.363636	136.3636	5	681.8182
					37	4813.676

$$\text{Consumer Price Index} = \frac{\text{weighted index}}{\text{Sum of weights}} = \frac{4813.676}{37} = 130.0993$$

In the simple example given above, the price index column in Year 2004, shows the average increase in prices between 2000 and 2004 as 130. This means that, on the average, prices increased by 30% during the period.

The CPIs can also be computed for different regions or cities to give an indication of differences in cost of living in the respective areas by comparison. Thus CPIs for major cities like Lagos, Port Harcourt, Kano, Abuja, etc will show the differences in cost of living.

The CPI is based on the concept of a cost of living index and is practical approximation of an ideal cost of living index.

Consumer Protection: Consumer protection is concerned with the protection of the consumer against substandard, inferior, or dangerous products, misleading advertisement, excessive charges and pricing, etc. It is the set of policies and measures aimed at regulating the products, services, methods, and standards of manufacturers, sellers, and advertisers to ensure quality and safety standards are met, fair pricing, honesty in packaging and advertising, etc. in the interests of the buyer. It consists of the setting of standards, product specifications, statement of the rights of the consumer, duties of the seller, laws, rules and regulations and mechanisms for enforcing them.

The United Nations Guidelines of 1985 set the framework for consumer rights protection for member countries worldwide. The Guidelines set forth the Rights of the Consumer as follows:

1. *The Right to Satisfaction of Basic Needs* Access to basic goods and services necessary for survival, such as food, water, energy, clothing, shelter, health-care, education and sanitation. Goods and services must meet the standard of quality promised such that there is value for money in the purchase.
2. The Right to Safety: Protection from hazardous products, production processes and services.
3. The Right to Information: Provision of information enabling informed consumer choice as well as protection from misleading or inaccurate advertising and labeling.
4. The Right to Choose: Access to variety of quality products and services at competitive prices.
5. The Right to Redress: Compensation for misrepresentation, shoddy goods and unsatisfactory public and private services, including the right to adequate legal representation
6. The Right to Consumer Education: Acquisition of the skills required to be an informed consumer throughout life
7. The Right to Consumer Representation: Advocacy of consumers' interest and the ability to take part in the formulation of

economic and other policies affecting consumers i.e. the right to be heard.
8. The Right to a Healthy Environment: Habitation is a place that is safe for present and future generations and which will enhance the quality of their lives.

Legislations
*   Sale of Goods Act: adapted from the English statute passed in 1893, it is the first law that seeks to protect the consumer. It provides that certain conditions that all goods sold by a trader must meet and asserts the right of the buyer to insist that goods bought by him must be:
    o   As described e.g. by advertisement, catalogue, brochure, etc.
    o   Of satisfactory quality.
    o   Fit for the purpose for which they are meant:
*   The Counterfeit and Fake Drugs Decree 1990. This Act prohibits the production, manufacture, importation, sale and distribution of any counterfeit, adulterated, banned or fake drugs. It also prohibits persons to sell any drug in an open market without due permission.
*   The Food and Drugs Act: protects the consumer by regulating the manufacture of drugs; prohibits misleading advertisement, packaging, and labeling of drugs.
*   The Poison and Pharmacy Act: regulates the compounding, sale, distribution, supply and dispensing of drugs and provides different levels of control for different categories of drugs and poisons.
*   Standards Organization of Nigeria Act: ensures that raw materials,

finished goods and factories meet set industrial standards.

- Hire Purchase Act. This law protects the hire purchaser against the excesses, cheating and exploitation of the seller.

In addition to normal law enforcement agencies, the government has set up specialized agencies to protect the consumer:

- Consumer Protection Council: The functions of the CPC is to bring offending companies and individuals to compensate and provide relief to consumers, where proven; rid the market of hazardous, dangerous and unsafe products; provide speedy redress to consumers complaints; sensitize consumers and manufacturers, importers, dealers and wholesalers to their rights and responsibilities; work with trade, industry and professional associations to develop and enforce quality standards designed to safeguard the interest of consumers.
- National Agency for Food and Drug Administration and Control (NAFDAC): instituted in 1994 to regulate and control the manufacture, importation, exportation, advertisement, distribution, sale and use of food, drugs, cosmetics, medical devices, chemicals and prepackaged water.
- Nigerian Communication Commission: protects users of telecommunications services against shoddy services and arbitrary charges.
- Standard Organization of Nigeria: specifying and enforcing Nigerian Industrial Standards (NIS); investigate into the quality of facilities, raw materials and finished products; establish a quality assurance system including de-/certification of factories, products and laboratories in Nigeria.

Consumer Activism: consumer protection groups formed to act as platforms that consumers may use to seek redress for grievances and advocate for their rights. In Nigeria, these groups include the Consumer Rights Advocacy League, and the Consumer Empowerment Organization of Nigeria (COEN).

Consumers' Sovereignty: the "supremacy" of the consumer in deciding what is produced and in what quantity through the exercise of his buying decisions. How much resources are allocated to the production of a particular good is determined by the consumers' demand, and prices rise or fall based on the consumers' choices. Even the monopolist, is subject to the sovereignty of the consumer, as he cannot fix the price at which to sell and the quantity to sell at the same time. He will either chose to fix the price and supply the quantity the market will take at that price or supply a certain amount and let the market decide the price.

Consumer's Surplus: Consumer surplus is the gain, by a consumer, of actually purchasing a good for less than he is willing to pay (reservation price). If, for example, a thirsty jogger is willing to pay N100.00 for a bottle of water, but was asked to pay N60.00, the consumer surplus is N100 – N60.00 i.e. N40.00. Consumer surplus is highest when sellers' economic profit is zero and zero when sellers can practice perfect price discrimination (i.e., selling each unit at buyer's reservation price). Consumer's surplus is an example of Economic Surplus.

Consumption: part of income used up or spent on immediate satisfaction i.e. the part of income not saved. The higher the level of consumption, the higher the multiplier effect. Consumption is dependent on, or is a function of income. Consumption is specified by the marginal propensity to consume (mpc).

In national income accounting, the total volume of private expenditure, denoted by C, in an economy during the course of the year.

Consumption Function: the relationship between consumption (C) and income, Y. Denoted by the formula: $C = a + bY$; where C = autonomous consumption; b = marginal propensity to consume.

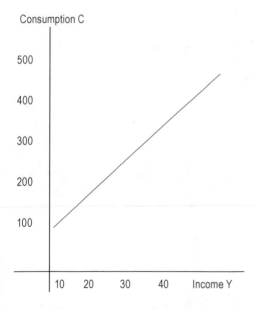

Consumption Line: the line, *PQ* in the diagram below, showing all possible combination of two goods a consumer can buy with a certain income or outlay.

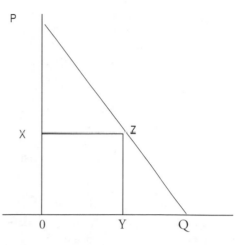

The consumer may decide to use his entire outlay on good P, he will buy 0P; he may instead decide to forgo good P and spend his entire income on good Q, buying quantity 0Q. Between these extremes, he may combine some quantity of both goods e.g. 0X of P and 0Y of Q, denoted by z on the Consumption Line.

Contract: a legal agreement between two or more parties that gives rise to enforceable rights and obligations. For an agreement to qualify as a contract, it must be enforceable by law. To be valid or enforceable by law, certain conditions must be met. These include

1. *Offer*: There must be an offer or proposal by one party (the offeror) to the other, the offeree.
2. *Acceptance*: the offer must have been accepted without conditions. If there exist elements of force i.e. duress or undue influence in either offer or acceptance, there is no contract.
3. *Consideration*: each party—the offeree and the offeror—must receive a benefit in return for their obligation under the agreement. 4. *Capacity*: parties must have the capacity to

enter into a contract. A contract with an underage (legal minor) is not enforceable.

5. *Legal*: the purpose of the contract must be legal. For example, an agreement to carry out an illegal act or that contravenes applicable regulations is not a contract.

6. *Required form*: certain contracts must be in specified form. A hire purchase contract must be in writing, for example.

Contractionary policy: A macroeconomic policy to slow down or moderate the level of economic activity when it is thought to be getting out of hand with inflationary tendencies. The overall aim is to reduce spending and investment by reducing the amount of money in circulation thereby reducing credit available and/or to increase taxes. This may be carried out through i) increasing interest rates ii) increasing the bank rate and other open market operations.

Contributory Pension: pension system under which the employer and the employee contribute to a common fund during the employees' work life so that he may become entitled to a pension upon retirement.

The Contributory Pension System replaced the Pay As You Go Defined Benefit System with the passage of the Pension Reform Act in 2004. The Defined Benefit Scheme was funded by the Federal Government through budgetary allocations, which proved unsustainable.

Under the new scheme, employees contribute a minimum of 7.5% of their Basic Salary, Housing and Transport Allowances (2.5% for the Military). Employers contribute 7.5% in the case of the Public Sector and 12.5%

in the case of the Military. The contributions go into a Retirement Savings Account (RSA) of the individual worker with a Pension Fund Administrator (PFA) of his choice. An individual's RSA remain even when the contributor changes place of work or employer.

The new pension scheme is a strictly regulated process with responsibilities shared between Pension Fund Administrators and Pension Fund Custodians both of which are overseen by the National Pension Commission.

Individual accounts that are privately managed by Pension Fund Administrators while the pension funds' assets are held by Pension Fund Custodians.

Controlling Interest: shareholding in a company that entitles the shareholder to control the management.

Convertibility: this term may be used in relation to bank notes and also in relation to foreign exchange. Bank notes are said to be convertible if they can be exchanged on demand for coin of full face value, as was obtainable under the gold standard.
A currency is described as convertible if it can be easily exchanged for other currencies without any restrictions.

Convertible Debentures: a long-term loan that may be converted to equity or ordinary shares.

Convertible Loan Stock: long-term capital, such as debentures, which may be converted, within a specified time frame, to ordinary shares.

Co-operative Society: a business organization owned by a group of individuals with common economic interest. There are three types of co-operative societies; producers co-operative, consumers' co-operative and credit and thrift co-operative societies.

1. Producers' Co-Operative Society: Producers of a particular commodity may decide to pool their resources together for the purposes of producing or marketing their products. This may enable small producers to producer on a large scale thereby benefit from economies of large scale. This will also enable them to jointly market their products and enjoy value-added services. For example, a producer s' co-operative society of farmers can buy, grade, package, store and distribute produce of the farmers. Individual members receive their money once the products are sold. Individual would not have been able to do all this alone.

2. Consumers' Co-Operative is formed by a group of people with the aim of obtaining low prices by buying in bulk or large quantity. Members pay a subscription fee and are entitled to a share of the profits which depends on the amount of purchases.

3. Credit And Thrift Co-Operative Is formed by people who wish to save money together so that loans can be given to members at relatively low interest rates. The co-operative also makes it easier for members to obtain loans from commercial banks.

Features and Characteristics of Co-Operative Societies

1. No maximum number of members of a co-operative society.
2. Unlimited liability

3. A co-operative society is not a separate legal entity.
4. The profits of a co-operative are not taxed by the government
5. Co-operatives are self-help organizations primarily concerned with the welfare of its members. The aim is not maximize profit unlike other business organizations.
6. Democracy. Every member has a say in the affairs of a co-operative. Members have equal rights and every member is entitled to one vote, and can stand for election into any office.
7. Members must take a minimum number of shares. This is how capital is raised for the co-operative.
8. All members bear the risk of the business together.
9. Profits are shared among members on the basis of patronage or purchases made from the co-operative.

Copyright: the exclusive right to reproduce a literary work or musical composition. It is assignable to another person in for a payment.

Corporate Affairs Commission (CAC): the Registrar of Companies in Nigeria. All corporate bodies are registered and issued certificates of incorporation by the CAC, and are required to make Annual Returns to it, among other requirements as specified under the Companies and Allied Matters Act.

Cost Curve: a graphical representation of the relationship between cost and output. Cost is plotted on the vertical axis against output on the horizontal axis.

A cost curve is derived from a cost function.

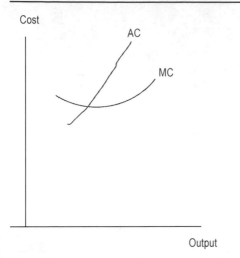

The cost curve shows that marginal cost (MC) and average cost (AC) are equal when MC is at a minimum. Before this point MC was falling, and AC is less than MC; after this point, it is on an upward trend. The output produced at the point when MC and AC are equal is the optimum output, because after this point addition to cost is greater than addition to revenue.

Cost, Insurance and Freight (c.i.f): a quotation on goods inclusive of cost of the goods, freight and insurance up the port of destination but excluding cost from port to the purchaser's premises.

Cost of Living: the amount required to afford the basic necessities of life. This may change overtime and may vary from one region or geographic area to another. This is measured through the Cost of Living Index, which is approximated by the Consumer Price Index.

Cost of Living Index: a measure of what is required to afford the basic necessities of life. A Consumer Price Index gives an approximate measure of a Cost-of-Living Index for a place at a point in time.

Cost Schedule: a table showing average cost, marginal cost, total cost etc., or any of these. Cost curves are derived from cost schedules.

Costs of Production: Money paid to factors of production for their contribution in the process of production; expenses incurred in the course of creating utility or satisfying want. The cost of production of a good cannot be specified unless it is related to a certain level of output. Cost per unit of output falls as output is increases. In the short-run, costs of production are either fixed or variables. In the long-run, all costs are variable. The production function specifies the relationship between costs of inputs, e.g. labour and capital and output. With the knowledge of this relationship, a cost schedule can be drawn as shown below:

- *Fixed Cost:* costs that remain constant (in the short run) as output increases or decreases. The cost of factory, installed machinery, salaries, rent and rates and other administrative expenses or costs as well as interest on loans remain constant whether the firm is producing at half of full capacity.

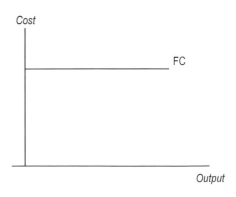

- *Variable Cost:* cost that vary or changes as output changes. Example are cost of raw material and wages of labour

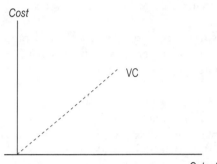

- *Total cost:* fixed cost plus variable cost.

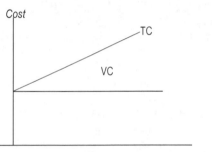

- *Average Cost:* the cost per unit of output produced. Initially, average cost decreases as output increases, giving rise to economies of scale. Ultimately, a point is reached where AC begins to rise; beyond this point, marginal cost is higher than AC. This means that addition to cost is greater than addition to cost, and the firm begins to incur losses.

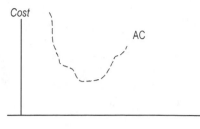

Mathematically,
AC = TC/Q

Output	FC	VC	TC	AC
a	b	c	(b+c)	TC/a
1	3	5	8	8
2	3	11	14	7
3	3	15	18	6
4	3	17	20	5
5	3	27	30	6
6	3	45	48	8

- *Marginal Cost:* the addition to total cost as output is increased by one unit.
$$MC = TC_2 - TC_2$$

Output	FC	VC	TC	MC
1	3	5	8	-
2	3	11	14	6
3	3	15	18	4
4	3	17	20	2
5	3	27	30	10
6	3	45	48	12

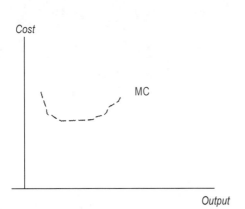

- *Average Fixed Cost (AFC)*: fixed cost per unit of output; total fixed costs divided by the number of units of output.

- *Average Variable Cost (AVC):* the variable cost per unit of output; Total Variable Cost divided by the number of units of output.

- *Average Total Cost (ATC):* total cost divided by output.

Cost-Push inflation: a sustained increase in the general price level (inflation) caused by increase in the cost of production. Cost-push inflation may be brought about by increase in the price of raw materials and other inputs of production. An increase in the price of petrol, for example, will increase cost of production across the various industries and cause the general price level to rise.

Cottage Industry: the production of goods from home for sale.

Coupon: the rate of interest on fixed income securities such as bonds and debenture.

Cover Note: a temporary insurance cover meant to bridge the gap before a comprehensive insurance policy is processed.

Crawling Peg: a type of flexible exchange rate that allows for very small movement in the rate of exchange in a year.

Credit: deferment or postponement of payment for value received. It is a form of financing. Credit is the grease of commerce ensuring that the wheels of production continue in motion. The availability of credit is a determinant of economic growth. This depends on the level of savings and the efficiency of financial intermediation in the economy, money market institutions (banks, co-operatives, thrift societies, finance houses) and capital market institutions (stock exchange, investment/merchant banks, insurance companies, etc.).

In the distributive trade, **trade credit** is an essential form of short-term finance. The producer may allow the wholesaler a period before payment or receive payment in advance from the wholesaler. The wholesaler in turn allows the retailer an interval, e.g. 30, 45, or 60 days, before payment. A well-capitalized wholesaler may even pay the producer in advance of taking delivery. The retailer may also extend credit to end-users to encourage sales. The producer, wholesaler and retailer recognize that they are partners, and that they need each other to be established and succeed; credit is an indicator of the level of trust and goodwill between them built overtime.

Bank Credit is usually in the form a loan or overdraft. Bank credit effectively increases the total purchasing power in the economy, and as such can impact on the general price level. The ability of banks to create credit must therefore be in tune with the monetary policy as managed by the central bank. The central bank ensures this through open market operations.

Credit Worthiness: the Six C's of Credit: assessment of a person's credit worthiness is usually based on a set of six factors, namely;

Character: a measure of the applicant's trustworthiness and integrity to honour his obligations.

Capacity: the ability to pay. Present and projected earnings vis-à-vis the amount of credit sought.

Conditions: likelihood of the applicant's job or business becoming adversely affected by general economic conditions; it entails a general assessment of the state of the local economy—inflation, unemployment, etc.

Collateral: a credit may be secured by an asset of value (collateral) which the lender may sell to recover or unsecured i.e. simply based on a promise to repay.

Credit: this refers to credit history i.e. how well the individual has handled his finances in the past demonstrating financial prudence and discipline or otherwise. This may be gleaned from personal interaction with the applicant.

Capital: the applicant's net worth, which may be indicated by assets or financial resources.

Sources of Credit
Hire Purchase: with a Hire Purchase facility a buyer/hirer can begin to use an asset before completing the payment. Payment is by scheduled installments during which

time the seller/vendor retains the title/ownership of the asset. After the paying the last installment, the hirer may take over the ownership. In this way a transport company, for example, may increase its fleet of vehicles without a huge initial capital outlay while boosting its revenue.

Mortgages: this relate to real estate financing. Mortgages are usually long-term in nature. It is secured form of credit as the property or building financed is used as the collateral for the amount extended. An new business location or factory may be financed by means of a mortgage, without adversely affecting business operations by allowing payment to be spread over a period of time.

Loans and Overdrafts: banks and finance houses gives advances to their customers, on short and long-term basis on structured terms (specified interest rates and tenor, etc.)

Rentals: a person or business may enjoy the service of an asset by way of rentals for a specified period of time. This may be particularly useful when an asset is required for a particular operation, time or as a stop-gap.

Credit Sales: the seller may agree to let the buyer take ownership and possession of the goods and for payment to be deferred or spread over a period of time.

Credit Card: a card issued by a bank to a customer after an assessment of his creditworthiness, entitling its holder to obtain credit from specified vendors up to a specified maximum amount. The card issuer essentially guarantees the card holder up to the agreed amount. The card-holder pays the bank at agreed regular intervals. Credit cards are a feature of electronic payment systems.

Credit Note: see under Commercial Documents.

Creeping Inflation: same as Persistent Inflation; see under inflation.

Cross Elasticity of Demand: This is the responsiveness of demand for a commodity to a change in price of another commodity. This happens with goods which are related in demand e.g. substitute and complimentary goods. For example, if two goods are substitutes, they tend to be in competitive demand, such that an increase in the price of one will bring about an increase in the quantity demanded of its substitute. Thus, a change in the price of beef will affect the demand for fish; the demand for petrol may increase or decrease due to a change in the price of diesel. Similarly, the demand for wigs may be affected by a change in the price of weave-on. The cross elasticity of demand is given by the formula:

$$= \frac{\%\ \text{change in quantity demanded of X}}{\%\ \text{change in price of Y}}$$

The cross elasticity of commodities X and Y are of particular importance to their respective producers in decisions relating to price and quantity to supply to the market.

Illustrative example

Commodity	Changes in Price	
	Previous Price	New Price
	=N=	=N=
Beef	50	75

Commodity	Changes in Quantity Demanded	
	Previous Qty	New Qty
	(KG)	(KG)
Fish	1000	3000

To determine the cross elasticity of demand for beef and fish:
Step 1; determine the percentage change in quantity demanded and price respectively:
Percentage change in quantity demanded:
Change in quantity demanded of fish

$$= 3000\ \text{kg} - 1000\text{kg} = 2000\text{kg}$$

Express as a percentage:

$$2000/1000 \times 100 = 200\%$$

Change in Price of beef

Price: Change in the price of beef:

$$N75 - N50 = N25$$

Express as a percentage:

$$25/50 \times 100 = 50\%$$

Therefore, cross elasticity of demand

$$= 200/50 = 4$$

Crowd-out: the tendency for government borrowing, e.g. to finance a budget deficit, to put upward pressure on interest rates, thereby leave little funds left (i.e. crowd out) for private sector borrowing.

Cumulative Preference shares: shares with guaranteed dividend, which accumulates if it is not paid. Dividends on these shares must be paid before any other dividends can be paid to other shareholders.

Currency: Paper bills (bank notes) and coins held by the public. Currencies, along with coins, are legal tender which people are obliged to accept as payment for goods and services and settlement of debt.

Currency Appreciation: An increase in the value of one currency relative to another currency. Appreciation occurs when, because of a change in exchange rates; a unit of one currency buys more units of another currency. This term is used when such an increase is brought about in the interaction of demand and supply in the foreign exchange market as opposed to a formal re-appraisal.

Currency Depreciation: A decline in the value of one currency relative to another currency due to market forces. Depreciation occurs when, because of a change in exchange rates, a unit of one currency buys fewer units of another currency.

Currency Devaluation: A deliberate or formal downward adjustment in the official exchange rate of a currency relative to other currencies. Devaluation is a last recourse to remedy a fundamental balance of payment disequilibrium. In such cases, the disequilibrium is because the currency is exchanging at a rate higher than its real value i.e. it is overvalued. Devaluation may therefore be deemed necessary. The effect of devaluation is to discourage imports by making them relatively more expensive and encourage exports by making them relatively cheaper or more competitive. In this way, equilibrium will be restored in the country's balance of payment.

For example, if a tonne of cotton costs N1, 000, and the rate of exchange of the US dollar to the Naira is $1 = N2, an American importer will pay $500 to buy a tonne of cotton from a Nigerian exporter. If the government decides to devalue the Naira so that the new exchange rate is $1 = N200, the American will now pay $5 for the same quantity of cotton. Nigerian exports

will now be cheaper and more competitive compared to those from other countries, and therefore exports may experience a boom, as Nigerian exports will compete more favourably with others. Conversely, imported goods will now become more expensive, and demand for locally made goods will increase.

Currency Revaluation: A deliberate or formal upward adjustment in the official exchange rate of a currency relative to other currencies. This hardly happens in practice, however, because of the balance of payments implication: making imports cheaper and exports less competitive.

Current Account: 1. A type of bank account from which withdrawals may be made by cheques and into which cheques can be paid. Interest is not earned on this type of account, and the bank charges a commission for withdrawals made. 2. That part of a country's *balance of payments accounts* which records the value of goods and services exported minus the value of goods and services imported. It consists of two parts; the visible trade section (where trade in goods are recorded) and the invisible trade section (where trade in services are recorded). See Balance of Payments.

Current Assets: very liquid assets which are as good as cash or can be easily converted to cash. Items under this classification in a balance sheet include cash, bank balance, accounts receivable/debts and closing stock

Current Liabilities: payments due to be made in the short-term such as accounts payable.

Current Ratio: the ratio of current assets to current liabilities.

$$= \frac{\text{Current Assets}}{\text{Current Liabilities}} : 1$$

It shows how well a business can meet its short-term liabilities or payment obligations out of is short-term assets. It is also referred to as 'working capital ratio.'

Customs Duties: tax imposed on goods imported into the country. Import duties are a form of indirect tax and provide a source of revenue for the government. As part of a country's commercial policy, there are used to regulate or restrict imported goods.

Customs Union: a form of economic integration in which member countries imposes no tariffs on goods traded among them and imposes a common external tariff on goods from non-members.

Customer Service: This refers to services designed to attract and to make sure they come back again. Customer service consists of 1. Pre-Sale Services and 2. After-Sale Services.

Pre-Sale services are services provided to prospective customers in order to encourage them to buy. This includes a) Granting of discount b) Granting of credit facilities including hire purchase. c).Personal attention to the individual concerns of the prospective customer; d) dispatching of price list, catalogue, brochure and other information to the prospective customer.

After-Sale Services: These are services rendered after the customer has made a purchase in order to encourage continued patronage.

After-Sale services include a) Home Delivery: the seller offers to transport the goods to the customer's location at no extra-cost. The seller of a power generating plant in Lagos, for example, may offer to deliver to a customer's factory in Lokoja b). Free-installation services: for example of equipment the seller of the power generating plant may offer installation.

c). Provision of Servicing, Repairs and Maintenance: the seller of cars may offer to insure a car for the first year.

d) Warranty: a manufacturer may undertake to repair or replace equipment if it is faulty under a specified period, e.g. three years, under certain terms and conditions.

Cyclical Fluctuations: see Trade Cycle

Cyclical Unemployment: Unemployment caused by a low level of aggregate demand associated with recession or depression phase of the business cycle. During a recession or depression, firms close down or cut back on production because of low demand and lay off workers.

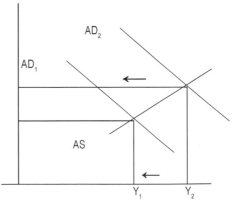

D

Dalasi: currency of Gambia; equal to 100 Bututs.

Death Rate: the number of deaths per thousand of the population in a year. The death rate is one of the determinants of the growth rate of the population, along with birth rate, immigration and emigration. Factors that affect death rate include the standard of living, availability of medical services/facilities, incidence of natural and man-made disasters, etc.

Debenture: long-term loan capital issued at a fixed rate of interest. Debenture holders are creditors, not owners or shareholders, therefore debenture interest must be paid before dividend to shareholders is considered. Debenture interest, indicated by the coupon rate, is a business expense and must be paid whether or not profit is made, unlike dividend which may or may not be paid. Debentures may be irredeemable or redeemable by the issuing company at a certain future date. Debentures may be secured on the company's assets in which case the holders have a lien on assets in the event of liquidation.

Debit Note: see under Commercial Documents.

Debt Buy Back: repurchase by the debtor of its own debt usually at a discount. This strategy was used by the Nigerian government under Gen Babangida to reduce the National Debt by buying at discounted values on the international capital market. This was discretely done through third parties. The National Debt was reduced by USD$5billion, mainly comprising of sums owed the London Club.

Debt Instrument: interest bearing financial security having specified interest payment and maturity (redemption) dates. Examples are debentures and preference shares. Debt instruments are evidenced by certificates which show their essential features.

Debt Management Office: the organization responsible for the management of Nigeria's international and domestic or local debt. The DMO is active in Nigeria's capital and money markets in its role to raise long-term and short term funds to fund budget deficits. This is through the issuance of bonds and treasury bills. The DMO was established in year 2000 before which time the nation's debt was managed by diverse departments in the Federal Ministry of Finance and the Central Bank. The DMO's functions includes debt recording and management activities, debt service forecasts; debt service payments; advising on debt negotiations as well as new borrowings.

Debt Sustainability Analysis (DSA): an assessment of a country's capacity to service its maturing debt servicing obligations. The level of external debt carries a higher weight relative to internal debt. Relevant factors include level of external reserves, exports receipts, government revenue, and debt-to-GDP ratio. It takes a dynamic approach that also includes an appraisal of the overall direction of government policies. The DSA gives an indication of financial stability. A Debt Sustainability Analysis is necessary to gauge a country's ability to attract foreign investment and financial assistance on the international capital market, from trading partners and international financial organizations like the International Monetary Fund and the World Bank Group.

Decreasing Economies of Scale or decreasing returns to scale: disadvantages of large-scale production; refers to a situation where long run average costs are increasing as output increases or when an increase in inputs brings about a less than proportionate increase in output. This means the firm is producing at a point where addition cost is more than addition to revenue or profit.

Decreasing Returns: See Diminishing Returns

Deductive Method: also known as the analytical, abstract or prior method; one of the methods (the other being the inductive method) used to derive generalizations in theory. The deductive method reasons from the general to the particular. Starting from a given hypothesis—e.g. that man is solely motivated by money—a conclusion is reached that, for example, a worker would demand the highest wages possible.

The following steps are followed using the deductive method:

1. *Perception of the problem:* the analyst must have a clear idea of the issue he is interested in investigating.
2. *Defining of terms:* a clear definition of terms and statement of assumptions.
3. *Derive hypothesis from assumptions:* on the basis of assumptions and premises, a hypothesis is stated.
4. *Testing of hypothesis:* verify hypothesis to test using statistical and other methods.

Criticism of the Deductive Method: the conclusions arrived at by the method are only as valid as the premises and assumptions from inferences are made. Where such assumptions are simplistic half-truths, the conclusions are bound to be facile and cannot withstand rigour.

Deed of Partnership: the governing document of a partnership. It contains the name of the business, method of admission of new members, amount of capital to be contributed by each member, how profit and losses are to be shared, responsibility for management by members, etc.

Deferred Payments: a function of money is to be able to facilitate the settlement of debt at a later date than on the date of a transaction. This derives from the fact that money is trusted to act as store of value.

Deferred Shares: *see Founder's Shares*

Deficit Financing: when government expenditure in a particular fiscal year exceeds its revenue. This may be considered the practical thing to do during a period of economic recession or depression with falling aggregate demand and unemployment. The government may reduce taxes while increasing expenditure in order to stimulate purchasing power and thereby spur investment/economic activity.

Deflation: persistent fall in the general price level; may be caused by weak aggregate demand which forces producers to reduce prices in order to sell their products. Businesses decline during period of deflation leading to low investment and unemployment. Deflation brings about an increase in the value of money as a given amount of money buys more goods and services. Creditors/lenders gain at the expense of borrowers/debtors. Fixed income earners benefit during a period of deflation while those whose incomes are not fixed are at a disadvantage. A combination of monetary and fiscal policy measures aimed at increasing purchasing power may be used to correct the situation. Monetary policy measures will be aimed at increasing the money supply through open market operations and raising the bank rate. Fiscal policy measures will include reducing taxes in order to increase purchasing power and encourage spending.

Deflationary Gap: the amount of investment, public and private, required to achieve full employment, where national output is less than full employment level; the amount by which aggregate demand is inadequate to achieve equilibrium national output or full employment i.e. the difference between equilibrium national income or output and aggregate demand. There is not enough demand for the available output of businesses leading to a downward pressure on the general price level. To bring the economy to equilibrium level, the government may use fiscal and monetary policy measures to stimulate purchasing power, for example, by reducing interest rates (thereby making it easier to obtain loans), and reducing taxes (thereby increasing disposable income). The government may also increase public expenditure e.g. by engaging in capital projects.

***Del Credere* Agent:** an agent who guarantees payments to his principal in return for a higher commission.

Delivery Order: see under Commercial Documents

Demand the quantity of the commodity consumers are ready and willing to buy at given prices and during a certain period. It is described as *effective demand* to differentiate it from wants which are not backed up by ability to pay. Note also that the prices are known and that it covers a definite period of time.

Individual and aggregate demand schedules and curves:

A demand schedule is a table showing the quantities of a commodity a consumer will buy at different prices. The table below shows a housewife's demand schedule for good.

Price per bag (Naira)	Quantity (bags per week)
100	10
110	8
120	5
130	3
140	2

Due to differences in tastes and incomes, demand schedules differ between individuals. Different individuals will demand different quantities at different prices. When the demands of all consumers in the market are combined we have the *aggregate or market demand.* The demand schedule can be plotted graphically to produce a *demand curve*. Price is plotted on the vertical (y – axis) and quantity demanded is plotted on the horizontal axis (x-axis). It is conventionally labeled DD.

Price

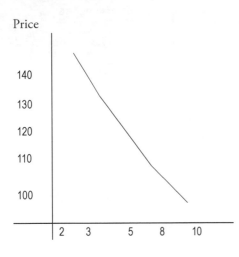

Quantity

The demand curve slopes from left to right i.e. it has a negative slope. This is a reflection of the **law of demand**: the _higher the price, the lower the quantity demanded_. This characterizes demand irrespective of tastes, preferences or income. All things being equal, more will be demanded at lower prices; less will be demanded as price increases. This is because as price rises, a commodity becomes expensive relative to its substitutes which are now demanded instead of it, and also less of it can be afforded due to the increase in prices.

Exceptional Demand Schedules and Curves: In certain situations more of a commodity is demanded at a higher price. This is an exceptional case, and in such situations the demand curve slopes from right to left, i.e. it has a positive slope, over a section of it or entirely.

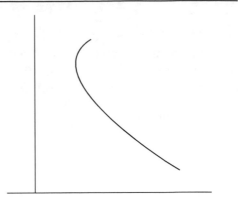

Exceptional demand curve   Abnormal demand curve with two slopes

Exceptional demand may be due to the type of good or due to peculiar circumstances.

1. *Articles of ostentation*: Luxury items such as tend to be more valuable at higher prices because the higher the price they command, the higher the *snob appeal*. They therefore tend to have exceptional demand schedules curves.

2. *Anticipation of changes in prices*: people will buy more at higher prices if they feel prices may rise further in the future. Also, less will be bought if they feel that prices may fall further in the immediate future. This is particularly true of the stock and shares of companies traded on the stock exchange. Dealers often look for shares with hidden potential or undervalued shares; they buy more of such shares at lower prices in anticipation of future rise in stock prices.

3. *Inferior good*: less of certain goods are bought as income increases. These are inferior goods or *giffen* goods. Examples include garri, used clothing, etc. which are consumed or used due to an inability to afford

better quality. An increase in the price of these commodities would lead to more being demanded, and less of other less essential commodities being demanded. In contrast, a fall in their prices would not lead to more being bought. Instead more of other commodities which could not previously be afforded will be bought.

4. *Rare commodities* such as antique furniture, paintings and manuscript have a positive demand slope as people tend to be willing to demand more at higher prices.

Demand, Determinants of, or Factors influencing the demand for a commodity

1. Price of the commodity: other things being equal, the higher the price of a good, the lower the demand for it and vice versa. If the price of good rises, the other goods of lower price will be substituted for it.

2. Price of other goods: price of goods that serve the same function (butter and margarine) or complement each other (tea and milk) affect the demand of the competing or complement.

3. New commodities e.g. may render a product obsolete and dated. For example, advent of colour television outmoded and outstripped demand for black and white TV.

4. Consumer's income: a person's demand depends on his income. He may decide on cheaper substitutes or purchase a more 'upscale' brand if his income increases.

5. Tastes and preferences: More of certain goods are demanded, and less of other is demanded by two individuals with identical incomes because of differences in tastes and preferences.

6. Fashion: People change their demand in line with the fashion of the day.

7. Expectation of future change in price.

8. Weather conditions: more of a particular good may be demanded and less of another due to weather conditions.

Demand, Types of

- Joint or complimentary Demand: demand for commodities that go together. Examples are cars and petrol, tea and sugar, etc.

- Competitive demand: demand for goods that are substitutes e.g. tea and coffee; butter and margarine.

- Derived demand: where the demand for a factor service or a (good) depends on the end-product which it is used to produce or obtain e.g. the demand for *factors of production*, *capital goods* and *money*

- Composite Demand: where a commodity is used for a more than one purpose. The demand for things like wood, for example, is composite because it is used for building construction as well as for furniture. Thus the price for wood depends on demand for both purposes. If demand for wood for construction purposes rises, the supply for furniture will reduce and bring about an increase in price.

Demand Deposit: American term for a Current Account at a bank, from which withdrawal may be made by means of cheque.

Demand, Exceptional: instances where more is demanded at higher prices than at lower prices.. This occurs in cases of inferior goods or so-called *giffen* goods, as well as articles of ostentation. A fear of future rise in prices may also bring this about. In such instances, the demand curve has a positive slope.

Demand for Money: desire to hold money as opposed to spending it. It is also referred to as *liquidity preference*. Unlike other commodities, money is not demanded for its own sake. Its demand *derives* from what it enables us to do; it is therefore said to have a *derived demand*. Lord Maynard Keynes identified three *motives* for the demand for money: 1. *Transactional motive*: this is the desire to hold money to enable us deal with day-to-day transactions such as transport fares, payment of bills, food stuffs, etc. 2. *Precautionary motive:* We also desire money for contingency or unforeseen circumstances. Such circumstances include accidents, major breakdown of one's vehicle, etc. 3. *Speculative motive:* this is the desire to hold money in order to take advantage of emerging investment opportunities. If people speculate that prices are likely to fall in the future, they will not make purchases in order to profit from the fall in prices. Similarly if interest rates are low, the desire to hold money for speculative purposes will be high.

Demographic Transition Theory: According to the demographic transition theory of population, countries go through three stages of demographic patterns based on population changes. This "theory" is *based on the history of Western European countries. Stage I: The Pre-Industrialization Stage*: At this stage, production is mainly primary, most people get married in their teens, the average family size is large, modern medical facilities are poor or non-existent, birth rate is high but death is equally high, thus there is stable growth rate. This is common to pre-industrial societies that are primitive society yet to experience economic modernization.

Stage II: The Industrial Stag: This is a period of population explosion as birth rates are higher than death rates. During this period the country or society is becoming industrialized, the work force is becoming increasingly specialized. Thus there is improved public and private healthcare, better diet, higher incomes, etc; as a result birth rate is higher than death rate giving rise to high life expectancy and a reduction in mortality rates. Most developing countries of the world are this stage. *Stage III: Post-industrial stage:* At the post-industrial stage of development, a country has very high standard of living, excellent medical facilities, life expectancy is high; the work force becomes highly specialized. Late marriage is common, and family size tends to be smaller. This leads to declining or low birth rates while better standard living standard and better medical conditions means low death rates leading to low or no population growth. Most developed countries of the world are at this stage of the transition. As a result of this, some of these countries are encouraging immigration in order to boost their work force.

Dependants: members of the population who are not part the economically active population (work or labour force). This may be because they are too young or too old.

Dependency Ratio: the ratio of dependants to the working population.

Depreciation: wear and tear of an capital asset over time. In national Income accounting allowance must be made for depreciation to derive Net National Product/Income/Output.

Depression: see Economic Depression

Deregulation: reduction or elimination, in some cases, of administrative controls on the types of businesses done, prices charged, and competition within an industry to enable a market-based allocation of resources. Regulation of the power and telecommunications sector in Nigeria meant that private investment was not allowed in these sectors. Commodity Boards used to dictate the price farmers could sell their produce. Similarly, what could be imported depended on the discretion of officials who issued import licenses. In the banking sector interest rate was administratively set by the Central Bank instead of being determined by the demand and supply for investment funds.

Regulation of certain industries is often a necessity because of their strategic nature or they are considered sensitive to national interest. However, it has been observed to distort prices and thereby bring about inefficient resource allocation. It sometimes gives bureaucrats undue power over economic agents, and breed corruption.

Deregulation, alongside liberalization, was the main thrust of the economic reforms that started under the Structural Adjustment Programme in 1986 in Nigeria, and which has continued since then. This has ended government monopoly of certain sectors such as telecommunications and power generation, and the elimination of Commodity Boards, which regulated agricultural production.

Devaluation: see currency devaluation.

Development Economics: branch of economics concerned with the study of the process of development of economies from subsistent communities with basic forms of organization to monetized, advanced societies with complex organization and technology

Development Finance Institutions: specialized banking institutions, owned and funded by the government, established to provide development finance to specific sectors of the economy. The DFIs in Nigeria are the Nigeria Export-Import Bank (NEXIM), Bank of Industry, Federal Mortgage Bank of Nigeria (FMBN), Infrastructure Bank (formerly the Urban Development Bank of Nigeria and the Bank of Agriculture (formerly, the Nigeria Agricultural Co-operative and Rural Development Bank).

These banks may be likened to the Korea's Development Banks which were instrumental to that country's success story. The government used these banks to support private firms that have attained some level of success on their own, and made them 'national champions' by providing them with credit. These firms, the *chaebol*,—include today's Samsung, LG, Hyundai, Daewoo etc.,—became the drivers of the country's industrial development. In the same way, China's Policy Banks—which carry out the policies set by the country's executive council to fund the country's development objectives e.g. from funding major infrastructure projects to supporting Chinese brands expand their markets and out-bid competitors world-wide. Unlike their Nigerian counterparts, however, the Chinese Policy Banks:

- Adequately capitalized with clearly defined mandates.
- Publish audited annual reports.
- Cheaply raise funds on the international capital market by issuing bonds.

Development Stocks: see Federal Government of Nigeria Development Stocks.

Diminishing Marginal Returns (law of) or law of variable proportions: Factors of production may be combined in different proportions to produce an output. There is however a limit to the output that may be achieved by simply increasing a factor while holding other factors constant or fixed. Diminishing returns is expressed in the law of diminishing returns which states that as increasing units of a factor of production are combined with one or more factors which are fixed in quantity, output might increase at first but a time will eventually be reached when addition to output (marginal product) of the variable factor will decline.

As the variable factor is increased, marginal product (MP) initially increases, due to increasing returns to scale; increase in the variable factor brings about a more than proportionate increase in output. Under this situation, the variable factor may be profitably increased until MP reaches a maximum, 16. At this point, factors of production are optimally combined. Beyond this point, MP falls, as output can no longer be increased by varying only one factor.

Fixed factor	Variable factor	Total product	Average Product	Marginal Product	Trend
4	1	1	1		
4	2	6	3	5	increasing returns
4	3	15	5	9	
4	4	32	8	17	
4	5	45	9	13	
4	6	48	8	3	diminishing returns
4	7	49	7	1	
4	8	49	6.1	0	
4	9	47	5.2	-2	negative returns
4	10	43	4.3	-4	

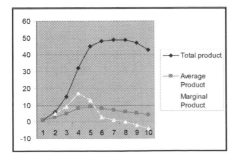

Decreasing returns to scale sets in after this point; increase in the variable factor gives a less than proportionate increase in output.

Between increasing and decreasing returns to scale, there is a period of constant returns to scale during which output changes by the same proportion as increases in input viz. a given percent increase in inputs brings about the same per cent increase in output.

The law of diminishing returns is applicable to all productive activities. In essence, it asserts that there is a limit to the amount of output which may be obtained by simply varying one factor of production while other factors are held constant. When that limit is reached, output can only be increased by varying or increasing all factors of production.

Diminishing Marginal Utility (Law of): is used to explain consumer behaviour; as more and more of a commodity is consumed, the satisfaction derived from consuming successive units (marginal utility) declines. While the total utility (satisfaction) derived by the consumer increases with each cup of ice cream taken, the additional satisfaction (marginal utility) from each successive cup declines until a point of saturation is reached.

Cups of ice-cream consumed	Total utility	**Marginal Utility (MU)**	Average Utility
1	10	10	10
2	18	8	9
3	24	6	8
4	29	5	7.25
5	32	2	6.4
6	33	1	5.5
7	33	0	4.71

Diminishing marginal utility is the basis of demand. As the consumer's satisfaction declines with each successive unit consumed, his valuation of each successive unit declines. Thus, he is only willing to buy more at lower prices; illustrating the law of demand, which is reflected in the demand schedule.

Dinar: currency of several Middle-Eastern and North African countries.

Direct Selling: a method of distribution which bypasses the middleman; the producer selling directly to the consumer.

Direct Services: occupations dealing with personal services and not related to distribution of goods e.g. doctors, teachers, lawyers, civil servants, judges, entertainers, soldiers, etc.

Direct tax: Amount levied by government on the incomes of individuals and firms, and on transfers of income and wealth. Examples: personal income tax, company income tax, capital gains tax.

Discretional income: what is left of a person's income after meeting all his basic needs and commitments—food, clothing, housing, rates, and direct taxes. See also disposable income.

Discount: 1. a reduction in the price of a good in order to boost sales or encourage prompt payment. This may be in different forms viz.

a. *Trade discount*: usually given to the middleman (wholesaler or retailer) to enable him make a profit; it is the difference between the buying price and the catalogue or list price; it is expressed as a percentage of the list price.

b. *Cash Discount* also known as rebate is the difference between cash price and the buying price. It is usually expressed as a percentage of the buying price. It is usually offered to encourage prompt payment.

2. The difference between the face value of a security (shares, stocks) and the market price, where the market price is less than the face value. This may be because of the present financial state of the company concerned.

3. A bill of exchange may be acquired for less than its face value (i.e. at a discount) prior to maturity, the amount of discount depending the time till maturity date as well as the risk of default.

Discount House: a financial institution or intermediary which specializes in dealing in money market (short-term) financial securities such as Treasury Bills, Treasury Certificates, commercial bills (like Bankers Acceptances and Commercial Papers), bank deposit certificates, etc. They are licensed by the central bank to deal on behalf of investors who are interested in buying or selling these securities.

Discount Houses play a central role in open market operations as the central bank gauges the money supply or the liquidity in the economy through the operations of the discount houses. The sale and redemption of short-term securities in open market operations is carried out through discount houses.

Services provided by Discount Houses:

(a) Securities trading: buying and selling of Treasury Bills, Treasury Bonds, Government Bonds, and Commercial Bills;

(b) Facilitating Open Market Operations (OMO) transactions by acting as the intermediary between the central bank and banks;

(c) Facilitating the issuance and sale of short term Government securities,

(d) Discount/re-discount services for Treasury Bills, Government Securities and other financial instruments;

(e) Short-term Financial Accommodation to banks in addition to accepting short-term investments from them;

(f) Short-term Financial Intermediation: acceptance of funds and placement of the funds in short-term financial securities like Commercial Papers, Bankers Acceptances, Government Securities;

(g) Personalized Wealth Management and portfolio management to high net-worth individuals;

(h) Portfolio Management services to Pension funds, Employee Schemes, Trustees of family settlements and charities.

Discretional Income: the amount of a person's income left after he has taken care of his basic needs and commitments such as food, shelter, clothing, rates and taxes.

Discriminating Monopoly: The charging of different prices to different groups of consumers for a similarly good or service. This is only possible under certain conditions. Firstly, it is not possible to transfer the good between the markets. Secondly, the price elasticity is different in the respective markets. Thirdly, the cost of keeping the markets separate is not too high. The monopolist practices price discrimination in order to maximize surplus profit. When the conditions are met, a monopolist may produce above that output where marginal cost equals marginal revenue. However, he supplies the profit maximizing output in the first market, and the balance in a second market at a price above his marginal cost.

Diseconomies of Scale: a situation where a firm's cost per unit of output (long run average costs) increases disproportionately as output increases. Diseconomies of scale are a disadvantage of large scale production; average cost begins to increase relative to average revenue when production is increased beyond the optimal output.

Disequilibrium: Imbalance. In the absence of rigidities, such a state is bound to be temporary as equilibrium will ultimately be reached. Disequilibrium may exist between demand and supply or between imports and exports in the balance of payments. Without interferences, market forces work towards a price at which supply and demand are equal i.e. equilibrium.

Disguised Unemployment or Hidden Unemployment: level of unemployment not apparent due to the number of people working part-time or retained by employers because they believe present slow-down in economic activity will not last for long.

Disposable Income: The income a person or household has left to spend after all direct taxes have been deducted from personal income. Disposable income may either be spent/consumed or saved.

Distribution, Commercial or Distributive Trade: production is not complete until the product reach the final consumer, and the process of distribution provides the channel through which the product passes from the factory to the individual or final consumer. The chain or process of distribution may be illustrated thus:

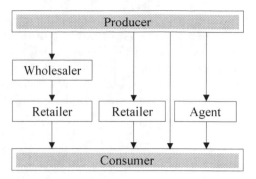

As shown, sometimes the manufacturer deals directly with the retailer. Large retail outlets, for example, buy directly from the manufacturer or from abroad and sell in retail units to the final consumer. Such retailers, however, offer limited services to the consumer. Occasionally, the producer may deal directly with the consumer. This is usually in the case of custom-made goods, where the goods are made to the order or specification of the customer, for example in tailoring. Aeroplanes are also made to the order of the customers e.g. airlines or high net worth individuals. In typical cases, the process is through the manufacturer to the wholesaler and the retailer before the good gets to the consumer.

The Wholesaler and Retailer are the middlemen or intermediaries in-between the producer and the final consumer. They perform the essential link between the producer and the consumer, and thus help to complete the process of production.

The Wholesaler: the wholesaler is a trader who buys in whole or bulk units and normally links the manufacturer with the retailer. He may sometimes deal directly with consumer, especially consumers who desire to buy in large or wholesale quantities. The following types of wholesalers may be identified; *national wholesaler*: this may be the manufacturer's national representative authorized to deal on his behalf nationally; *Regional wholesaler*, who may cover a state or states; *local wholesaler*, who may cover a town or locality; *importers* who buy directly from producers abroad for onward sale to local wholesalers.

Functions of the wholesaler to the manufacturer

1. *Buying in bulk from the producer*: The wholesaler can afford to buy in bulk from the manufacturer because he has the capital. This enables the manufacturer to concentrate on his primary task of production. Without the wholesaler the manufacturer will have to deal with a large number of retailers buying small quantities or a multitude of consumers buying even smaller quantities. This will be a huge distraction.

2. *Market information*: Keeping manufacturers informed of the state of the market. This enables the manufacturer to respond effectively to the market situation, for example, to adjust to changes in taste, fashion or preferences.

3. *Buying in bulk:* by buying in bulk, the wholesaler relieves the manufacturer of warehouse space to continue production and the time and expense of dealing with thousands of orders from retailers.

4. *Warehousing:* by warehousing the goods, the factory is free of produced goods so that production can continue ahead of demand.

5. *Financing*: by paying the manufacturer in cash in advance, the manufacturer has needed to cash to finance operations. Even when he does not pay in advance, the manufacturer can use confirmed orders from the wholesaler to secure short-term loans from his bank.

6. *Completion of production*: the wholesaler sometimes completes production of certain goods by blending, sorting, packaging, etc.

7. *Transportation:* the goods are often conveyed from the factory or plant to warehouse by the wholesaler's trucks and vans. This saves the manufacturer transport and logistics expenses and problems.

8. *Branding*: the wholesaler sometimes collects goods from numerous small producers and markets them in his own trade name or brand.

9. *Advertising:* the wholesaler most times undertakes advertisement of goods in his area.

10. *Trade Promotion and Exhibitions:* sometimes the wholesaler joins with manufacturer to hold trade promotions and exhibitions.

11. *Risk bearing:* By buying and paying the manufacturer in advance, the wholesaler bears the risk of fall in prices

Functions of the Wholesaler to the Retailer

1. *Breaking the bulk for the retailer:* The wholesaler sells in smaller quantities the retailer can afford. This makes it possible for the retailer to stock the different varieties consumers require

2. *Convenient Location*: the wholesaler is usually closer to the retailer in terms of physical location.

3. *Convenient Quantities*: the wholesaler makes it possible for the retailer in smaller quantities that he can afford.

4. *Credit facilities*: the retailer often buys on credit terms from the wholesaler; allowing the retailer to pay after making sales. In this way,

the wholesaler finances the business of the retailer.

5. *Stabilization of prices:* By holding stock of goods and allowing a regular supply in to the market, the wholesaler prevents fluctuation in prices.

6. *Preparation:* the goods are prepared for selling by the grading, pre-packing, and sorting carried out by the wholesaler. The retailer is not equipped to handle this function.

7. *Ready stocks:* by stocks of goods held by the wholesaler assures the retailer of ready stocks and supplies.

Functions of the Retailer

1. *Unit Sales:* The retailer makes it possible for the consumer to buy in small units. Without the retailer, consumers would have to buy in large quantities from the wholesaler or manufacturer.

2. *Convenience to the consumer:* The retailer makes goods available at convenient locations to the consumers. Without the retailer consumers may have to travel long distances to make their purchases.

3. *Variety to the consumer:* the retailer stores a variety of goods in the shop, making it possible for the consumer to obtain a number of his needs at one shop.

4. *Credit facilities to the consumer:* The retailer sometimes sells on credit to the consumer, on weekly, monthly or hire purchase basis.

5. *After-sales services:* In the sale of technical goods, e.g. electronics and machines, retailers provide necessary after-sale and maintenance services.

6. *Market information:* the wholesaler and manufacturer are informed of market situations by the retailer as he is closest to the consumers. Such market information is necessary to know which products are performing well in the market and which are not.

The Role of Co-operatives in Distribution

1. Direct marketing: Consumers' co-operatives buy in bulk from manufacturers and sell at retail prices to members and non-members. Thereby doing without the middlemen.

2. Credit facilities

3. Connect consumers to producers

4. Stabilizing prices

5. Fighting hoarding

6. Advice consumers and buyers

The Role of Government Agencies in Product Distribution in Nigeria The federal government and various state governments in Nigeria have, at various times, set up agencies to ensure the availability as well low prices of essential commodities. These include Nigerian National Supply Company (NNSC), established by the federal government in 1972. It imported and distributed essential commodities through co-operatives, government ministries, appointed distributors as well as directly to the public. In this way it helped to ensure the availability of essential items at affordable prices, at least for a while. The NNSC failed to achieve the objective for which it was established i.e. to keep prices down. In addition, the company was soon overwhelmed by the problems of corruption and embezzlement like most public corporations or parastatals. For these two reasons, as well as poor public finances at the time, the NNSC was closed in 1986 during the Structural Adjustment Programme. Petroleum Trust Fund was established in 1994 and was scrapped in 1999. Like the NNSC, it imported and distributed essential commodities through various channels across the federation.

The Problems of Distributive Trade in West Africa

1. Poor transportation system: Some areas of West Africa are not accessible because of the undeveloped transportation (road, railway network) system in West Africa. A good railway system would make it possible to move goods over long distances at low cost. Poor road network mean that it is difficult and expensive to move agricultural products from rural to urban centres, and to move manufactured goods from urban to rural areas at low cost.

2. Too many middlemen: the chain of distribution is long, with several middlemen before the good reaches the final consumer. This is due to the poor state of the transportation system. This adds to the final price of the goods.

3. Hoarding: hoarding is the act of storing up goods in order to create artificial shortage so as to bring about increase in prices. Middlemen often take undue advantage of market situations by hoarding goods.

4. Low demand: effective demand is low because many people are low income earners. Though many people are in need of the goods, few can afford them. This reduces the market to a small fraction.

5. Inadequate of Credit Facilities: it is difficult for entrepreneurs to raise necessary capital to finance their business ideas because they do not have necessary collateral security. Because of this the distributive trade is dominated by few, very large organizations.

1. *Inadequate Storage Facilities*: Preservation of farm produce is hampered by inadequate storage facilities. This leads to glut in during harvest season and shortage during the planting season.

2. *Undeveloped Commercial Services*: commercial services such as banking, insurance, market research, advertising, warehousing, and transportation necessary to support industry generally. The undeveloped state of these services in West African countries severely hampers business generally.

Distribution of (National) Income: the way rewards for participating in production (rent, interest, wage/salary and profit) is distributed among the various owners of factors of production. The distribution of national income is described as equitable when the various owners are receiving a fair share of the national income; or inequitable when owners of a factor e.g. capital is receiving a more than proportionate share of the national income. In such instance, the government may use fiscal policy to re-distribute national income by taxing the rich and using proceeds to provide public facilities that benefit all.

Distributor: a wholesaler or middleman.

Diversification: spread of investment in several industries or portfolio. This is usually done to minimize the risk of putting all eggs in a single basket.

Divestment: sale of investment.

Dividend: share of profit paid to shareholders by a company. It is proposed by the management of the company for approval by the shareholders. Unlike interest on long-term capital such as debentures, interest is not fixed, and in some years it may not be paid, if the management decides to transfer all of the year's profit to reserves or in years when losses are made.

Dividend Warrant: a draft issued by a limited liability company in favour of a shareholder for the amount of dividend due to the shareholder for a particular period.

Division of Labour: Division of labour is a system of production in which the production process is broken down into different stages so that each stage is undertaken by one person or group of persons. For example, in the a tailoring or garment making process, when division of labour is applied, the different stages of cutting, weaving, sewing, ironing and packaging is handled by different workers.

Division of labour become increasingly evident as the society or community develops. Initially, everybody is a jack-of-all-trades: killing his own meat, planting his own food, building his own house, making his own cloth, etc. As the community develops, some decides to do one or two things e.g. hunting or farming, exchanging his output for those of his neighbour. This increases the total output of goods produced and affords everybody a better standard of life. Even further, within each occupation, people decide to perform only certain

specializations e.g. carpentry, iron-working, plumbing, etc. The quality and quantity of output is further increased leading even higher standard of life as division of labour is applied within farming or woodworking or tailoring. A tailor may make a shirt alone; another may have a few workers/apprentices between whom the different tasks are divided in a workshop. The output is for the immediate or nearby market. In shirt-making factory, division of labour is applied with the different tasks of shirt making performed by specialized workers who use machines to perform the various tasks to mass produce shirts in commercial quantities for nearby and far-away markets.

Division of labour therefore gives rise to specialization as workers are required to work in particular area of work.

Adam Smith, the father of economics, explained division of labour in his book *"The Wealth of Nations"* published in 1776. In his book Adam Smith identified 18 different stages in the production of pins. He explained that when the 18 different stages were handled by different workers instead of one, a total of 48,000 pins were produced instead of 20 pins per day.

Advantages of Division of Labour

1. *Increase in output:* more is produced when division of labour is applied e.g. from 20 pins to 48,000 pins per day in the example cited by Adam Smith.

2. *Greater Productivity:* productivity means output per worker. For example, 18 workers produced 48,000 pins means that output per worker was 2,666.67 (i.e. 48000/18)

3. *Create Employment Opportunities:* breaking down the production process means that more workers are

required to handle the various stages. In making a shirt, for example, different workers are required for cutting, weaving, sewing, fixing buttons, ironing, packaging, etc. respectively instead of one.

4. *Proficiency*: As workers now handle only one area of the production process, they develop mastery; they work faster and make fewer mistakes, resulting in efficiency, achieving more in less time.

5. *Less Fatigue*: With division of labour, the process of production is systematized as the flow of work is arranged so that the work moves from one stage to another; it is the product or article that moves from one worker to another instead of the worker moving from one position to another. Thus the worker conserves his energy enabling him to work longer as well as concentrate on his task.

6. *Improved Quality:* with specialization, workers become adept at their work resulting in a higher quality of output.

7. *Use of Machines:* with division it is easier to mechanize the production *process.*

Disadvantages of Division of Labour
1. *Monotony*: Having to perform the same task repeatedly everyday makes the job un-interesting, dull and un-exciting.

2. *Loss of Craftsmanship*: with division of labour, workers become mere machine attendants instead of craftsmen known for their unique styles.

3. *Risk of Unemployment:* with specialization, a worker's skill becomes highly specialized in one area. For example, he might become just a cutter or weaver instead of a tailor because he has been trained to work as a cutter in a shirt-making factory for years. If he should lose his job, chances of employment are reduced as his usefulness is limited.

4. *Alienation of Production:* workers can no longer identify the product with themselves as individuals.

5. *Danger of Standardization*: with division of labour, producers find it impossible to cater to individual taste as products are now standardized as a result of mass production.

Limitation of Division of Labour
With division of labour, mass production is achieved. However, this is only sensible if there is market or demand for the products. For example, if the demand for pins is only 20, it will not make sense for 48,000 pins to be produced. Thus, division of labour is limited by the market.

Dormant Partner: member of Partnership business who is not actively involved in the management. A dormant or sleeping partner may be equally liable for the partnerships debt.

Double Counting: in National Income accounting, the danger of including the value of inputs as well as the final output of which they form a part of separately. In order to avoid this, only the value-added is accounted taken. Similarly, when using the income approach, transfer payments and cash gifts are not added as they constitute part of income re-distributed.

Drawee: a bank on which a cheque is drawn. In the case of a bill of exchange, it is the debtor and acceptor of the bill.

Drawer: the person who writes a document. In the case of a cheque it is the debtor while for a bill of exchange it is the creditor.

Drawings: a book-keeping term for cash withdrawn by the owner or partner of business.

Dumping: the act of selling goods in foreign markets at prices below cost of production in the exporting country. It is an example of price discrimination; the seller may have recovered all fixed costs in the home market. Dumping often give rise to calls for protection in the importing country. This may be effected by imposition of tariffs. Imposition of tariffs on such imports may raise the price to levels high enough for local firms to compete with them.

Duopoly: a form of imperfect market where there are only two suppliers; a form of oligopoly.

Duopsony: a market situation with only two buyers for a good or service.

Dutch Auction: an auction where the auctioneer calls out a high price then keeps lowering it until there is a buyer

Dutch Disease or Resource Curse: The maladjustments in a country's economic system that results from an upsurge in inflow of foreign currency due, but not limited to, natural resource such as crude oil. The discovery and exploitation of such natural resource creates a false sense of wealth, and finances a level of consumption that is out of proportion to the country's productive or industrial base and level of economic development. A false sense of status become quickly entrenched in the outlook and expectations of the people and its government as the currency become overvalued, making imports cheap and exports uncompetitive. The industrial sector, with products incapable of competing against cheap imports and uncompetitive in foreign markets, shrinks or the growth of a nascent one is arrested. In the long-run, the easy money corrupts the economic and political systems and the elite, as cronyism, with its host of vices, replaces enterprise and its concomitant virtues, as amply illustrated by the Nigerian experience.

Oil revenue made Nigeria suddenly 'rich' in the 1970s, when crude oil prices went from under $5 in 1973 to over $37 per barrel in 1980; civil servants salaries were revised upwards by 100%, as the Naira appreciated in value against the British pound and the United States dollar. That meant Nigerian produce became more expensive than British products. Imports ballooned as the famous groundnuts pyramids of Kano vanished. Petrodollars quickly eroded agricultural commodity export and the economy became a mono-product one. The industrial base of the economy was stifled at its infant stage.

Petrodollars financed a consumerist lifestyle of the middle class.

The term, *dutch disease*, derives from the experience of the Netherland when natural gas was discovered in that country in the 1960s. Britain experienced similar experience in the late 1970s as its competitive edge was eroded with the increase in the exchange rate of the pound sterling as crude oil prices soared. The exploitation of North Sea oil had made the country a net exporter of crude oil.

E

East Caribbean dollar is the currency of: Antigua and Barbuda, Dominica, Grenada, Saint Kitts and Nevis, Saint Lucia, Saint Vincent and the Grenadines, Anguilla and Montserrat. It is sub-divided into 100 cents and pegged to the US dollar.

Earned Income: income or payments received from economic activities i.e. for production and distribution of goods and services. The term is used by tax authorities to distinguish income from paid employment, as an employee or self-employed, from income from investments such as interest and dividends.

E-Banking: electronic banking such as Debit and Credit Card, Automated Teller Machine (ATM), Internet Banking, Mobile Banking, Point of Sale Devices, Electronic Funds Transfer, etc.

E-Business (electronic business) is the conduct of business by electronic means; it involves buying and selling (e-commerce) as well as servicing customers and collaborating with business partners. Increased security of e-payment systems, which enable payment over the internet have contributed to the growth of e-business. Websites of organizations of all manners— manufacturers, retailers, schools, etc, are designed increasingly to be interactive and contain features which enable would-be customers to interact in real-time. Amazon.com Inc, e-Bay and Dell Computers are example of companies which have used the internet to offer their goods and services to their customers successfully.

E-Commerce: part of e-business; commercial activity facilitated by electronic means. Electronic Data Interchange (EDI), Electronic Funds Transfer (EFT), credit cards, Automated Teller Machines, and electronic banking, etc. were among the earliest tools which have now been dominated by the Internet. These technologies make it possible for business-to-business (B2B) and business-to-consumer (B2C) transactions to take place via computer networks. Access to electronic content can be secured to allow download or merchandise purchased and shipped, upon payment. With e-Commerce, manufacturers can bypass middleman to deal directly with the consumer.

E-tailing: short for "electronic retailing," is the selling of retail goods via the World Wide Web or Internet. Customers order goods through a retailer's website and make payments for them electronically e.g. through a debit or credit card. It is an example of business-to-consumer (B2C) transaction.

E-payment: electronic payment; payment systems that enable shoppers to pay for goods and services electronically. E--payment systems facilitate e-commerce. Examples are Point-of-Sale (POS) terminals, and electronic transfers.

Economic Commission for Africa: An organ of the United Nations Organization, founded in 1958. The ECA's mandate is to promote the economic and social development, foster interregional integration and promote international cooperation among its member countries. The organization focuses on five key areas in pursuit of its mandate, namely:

- Facilitating economic and social policy analysis;
- Ensuring food security and sustainable development;
- Strengthening development management;
- Harnessing information for development; and
- Promoting regional cooperation and integration.

It pursues its set objectives by carrying out the following activities, among others technical advisory services to member countries and sub-regional organizations in support of spatial information technologies; research and studies for advocacy and policy analysis; organizing seminars, workshops, expert group meetings and conferences; and establishing, maintaining and disseminating regional databases on mapping, spatial baseline information programmes, and training

Its headquarters is in Addis Ababa, Ethiopia with sub-regional offices in North, East, Central, West and Southern Africa.

Economic Depression: A time of severe stagnation in economic activity. It is characterized by high levels of unemployment, deflation, declines in income, production, and commercial activities and currency devaluation. These results in low aggregate demand, low investment, and price deflation, financial and banking contagion which further reinforce the situation. In all, Gross Domestic Product contracts by at least 10 per cent for at least two years.

The Great Depression, which started in the United States, triggered by the stock market crash of October 1929, and affected all the major world economies at the time, is the defining example. In the United States output contracted by more than 30 per cent, unemployment reached record levels of 25 per cent, consumer prices fell by as much, and more than half of the banks failed.

Causes:
Various explanations of the probable causes have ranged from excessive stock market speculation which ultimately led to the crash of prices in October 1929 to widespread protectionism in trade policies at the time to the international monetary system at the time, the gold standard.

At the end of the World War 1, the exchange rates of currencies were misaligned to their underlying economies. In order to protect the fixed exchange rate of their currencies, countries resorted to protectionist trade practices, erecting tariff barriers and deflating their economies through fiscal and monetary policies. Against this background, what might have been a normal business cycle downturn snowballed into the great depression.

The 1920s was a period of boom for the United States economy. Americans were busy living the American Dream—buying cars and new innovations and appliances—radios, television, electric power, etc. and speculating on the stock market—on credit. It was a prosperous period with high euphoria which led to intense speculation and over-investment on the stocks of technological and financial firms on the stock exchange. This induced an economic bubble financed by margin loans. There was therefore a high level of unsustainable level of debt overhang which came to a head in October 1929. From then onward, it was a precipitous slide downwards for the economy at large.

The stock market crash caused widespread panic and exposed banks, with high margin loans, which could not be paid back. Loss of confidence led to panic withdrawal which led to bank failure on a monumental scale. The central bank, the Federal Reserve, refused or was unable to support failing banks. Massive bank failure led to credit crunch which undermined business confidence and investment. Businesses closed down and laid off workers. Investment ceased.

Business and general confidence were further hammered by the drought in the Great Plains of the United States which meant that farmers could not depend on their farms to feed. Many families were displaced and mass migration ensued.

In Europe, the pattern of plunging stock prices, panic bank withdrawals and credit crisis was replicated. Britain had returned to the gold standard at the pre-WWI pound exchange rate. In view of the present realities, the pound was over-valued, and the country's trade was being impacted negatively. The government was forced to leave the gold standard and devalue the pound. In Germany, Poland and Hungary, hyperinflation led to replacement of currencies.

Bank failures and over-reaction e.g. in the erection of trade barriers and retaliatory measures by other governments aggravated the situation into the worst economic collapse of the industrial age.

The effect of all this was a general deflation in asset and commodity prices, drying up of credit and disruption of business which summed up to widespread unemployment reaching 34 per cent in Germany.

At the initial stages, the view of economists like Joseph Schumpeter of the Austrian School, that it was best for the government to do nothing and that the depression must be left to run its course was dominant and informed the stance of President Herbert Hoover of the United States. This practically ensured the election of Frederick Delano Roosevelt who proposed a so-called 'New Deal' stimulus program, an ambitious fiscal program to stimulate the economy.

Pre-occupation with a balancing the budget, however, meant that the economy did not fully recover until the re-armament program for World War II.

John Maynard Keynes' *"The General Theory of Employment, Interest, and Money"*— the foundation of macroeconomics—was published in 1936 in response to the Great Depression. In it, the author attempted an explanation and solution. In contrast to the view of the classical economics view that the economy should be left to find its equilibrium, Keynes stated that it is possible for the economy to remain in a state of permanent disequilibrium with aggregate demand falling short of aggregate supply due to market rigidities and leakages. He advocated the use of fiscal policy to increase purchasing power—including tax cuts, government expenditure i.e. deficit budgeting—may be necessary to bring the economy to equilibrium.

Economic Development: An increase in a country's *capacity* to produce goods and services. It is indicated by increasing value-added in the output of goods and services, through the transformation of its production profile from mainly primary (pre-industrial) production through secondary (industrial) production to tertiary (post-industrial) production overtime.

Increasing value added means, for example, a piece of timber that would have ended up being used as firewood, with improved capacity that comes with economic development, that same timber, is converted into a piece of high-quality furniture worth thousands in monetary value. With economic development, production becomes increasingly mechanized; manufactured and processed goods increase as a percentage of national output, and as result, quality of life improves overall. The economy evolves from a generally rural to an urban, cosmopolitan one. It is reflected in improved standard of living i.e. increased access to electricity, potable water, quality medical services, higher literacy level, etc. Economic development is qualitative as opposed to economic growth which connotes quantitative increases in national output.

Economic Development, Stages In: As identified by Economics Nobel Laureate W.W. Rostow, there are five distinct stages in the journey to emergence as a developed economy:

1. Traditional Society: subsistent agriculture is dominant; technology is basic and rudimentary; production is labour-intensive; little or no specialization and exchange is mainly by barter.

2. Transitional Stage: prelude to take-off; use of means of exchange, specialization, existence of a basic transport infrastructure; structured educational system; beginning of an enterprise culture; beginning of a savings and investment culture and financial system; emergence of organized political and economic institutions; external trade in primary products.

3. Take-off: this stage is characterized by factory organization with increasing mechanization and the use of division of labour in production; emergence of an industrial or secondary sector as the ratio of manufactured goods to national output increase. Capital investment per capita increase; the emergence of a middle class.

4. Drive to Maturity: entrenchment of secondary industries with diversification of the industrial base; widespread use of technology; deepening of the financial system; increasing urbanization. Increasingly distinct service sector superstructure on the industrial substructure. Increasing export orientation and reduced dependence on imports.

5. High Mass Production and Consumption: cosmopolitan society with a dominant tertiary sector; very high level of specialization of labour; high standard of living and high per capita income.

Economic Good: any good or service which must be paid for by the individual or by the community. The production and distribution of economic goods is the subject matter of economics because the problems of scarcity arise because of them.

Economic Growth: increase in the output of goods and services (national output) or national income. It is measured by the change in Gross National Product or Gross Domestic Product between two periods. Economic growth is characterized by

1. Increase in investment and business activities: economic growth is seen in the general level of business activities in the economy. In a growing economy, investment and productive activities are increasing.
2. Increase in employment: as a result of increasing business activities, more people are being employed.
3. High Demand: aggregate demand for goods and services is high; people have the purchasing power to buy the output of goods and services of businesses. This may mean a low or moderate level of inflation.

Increase in the gross domestic product year-on-year may be brought about by the following:

1. Export earnings of a mineral resource like crude oil e.g. Nigeria and Arab countries. These countries run the risk of the so-called Dutch disease or resource curse where high export receipts from a mineral resource stunt the development of a viable industrial base by overvaluation of the exchange rate which effectively subsidizes unsustainably high import of consumer goods while weakening competitiveness of locally manufactured goods within the country and abroad.
2. Production of consumer goods for export: the model followed by Japan and the Tiger economies of South East Asia, viz. South Korea, Taiwan, Malaysia, etc. that has successfully transformed these countries.
3. Production of consumer goods for local market e.g. Brazil and India. Taking advantage of huge internal market for an import substitution industrialization strategy with measures to protect local industries.
4. Investment in capital infrastructure: This is usually State-led. The route effectively followed by the leadership to transform Russia to catch-up with Western nations in the 1930s. In more recent times, China has combined this with encouragement of foreign investment, high level of human capital development and a stable political environment to engender a veritable workshop of the world achieving double rates of economic growth for decades.

Economic growth should ultimately bring about a maturation of the several sectors of the economy i.e. a transformation of the production profile of the economy from one dominated by primary to one dominated by secondary and tertiary production. Where this does not happen, there is growth without development.

As is clear from the tables below, while the Nigerian economy may have recorded year-on-year economic growth between 1975 and 2005, with increase in output of goods and services from N14, 410.70 to N415,397.62, economic development has, at best, been most modest; national output is still dominated by primary products, accounting for over 65 per cent, share of manufacturing actually declined from over 10 per cent to under 7 per cent

Economic Growth and Development, Determinants of:

1. Capital: Capital funds are central to funding production activities. In the initial stages of development, capital may have to be imported in the form of borrowing, grants and development aid to break from the trap of the vicious circle of poverty. In earlier times, this usually took the form of colonial expropriation.

2. Technological Progress: improvement in technology spurs and sustains economic growth by bringing about greater productivity; growth in value-added and surplus which are the sources of economic development and higher standard of living. In the initial stages, not a few countries have unashamedly and aggressively copied foreign technologies.

3. Quality of Human Resources: An educated, well trained and disciplined workforce makes all the difference in the business of value-creation i.e. production. Efficient and effective utilization of the factors of production is dependent on the productivity of human capital; the higher the quality of education and training of the workforce, the greater the productivity and the quality and quantity of output. Countries with relatively modest amount of natural resources have recorded high levels of economic growth and development due to the high quality of their workforce. Like capital funds, foreign expertise may have to be imported at the initial stages, while developing a first-rate educational and human capital training/ development system.

4. Availability of Natural Resources: fertile land, mineral deposits, such as crude oil, limestone, bauxite, etc. are vital raw materials for industry and source of foreign exchange while human population translate to markets; all of which are needed to generate economic activities.

5. Efficient Allocation of Resources: resource allocation is the determination of what to produce with available resources. This may be by free market forces of demand and supply or by planning committees. Generally, experience has shown interacting market forces to be more efficient in sustaining growth in the long-term. Market forces, however, are prone to market failure, and may not be particularly effective in prioritizing resources to key areas which are fundamental to facilitate developmental take-off of the industrial sector. Thus a level of government intervention may be necessary.

Nigeria: Analysis of GDP, 2005		
Activity Sector	GDP 2005 (N' millions)	Percentage of National output (GDP)
Primary	370, 404.59	65.8
Secondary	28, 764.93	6.4
Tertiary	16, 228. 10	27.8
GDP	415,397.62	100.00

Nigeria: Analysis of GDP, 1975		
Activity Sector	GDP 1975 (N' millions)	Percentage of National output (GDP)
Primary	9, 928.97	68.90
Secondary	1,498.72	10.4
Tertiary	2,983.02	20.7
GDP	14, 410.70	100.00
Source: National Bureau of Statistics		

INDIA: Analysis of GDP		
Activity Sector	Percentage of National output (GDP)	Percentage of National output (GDP)
	1973	2003
Primary	45	25
Secondary	20	20
Tertiary	35	55
	100	100

How much of economic growth has translated to economic development can be observed in changes in the structure of the economies of India and Nigeria as illustrated in the tables above. Development has resulted in the reduction of the percentage of primary production and increase in secondary production between 1973 and 2003 for the Indian economy. For Nigeria, primary production is still dominant at 65.8 per cent.

6. Rate of Capital Formation: social infrastructure like transport systems, telecommunication systems, electric power, and investment capital are critical to catalyze the industrialization process. This is the aim of national development plans.

7. Quality of Political and Social Structures and Institutions: economic development cannot take place amidst political and social uncertainty and disorder. All the factors listed above must be underpinned by institutionalized arrangements and sustainable governance rules in way that ensures security of life and property.

Economic Planning: the process of prioritizing national expenditure usually under definite time frames. Economic planning is part of the process of charting the course of economic development by the government so that resources and efforts are marshaled towards definite objectives. Economic planning is emphasized under communist economic systems, where the State takes all economic decisions and their implementation. Under capitalist systems, the State often limits itself to regulation, at best. Many developing countries have embraced economic planning in their effort to jump start their economies and spur growth. Nigeria had five National Development Plans between 1962 and 1985. After 1985, national development plans were replaced by three-year rolling plans which are now termed Medium-Term Expenditure Framework (MTEF).

Economic Problem of Society, Basic: see Basic Economic Problem of Society

Economic Integration: the coming together of two or more countries to promote common economic interests e.g. for increased trade between them.

Economic integration may be in the form of a Free Trade Area, Customs Union, Common Market, and Economic Union or Community. Production is only limited by the size of the market. The larger the market, the greater the economies of scale, the lower the unit cost of production, leading to higher standard of living for all. Countries therefore stand to reap advantages by reducing barriers to trade between them through co-operation. From removal of barriers to movement of goods and peoples and factors of production between them, co-operation may ultimately cover co-ordination of fiscal and monetary policies. Economic integration moves in phases from PTA (preferential trade area); free trade area (FTA); Customs Union; Common Market; Economic Union to Monetary Union

Economic Rent: a payment made to a resource in excess of what is required to elicit its supply. The payment arises from current supply scarcity or legacy benefits that are difficult to do away with. It is needed to determine the employment but not the availability of that resource.

Economic Stabilization Programme: austerity or belt-tightening measures put forward by the Shagari administration in Nigeria in 1982, in response to fiscal and balance of payment deficits brought about by highly reduced exports revenue as crude oil prices hit the bottom due to supply glut globally. These were preceded by austerity measures put in place by the preceding military government which were abandoned by the Shagari administration, when crude oil prices briefly revived in the wake of the Iran-Iraq war. The new civilian administration increased government expenditure and the national debt. Thus, when crude oil prices crashed after the war

in the Middle East, government finances were left in jeopardy. The Economic Stabilization measures were meant to curb government recurrent expenditure as well as increase government revenue in order to bring about balance in the budget and equilibrium in the balance of payments. They reveal the underlying paradigm of economic regulation at the time, as they consist of direct, physical administrative controls as oppose to indirect control via reliance on market forces.

Below is a summary of the stabilization measures announced by the President on 21 April 1982:

1. Exchange Control Measures: Measures introduced to control foreign exchange include:
    a. Reduction of Basic Travel Allowance (BTA) from ₦800.00 to ₦500.00 per person per annum.
    b. Reduction of business travel allowance from ₦3,000.00 to ₦2,500. per annum for registered companies;
    c. Restricting the number of pilgrims to perform the Hajji in 1982 to a maximum of 50,000 persons.
    d. Centralization of registration of Form 'M' in the Central Bank's Headquarters.
    e. Introduction of pre-shipment inspection for frozen and canned fish and reintroduction of pre-shipment inspection for spare parts, raw materials and books.
2. Monetary Measures:
    a. Limits on total central bank foreign exchange disbursements.

b. Limits on bank credit to the private sector were progressively lowered, and administered bank lending rates were raised.

c. As part of the monetary policy, all interest rates were revised upwards across the board by two percentage points from their existing levels, but later in the year in November 1982, they were reduced by one percentage point.

3. Fiscal measures

a. increase in petroleum products prices and utility tariffs,

b. Freeze on wages and salaries in the public sector.

c. Freeze on capital expenditure,

d. Restriction on foreign borrowing by state and local governments.

e. Tightening of import controls and significant increases in customs tariffs.

f. The introduction of an advance import deposit scheme.

g. Imposition of import ban on frozen chicken and gaming machines.

h. Removal of 29 commodities from open general license to specific import license requirement.

i. Introduction of new and increase in import duties for over 45 items.

j. Increase in excise duties from 5 to 45 per cent on non-essential commodities like cigarettes, towels, fabrics, cosmetics and perfumes, and paper napkins, electric fans, locks, bicycles and motor cycles.

k. Increased remuneration, improved equipment and training for customs officers; intensification of anti-smuggling activities such as raids on market, seaport and airport raids, etc.

These measures proved to be little more than palliatives in view of the fundamental problems facing the economy. Government's financial situation worsened and the Central Bank could not meet foreign exchange payments. Soon the country's trading partners refused to open letters of credit in favour of Nigerian importers. The deteriorating economic situation ultimately led to the overthrow of the government on December 1983. Measures taken by the succeeding government were founded on the same paradigm of a public-sector-driven economy, managed by administrative controls as opposed to regulations based on market signaling; there were no measures to contend with the over-valued exchange rate of the naira or policies to attract foreign investment. Measure taken failed to elicit confidence from the country's trading partners, creditors and the International Monetary Fund and World Bank to give the required support. Ultimately, there was another change in government, in 1985. The festering economic situation set the stage for implementation of the Structural Adjustment Programme in 1986.

Economics: the study of the creation and sustenance of wealth i.e. goods and services desired for human satisfaction. This is necessary because of the reality of having to satisfy limitless human wants out of limited resources. Because resources are limited relative to the human wants, resources are said to be relatively scarce. This relative scarcity of resources is faced by all economic units—the individual, household, business organization, and governments—and necessitates the making of choices. The essence of the study of economics is to proffer analysis and perspectives for these units to make the most of the resources available to them.

Economics may be traced to the Physiocrats, a group of French philosophers who put forward a theory of circular flow of income and output in the 18th century, as the beginning of the Industrial Revolution, and advocated minimal government role in the management of the economy or *laissez-faire*. The beginning of Economics as a subject of study, distinct from other social sciences, however, dates from Adam Smith's book *"An Enquiry into the Nature and Causes of the Wealth of Nations"* published in 1776. The Scottish philosopher, who came to be known as the father of Economics, identified land, labour and capital as factors of production; examined the impact of division of labour on output.

Adam Smith stressed that the more wealth is created in a sustainable way and the society as a whole is better off, when people are left to pursue their own individual interests, with minimal government supervision or regulation. This meant that the fundamental issues of 'What to Produce', 'How to Produce' and 'For whom to Produce' by the society or economic system, are better left to be decided by 'the invisible hand' as revealed by the forces of demand and supply for goods and services. Thus, Adam Smith laid the theoretical foundation for the capitalist or free market economy

Adam Smith, David Ricardo, Jean Baptiste Say, John Stuart Mill, and Reverend Thomas Malthus constituted the Classical School of Economic thought that held the view that prices and wages, in a free economy, are flexible and will always adjust towards equilibrium.

Thomas Robert Malthus was an Anglican clergyman, whose *Principle of Population* (full title: *An Essay on the Principle of Population as it Affects the Future Improvement of Society)*, published in 1789, is the most famous of his many writings. His submissions were to influence the work of Charles Darwin.

He predicted, wrongly, the onset of the law of diminishing returns as the population of England exploded against the backdrop of the Industrial Revolution. His gloomy outlook was to earn Economics the "dismal science" tag from Thomas Carlyle.

David Ricardo is best known for his work on the theory of Comparative Advantage as the basis of (free) international trade. He also set forth a Labour Theory of Value in his *Principles of Political Economy and Taxation* published in 1817, which foreshadowed the work of Karl Marx.

John Stuart Mill's *"Principle of Political Economy"* was published in 1848, building on the work of Ricardo and Malthus.

From its beginnings in philosophy, the introduction of mathematical tools of analysis has marked the emergence of Neo-Classical Economics.

The Great Depression of the major world economies in the 1930s was a major challenge for which economic theory was hard pressed for explanations. This was to come from British economist John Maynard Keynes in his book *"The General Theory of Employment, Interest, and Money"* published in 1936. The book was the beginning of what has become known as Keynesian economics, the basis of macroeconomics.

The work of Keynes, along with those of Alfred Marshall and others which introduced empirical tools of analysis into economics belongs to the Neo-Classical school of economics.

Economics, Definitions of: the central theme of definitions of Economics by the classical economists was "wealth". According to Adam Smith, political economy as the subject was then known, is *"an inquiry into the nature and causes of the wealth of nations"*.

To John Stuart Mill economics is *"science of production, distribution, and consumption of wealth"*.

In his influential book "Principles of Economics", published in 1890, Alfred Marshall defined economics as *"the study of man in the ordinary business of life. It enquires how he gets his income and how he uses it. Thus, it is on the one side, the study of wealth and on the other and more important side, a part of the study of man"*.

Marshall's definition was widely accepted for a long time. It broadened the scope of the subject beyond a preoccupation with wealth to include the study of man in his quest to make the most of his resources/income.

This view anticipated the evolution of the subject as its the scope broadened beyond the narrow preoccupation with "wealth" to include the concept of "material welfare" of man.

In 1932, Lord Robbins published *'Nature and Significance of Economic Science'* in which he defined Economics as "the science which studies human behaviour as a relationship between ends and scarce means which have alternative uses". 'Ends' refer to human wants, and 'means' refers to resources. Robbins' analytical definition has since replaced Marshall's descriptive definition.

Economics aim to explain the behaviour and interaction of economic units—individuals, households, business units, and governments as well as how economies work. The essence of economic analysis is to enable economic units and economies function better. In carrying out his work, the economist has increasingly sought to use empirical methods as much as possible.

Primarily, economics is sub-divided into *microeconomics*, which is concerned with individual economic units such as consumers, households and business firms, and *macroeconomics*, which focuses on the economy as a whole, dealing with issues like unemployment, inflation, monetary and fiscal policies; economic growth and development, etc.

Economics, Basic Concepts of: the concepts of Wants, Resources, Scarcity, Choice, Scale of Preference, Opportunity or Real Cost.

- *Wants* refer to cars, houses, telephones, transportation, entertainment, education, etc, that is *goods and services desired for consumption*. Wants are unlimited or endless and insatiable. Wants are also referred to as *ends.*

- *Resources* are the *means* with which wants are satisfied. Examples are land, labour, capital, time, money, etc. Compared to wants, resources are not enough resources, i.e. resources are limited or relatively scarce.

- **Scarcity** means *limited in supply*. Whereas wants are unlimited, the resources required to satisfy them are limited. This is the central issue in economics: how to use limited resources to satisfy unlimited wants.
- **Choice:** Since resources are scarce relative (or compared) to wants, we must choose which of our wants we need to satisfy, and which to forgo or sacrifice.
- **Scale of Preference** is an ordered list of wants with the most important coming first. A scale of preference is necessary because we cannot satisfy all our wants, since resources are limited in supply. Therefore we have to order our wants in order of importance or priority to us. Thus, we draw up a scale of preference to rank our wants into 1st, 2nd, 3rd, 4th, 5th, etc. in order of priority and importance to us.
- **Opportunity or Real Cost:** To purchase or produce a product (or service) means we have to forgo another product (or service). Opportunity cost is a way of expressing the cost of choice in terms of the product (or service) we have to forgo in order to obtain it.

For example, if Tega has N100, and chooses to purchase a notebook instead of ice-cream, the opportunity cost of the notebook is the ice-cream she did not buy.

Similarly, if a farmer decides to grow cash crops instead of food crops, the real cost (or opportunity cost) of growing cash crops is the food crops forgone.

The concepts of want, resources, scarcity, choice, scale of preference and opportunity cost are all very important to individuals, households, firms and the government. Individuals, households, business firms and the government are economic units. They are constantly faced with the problem of unlimited wants against limited or scarce resources with which to satisfy them. Thus, they all must **choose** which want to satisfy, list them in order of priority or preference **(scale of preference)**, and forgo one **(opportunity cost)** want in order to satisfy another.

Economic Reforms: measures taken to bring about a more efficient and effective allocation of resources and to improve the productivity of an economy evidenced by high level of business activities, employment opportunities, improved living standards, low inflation, etc. Economic reforms may be prompted by economic stagnation, chronic inflation/stagflation and unemployment, balance of payment crisis, fiscal crisis/poor state of government finances, etc. In the 1980s, measures to reduce the role of the State in the running of the economy and to rely on market forces gained ascendancy across the world. These measures entail reduction of government role in the economy, increased reliance on market forces in the management of the economy, deregulation of exchange rates and interest rates, incentives to attract foreign capital, trade liberalization, privatization of government-owned enterprises; removal of foreign exchange controls, etc.

Perhaps arising out of global economic difficulties of the 1970s, not least following from the OPEC oil shock, efficiency of resource use increasingly began to overshadow ideology in national politics in the 1980s. Economic realities took the front burner over conspiracy theories of imperialism. In Britain, Thatcher came to power in 1979 and practically set the tone with her program of privatization and economic rationalism. With Reaganomics in the United States, economic rationalism was to reverberate through the IMF and World Bank and ultimately coalesced in the Washington Consensus, a set of economic reform proposals that the IMF obliged countries in need of its support to administer.

The dominant themes of economic development strategies before 1980s—nationalism, indigenization, protectionism, self-sufficiency, economic planning and controls—gave way to a market paradigm: privatization, trade liberalization, export promotion, fiscal discipline, deregulation, etc. in the face of economic stagnation.

Economic challenges forced countries like Argentina, Brazil, India, Nigeria, and Ghana among others to begin to undo the import substitution industrialization strategies.

China started a series of steps, under Deng Xiaoping in 1978, that were to make the communist country the highest recipient of foreign direct investment.

In the Soviet Union, Mikhail Gorbachev came to power in 1985, and proposed a set of economic reforms—*perestroika,* designed to end shortages and economic difficulties.

Issues that have been thrown up in the process of economic reforms include:

Pace of Reforms: should economic reforms be an incremental and gradual process or should by shock therapy?

Order of Reforms: should economic reforms precede political reforms or can they done simultaneously? The Soviets' experience would ordinarily seem to suggest that economic and political reforms cannot be successfully undertaken together. A conclusion which looks consistent with the Chinese experience: tremendous success with economic reforms has been against a background of stagnancy in the political sphere.

Economic Recovery Program (ERP): Structural Adjustment in Ghana, launched in 1983.

Falling commodity (cocoa, gold, diamond, bauxite, etc.) prices meant that the socialist policies of the Nkrumah era became a huge unsustainable burden on the State. By the 1980s, the Ghanaian economy was grinding practically to a halt with fiscal and balance of payment crises. Perhaps the lasting legacy of these policies was the sense of entitlement that it induced among the people who saw government as great provider 'big-daddy'.

The need for reforms was acknowledged as early as 1966, when the government of General A.K. Ankrah recognized the unsustainability of import substitution strategy of the Nkrumah era and engaged with the International Monetary Fund, agreeing to trade liberalization, removal of subsidies, fiscal and monetary discipline, and devaluation of the cedi, popular resistance to reforms ensured the evil day was postponed through a succession of violent changes in government lasting almost three decades during which time Ghanaians became economic refugees in neighbouring West African countries.

In face of deterioration in government finances, the resistance to reforms meant that government was sustained by foreign loans through the 1970s, while the overvalued cedi ensured that smuggling boomed and continued loss of government revenue. The hands of successive governments were tied with popular resistance against any sort of reforms. The economic situation worsened with high unemployment, high inflation, with widespread scarcity of essential commodities which the government could no longer afford to import.

It was against this background that Jerry Rawlings and his Provisional National Defence Council (PNDC) came to power in 1981. He proclaimed a revolution, convinced that the problem with the economy was corruption and mismanagement. After a period of fighting the symptoms of the crisis with seizures and selling off of goods from traders accused of hoarding by vigilantes, currency confiscation and liquidation of politicians, the government had to confront the structural nature of the economic difficulties facing the country.

In particular, a severe drought, mass deportation of Ghanaians from Nigeria in 1983 and the fact that help was not forthcoming from the East bloc countries, the government was forced to re-think its populist stance. Rawlings came to the conclusion that 'Populist nonsense must give way to popular sense', and did a U-turn by agreeing to IMF and World Bank conditions in exchange for financial assistance.

Primarily the objective of the ERP was to put the economy on the path of sustainable growth. This entailed restructuring of economic institutions, increasing export earnings, reducing inflation, increasing the availability of consumer goods, etc. These objectives were pursued through devaluation of the cedi; privatization of state owned enterprises; liberalization of trade and reduction of direct controls.

ERP I (1984-1986): Stabilization

In the first phase of the ERP, 1983-1986, the objective was to reduce foreign debt and improve the balance of payment position. Measures were taken to increase tax collection, reduce government expenditure, and reduce subsidies. The government stopped direct determination of the exchange rate, subjecting it to auction, effectively devaluing the currency.

ERP II (1987-1989): Rehabilitation

The second phase (1987-89) Private foreign exchange bureaus were permitted in 1988 further devaluing the cedi and reducing the gap between the official rate and the parallel market rates.

ERP III (1989-1993): Liberalization and Growth:

entailed divestiture from state-owned enterprises/privatization and further devaluation of the cedi through foreign exchange market reform.

Devaluation saw the value of the cedi go from ¢90 to US$1 in 1986 to ¢720 in 1993 to ¢1,023 in 1994 to ¢9,500 in 2007. This was achieved through open auction, the interbank market and ultimately free flotation mechanism.

Steps taken reassured the country's trading partners and donors leading to increased official development assistance (ODA), which enabled the government to embark on infrastructure rehabilitation.

An investment Code, targeting FDI, was introduced.

As a result, inflation was reduced to 30 per cent from an average of 123 per cent before ERP.

The budget deficit was reduced from 6.3 percent to 0.1 percent of GDP between 1982 by 1986; foreign debt servicing arrears were practically eliminated and the balance of payment and the current account recorded a surplus for three years to 1990. Devaluation reduced smuggling and boosted exports. It also made essential commodities available, though expensive.

The divestiture/privatization program saw the establishment of the Ghana Stock Exchange which began operations in 1990.

The government liquidated unviable state-owned enterprises and sold its interest in several others including Ghana Telecom and Accra Breweries.

In 1994, the government sold part of its 55 per cent shares in Ashanti Goldfield Corporation (AGC) to Lonmin of South Africa under a share flotation that it listed on the Ghana and London Stock Exchanges. In 1996, AGC became the fisrt African company to be listed on the New York Stock Exchange.

The ERP measures faced intense opposition and were enforced under a violent, repressive and autocratic order to put it mildly. It has not been a total success story, like everywhere else—Nigeria, Chile, Zimbabwe, Philippines, etc.—where these measures has been implemented. The question remains though whether these economies would have been better off without Structural Adjustment.

Economic Sanctions: punitive measures imposed, usually on a country by another or group of countries, intended to bring about a change in policies or a course of action.

Economic Surplus: refers to Consumer's Surplus and Producer's Surplus.

Economic System: the system by which resources are allocated between competing or alternative uses in an economy. An economic system addresses the basic economic questions of *what to produce, how to produce* and *for whom to produce.* Examples: capitalism and socialism.

Economic Union: the ultimate form of economic integration of sovereign states combining features of a currency union and a common market. Members share a currency as well as allow free movement of goods, capital and labour among them. Example is the European Union.

Economies of Scale: the advantages of large-scale production or the advantages a firm enjoys as a result increasing its scale of production. These economies make it possible for big firms or companies to produce at lower average unit costs. Where these advantages arise because of changes inside or within the firm, they are referred to as internal economies to distinguish them from *external economies* which arise from outside the firm e.g. from localization of an industry.

Internal economies:
- *Managerial Economies:* bigger firms can afford to employ highly qualified

staff. This leads to more efficient operations and quality of output.

- *Technical Economies*: big firms can afford to employ specialized machinery and take advantage of division of labour in production. Output per worker is thereby increased.
- *Commercial Economies:* A large firm can afford to buy in very large commercial quantities or in bulk and thereby enjoy discounts. They can also afford to engage consultants/experts to conduct market research to inform product design and sales campaign. They can also engage in advertisement in different media as unit cost of output is minimized because of their large output.
- *Financial Economies:* large firms can borrow at much lower rates of interest than smaller firms because creditors consider them less risky. Besides, they have assets that they can pledge as security or collateral. Also, large firms can raise long-term capital by issuing shares or debentures on the capital market.
- *Welfare Economies:* the larger a firm is, the more its ability to cater to the welfare of its human capital, and this contributes to higher morale which leads to greater efficiency and effectiveness. Big firms usually have staff cooperative societies, staff club, housing estates.

ECOWAS: the Economic Community of West African States; a common market of West African countries established in 1975 comprising of the Republic of Benin, Burkina Faso, Cape Verde, Cote d'Ivoire, The Gambia, Ghana, Guinea, Guinea-Bissau, Liberia, Mali, Niger, Nigeria, Sierra Leone, Senegal and Togo. Fifteen West African countries signed the Treaty of Lagos establishing ECOWAS on May 28, 1978. This was followed with the signing of protocols in Lome, Togo in November, 1976. In 1993, a revised treaty was signed to extend co-operation among member states. The revised treaty provides for the establishment of a common market and single currency, a West African parliament, an Economic and Social Council (ECOSOC), and an ECOWAS court to enforce decisions of the Community.

Objectives

1. To remove trade restrictions between member states,
2. Free movement of goods, labour and capital between member states,
3. Common tariff structure and commercial policy (customs union) against non-members,
4. To promote development of infrastructure—transport and communications, energy, trade and payments, between member states.

Benefits of ECOWAS

1. Larger markets for goods and services
1. Higher level of investment: due to a wider market
2. Higher standard of living through increased trade with more goods and services available to residents and citizens
3. Greater specialization among member countries
4. More job opportunities.

Problems

1. Low level of trade between members: the economies of member countries export almost the same products—primary commodities, and demand

manufactured goods in return. Thus the economies compete against one another.

2. Dependence on revenues from import duties: revenues from import duties constitute a large proportion of revenue of member countries. This makes member countries unwilling to remove trade restrictions between them.

3. Colonial influence: trade relations with former colonial masters remain strong and higher than trade between member states. The Francophone countries have an economic organization which ties them to France through the common currency, the CFA franc. They are thus minimally committed to ECOWAS.

4. Underdeveloped infrastructure: road and communication network between member countries are poor and underdeveloped. This makes trade between countries difficult and expensive.

5. Political instability: frequent leadership changes in member countries occasioned by coups, and social and civil strife have impeded the development of the organization.

6. Fear of domination by small countries: smaller countries are intimidated by the size of Nigeria with its huge population and vast natural resources. This reduces their enthusiasm and commitment to the organization

Achievements of ECOWAS
- ECOWAS Passport: the aim of free movement of people and trade between member states has been greatly enhanced by the creation of the ECOWAS Passport which enables the free movement of citizens without visa and residence in member countries within ninety days.
- Establishment of the West African Monetary Institute
- Hydro-electric dams in some member countries; thermal plants in Nigeria, Cote d'Ivoire, Ghana, Benin and Togo to be powered with natural gas from Nigeria.
- Establishment of the West African Health Organization (WAHO)
- Construction of 9000km of major roads and 11,000km feeder roads

Challenges of ECOWAS
- Underfunding and understaffing
- Non-Ratification and non-Implementation of adopted Protocols
- Poor Infrastructure

In view
- Harmonization of monetary and fiscal policies
- Harmonized payment systems
- Common currency, *ECO*

Effective Demand: demand for a commodity backed by the ability to purchase it.

Elasticity: the responsiveness of demand, supply or income to a change in price of a commodity.

Elasticity of Demand: (also *price elasticity of demand*) is the responsiveness of demand to a change in price of a commodity; the percentage change in the quantity demanded of a good divided by percentage change in its own price. Demand is *elastic* when a change in price brings about a bigger increase in quantity demanded. Demand is *inelastic* when a change, (e.g. X,) in price brings about a lesser change (of less than X) in quantity demanded; elasticity is said to be *unitary* if a change in price brings about the same degree of change in quantity demanded.

Elasticity of demand is given by the formula:

$$\frac{\text{Percentage change in quantity demanded}}{\text{Percentage change price}}$$

When elasticity is perfect, elasticity is equal to infinity;

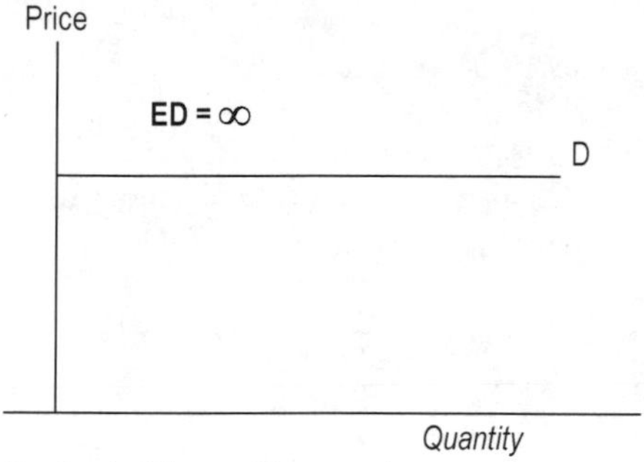

Price

ED = ∞

D

Quantity

Perfectly Elastic Demand

When inelasticity is perfect, elasticity is equal to zero:

Perfectly Inelastic Demand

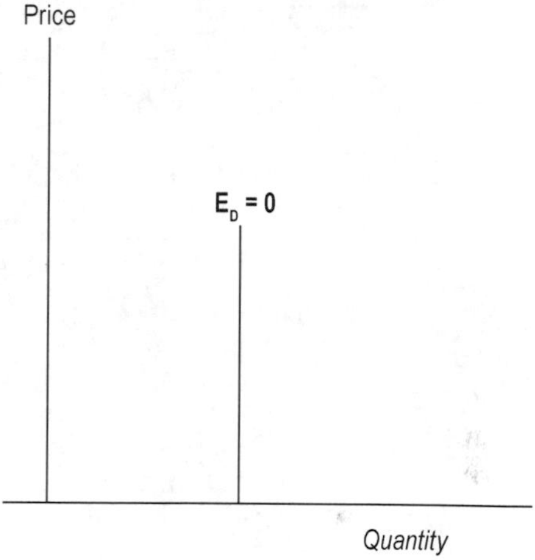

Price

$E_D = 0$

Quantity

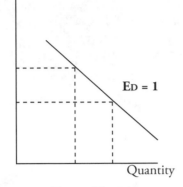

Unitary Elasticity

Unitary elasticity
- Change in price results in proportionate change in DD.

- X % change in price = X % change in DD,

- Total expenditure on the good unchanged.

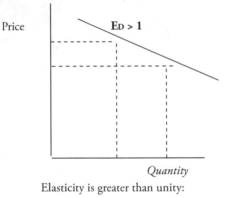

Elasticity is greater than unity:

Elasticity is greater than unity:
- Change in price results in more than proportionate change in DD

- % change in price is greater than % change in DD

- Total expenditure on the good is less than before.

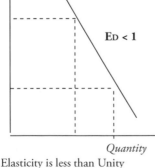

Elasticity is less than Unity

Elasticity is less than Unity
- Change in price results in less than proportionate change in DD

- % change in price is less than % change in DD

- Total expenditure on the good is more than before

Elaticity of Demand: Determinants

1. *Availability of Substitutes*: if a commodity has substitutes within the same price range, the more elastic its price demand will be. The demand for salt will remain inelastic as there are no other commodities that can be substituted in its place.

2. *Degree of Necessity*: the more a good is thought of as indispensable by a person, the more inelastic his demand tend to be.

3. *Time:* response to change in price may not be immediate as people may demand the same quantity as before being reluctant to substitute other goods in their place. With time, adjustment may be made in taste, bringing about changes in quantity demanded.

4. *Income:* the higher a person's income, the more inelastic his demand for goods tend to be generally. Conversely, the lower a person's income, the more elastic his demand tend to be.

5. *Habit*: the more a person's demand for a good is borne out of habit, the more inelastic their demand.

Elasticity of Supply: the responsiveness of supply to a change in price. The elasticity of supply is given by the formula:

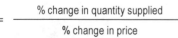

$$= \frac{\% \text{ change in quantity supplied}}{\% \text{ change in price}}$$

If the price of commodity increase from N50 to N55, and as a result supply increases from 100kilos to 120kilos, the elasticity of supply may be calculated thus,

Change in price = 55-50 = 5

Percentage increase in price
= 5/50 x 100 = 10%
Change in quantity supply
= 120 – 100 = 20
Percentage change in quantity supplied
= 20/100 x 100 = 20%
Elasticity of supply
= 20%/10% = 2

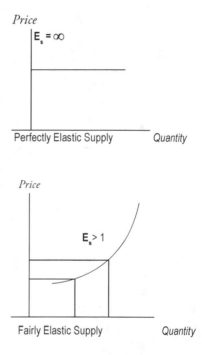

Perfectly Elastic Supply   Quantity

Fairly Elastic Supply   Quantity

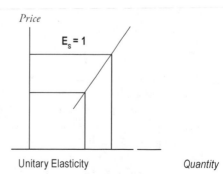

Unitary Elasticity   Quantity

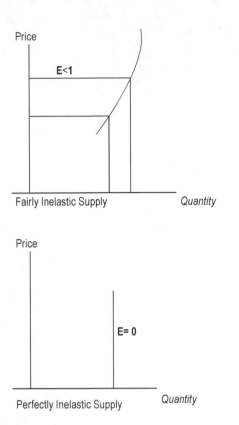

Fairly Inelastic Supply

Perfectly Inelastic Supply

production of a variety of output with little or no cost, supply will tend to be elastic. For example, a furniture maker can respond to market changes by producing more office desks and less home furniture.

3. Availability of Factors of Production: the easier required inputs for production can be procured, the more elastic supply will be. For example, if materials are locally available, supply will be more responsive to change in price. On the other hand, if imported materials are used in production, supply will tend to be inelastic.

4. Spare Production Capacity: an industry or firm with spare capacity can increase capacity in response to market conditions. Where this is not the case, supply will tend to be inelastic.

Embargo: the prohibition of the import a certain good into a country.

Emigration: the movement of people from a region or country into another. Emigration is one the determinants of population, along with immigration, birth rate and death rate. People move from an area for economic and political reasons.

Elasticity, Cross: see Cross Elasticity of Demand

Elasticity, Income: see Income Elasticity of demand

Endogenous Change: a change arising from within such as a change in demand brought about by change in price. This contrasts with changes in external factors like fashion or weather.

Elasticity of Supply: Determinants

1. Time Required to Produce: The time it takes to increase or decrease production and supply varies between industries. The longer the time between the commencement of production and supply, the more inelastic supply tend to be. For agricultural produce, the response of supply to change in demand will be minimal as output and supply is the determined by decisions made in the planting season. In other cases supply can be adjusted in the short-term.

2. Ease of Substitution of Factors of Production: the inputs or factors of production can be used for the

Endowment Policy: an assurance policy under which the sum assured is paid after a fixed number of years or at the death of the assured, whichever comes first. Endowment policies are a form of targeted savings, and are often used to provide for financial commitments such as children's education.

Entrepreneurship: see under Factors of Production.

Equilibrium: A state of balance between factors affecting a system such that there is no tendency for change. Equilibrium theory states that forces are set in motion to bring a system back to equilibrium whenever there is a disturbance.

Equilibrium output/of a Firm: the output at which a firm's profit is maximized or loss minimized. At this output, marginal revenue is equal to marginal cost (MR=MC), and the Average Cost curve is rising. When MR=MC but AC is falling or trending downward, equilibrium output has not been reached and the firm may continue to increase output until AC is on the upward trend, and MR=MC; the MC curve cutting the MR curve from below. Beyond this point, increase in output or production adds more to cost than revenue, so that loss is incurred. At this point there is no incentive to change scale of production and organization.

Equilibrium of an Individual/Consumer: an individual has arrived at a point of equilibrium where his outlay is expended in way that his utility is maximized. At this point, the consumer cannot increase his total utility by substituting one commodity for another. Under the Cardinalist Theory of Consumer Behaviour, where only one commodity is involved, the consumer will maximize his utility at the point where the

marginal utility of the commodity is equal to the price of the commodity, i.e. Marginal Utility of good = Price of good. Where more than one good are involved, the consumer will be at equilibrium when

$$\frac{\text{MU of good X}}{\text{Price of good X}} = \frac{\text{MU of good Y}}{\text{Price of good Y}}$$

where, MU refers to Marginal Utility.

Under the Ordinalist Theory of Consumer Behaviour, equilibrium of the consumer is illustrated by indifference curve. In the diagram below, the consumer is at equilibrium where the indifference curve is tangential to the budget line. This is when he is having four units of good x and 10 units of y, illustrated by point T.

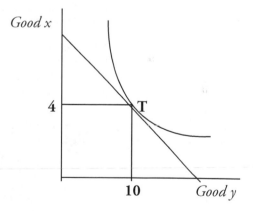

Equilibrium of an Industry: A state where new firms are not attracted into and where old firms do not want to leave an industry.

Equilibrium National Income: national income is at equilibrium when aggregate demand is equal to aggregate supply; there is neither a deflationary nor an inflationary gap. Aggregate demand or expenditure is the sum of the total amount spent by consumers

(C), business on investment (I), government on purchase (G) and foreigners on net exports (X-M). At any point in time, this total may be less than, equal to or more than national output or aggregate supply. Where aggregate demand is less than the national output, producers will have unwanted inventories. This will signal producers to cut back on production and investment until the point of equilibrium is reached. On the other hand, if aggregate demand is more than aggregate supply, producers will discover that desired inventories are being sold. This will signal increased investment and expansion of output until the higher level of demand is matched, national income equilibrium is reached.

When national income is at equilibrium, total **injections** into the circular flow of income are equal to **leakages**.

Equilibrium Price: the market-clearing price at which demand is equal to supply. At the equilibrium price, quantity demanded is equal to quantity supplied. Below the equilibrium price, supply is less than demand and there are shortages; above the equilibrium price, supply is more than demand resulting in a market glut or surplus.

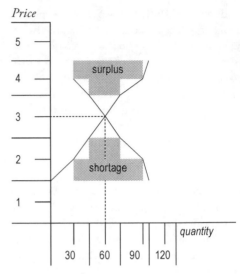

Equities: same as Ordinary Shares.

Euro: the official currency of the Eurozone countries, established by the Treaty on European Union or Maastricht Treaty of 1993. These countries, comprising Austria, Belgium, Cyprus, Estonia, Finland, France, Germany, Greece, Ireland, Italy, Latvia, Luxembourg, Malta, the Netherlands, Portugal, Slovakia, Slovenia, and Spain, meet the euro convergence criteria.

The euro was initially introduced as an accounting currency on January 1, 1999, three years before bank notes and coins were introduced on January 1, 2002. The currency is managed by the European Central Bank, based in Frankfurt, Germany. The CFA franc, the currency of certain West and Central African countries, is fixed or pegged to the euro. The CFA was pegged to the French franc before the introduction of the euro.

With Germany at the core of the European Monetary Union, the euro built on the strength of the Deutsche Mark, and has become a reserve currency in several countries.

The single currency is a symbol of European economic union, and a key instrument of the integration of the European economies: it has removed exchange rate risks and reduced cost of transactions across international borders among member countries.

European Union (EU): a political and economic union between 28 European countries, created by the Treaty on European Union (Maastricht Treaty) on November 1st, 1993. Eighteen of these countries (Austria, Belgium, Cyprus, Estonia, Finland, France, Germany, Greece, Ireland, Italy, Latvia, Luxembourg, Malta, the Netherlands, Portugal, Slovakia, Slovenia, and Spain.) are members of a monetary union, the Eurozone, with a common currency, the euro, administered by the European Central Bank. Its headquarters is in Brussels, the Belgian capital. The EU is the most evolved co-operation among sovereign states in the world.

The history of the EU dates back to the European Coal and Steel Community (ECSC) formed in 1950, building on the co-operation and co-ordination during the European Recovery Program (Marshall Plan), with the desire to prevent recurrence of the First and Second World Wars by binding or uniting European countries into a sort of federal system. The ECSC was a free trade area for iron ore, steel and coal among the six founding members - Belgium, France, Germany, Italy, Luxembourg and the Netherlands. These countries effectively decided to co-manage these key resources which are central to military and industrial needs to prevent re-armament programs.

The ECSC became the European Economic Community (EEC) with the signing of the Treaty of Rome in 1957. The EEC targeted the creation of a single or common market where people, capital, goods and services move without barriers and a customs union where customs duties, tariffs and other trade barriers are abolished between member countries and a common external tariff apply against non-members. The EU strives to ensure a level playing ground for economic agents by overseeing antitrust issues, scrutinizing mergers, and breaking up oligopolistic cartels and preventing monopolies and State aid.

The Common Agricultural Policy (CAP) designed to guarantee food security and protect agriculture and farmers, through a system of subsidies and interventions, from economic realities and challenges, came into force in 1962.

After the collapse of the Bretton Woods regime of fixed exchange rates, the Exchange Rate Mechanism (ERM) was created in 1972, to maintain monetary stability by allowing member currencies fluctuate against each other within narrow limits. This was the forerunner to a monetary union and common currency.

The European Central Bank was established in 1998, and took –off with the introduction of the euro in 1999. The euro remained an accounting currency until 2002, when euro paper currency and coins replaced the national currencies. The ECB is the issuer of the euro and its main charge is to maintain price stability within the Eurozone (EU countries that have adopted the euro).

The EU is the most advanced and functional co-operation between sovereign countries. Areas of co-operation cuts across agriculture, environment, education, energy, foreign policy, etc. anchored by institutions such as the European Commission, the executive arm; the European Council responsible for the EU's overall political direction; a directly elected European Parliament; the Council of the European Union, representing individual member countries; the Court of Justice of the European Union; the European Court of Auditors which checks the financing of the EU's activities; the European Central Bank responsible for monetary policy; the European Investment Bank finances investment projects; the European Ombudsman investigates complaints about maladministration by EU institutions and bodies.

Excess Demand: shortage; the excess of quantity demanded over quantity supplied at a given price; situation at any point below the equilibrium price; arises when quantity demanded is higher than quantity supplied.

Excess Supply: The excess of quantity supplied over quantity demanded at a given price. Also known as surplus.

Exchange Control, Foreign: control and restrictions imposed by a government on purchase/sale/possession of foreign currencies. Government may assume the sole right to purchase, sell and possess foreign exchange. Thus all receipts in foreign currencies are required to be sold to the government at a fixed rate of exchange.

An Exchange Control regime is usually characterized by the following features:
- A fixed exchange rate.
- A dual exchange rate regime.

- A ban on the use and possession of foreign currency within the country.
- Reporting of all earnings in foreign currency.
- Restrictions on the movement of foreign currencies in and out of the country.

Exchange Controls are a rationing stratagem usually necessitated by a shortage of foreign exchange earnings by the government. They have increasingly become outdated by the bandwagon of deregulation, liberalization and globalization with free capital flows across national boundaries. The absence of controls across countries magnified the Asian Currency Crisis of 1997 in many countries of that continent, and the swift imposition of same by the Malaysian government helped to reduce the impact of the crisis on that economy.

In Nigeria, the Exchange Control Act of 1962 was one of the many features of direct controls/regulations that were removed with the advent of structural adjustment program that started in 1986.

Exchange Rate: the rate at which one country's currency is expressed in terms of another. The exchange rate is a key index like interest rate, and it is actively manipulated by the government in the management of the economy. The exchange rate gives an indication of the strength of the underlying economy.

The exchange rate is a key part of a country's economic policy as it determines the competitiveness of its exports in international markets. The higher the exchange rate the more expensive the country's exports will be. Conversely, the lower the rate of exchange the cheaper imports will be. In other words, a high exchange rate discourages exports and encourages imports. A low exchange rate has the opposite effect. The exchange rate therefore directly impacts on the balance of payment.

A rate of exchange is said to be over— or under-valued where it is pegged at a value above or below its equilibrium rate i.e. the rate that equate its demand to its supply in an open market. As an index of the productive capacity of the economy, it is said to be over or under-valued when the rate does not give a fair reflection of the underlying productive capacity of the economy. An overvalued exchange rate overstates the economy's present productive capacity while an undervalued exchange understates it.

For example, when Britain's decision to return to the pre-WWI exchange rate at the end of the war, resulted in high interest rates and caused the economy to years of growth until the pound was devalued in 1931.

A country's economic managers may deliberately decide to maintain the exchange rate at an undervalued rate as part of the country's overall industrial development strategy, i.e. to foster import substitution while ensuring the country's exports are competitively priced in foreign markets. For example, a central part of the economic development strategy of the export-driven economies of the 'tiger' economies of Asia, for example, has been to ensure that the exchange rate is undervalued relative to major world currencies like the United States dollar and the pound sterling. This meant their exports were competitive in foreign markets and at the same time imports were expensive relative to local substitutes. Thus

undervalued currencies were used to lynch-pin industrial development strategy.

An overvalued exchange rate is the essential feature of the 'resource curse', when it arises from robust foreign exchange earnings from the exports of a primary resource such as crude oil, whose exploitation and export usually fail to integrate with other sectors of the economy, and foster their development. Strong external reserves and balance of payments position resulting from robust foreign exchange earnings may strengthen the country's currency relative to other currencies but misalign it with the true state of the country's economic development. Such foreign exchange earnings may enable the country to live above its extant means by financing mass importation which it implicitly subsidize to the lasting detriment of the country's own nascent industrial sector. An over-valued exchange rate gives an illusion of economic prosperity while undermining the basis for one in the long-term.

A country may officially fix or peg its exchange rate at a pre-determined rate or subject it to market forces by allowing it to float against other currencies in the foreign exchange market.

Fixed exchange rate offers economic stability and facilitates international trade as it eliminates exchange rate risk. However, it reduces the impact of monetary policy and control over interest rates. This is because a certain rate of exchange necessarily dictates a certain monetary stance. In addition, there is a tendency for the exchange rate to be over- or undervalued with telling impact on the economy.

Floating exchange rate enables policy makers and economic agents to see a truer picture of the economy and affords the leverage of monetary policy in the management of the economy. This has become a constant feature of economic reforms in most countries, and is a condition for securing the financial assistance of the International Monetary Fund. However, there is ever present tendency for inflation. Thus, where floating exchange rate system is usually accompanied by some form of exchange rate control/management.

This may entail controls over capital flows coming into and leaving the country and discretionary intervention in the foreign exchange market to ensure the rate stays within certain bands of fluctuation. Such discretionary management is often within an overall economic development or management strategy, for example, to ensure international competitiveness or in view of its effects on the general price level.

Determinants of Exchange Rate: under a floating exchange rate regime, the exchange rate is the product of the demand for and supply of the currency relative to that of its trading partners. In the absence of intervention in the foreign exchange market, the factors below directly determine the strength of the market forces for the currency:

1. ***Interest Rates***: high interest rate means high rates of return on investment, other things being equal. This may attract foreign capital and cause the exchange rate to rise.

2. ***Current Account Balance***: a deficit in the current account of the balance of payment means the country is not earning enough from its exports to cover its imports. The country is demanding foreign currency more than it is receiving from its exports. There is therefore excess demand for foreign currency, and this will tend to lower the exchange rate. Conversely, a surplus in the current account will tend to increase the exchange rate, other things being equal.

3. ***External Reserves***: where a country builds up reserve of foreign currency from surpluses from trade, it is able to withstand demand for foreign currency and thereby sustain a desired rate of exchange than it would otherwise. High crude oil prices (Nigeria's major export) in the 1970s helped the Naira appreciate against major currencies to the point of over-valuation, as the exchange rate gave a false reflection of the productive capacity of the economy.

4. ***Terms of Trade:*** if the prices of a country's exports increase relative to imports, means improvement in terms of trade and greater demand for the country's currency. This will increase the exchange rate. On the other hand, if the prices of imports increase more than increases in the prices of its exports, the demand for foreign currency will be high, and lower the exchange rate.

5. ***National Debt***: the higher the national debt of a country, as a percentage of its GDP, the higher the likelihood of default, therefore the less attractive the country is to foreign capital and the higher the outflow of foreign currency through external debt servicing. This reduces supply of foreign currency and thereby exerts downward pressure on the exchange rate.

6. **Economic Performance**: where the economy of country is conducive to investment, it will attract foreign investors and encourage local investors to invest in the country. This will increase supply for foreign capital or currency relative to demand for the local currency thereby boosting the exchange rate. On the other hand, where the political and economic situation of a country is perceived to be risky or unfriendly to investment, there will be capital flight from the country. This will exert downward pressure on the exchange rate

7. **Exchange Controls**: the government through the central bank may seek to manage the exchange rate at a certain rate rather than leave it entirely in to be determined by market forces. Exchange controls may be in the form of exchange restrictions and intervention in the market. Under an exchange restriction regime possession of foreign currency is subject to government approval. This was used by the Nigerian government prior to the Structural Adjustment Programme in 1986 when the Second-tier Foreign Exchange Market (SFEM) was put in place. In recent times, the central bank has sought to manage the exchange rate of the Naira by intervening in the market by buying and selling foreign currencies in the so-called Dutch Auction System (DAS).

Exchange Rate of the Naira:

The naira was pegged to the British pound sterling until 1967 when the pound was devalued by the Bank of England. Thereafter it became pegged to the United States dollar. After the United States left the gold standard and devalued the dollar, certain adjustments were made to the rate, and in 1978, the naira rate was related to a basket of 12 currencies until 1985 when this approach was abandoned for the United States dollar.

Until the devaluation of the naira with the implementation of the Structural Adjustment Program in 1986, the naira exchange rate gave a false, strong impression of the underlying economy, exchanging at between 0.6 and 0.9 to the United States dollar. This was against the backdrop of the oil boom of the early 1970s which boosted foreign exchange receipts and reserves.

The crash in crude oil prices brought about a reality check with the introduction of exchange control measures in 1982 under the Economic Stabilization Program. The succeeding government followed with even stricter controls but these were not able to bring about any sustainable change either, until the introduction of Second-tier Foreign Exchange Market (SFEM) as part of the Structural Adjustment Programme reform package in September, 1986. Since that time, the determination of the naira exchange rate and allocation of foreign exchange has been based on market forces, as modified by discretionary interventions by the CBN. A first-tier rate which was administratively determined was applied to external debt repayment/servicing and obligations to international organizations. In 1987, the first and second-tiers were merged in a reconstituted Foreign Exchange Market, (FEM) at ₦3.74: $1.00.

Since the devaluation of the naira in the first SFEM session, the naira has steadily depreciated from the initial N22 to the USDollar to almost ₦160. In 1989, the Bureaux de Change were introduced to accommodate small users of foreign exchange in the bid to reduce the relevance of the parallel market and to close the parallel market premium. However, the fundamental issue remain the fact that the country's demand for foreign exchange continue to be higher than supply of same—huge import bill relative to its export earnings—which continue to impact the exchange rate of the naira. Improvement in crude oil price, in recent years, has enabled the accumulation of reserves which has enabled the CBN to meet demand and effectively intervene in the foreign exchange market. This has meant a reduction in the rate of depreciation and in the parallel market premium. Thus, the CBN has been able to ensure the rate stays within ₦150—₦160 band to the United States dollar.

Year	Official Rate Naira ₦: USD$	Parallel Market Naira ₦: USD$
1980	0.50	0.9
1985	1.00	3.79
1986	3.60	4.17
1990	8.04	9.61
1993	22.05	36.23
1999	93.95	99.2
2003	129.30	135
2005	131.10	140
2009	122.50	n.a
2011	158.00	n.a
2012	158.00	n.a
Source: Central Bank of Nigeria		

Exogenous Change: change induced or brought about from the outside; a non-economic change affecting economic conditions. Political or security situation may impact positively or negatively on the economy to, for example, attract or deter foreign investment.

Expansionary Fiscal policy: A policy to increase governmental expenditure and/or to decrease tax in order to boost or expand business activity. Expansionary policy may be used to check deflation in the economy. See also fiscal policy.

Expansionary monetary policy: A monetary policy designed to expand the growth of money and credit in the economy. See also monetary policy.

Expenditure Method or approach: one of the method of accounting for national income; see under National income Accounting.

External Debt: part of the national debt owed to other countries or foreigners. Unlike internal debt, servicing of the external debt i.e. payment of interest and principal, form part of the balance of payment. Thus, beyond certain point, it may be deemed unsustainable, and reduce the confidence of trading partners to do business with the country concerned. This is because, there is a limit to how much debt a country's economy can sustain at any point in time. Beyond such a point, speculations of default may arise, and this is bound to self-fulfill. The country's managers are left without any margin of error. At the slightest excuse, foreign debt holders will off-load or sell off their stock and compound the situation, impacting on the stability of banks, and the exchange rate.

Export Credit Guarantee: a guarantee provided to banks in respect of credit given to exporters in support of the export of goods and services from Nigeria. It also enables Nigerian exporters to access credit internationally on terms that are more competitive than that offered within the local market. This a facility offered by the Nigerian Export Import (NEXIM) Bank as part of incentives to encourage the growth of the export sector.

Export Credit Insurance: insurance policy that covers exporters against risk of non-payment by buyers. This facility is offered by the Nigeria Export-Import (NEXIM) Bank as part of incentives to encourage the growth of the export sector.

Export Processing Zone (EPZ): see Free Trade Zone (FTZ)

Export Trade: selling abroad. One of the two branches of Foreign Trade, along with Import Trade. Export trade is divided into trade in visible items i.e. goods, and trade in services (invisible items) such as financial services (banking, insurance, etc.), and transportation such as aviation and shipping, tourism, etc.

Ex-Rights: shares or prices so quoted indicates that the prices excludes rights to any "rights" issue that has been or shall soon be made.

Ex-Ship: when goods are sold under this term of sale, the seller bears the risk until the goods have been properly loaded from the ship.

External Economies of Scale: economies that accrue to a firm from the outside e.g. as result of being located close to firms in the same industry or being located in an industrial estate. These economies or advantages do not arise out of any direct action of the firm.

Externalities: unintended or spillover effect of the production or consumption of a good by third parties; social costs or benefits which affect those not directly involved in the production or consumption of a good or service. Examples are pollution from a factory, congestion or cigarette smoke. Neighbours of a factory may endure noise pollution and traffic congestion resulting from the company's operations. On the positive side, they may also enjoy illumination from its perimeter lighting. As externalities are not usually compensated for by the market forces, they are cited as an example of market failure, and may necessitate government intervention in the form of regulation or taxation to ameliorate or remedy.

Extractive Industry: same as Primary Production.

Ex-warehouse: a quotation so given shows the price excluding delivery charges.

F

FAAC: the Federation Account Allocation Committee responsible for sharing federally collected revenue between the three tiers of government—Federal, State and Local Government—in Nigeria.

FAAN: see Federal Airport Authority of Nigeria.

Factor Cost: output measured in terms of the cost of the factors of production used. This is distinct from output at market prices because of indirect taxes and subsidies. National output may be measured at factor cost or market prices.

Factor Mobility: the ease with which factors of production can be transferred from one form of employment to another (occupational mobility), and from place to place (geographical mobility). Land is the least mobile factor while labour is the most mobile. Factor mobility is related to factor specificity

Factors of Production: inputs required for production to take place: land, labour, capital and entrepreneur.
- *Land:* natural resources; all natural or non-man made factors or "gifts of nature"—wind, lakes, rivers, sunlight, etc—which are economically useful in the production of goods and services. Land is fixed in supply and immobile; it is practically fixed in supply, and is subject to the law of

diminishing returns. The reward for land as a factor of production is *rent*.
- *Labour:* human resources. The economically productive capabilities of humans, their physical and mental talents as applied to the production of goods and services. Labour may be skilled, semi-skilled and unskilled. Labour is the most mobile factor of production. The reward of labour as factor of production is *wages/salary*.
- *Capital:* material resources used in production; man-made factor of production: factories, machinery and equipment, structures and inventories, that is, goods produced for use in further production. Capital is the total property of a business. The reward for capital is interest.

Types of capital:
- *Fixed capital:* these are long-term assets or producer goods that do not change form in the course of production; Examples are buildings, plant and equipment, cars and trucks, etc. They are durable in nature and can be used over a long period during which they depreciate in value before they are eventually scrapped.
- *Circulating or working capital:* this refers to liquid asset or cash required to keep the business going. Working capital is used up during production e.g. in paying maintenance expenses, raw materials, salaries, etc.

- *Social capital:* this refers to social infrastructure provided by the state that assists in production e.g. electricity, road and railway network, telecommunication networks, hospitals, schools, etc. They are not directly used in production but they facilitate and greatly enhance efficiency and effectiveness of the process of production. The more social capital a country has the greater its production.
- **Entrepreneurship**: the initiator of process of production. The factor of production responsible for the organization and management of production. As well as making the usual business decisions, entrepreneurship is often associated with the functions of innovation and bearing of risks. Also referred to as enterprise.

Factor Specificity: A factor is said to be specific if it is so specialized that it cannot be employed for any other purpose other than that for which it was originally designed or used for. Unskilled labour is non-specific as the time required is short unlike skilled labour which can be highly specific due to the long period of training and education, in the case of professionals like doctors or lawyers, or natural talent required, in the case of an artist. Capital, in the form of machinery, can be highly specific and immobile, for example a crude oil refinery cannot be used for any other purpose. On the other hand, a building can easily be converted from a factory to a warehouse or worship centre.

Factory: place where production takes place in an organized and structured way. The factory system is one the features of the industrial and capitalist economy where goods are mass produced, with specialized labour for distant markets as opposed to the pre-industrial economy where production took place at home for domestic consumption or local market.

Fair Trade: the idea that trade—often in the context of international trade—should be fair in terms of

Fascism: a political system that stresses extreme nationalism with military strength and national prestige superseding all other considerations.

Federal Airport Authority of Nigeria (FAAN): the FAAN is the government body established to manage airports in the country. The international airports, Murtala Mohammed, Lagos, Nnamdi Azikiwe, Abuja, Aminu Kano, Kano and Port Harcourt, and other airports. It provides facilities required for the effective utilization of airports such as hangars, runways, and collaborates with security agencies to ensure adequate security of goods and persons at the airports. The FAAN is under the Ministry of Aviation.

Functions of the FAAN

1. Develop, provide and maintain airports.
2. Provide necessary services for providers and users of aviation services.
3. Provide facilities—office complexes, shopping malls, hangars, towers, lounges, trolleys, conveniences—for safe, orderly, efficient and effective operation of air transport services;
4. Ensuring the serviceability of airport facilities, Runway, Apron, Terminal facilities, access roads, etc.

5. Provide a conducive atmosphere and conditions for the use of the country's airports by airlines and passengers e.g. in terms of management of aircraft, vehicular and human traffic; environmental sanitation.
6. Provide accommodation and other facilities for the effective handling of passengers and freight.
7. Provide security at all airports in collaboration with other government agencies.

Federal Government of Nigeria (FGN) Bonds long-term interest bearing debt securities issued by the Federal Government of Nigeria through the Debt Management Office, with tenors between two and ten years. They are used by the government to finance budget deficits and raise money for capital projects. The bonds are listed and traded on the floors of the Nigerian Stock Exchange (NSE). Upon issuance, bonds become part of the domestic debt stock, and the buyers/subscribers—banks, discount houses, and pension funds managers, high net worth individuals, among others—effectively become creditors to the government. As sovereign debt backed with Federal might, risk of default is nil.

Bonds are an effective monetary policy tool in financing budget deficits without increasing the money in circulation with its inflationary implications. For example, the government financed the payment of N75billion of pension arrears in 2006 by issuing bonds, rather than increase the money supply by this amount and risk inflation.

The government has increasingly resorted to the use of market source of funding in its efforts towards a more rational management of its fiscal operations, and the development and growth of the capital market.

Federal Government of Nigeria Development Stocks: long-term interest—bearing debt instruments issued by the Federal Government to finance its development projects, with tenors of between two and twenty five years.

Federal Reserve Bank: central banking in the United States is the function of the Federal Reserve System which comprises twelve Federal Reserve Districts each with its own Reserve Bank. Each district Reserve Bank holds the reserve requirement of its member commercial banks. Monetary policy is co-ordinated through the Federal Reserve Board in Washington.

Federal Mortgage Bank of Nigeria (FMBN): a development finance institution, responsible for the administration of the National Housing Trust Fund, which may be accessed by individual subscribers through the primary mortgage banks.

Fertility Rate: number of births per thousand women of child-bearing age. It is statistic used in projecting population growth.

Fiat money: Money by law; because the government declares it legal tender. Fiat money may have little or no intrinsic value in itself; usually taking the form of tokens or pieces of paper; and is not redeemable for any commodity. This contrasts with Commodity Money such as salt, cigarette, etc.

Fiduciary Issue: money that cannot be converted to any real commodity such as silver or gold. Under the gold standard and the Bretton Wood "gold-exchange" standard monetary systems, money could be converted upon demand to gold at a pre-determined rate. Money thus had an intrinsic value in itself. After the collapse of the gold standard and the end of the Bretton Woods system of fixed exchange rates in 1973, money has ceased to be backed by any real commodity like gold or silver. Modern money is legal tender; backed the force of law as a means of exchange not by a promise to exchange it for real value.

Financial Economies: advantages enjoyed by a large firm by being to borrow money more cheaply than small firms. This is because it can offer collateral for its loans or debentures and issue shares through the Stock Exchange.

Financial Institutions: Financial institutions are companies or institutions that perform the function of financial intermediation in the economy. Financial intermediation is the process of taking money from sectors with financial surpluses (lenders) and making it available to sectors in financial deficit (borrowers), i.e., sectors that do not have enough money or credit. Financial institutions therefore interface between lenders and borrowers. They comprise banks (i.e. commercial, development, investment, mortgage, microfinance, savings and loans, etc) acceptance and discount houses, insurance companies, pension funds, the stock market, etc.

Money and credit are to the economy what blood is to a biological system. The level of development of an economy can be gauged by the level of development, depth and relevance of its financial system to the economy. The financial system ensures the proper functioning of the economy by ensuring that money and credit circulate through the various sectors of the economy. The role of financial intermediaries is vital for two important reasons. Firstly, they make investment funds available, by pooling savings from various sectors. Secondly, it provides credit to facilitate production and the exchange of goods and services, without which the velocity of economic activities will be slow, at best.

Beginning with the reforms entailed in the structural adjustment programme of 1986-1992, the Nigerian financial system has evolved in terms of changes in ownership structure of its institutions, the depth and breadth of instruments used, the number of institutions and the regulatory framework within which the system operates.

The liberalization of the financial system marked by removal of exchange controls in 1987 and the deregulation of interest rates in 1991 boosted competition among financial institutions, and the increasing dependence on indirect tools of monetary control-cash reserve requirements, liquidity ratios, open market operation, etc—enhanced the role of financial institutions in the economy.

Liberalization saw an increase in the number of banks and finance houses, and in no time excesses became glaring. Number of banks increased from 40 in 1985 to 120 in 1993; by 1998, distress has reduced this number to 89. The need to strengthen regulation of the industry, enforce ethics and protect depositors saw the granting of autonomy to the Central Bank of Nigeria in 1991 and the enactment of the Banks and Other Financial Institutions Decree, and the establishment of the Nigerian Deposit Insurance Corporation (NDIC) in 1988.

The Securities and Exchange Commission was also established during this time to oversee and regulate the capital market with powers to approve new stock exchanges.

The practice of insurance was strengthened with the establishment of the Nigerian Insurance Commission (NAICOM) to replace the Nigerian Insurance Supervisory Board (NISB).

Earlier, in 1990, the CBN had implemented the Bank of International Settlement's risk weighted measure of capital adequacy for Nigerian banks. The minimum capital requirement for banks was raised to N500m for both commercial and merchant banks. The concept of universal banking was adopted in 2001 and the minimum capital was further revised upwards to N2billion.

In order to increase the capacity of banks and meet the development challenges of the economy, the minimum capital requirement was further increased to N25billion in 2004. This resulted in mergers and acquisitions that brought the number of banks from 89 to 25 through consolidation, bringing about larger and stronger institutions with competitive relevance in the West African sub-region and beyond. Consolidation brought about greater regulatory challenges ultimately leading to the formation of the Asset Management Company of Nigeria (AMCON) in 2011.

Financial Intermediaries see Financial Institutions.

Finance House: institutions that specialize in short-term, financial intermediation. They mobilize funds from the investing public in form of borrowing and provide facilities for Local Purchase Order (LPO) and project financing, equipment leasing and debt factoring, among others. They are under the direct control and supervision of the Central Bank of Nigeria.

Firm: A business unit or company formed to carry out certain economic activity as a going-concern; where factors of production are organized and input are transformed to create goods and services for human satisfaction. It may a private enterprise, taking the form of a sole proprietorship, partnership or a joint-stock company or a public enterprise.

Fiscal Policy: The use of government revenue and expenditure to control the economy in order to maximize national income or achieve desired objectives in levels of employment, control the general price level (inflation/deflation), international trade (balance of payments), level of economic activity (boom and recession/depression), etc. Fiscal policy is laid out in the national budget, and taxation is a central fiscal policy tool. The government may increase taxes to reduce purchasing power in the economy, and thereby curb demand-pull inflation. If the economy is experiencing deflation, the government may reduce taxes to increase disposable income, and thereby stimulate economic activity. Import and export duties may also be used to regulate international trade by reducing export duties and increasing import duties as may be desired in the balance of payments. Fiscal policy may also be used to redistribute national income by taxing the rich and using the tax revenue to provide facilities for all.

Fiscal policy instruments or tools used by the government to control or regulate the economy are taxes and government expenditure. The essence of fiscal policy is to bring about desired outcomes in the general price level, employment, investment, national output/income, international trade, etc.

Objectives of fiscal policy

1. *Revenue*: tax receipts provide government with its main source of revenue required for the administration of the country.

2. *Redistribution of income:* government may fiscal policy measures such as taxes to redistribute income between owners of the factors of production so as to bring about a more equitable distribution of the national income. This may be achieved by taxing owners of capital who receive a disproportionate share of the rewards of production and using the receipts to provide social amenities for all.

3. *To manage the general price level*: a sustained increase/decrease in the general price level may be controlled by increasing or decreasing the amount of money in circulation by the use of taxes. Inflation may result when there is too much money chasing too few goods. In such a situation the government may reduce the amount of money in circulation by increasing taxes. During a period of deflation, the amount of money in circulation may be increased by reducing taxes.

4. *Balance of Payment adjustment*: a country is experiencing unfavourable balance of payment when its imports exceed exports. Such a situation is not sustainable, and the government will need to take necessary measures to correct the imbalance. Fiscal policy measures may be used to discourage imports and encourage exports. Import duties and tariffs may be imposed to discourage or make imported goods relatively expensive. The government may also reduce or abolish export duties to encourage exports.

5. *To stimulate the economy from recession/depression:* where aggregate demand is weak, it means that people do not have enough purchasing power to buy the output of firms. Where firms cannot sell their products, they are not able to invest and employ people, resulting in a slowdown of the economy, characterized by high unemployment i.e. a recession or depression, if the slow-down severe. In such a situation, the government may reduce taxes in order to increase purchasing power, and thereby bolster aggregate demand.

Fiscal Year: financial year; the period covered by a budget.

Fisher Equation: an alternative term for the Equation of Exchange, which attempts to express the Quantity Theory of Money algebraically. It states that

$$MV = PT$$
where,
M = Money Supply;
V = Velocity of Circulation of money (the number of times money changes hands);
P = Average Price Level;
T = Volume of Transactions of Goods and Services.

The Fisher Equation is an algebraic expression of the Quantity Theory of Money, which states that there is a direct relationship between increases in the money supply and increases prices.

The Fisher Equation is named after the American economist, Irving Fisher, who refined the Equation of Exchange, by adding two new variables; the average price level (P) and the volume of transactions (T).

Fixed Costs: in the short-run analysis of the firm, production costs that do not change as output changes. If a bakery increases output of bread from 500 loaves per day to 700 per day, certain costs like factory rent, cost of machinery, manager's salary, interest on loan, etc, will remain unchanged or fixed. Some costs are fixed in the short-run but in the long-run all costs are variable.

Fixed Assets: assets with a long-term lifespan, bought for use in production, not for re-sale; they do not change form in the process of production. Items under this classification in a company's Balance Sheet include land and buildings, plant and machinery, furniture and fittings. Fixed assets are depreciated to account for their contribution to production. Yearly depreciation is written-off to the Profit and Loss Account.

Fixed Capital: same as Fixed Assets

Fixed Costs: costs which do not vary as output changes such as cost of installed machinery, buildings, and other fixed assets. Rent and rates and administration expenses also remain constant over a range of output. The distinction between fixed and variable costs is only in the short-term as all costs are variable in the long-term: installed capacity may be expanded or reduced in the long-term.

Fixed Exchange Rate: where the exchange rate of a currency is pegged or allowed to move within a narrow band. This is as opposed to fluctuating exchange rate which is subject to market forces in the foreign exchange market.

Flexible Exchange Rate: system of exchange rates where the rate of exchange is allowed to fluctuate within a pre-determined band.

Flight of Capital: rapid outflow of financial assets from country. This is usually because of loss of confidence by investors due to economic conditions e.g. fear of devaluation/ material depreciation of the currency, fear of nationalization, questions over the ability of the government to meet its maturing obligations to trading partners/creditors, etc. Foreign portfolio investment, unlike foreign direct investment, is particularly prone to flight. See Foreign Capital.

Floating Charge: according to the terms of agreement, the claim of a creditor, e.g. a debenture holder, over any asset of a business, as opposed to a fixed charge which relates to a particular asset.

f.o.b: see Free on Board.

Food and Agricultural Organization (FAO): an agency of the United Nations Organization with a mandate to work toward the attainment of global food security by promoting agricultural development, improving nutrition. The Organization offers direct development assistance, collects, analyzing and disseminating information, providing policy and planning advice to governments and acting as an international forum for sharing ideas on food and agriculture issues.

Force Majeure: a clause in a contract that frees parties from obligations or liabilities when an extraordinary event or circumstance beyond the control of the parties such as war, civil unrest, strike or an 'act of God' (natural disaster) prevents any or both parties from fulfilling their duties under the contract.

Foreign Capital: foreign capital is of categories: foreign direct (FDI) and foreign portfolio investment (FPI). The lower the rate of savings in a country, the greater the reliance on foreign capital for development. The creation of an environment conducive and attractive to foreign capital is a key objective of economic reforms championed by the International Monetary Fund and the World Bank. Reforms have sought to create conditions to attract foreign capital to fuel economic growth. However, where huge foreign capital inflows consist mostly of portfolio investment, and not matched in increased productive capacity from direct investment in the traded-goods sector, a potentially volatile situation may be created. In the context of economic liberalization and globalization, huge amounts of capital can be moved across international borders at short notice leaving a country prostrate, and precipitating an economic crisis. Any development, pronouncement or issue that suggests or is suspected to bring about a change in interest and/or exchange rates in the context of certain underlying factors could easily affect investment sentiment and confidence, and lead to massive capital flight from a country at short notice. In Mexico, in 1994, a combination of ultimately incompatible monetary and exchange rate policies came to a head with the devaluation of the currency, the peso, to undermine investors' confidence. This triggered massive capital flight that led to a financial crisis that practically grounded the economy. In 1997, when portfolio investors doubted the ability of the Thai government to meet its foreign

debt servicing obligations, panic among investors snowballed, ultimately herding out in droves across Asia almost resulting in a global meltdown.

Foreign Direct Investment: significant long-term investment in productive assets e.g. buildings, machinery, factories, etc. or ordinary shares of a company by non-residents or foreigners. Such investment is characterized by involvement in management of the company and directly creates employment opportunities. This is usually done by multinational corporations as opposed to financial institutions who favour portfolio investment. Increasing cost of labour in their home country and the quest for new markets are motivating factors to invest abroad.

Attraction of FDI has become of the objectives of structural reforms in many developing countries since the 1980s in sharp contrast to times when import substitution industrialization and economic self-sufficiency was the popular route for economic development.

One of the factors behind the transformation of the newly industrialized countries like South Korea and Taiwan has been their ability to attract foreign capital from the United States and Europe.

China is living up to its potential of becoming the dominant world economy due to ability to make itself the workshop of the world by attracting multinationals to set factories there to take advantage of its low labour costs and immense internal market.

In contrast foreign portfolio investment is short-term in nature, and is limited to investment in stocks, bonds and shares of companies listed on the Stock Exchange.

FDI, Benefits of

Foreign direct capital brings with it technical expertise and management know-how all of which most developing countries direly need to break from the vicious circle of underdevelopment.

1. Employment: FDI impact on the local economies where there are situated providing direct and indirect employment opportunities.

2. Technology: by providing machinery and equipment, capital-intensive technology, marketing knowledge, new information technology, distribution and logistic support, etc., FDI helps to build local industrial capabilities, the development of a pool of trained labour, adoption of a new set of technologies.

3. Training: MNCs offers opportunities in managerial skills e.g. new systems of organization and management, and exposure to international standards to employees.

FDI, Determinants of:

1. The market size and growth in the host country: A country's population, real GDP, GDP growth rate, GDP per capita tend to attract more FDI due to larger potential demand and lower costs due to scale economies. This is the case with China; it has a huge internal market, a fast growing middle class.

2. Economic stability and growth prospects: stable macroeconomic condition indicated by real GDP growth rate, industrial production index, inflation rates, exchange rates

and interest rates tend to receive high FDI inflows than one characterized by a volatile indices.

3. Labour costs: High wage rates, high level of labour union activities and industrial action, etc., deter FDI inflows. One of the reasons multinational corporations outsource manufacturing plants from their home countries is the rising cost of labour.

4. Infrastructure: the presence of well-maintained quality infrastructure—electricity, water, transportation, and telecommunications reduces cost of doing business, increase marginal productivity of capital and therefore attracts multinationals.

5. Trade openness: Trade openness, meaning the degree of liberalization of trade regime of the host country, is regarded as a very important factor that promotes FDI. Much FDI is export oriented.

6. Political stability: Political instability and frequent occurrence of civil disorder create an unfavourable business climate which seriously erodes the risk-averse foreign investor's confidence.

7. Human capital: A country with a more educated and skilled labour force that can learn and adopt new technology faster will be more productive, less need for training and lower turnover. Technical skills and exposure to technology tend to be low in most African countries, due to an education system that stresses academic and clerical skills over technical prowess, negatively impacting productivity. This is another attraction of Asian countries in attracting FDI.

8. Natural resource endowment: Countries that are endowed with natural resources would receive more resource-seeking FDI, ceteris paribus.

9. Herding Effect: The presence of other multinational companies in a country is an indicator of a friendly business climate. The decision to enter into a country can be partly justified by the fortunes of other MNCs in the country.

10. Exchange Rate Valuation: A weaker real exchange rate means firms can take advantage of relatively low prices in host markets to purchase facilities or, if production is re-exported, to increase home-country profits on goods sent to a third market. One of the secrets of China's success is that its currency is pegged to the United States dollar at an under-valued rate.

11. Political stability: a political environment characterized by civic disorder, riots, terrorism, and the like deters potential foreign investors.

12. Institutions: poor administrative institutions usually mean poor regulatory framework, bureaucratic hurdles and red tape, lack of judicial transparency, and high levels of corruption which adds to investment costs and lowers profits.

FDI in Nigeria

Foreign Direct Investment was un-restricted until the NEPD (indigenization) decrees of 1972 and 1977. These laws raised the threshold for foreign investment by reserving certain businesses for Nigerians and restricting foreign ownership to 40 per cent. The implementation of these laws caused some foreign firms, such as IBM, to divest from the country.

Reforms under SAP saw the relaxation with the amendment in 1989. The indigenization decrees were eventually repealed with the passage of Nigerian Investment Promotion Decree of 1995. This law allows 100 per cent FDI in any business, except those concerned with arms, narcotics and military wares, and established the Nigeria Investment Promotion Commission as a body to facilitate and promote foreign investment in Nigeria.

• The Foreign Exchange (Monitoring and Miscellaneous Provisions) Act was also passed in 1995 to encourage FDI by enabling free transfer of foreign exchange and repatriation of funds by foreign investors.

These laws coupled with the return to democratic rule in 1999 increased the inflow of FDI into the country. Deregulation of the telecommunications in 2001, saw the entrance of MTN, Econet and Etisalat all foreign companies. Similar deregulation and reforms of ports saw the award of a concession to APM Terminals manage the Apapa port in Lagos in 2006.

• Setting up of Export Processing Zones: The Nigeria Free Zone Act was passed in 1992. The law enabled the establishment of the Nigerian Export Processing Zone Authority (NEPZA) to attract multinational corporations to set up in the country. See Free Trade Zone.

• The National Economic Empowerment Development Strategy (NEEDS) specifically aims to attract FDI with special focus on Nigerians and Africans in Diaspora.

• Bilateral Investment Promotion and Protection Agreements: the government has signed and ratified with some countries to reduce perceived risk in order to encourage investment from their nationals. These countries include the United Kingdom, France, Netherlands and Korea. The treaties contain guarantees of national treatment of foreign investors, most favoured nation (MFN) provisions, fair and equitable treatment and standard guarantees for unrestricted repatriation of investment and returns.

Foreign Exchange Management/Policy: the management of the price of a country's currency value i.e. exchange rate to ensure that it is line with overall macro-economic objectives in terms of economic development viz. export promotion/ industrialization, general price level, balance of payment, etc. This might entail a policy to ensure the currency's value is kept at a certain rate to major currencies with the aim of ensuring imports are cheap or conversely that the country's exports are competitive in foreign markets and locally produced goods are cheap compared to imports. There is also the challenge of ensuring that the exchange rate does not translate to high interest rates within the country. A country's exchange rate may be administratively set or it may be subjected to the market forces to determine it. However, the monetary authorities may need to intervene in the market to ensure the rate stays within certain bands in view of set macro-economic goals. Exchange controls and import licensing are common under a non-market determined exchange management system, such as existed in Nigeria before 1986.

Foreign Exchange Market: the market for the buying and selling of foreign currencies. In the foreign exchange market, the forces of demand and supply for foreign currencies interact to determine the exchange rate. In Nigeria, this comprises the official window such as the Dutch Auction System, the inter-bank market and the bureaux de change. There is also the parallel or black market which emerged during the exchange control era, and continues to exist due to shortage of foreign exchange.

Foreign Exchange Market System: the mechanism used in determining the rate of exchange between currencies. Types of foreign exchange systems include the gold standard, fixed exchange system, and freely fluctuating exchange system. These may be classified into managed currency systems and market-based systems.

The rate at which a currency is exchanged in terms of other currencies depends on the relative demand and supply for it. The more a country imports, relative to its exports, the higher the demand for its currency hence lower the exchange rate will be, and vice versa. Thus, the exchange rate will be a reflection of the relative economic performance of the economy, if it is determined by market forces. However, government often finds it necessary to intervene to maintain the value within certain limits in alignment with its overall economic management/development strategy. For example, the export-driven development strategy of South East Asian countries dictated a need to keep the value of the currencies low, even undervalued, to ensure their exports remain competitive. On the other hand, countries that pursue import-substitution economic development strategy tend to keep their currencies at high rates of exchange relative to other currencies as this will keep cost of imported inputs cheap.

An overvalued exchange rate cannot be sustained, however, as it will lead to a fundamental disequilibrium in the balance of payments position overtime.

In Nigeria, a fixed exchange regime was in place under the Exchange Control Act of 1962 until the advent of structural economic reforms when the value of the naira was left to market forces to determine. The liberalization of the foreign exchange rate market i.e. post-Exchange Control era, began in 1986 with the Second-tier Foreign Exchange Market (SFEM). Limited controls were re-introduced with the Autonomous Foreign Exchange Market (AFEM) in 1995 due to volatility of the rate with the pegging of the exchange rate and centralization of the market at the Central Bank. Liberalization resumed with the Inter-bank Foreign Exchange Market (IFEM) in 1999. Even though these mechanisms allowed the participation of Bureaux de Change in the foreign exchange market they did not succeed in eliminating a parallel market which continued to exploit scarcity of foreign exchange and bureaucratic procedures.

Foreign Portfolio Investment: investment in shares and financial securities by foreign nationals which do not result in involvement in management of concerned enterprises.

Founder's (Deferred or Management) Shares: shares reserved for the promoters or founders of a business. They usually have favourable powers of control and voting. They may be used by the founders of a private company to retain control and takeover by outsiders upon being converted to a public company. The claim on profit as well as on capital repayment in the event of a winding down, of this class of shares usually comes after all others, though, claims of ordinary shareholders, for example, may be limited to a certain percentage.

Free Competition: an environment of Perfect Competition where market forces interact with no interference or intervention by the State

Free Economy: an economic system in which the basic economic questions of what to produce, how to produce and for whom to produce are determine by the (*"invisible hand"*) interaction of demand and supply in the market. In practice, there is no country where the state or government does not play a role in the economic system. Market failure—the short comings of the market—is acknowledged even as economic liberalization and deregulation aim at ensuring market forces are not distorted in allocation of resources.

Free Enterprise: an economic system where individuals can own factors of production and freely act as economic agents following the dictates of market conditions indicated by demand and supply forces without interference from the State or government.

Free Floating Exchange Rates: see Foreign Exchange Systems

Free Goods: goods, which have no opportunity cost, e.g. air. Such goods are in unlimited supply, that is, not scarce nor made out of scarce resources. Therefore, unlike economic goods are not subject to forces of demand and supply. Free goods present no problem of scarcity and are thus outside of the subject-matter of economics.

Freehold: real estate whose owner is not subject to payment of rent or other charges.

Contrast leasehold.

Free on Board (f.o.b): quotation inclusive of cost of carriage from supplier's premises to the port of dispatch, other cost being borne by the purchaser.

Free on Rail (f.o.r): prices quoted on these terms are inclusive of carriage from the sellers premises up to the railway station from which the goods are despatched. The buyer is responsible for the railway charges.

Free Port: Ports where goods meant for re-export are not subject to customs duty.

Free Rider Problem: a situation where people consume more than their fair share or pay less than their fair share of a common resource. Tax evaders pose a free rider problem as they free-ride or enjoy the services made possible by the payment of taxes as much as those who pay their taxes.

Free Trade: there is said to be free trade between countries when trade between trade is left to the forces of demand and supply without artificial restrictions such as tariffs, customs duties, quotas, import duties, import licensing, bans and embargoes, foreign exchange control, etc. Consumer's welfare will be highest—at least in theory—when countries specialize in their area of comparative advantage and freely trade with each other, according to the theory of comparative advantage. However, countries are political units competitively engaged with each other giving rise to desire for self-sufficiency, relative economic and political might, etc. Besides, the issue of comparative advantage is hardly static, and it is the desire of every country to develop to its full potential. Economic groupings such as Economic Community of West African States (ECOWAS), the European Union, and the North American Free Trade Agreement (NAFTA), etc, are founded on the recognition of the economic benefits of free trade. The World Trade Organization, which evolved from the General Agreement on Tariff and Trade (GATT), was founded to promote free trade by reducing trade restrictions.

Advantages of Free trade
Greater world output: overall global output of goods and services is higher when countries trade freely with each other as there is maximum market for goods and services. The global economy is therefore better off when trade is not restricted.

Higher standard of living: residents of countries that engage in free trade have a higher standard of living as they have access to greater variety of goods beyond what their local producers can offer.

Bigger markets: with free trade, firms are not limited to their home market. They have access to bigger international markets which enable them to produce cheaper due to economies of large scale production.

Lower prices, better quality: free trade brings about lower prices and improved quality due to more efficient use of resources brought by competition.

Disadvantage of Free trade
Unfair competition: countries are at different stage of economic development, and free trade may be in favour of the more advanced country with advanced technology and superior labour force. On the other hand, a developing country may have an unfair advantage due to its relatively cheap labour.

Encouragement of dumping: free trade encourages countries to dump their products in the local market by selling below cost of production in the importing country to the detriment of local producers. This act must be counteracted by restricting trade.

Dependency: free trade does not encourage a country to be self-reliant resulting in dependence. For certain strategic industries this is not acceptable.

Non-essential and dangerous imports: if trade is not regulated and restricted in certain areas, the country will be flooded with non-essentials and imports which are not in the public interest like goods sub-standard products.

Free Trade Area: an area comprising a group of countries, with contiguous international borders, that have agreed to allow trade between them without imposing duties. This may be the first stage in evolving economic integration. Example is the North American Free Trade Area (NAFTA) comprising Mexico, United States of America and Canada

Free Trade Zone (FTZ) or Export Processing Zones (EPZ): are specially designated areas with specially built infrastructure—transportation, warehouses, uninterrupted power supply, water supply and advanced telecommunication facilities— where raw materials and components may be imported for manufacturing or assembly into finished goods and re-exported. Incentives granted to offices and factories set-up in an FTZ may include minimal bureaucratic requirements, rent-free land, tax holidays, and exemption from local taxes, foreign exchange restrictions, customs and tariffs. The purpose is to attract foreign direct investment by multinational corporations (MNC) to set up factories to mass produce goods like clothes, shoes, electronics, etc for export. FTZ may be used to stimulate the development of a remote and underdeveloped area of a country, and are often located near seaports, international airports and national border region.

The development of FTZ in Nigeria was made possible with the passing of the Nigeria Free Zone Act in 1992 which established the Nigeria Export Processing Zone Authority (NEPZA). The first FTZ in the country, the Calabar FTZ, was commissioned in 2001. Others completed and operational include the Onne Oil and Gas, Kano, Maitagari, Tinapa and Lekki FTZs.

Frictional Unemployment: Short-term joblessness due to time taken to secure a new job. A person who leaves a job to find something better is considered frictionally unemployed. This type of unemployment characterizes workers subject to seasonal work (e.g., construction, agricultural, recreational workers, etc.). There is bound to be a degree of frictional unemployment even during period of full employment.

Functional Relationship: variables are said to have a functional relationship if a change in one results in a change in the other. Demand, for example, is a function of price.

Fundamental Disequilibrium: an unfavourable or adverse balance of payment position due to an overvalued rate of exchange relative to other currencies. Imports become cheaper and exports become less competitive. Where the exchange rate is determined by the market, it may adjust overtime, barring intervention by the monetary authority i.e. the central bank.

Devaluation may be the ultimate recourse where the exchange rate is pegged. The foreign exchange rate may not reflect the relative strength of its economy vis-à-vis other currencies due to a number of factors. For example, when Britain returned to the gold standard at the pre-WWI exchange rate of the pound, in 1925, the government discounted the effect of the war on the economy; the pound was therefore over-valued at the old rate. This put the country at a disadvantage in international trade. This was not a sustainable position, and the government was forced to devalue the pound in 1931.

A currency may appreciate against currencies over time on the back of foreign exchange earnings from mineral resource exports as opposed to overall economic performance. The true situation may not be apparent so long as the price of the mineral produce remains high. By the time the price does finally crash, the country may have gotten used to an import bill that it cannot sustain, resulting in a fundamental disequilibrium.

G

Galloping Inflation: same as hyperinflation

GATT (General Agreement on Tariff and Trade): conference of countries with the aim of reducing import duties and other import restrictions in order to expand trade between them. GATT has been replaced by the World Trade Organization.

Garnishee Order: a court order issued at the instance of a creditor requiring a third party, known as the garnishee, owing money to debtor, not to make any payment to the debtor until directed to do so by the court.

GDP: See Gross Domestic Product

Gearing: this refers to the ratio of external long-term funds, such as debentures, with prior fixed charges, to other types of long-term funds such as shares in a company's balance sheet. Fixed charges on debentures and certain preference shares are paid first before dividend are paid to ordinary shareholders. Where such fixed prior charges are high, and take a major part of profit leaving little for ordinary shareholders, gearing is said to be high. Gearing is said to be low if the prior charges are low.

General Average: in maritime insurance, this refers to loss incurred by the captain of a ship in order to preserve the ship and its cargo from further loss, for example, in a storm. In an emergency, the captain may decide to throw overboard some of the cargo in order to preserve his ship's integrity or extra charges may be incurred to tow the ship to safety. In these instances, owners of cargo who have not insured against such risk may partly bear the loss, along with the ship owners, in the form of general average contribution, calculated in proportion to the value of their cargo.

General Crossing: two parallel lines drawn across the face of a cheque without restrictions to a particular bank. Cash is not paid on such a cheque. Compare *Special Crossing*.

General Partner: a member of a partnership who is actively involved in the management of the enterprise.

General Strike: an industrial action involving all trade unions. In Nigeria, this has been called by the two umbrella trade unions, the Nigeria Labour Congress and the Trade Union Congress, to protest government policies such as removal of fuel subsidy or for a revision of the minimum wage. Such strikes usually paralyses the economy.

Geographical Mobility: the ease with which a factor of production can be move from one place to another. Labour is the most mobile factor of production while land is the least mobile. Capital transfers between national borders have usually been subject to legal regulations but these have become increasingly relaxed in the face of globalization.

Geometric Progression: a series increasing by a multiple. For example, 2, 6, 18, 54 . . . Contrast Arithmetic Progression.

Giffen Goods: goods for which demand increases as prices increase. This is usually the case for basic necessities among very low income groups. An increase in the price of certain necessities may result in the reduction in demand for more expensive goods, while the demand for the necessities is increased. Giffen goods have exceptional demand curves over a section showing a direct relationship between quantity demanded and price. The term is after Sir R. Giffen, who was the first to make the observation.

Gifts of Nature: a feature or characteristic of natural resources—rivers, lakes, wind, sunlight, etc—described together as 'land', as a factor of production.

Gilt-edged (securities): a financial security with a minimum risk of default of payment of interest such as bonds issued by sovereign governments.

Globalization: world-wide integration of economies and societies due to free flow of ideas, people, capital, goods and services. Advances in communication technology and transportation have essentially driven the process beginning with the invention of the telegram and steamship, following the Industrial Revolution in Europe and the opening up of the then so-called New World. The process has been accelerated by the internet which has drastically reduced the cost of communication across the globe and turned it into a single market place or "global village".

GNP: see Gross National Product.

Going Concern: the capacity of a business enterprise to continue to make profit in perpetual succession. Where a company's going concern status is threatened, it means it is going bankrupt.

Gold Exchange Standard: a monetary system in which a country maintains its reserves at a fixed exchange rate in the currency of another country which is on the **gold standard.** The currency of the country on gold-exchange standard is thus convertible to gold without the country having to maintain a reserve of gold.

This monetary system is what obtains presently with most countries holding their reserves in United States dollars, British Pounds sterling, and increasingly, the Chinese yuan/ renminbi.

Gold Reserves: part of a country's external assets or international reserves held to underpin its monetary system/banks/ national currency. Gold Reserves may also be used to make payments when there is an adverse balance of payment. It underlies the country's relative economic strength. Reserves are also held in international reserve currencies (such as the United States dollar, British Pound sterling, Japanese yen and Chinese yuan), Special Drawing Rights (SDR), and bonds.

Under the Gold Standard, countries were required to maintain gold reserves equal to the amount of money in circulation.

Gold Standard: A monetary system in which the value of the currency is related/ anchored directly or indirectly to the value of gold.

Three variants may be identified:

- The gold specie standard: under which gold coins circulated as a means of exchange or money or the means of exchange was associated with gold coins.
- The gold bullion standard: the government guarantees to exchange a unit of currency/money for gold on demand.
- The gold-exchange standard: the government warrants to exchange cash at a fixed rate of exchange with the currency of a country on the gold (specie or bullion) standard.

The gold standard existed in various forms in the world's major economies between the 1880s and 1971, when the United States was forced by a combination of economic constraints to abandon it.

Under the gold standard money, has value in itself, i.e., intrinsically, as it can be exchanged for its worth in gold. The value of money in circulation is therefore limited to the value of gold held in stock as opposed to the value of goods and services. This meant that governments cannot print money at will; for every currency note printed, there has to be the equivalent in gold held in reserves. This was practically a hold on inflation. Indeed during the period of the gold standard, inflation was practically non-existent.

While this may restrain any upward pressure in the general price level, i.e. inflation, as it restricts the ability of the central bank to expand the money supply, there is the tendency of money supply not keeping pace with increase in national output, thus leading to deflation and attendant unemployment, which may be chronic or long-lasting. The limited ability of the central bank over the money supply also mean monetary policy is of no effect; it was not a tool available to the central bank to manage or regulate economic activities.

The gold standard also impacted on international trade by automatically adjusting balance of payment disequilibria between countries. A balance of payment deficit has to be covered by gold reserves, automatically reducing the amount of gold reserves backing up the money in circulation. The central bank would thus be forced to enforce a policy of credit contraction, for example, by raising the bank rate, and thereby reduce the amount of money in circulation. A reduction in money in circulation would cause a reduction in aggregate demand, a fall in prices, reduce demand for imports. At the same, exports become cheaper. This process will continue until the deficit is covered and equilibrium is restored.

The opposite process would be set in operation in the case of a balance of payment surplus: excess reserves would force the central bank to enforce an expansionary credit policy. This would stimulate demand for imports even as exports become less competitive, until equilibrium is restored.

Since countries under the gold standard valued their currencies in terms gold, a fixed rate of exchange was in effect between currencies. For example, if country X valued its currency at 100 grains of gold and country Y valued it own at 50 grains, a rate of 2: 1 existed between the respective currencies. This practically eliminated foreign exchange risk as a consideration in international trade and commerce. This greatly facilitated international trade, movement of capital as well as labour between countries; indeed the gold standard underpinned a period of globalization that took place prior to the First World War. Foreign investment from Great Britain flowed into the New World of United States, Canada and Australia to finance industries and infrastructure. Under the gold standard, international capital markets burgeoned and expanded, channeling finance from capital—rich to resource-rich countries because with it as the benchmark, investors feel safe to invest in distant economies.

The merits and demerits of the gold standard can therefore be enumerated as follows: i) it practically ruled out inflation as arbitrary printing or minting of money was not possible because this has to be accommodated with an increase in gold stock; ii) it eliminated foreign exchange risk in international trade and thereby facilitated free movement of goods, capital and labour between countries, raising living standards globally in the process; iii) it automatically ensured balance of payment equilibrium between countries.

On the other hand, its disadvantages were i) the money supply, being tied to the amount of gold stock, cannot be adjusted in tandem with national output; ii) monetary policy could not be used to regulate the level economic activity as this depended on the inflow or outflow of gold into the economy.

Furthermore, a major drawback of the gold standard was that, the world economy was regulated by the business cycle (finance and employment conditions) of the dominant economy, of the time: Great Britain. Before the First World War, Great Britain was the world's strongest economy and London was the financial capital of the world. The

British economy was however severely weakened by the War, and its return to the gold standard after the War, at the pre-war exchange rate could not be sustained. At this rate, British exports were not competitive, while imports became cheap. This resulted in deflation which negatively impacted on production and output, resulting in high unemployment and recession. The British economy contracted. A budget deficit in 1931 further weakened confidence in the British pound leading to withdrawal of credit and trade loans from London. Under these circumstances, Great Britain devalued the pound and withdrew from the gold standard in 1931 in the middle of the Great Depression.

After the Second World War, in order to put in place a new international monetary system, the world's major economies met in Bretton Woods, New Hampshire, in the United States. The outcome was the Bretton Woods system of fixed exchange rates anchored by the United States dollar. Under the Bretton Woods system, United States dollar was fixed to gold at $35 while other countries fixed their currencies to the U.S. dollar.

This meant that the U.S. dollar was backed by gold reserves. This ultimately became unsustainable by 1971, in the light of mounting U.S. balance of payment trade deficits with its trading partners such as Japan and Germany, and consequent overvaluation of the United States dollar. In 1971, the U.S. government ended the convertibility of the dollar into gold for foreign governments.

While the gold standard, practically guaranteed low inflation, and stable exchange rates, it also meant that government surrendered the power to regulate economic activity. For example, it could do practically nothing even during periods of high unemployment. See Bretton Woods System

Goodwill: an intangible asset of business accounting for the difference between the sum of its net assets and its sale value, as a going concern. Over the course of its existence, a business may acquire a certain 'something special' or edge in its market and industry that enable it to earn a premium on its tangible assets. Goodwill may appear in the balance sheet of a company that has paid a premium on the net assets of a business it has taken over. It is recommended practice to write off the value over a short period of time.

Government Intervention: even in a free market economy, government often has to interfere in the workings of forces and demand and supply for the overall welfare of the economy. Specifically, the government intervenes in the following ways:

1. Fiscal Policy: the manipulation or use of the government expenditure and taxation to steer the economy in desired direction; to moderate economic activity, create jobs, manage the general price level, etc.
2. Monetary Policy: the regulation of the money supply to bring about desired outcomes in interest rates, regulate the general price level (deflation/inflation), etc.
3. Provision of Infrastructure: investment in social capital such as roads, bridges, telecommunications systems, electricity, etc. to increase productive activity.
4. Provision of Merit Goods: the free provision or subsidization of public

health immunization, libraries, public galleries, etc.
5. Protection from Externalities: limiting the unintended effects of production such as pollution by taxation or regulation.
6. Regulation: laying down and enforcing the rules of engagement for economic agents to ensure fair competition.

Great Depression: the period between 1929 and 1935, where economic activity was at a very low ebb worldwide, at least in most of the developed world, with high levels of unemployment, deflation and low business activity. It was triggered by the Stock market crash in October 1929, which led to a collapse of the banking system, which the central bank, the Federal Reserve, fail to stem, negatively impacting on money supply, credit availability and business sentiment and consumer confidence. All this was further compounded by serious drought that made subsistence almost impossible causing mass exodus from eastern states of the United States. Reactionary trade protection measures such as erection of tariffs compounded the problem.

People were enthralled by new manufactures and appliances that were just becoming standard features of the consumerist lifestyle. The stock market was seen as easy route to fortune and margin loans were easily accessible.

The crash came against a backdrop of post-WW1 economic expansion that saw huge increase in productive capacity in new industries beyond demand, and easy credit.

Meanwhile increase in money supply to finance war and reconstruction and attendant hyperinflationary pressures has led to the replacement of currencies in Germany, Austria and Russia among others.

The effects of the pound's over-valued exchange rate in view of these realities hit the British economy hard. In 1931, Britain left the gold standard and devalued the pound. Others promptly followed, and competitive devaluation of currencies ensued. Those left on the gold standard—the United States, France, Holland, Switzerland, and Belgium—soon find themselves at a competitive disadvantage and followed suit: the others followed as the United States left the gold standard in 1933 and devalued the dollar as deflation reached 25 per cent in that country.

Full recovery was not to be until rearmament program for the Second World War.

Lessons/Fall-outs of the Great Depression
One of the legacies of the Great Depression is the acknowledgement of the need to intervene to prevent bank collapse in order to avoid a snowball effect on the real economy. Thus the Federal Reserve quickly intervened following the Stock market crash in 1987 and again 2008 following the collapse of Lehman Brothers to avoid a repeat of the history lesson.

Capital market regulator and bank deposit insurance which have become standard features in most financial systems dates back to the setting up of the Securities and Exchange Commission and the Federal Deposit Insurance Corporation by the Roosevelt administration following the Great Depression.

More Active Government Involvement in the Economy: Mass unemployment, deflation, near-zero business activity writ large the weaknesses of the capitalist system and brought Karl Marx's dire warning of 'class struggle' and the threat of 'revolution' to bold relief. From the New Deal in the United States to Bolshevism in the USSR to Fascist Italy to National Socialism in Germany, governments everywhere began to take a more active role in the running of the economy. State planning, protectionist trade policies, state funding of industry and agriculture became widespread. The tide was not to turn until after the OPEC oil shock, and the worldwide recession that followed it. The global recession that followed the OPEC oil shock gave rise to Thatcherism/Reaganomics, the Washington Consensus and the Structural Adjustment Policies in the 1980s. See also Economic Depression.

Green Revolution: an agriculture development Program of the Shehu Shagari administration in the Fourth National (Economic) Development Plan of Nigeria. : successor to the Operation Feed the Nation (OFN); under this programme, more River Basin Development Authorities were established. The scope was expanded beyond individual to include corporate organizations; corporate organizations were encouraged to invest in agriculture by incentives such as tax relief and duty-free importation of farm machinery. Agricultural infrastructure such as processing and storage facilities was built.

Gresham's Law: "bad money drives out good money"; the tendency of bad money (e.g. debased coins) in circulation to ultimately eliminate good money (e.g. coins with intrinsic value) from circulation by encouraging holders of good money to debase their holdings. Attributed to Sir Thomas Gresham.

Gross Domestic Product (GDP): In National Income Accounting; the total monetary value of a nation's output of goods and services produced <u>within</u> a nation's physical borders, in a year. Output of goods and services produced within the country whether by citizens or foreigners are included. Three different methods may be used to arrive at this figure. These are the output, income and expenditure methods (see entries) respectively. GDP minus depreciation (capital consumption or wear and tear of machinery) = Net Domestic Product (NDP). GDP may be calculated at market prices or at factor costs. GDP *plus* net income from abroad *equals* GNP (Gross National Product).

Gross National Product (GNP): The total output of goods and services by a country's nationals in a given calendar year. GNP includes the production or incomes of citizens or nationals of the country wherever they may be in the world but excludes the production or incomes of foreigners within the country.

- GNP = GDP + Net Property Income from abroad: *(sum of rent, interest and dividend received from abroad from less amount paid to foreigners).*

Nigeria's GDP at Current Basic Prices				
Activity Sector	2011		2012	
	%	N'Millions	%	N'Millions
Crop Production	27.60	10,323,648.69	29.51	11,965,513.67
Livestock	2.02	756,030.85	2.13	863,546.24
Forestry	0.37	140,184.40	0.39	156,553.54
Fishing	1.00	373,570.19	1.06	428,229.01
Coal Mining		0.84		0.99
Crude Petroleum And Natural Gas	40.85	15,285,004.21	37.00	15,004,619.95
Metal Ores		45.06		54.42
Quarrying And Other Mining	0.14	52,412.32	0.15	59,333.33
Oil Refining	0.19	70,693.43	0.20	80,135.56
Cement	0.07	25,789.82	0.075	30,213.96
Other Manufacturing	1.60	598,330.90	1.61	651,117.48
Electricity	0.20	77,444.00	0.22	87,389.33
Water	0.01	3,286.10	0.01	3,915.94
Building And Construction	1.22	456,284.91	1.33	539,676.12
Wholesale And Retail Trade	14.40	5,385,815.10	15.50	6,284,923.68
Hotel And Restaurants	0.35	130,821.02	0.37	151,813.86
Road Transport	1.41	529,193.39	1.53	621,214.30
Rail Transport And Pipelines		11.65		13.42
Water Transport	0.004	1,508.65		1,736.27
Air Transport	0.018	6,579.88	0.019	7,696.55
Transport Services	0.076	28,498.61	0.082	33,121.74
Telecommunications	0.78	292,539.10	0.82	331,502.79
Post	0.005	1,947.44	0.01	2,199.08
Financial Services	1.74	650,865.63	1.52	615,822.47
Insurances	0.046	17,362.45	0.045	20,209.23
Real Estate	3.81	1,424,064.88	4.21	1,708,645.69
Business Services	0.24	91,236.67	0.26	104,700.42
Public Administration	0.68	253,332.33	0.71	288,075.17
Education	0.18	65,482.34	0.19	76,893.58
Health	0.038	14,238.27	0.04	16,084.02
Private Non-Profit Organization	0.0007	276.54	0.0008	327.98
Other Services	0.94	350,167.22	1.00	405,328.81
Broadcasting	0.009	3,193.72	0.09	3,491.32
GDP Current basic Prices	100.00	37,409,860.61	100.00	40,544,099.92
Net Indirect tax		607,100.02		637,517.15
GDP at Market Prices		38,016,960.63		41,181,617.09
Source: National Bureau of Statistics				

Gross Profit: the difference between a product's purchase price and its selling price i.e. profit before any expenses incurred in making the sale are deducted or accounted for. The gross profit of a business for a specified period is calculated by drawing up a Trading Account, and in order to do this stock-taking at the beginning and at the close of the period in necessary.

TRADING ACCOUNT
for the year ended 31 December 2012

Sales		₦200,000.00
less: Return Inwards		(15,000.00)
		185,000.00
Opening Stock	50,000.00	
Purchases	100,000.00	
	150,000.00	
less: Closing Stock	(40,000.00)	(110,000.00)
Gross Profit		**75,000.00**

Gross Profit Margin: the ratio of gross profit (Sales less cost of goods sold/cost of sales) to net sales. It shows the percentage by which gross profit exceed cost of production/sales. It shows the profitability of a business before overhead costs. It is a test of profitability; the higher the ratio, the more efficient and profitable the business is.

$$\text{G.P. Margin} = \frac{\text{Gross Profit}}{\text{Revenue}} \times 100$$

$$= \frac{\text{Revenue} - \text{COGS}}{\text{Revenue}} \times 100$$

COGS = Cost of goods sold
Given sales of N200,000.00 and Cost of Goods Sold of N110,000.00,

$$\text{G P M} = \frac{200,000 - 110,000}{200,000}$$

$$= 0.45 = 45\%$$

This means that the firm has 45%, less than half, of its revenue to cover operational expenses and profit.

Group Life Assurance: life assurance policy taken by employers to provide payments to employees who suffer temporary or permanent disability or to their dependants in case of death while in employment. This policy is mandatory for employers who desire to join the Pension Scheme in Nigeria.

Group of Eight: the world's wealthiest eight countries comprising Canada, France, Germany, Italy, Japan, Russia, United Kingdom and the United States. The European Union is a non-enumerated member. Together these countries account for over fifty per cent of the world's output. The group meets annually, under the G8 Summit, to deliberate on issues of global concern such as economic growth, global security, energy, and terrorism, etc. Other countries may be invited to attend the summit as non-participants. The G8 does not have a mechanism of enforcing its decisions on members, and it is often criticized for being limited in its membership, and not taking into account the increasing influence of the huge economies of China and India.

Group of Ten (G10): ten countries— Belgium, Canada, France, West Germany, Holland, Italy, Japan, Sweden, United Kingdom and the United States—that agreed in 1962 to lend to the International Monetary Fund (IMF) to increase its capacity, if need be.

Growth: see Economic Growth

Guarantee: 1. an undertaking given by a manufacturer in respect of the quality of its product. The guarantee may be for a specific period of time within which the product may be returned, in case of any defects. Same as Warranty. 2. a company may be limited by guarantee of the members. In case of winding-up of the company, members are liable to the extent of their guarantee. The name of the company is required to end with GTE to denote the fact.

Guarantor: a person who guarantees to pay a loan, if the borrower fails to do so.

H

Hidden Unemployment: disguised unemployment or under-employment. Under-employment is a situation when people are employed doing jobs for which they are over qualified because they could not find the job for which they are qualified. For example, when an unemployed engineer converts his vehicle into a taxi in order to makes ends meet. It is described as disguised because it is not obvious: the engineer is actually unemployed.

HIPC Highly Indebted Poor Countries: countries considered to be at the brink of insolvency in view of their high debt-to-exports/revenue ratio. The HIPC Initiative is an International Monetary Fund programme started in 1996 under which qualifying countries may be assisted—via debt relief/forgiveness and low interest loans—to reduce their debt to sustainable levels. To be eligible for HIPC classification and qualify for relief, a country must meet certain economic management targets, which often translates to economic reforms to put the economy on a path of sustainable growth. See Sustainable Debt.

Hire Purchase: a contract between a buyer and a seller which allows the buyer to take physical possession of the goods upon the payment of a percentage of the purchase price as deposit while the balance is spread over a period. The seller retains the right of ownership over the goods until the last installment is made.

Holding Company: a financial company with controlling interest in other companies. Controlling interest is shareholding in excess of 50%. The companies in which a holding company has interest may be in diverse or unrelated industries.

Horizontal Integration: merger of firms in the same stage of production.

Home Trade: also internal trade; trade within a country. It contrasts with Foreign or International Trade. Home trade is divided into Retail and Wholesale Trades.

Human Capital: labour as a factor of production; the manual, mental, creative human effort used in production of goods and services. The quality of human capital makes difference between companies, regions or countries with comparable capital or natural resources. The quality of human capital is a complex product of historical, training/educational, intellectual, cultural and spiritual factors.

Human Development Index (HDI): a composite measure of the quality of life taking into consideration income, education, human life expectancy, and access to clean water. It has been compiled by the United Nations Development Program since 1990. Norway, Iceland and Japan have topped HDI rankings multiple times. It is an alternative to quantitative statistics such as per capita income and Gross Domestic Product.

Hyperinflation: an alternative term for runaway or galloping inflation. This is often brought about by excessive increase in the money supply relative to available goods and services. Too much money in circulation makes money lose value as prices increase on a daily basis. People lose confidence in money as a store of value, and exchange financial assets such as bank deposits, shares and other securities for real goods. People also increasingly prefer other commodities as a medium of exchange resorting to barter until the currency is withdrawn and replaced by another. This has happened in Hungary, Germany, Argentina, Brazil, Zimbabwe and other countries when government resorted to printing money to finance its activities.

I

(ICRC): see Infrastructure Concession and Regulatory Commission.

IMF Conditions or Conditionalities: conditions specified by the IMF for countries to meet before they can receive assistance from the fund. According to the Fund, these conditions are necessary to ensure that countries do not repeat the mistakes which make them require its assistance in the first place. These conditions are therefore supposedly intended to put the countries on the path of sustainable development by removing distortions which bring about inefficient allocation of resources, wasteful expenditures e.g. on white elephant projects, fiscal indiscipline, etc. These conditions include realistic exchange rate, which often translate to mean devaluation for most developing countries; liberalization of international trade; deregulation of interest rates; privatization and commercialization of public corporations, removal of subsidies, among others, etc distilled in the so-called Washington Consensus. The implementation of these measures at a time has often meant severe hardship for the populace and a near total collapse of the social sector in the reforming countries. See Economic Reforms.

Import Substitution Industrialization (ISI): an inward-looking economic development strategy that aims to make a country self-sufficient by setting up industries producing goods that are being imported. ISI is characterized by active government investment and control of the economy. The implementation of ISI entailed the following—subsidization of local industries; Protectionist trade policy: high tariffs and quotas on imports; State control/ownership of key industries; Exchange controls: regulation of foreign exchange dealings and investments; administratively determined exchange rates;

Pervasive import controls and licensing; Administrative controls e.g. of interest rates and price controls; Indigenization and Nationalization of enterprises; Reservation of certain sector and restriction in the growth of large firms; Subsidies for state owned firms; Allocation of credit to state firms

This involved putting a lot of discretionary powers in the hands of State employees who would more often than not get in the way objective market forces and distort market signals. This translated to a massive state bureaucracy that was invariably overwhelmed with its own labyrinthine processes, which proved a fertile ground for corruption.

This was the prevalent development strategy in the 1960s up to the 1980s. Countries that followed this path included Brazil, India and Nigeria.

This strategy contrasts with the outward-looking developing strategy which stresses competition, the development of a private sector; producing for export and trade with the outside world with the government acting the role of a referee rather than a player in the economy.

The relative effectiveness of these strategies is seen in the contrasting results of the countries that followed them.

India, Brazil and Nigeria with massive human and natural endowments were hobbled by the ISI strategy from experiencing the economic growth rate of South Korea and Taiwan which saw them transformed from poor, impoverished to achievement of developed country status in decades.

Economic difficulties in the 1980s prompted reforms that rolled back the State for trade liberalization and deregulation policies across countries.

Immigration: the movement of people into a country or area. It is one of the determinants of the size of population. People may be caused to move to a country because of attraction of economic opportunities e.g. in search of employment or investment opportunities or as refugees in search of a safe haven from persecution, war or famine. The movement of people out of a geographical area or country is referred to as *emigration*, and when this is offset against immigration, *net migration* is obtained. Net migration plus *natural growth rate* (birth rate less death rate) of the population gives the population growth rate. Because immigration is one of the determinants of population, government must have policies to control it. Thus it might be necessary for a country to encourage immigration in order to ensure an adequate work force, or discourage immigration where the working population is adequate, and avoid a strain on resources/facilities.

Imperfect Competition: any market situation where a buyer(s) or seller(s) has some form of influence in the determination of the price of their product due to barriers to entry such as large amount of capital required to set up or branding and patents among others. At least one of the following conditions are met when firms are in imperfect competition environment: (a) one producer/seller (monopoly) or a combination of producers/sellers (oligopoly/duopoly) accounts for a large percentage of the industry output giving making him a price leader or (b) each seller commands a certain level of loyalty among consumers due to product differentiation arising from branding or patent rights (monopolistic competition). This is often the case in real life market conditions as buyers usually prefer certain brands to others and are often not aware of all necessary information before making buying decisions. Imperfect competition is characterized by the absence of conditions for perfect competition viz. freedom of entry and exit, homogeneity of product, multitude of sellers and buyers and free flow of information so that no one or more buyers or sellers are important enough to have an influence on price. See monopoly, oligopoly, monopolistic competition, monopsony, oligopsony.

Imperfect Market: Any market where the conditions for a perfect market are not met viz. i) the commodity is not homogenous i.e. there is product differentiation or branding; ii) the market price can be influenced by a seller or a combination of sellers; iii) there is no free flow of information between buyers and sellers; iv) the commodity is not easily transferred; and v) there is discrimination among buyers i.e. certain buyers receive favourable treatment. An imperfect market is the general case in real life as there are only a few instances where perfect market are met, the stock exchange and in open foreign exchange markets being examples.

Import Duties: indirect tax imposed on goods being brought into a country. Reasons for imposing import duty include raising of revenue for the government, discouraging the importation of those goods on which it is imposed and to bring about a more favourable balance of trade, and/or to protect infant industries, etc.

Import License: under certain systems of foreign exchange control, importers can only be granted foreign currency allowed by the government/central bank. Thus an importer must secure an import license in order to have foreign currency to import. It is an example of administrative control as opposed to a market-driven control, and is a rationing tool used in times of shortage of foreign exchange.

The import license system was what obtained in Nigeria until the advent of the Structural Adjustment Programme in 1986. Since then, access to foreign currency has been through various open mechanisms such as the Second-tier Foreign Exchange System, Dutch Auction System, etc.

Import Quotas: a restriction of the total amount of a commodity that can be brought into a country during a certain period, e.g. fiscal year. It is an alternative to tariff.

Import tariff: barriers imposed on goods being brought into the country e.g. import duty, import bans, quotas, etc.

Imprest Account: sum provided for petty cash expenses. Periodically, the account is credited to bring the balance back to the agreed sum.

Income effect: The effect of a change in income on the quantity of a good or service consumed. A change in the price of a good brings about a change in the real income of the consumer (*income effect*) because he is now able to buy more (or less) than before, and alter the relative prices of the goods (*substitution effect*).

Incidence of Taxation: A measure of who ultimately bears the burden of a tax. The person who actually pays a tax may not be the person on whom it was levied; the person on whom a tax is levied may shift the burden or incidence to another person or persons. The incidence of a direct tax cannot be shifted by the person on whom it is imposed. The incidence of an indirect tax can be shifted depending on the price elasticity of demand of the good on which it is imposed. The producer or seller of a commodity on which an indirect tax is imposed may shift the burden or incidence of tax to the consumer of the commodity. This means the consumer may pay part or all of the tax.

- When the price elasticity of demand is perfectly elastic, the seller/producer cannot shift the burden of tax as the consumer will refuse the smallest increase in the price. The seller must therefore bear the entire burden of the tax.

- When the price elasticity of demand is perfectly inelastic, the consumer buys the same at the higher price; seller is able to shift the entire burden (100%) of the tax to the buyer by increasing the price of the commodity by the full amount of the tax without any decrease in demand.

- Where the price elasticity of demand is unitary, the quantity demanded falls by the same proportion as the increase in price seller will be able to shift 50% of the tax to the buyer.

- When the price elasticity of demand is moderately elastic, the seller will bear a greater percentage of the tax than the buyer.

In the diagrams below, imposition of tax causes a shift of the supply curve from SS to S_1S_1 and a new equilibrium price at L from the initial price at K. Quantity demanded falls from Y to X and price rises from K to L as a result of the imposition of an indirect tax. After paying the tax the seller is left with J

Incidence of tax when demand is elastic: the seller bears a smaller fraction (KGJH) of the tax than the buyer (LFGK).

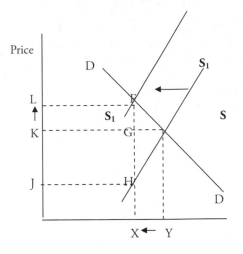

Incidence of tax when demand is perfectly elastic: upon the imposition of the indirect tax, there is a sharp fall in quantity demanded (from Y to X) but price remains the same; the entire burden of the tax is borne by the seller.

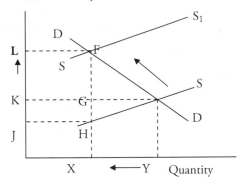

Incidence of tax when demand is inelastic; the buyer bears the bigger (KGHJ) fraction of the tax than the seller (LFGK)

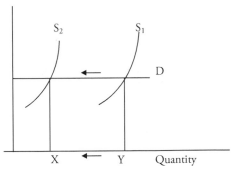

Incidence of tax when demand is perfectly inelastic: quantity demanded remains the same, in spite of the price increase (from K to L) as a result of the imposition of the indirect tax; the seller is able to shift the entire burden to the buyer.

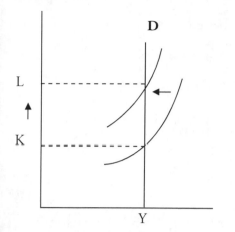

Income Determination: The national income of a country is determined by the level of real capital investment. Real capital investment itself depends on marginal propensity to consume, level of savings, interest rates, marginal efficiency of capital, government policies, and business climate/expectations. See National Income.

Income Effect: one of the effects a change in the price of a commodity is to bring about an increase in real income of the consumer, if the price falls, as more can now be afforded, or a decrease in real income, if price rises. See also Substitution Effect.

Income Elasticity of Demand: responsiveness of demand to a change in income.

$$= \frac{\% \text{ change in quantity demanded}}{\% \text{ change in income}}$$

The income elasticity of a *normal good* is positive (more is demanded as income increases) while that of an *inferior good* is negative (less is demanded as income increases).

Income, Nominal: income in money terms. Nominal income is subject to **money**

illusion as its purchasing power is subject to changes in the general price level: an increase in salary from N30,000.00 to N60,000.00 does not necessarily mean that the consumer can now afford twice as many goods and services as before.

Income, Real: income expressed in terms of its purchasing power i.e. goods and services it can buy.

Income Method or approach: in national income accounting, the sum of all incomes earned by factors of production during the year. Using this method Gross National income/product = the sum of rent, interest, wages and salaries and profits during the year. All transfer payments e.g. gifts, donations, bursary awards, scholarships, social security payments, pensions and gratuities, etc, must be excluded to avoid double counting. Problem of the income approach include the determination of the value of 1. Incomes which are not documented e.g. by those who are employed in the informal sector; 2. rent of owner-occupied houses.

Increasing Returns to Scale: Economies of scale; a situation where long run average costs are falling as output is increasing.

Indirect Taxes: tax levied on goods and services. Indirect tax may be avoided by not buying goods or services on which they are imposed. Examples include value-added tax, import and export duties, excise duties, etc.

Indifference Curve: it is a concept used to analyze consumer behaviour. It is a curve showing all possible combinations of two goods among which the consumer derives the same level of satisfaction and is therefore indifferent between them. The curve is derived from an indifference schedule showing the various combinations of two commodities from which the consumer derives the same level of satisfaction:

Combination	Units of X	Units of Y
A	1	50
B	2	35
C	3	25
D	4	15
E	5	10

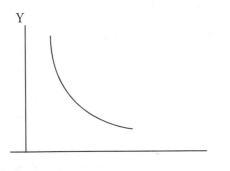

In order to maintain the same level of satisfaction among the different combinations, for a give level of income, one of the commodities has to be given up to have more of the other; increasingly less of good Y is given up for each unit of good X as diminishing marginal utility sets in: the less of good in the combination, the higher the marginal utility derived. This defines the slope of the indifference curve, the *marginal rate of substitution.*

Several curves, together called an indifference map, from different indifferent schedules, may be drawn on the same axis for different levels of income. While the consumer derives the same level of satisfaction from points on the same curve, he derives greater levels of satisfaction from curves to the right. He therefore prefers combinations on indifference curves to the right.

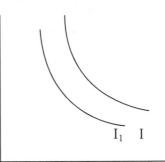

However, not all combinations on any curve are a rational allocation of the consumer's income while other combinations may be unaffordable given the consumer's present income. The best combination, given the consumer's income, is the combination that is tangential to the budget line:

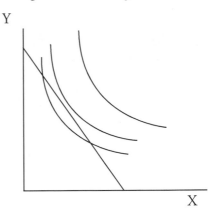

Characteristics of Indifference Curves

1. Indifference curves slope downward from left to the right, indicating that as more of one commodity is consumed, less of the other is consumed in order to stay on the same on the same level of satisfaction. The slope of the indifference

curve is called the *marginal rate of substitution*, written MRSxy.

2. Indifference curve are convex to the origin.
3. Indifference curves do not intersect and cannot cannot be vertical or U-shape

Indifference Map: a collection or series of indifference curves. The indifference curve to the right represents a superior combination to the on the left, and the consumer prefers it to the on its left. Thus, the consumer prefers every combination on I_2 to those on I_1, similarly every combination on I_3 is preferred to every combination on I_2.

Inductive Process/Method (of Analysis): the empirical method of analysis, which reasons from specific to the general. The process entails

- Observation,
- Formation of Hypothesis,
- Data Collection,
- Experimentation,
- Analysis of data, and
- Generalization.

The Inductive Method contrasts with and complements the Deductive Method of Analysis.

Industrial Action: umbrella term used to describe methods used by trade unions to press their demands such as strikes, work-to-rule, picketing, etc.

Industrial Revolution: the transformation of an underdeveloped economy with preponderance of primary production and rudimentary technology to an industrialized one. It is a process that marks the transformation of the economy and society from a relatively rural, peasant, and subsistent one into an urban, industrial, and commercial economy.

Spreading from England, Europe and the United States were the first to experience an industrial revolution in the nineteenth century. The Japanese, Russian, and South Korean economies have undergone similar transformations through a more deliberate planning and mobilization of capital resources by the government of these countries in the later centuries.

A series of inventions and innovations that made mass production possible in the mid-eighteenth century—roughly put anywhere between 1780 and 1820—made Britain the first country to experience an Industrial Revolution. These inventions impacted power, transport, iron and steel, and saw the emergence of division of labour and factory system of production which together made mass production possible. The textile industry was the first industry to be directly impacted.

The industrial revolution in England was the result of certain critical factors, without which the various inventions and innovations would have been ahead of their time, and of little use. These factors include the following:

1.) Constitutional order: Britain was the first country to establish a constitutional monarchy with the Glorious Revolution in 1688; a century before the French Revolution, and two centuries before Otto von Bismarck and the unification of the German States.
2. Markets to absorb what was produced. The British Empire was on the ascendant with the world—the

'New World', Asia and Africa—at its feet.

2.) Capital to finance production. Trading opportunities reached new levels from the 1500s upwards, and saw to the accumulation of capital on a massive scale with the emergence of a capitalist middle class, comprising of merchants and bankers, who provided much needed credit for commerce and industry. Profits from companies with royal charter to exploit colonial resources and trade poured into Britain to found banks, and finance the construction of infrastructure such as turnpike roads, canals, and research.

3. Institutional development: the establishment of the Bank of England in 1694, Lloyds of London in 1689 and the London Stock Exchange in1698, ensured that things were done in a sustainable and systematic manner, and not dependent on any particular individual or group of individuals.

4. Abundantly Cheap Labour: As submitted by Eric E. Williams, former prime minister of Trinidad and Tobago in his thesis, the British economy was the beneficiary of the infamous transatlantic slave trade which supplied extremely cheap labour to work in British plantations in the West Indies and the Americas.

5. Cheap Raw Material: the plantations in the West Indies and Americas provided abundant essential input for British industry.

Industrialization: The use of machines in production or mechanization of the production process, making large scale or mass production possible. It is a phase or stage in the economic development process where production moves from the primary or extractive stage (where most production consists of agricultural or primary production). It is measured by the percentage of national output that consists of processed output.

For industrialization to take place, certain conditions must be present. Together these conditions serve to create an environment where economic activities can thrive sustainably. These pre-requisites of industrialization are the essence of socio-economic development strategies:

1. *Capital Accumulation:* capital is central to production activities, and in the initial circumstances countries are in a deficit of the financial resources required to exploit their natural resources. A country may be trapped in a *vicious circle of poverty or under-development* unless it imports capital to jump start the development process. There may therefore be recourse to foreign capital in form of loans, grants or aid from other countries, international creditors or development institutions like the World Bank. In addition to these, government seeks to implement laws and regulations that will attract foreign investment through reforms. In this way China has succeeded in making the country the workshop of the world, with major world renown organizations having at least a factory in that country.

2. *Infrastructural development:* road network, transport and communication systems, electric power, are essential for businesses to succeed. They lower costs of production and of doing business

and thereby engender entrepreneurial activities.

Since independence Nigeria, through its National Development Plans, established hydropower plants, but these have fell short as the supply has fell short for demand for electric power. Industrialization has thus been seriously hampered by unsteady power supply. The power sector was one of the last to be deregulated and reforms are aimed at attracting foreign direct investment. Telecommunication was given a serious boost with the deregulation of that sector which saw an influx of foreign direct investment. The transportation system in the country still remains largely rudimentary and unorganized. The rail lines remain essentially the same since before independence.

3. *Enabling Legislations and Regulations*: Laws can promote or hamper business activities. The legal and judicial system must be able to regulate business activities and to protect property rights. The concept of the joint stock company with limited liability for shareholders, for example, was a major innovation that contributed immeasurably to modern industrial organizations. In Nigeria, before the promulgation of the Companies and Allied Matters and the Banks and Other Financial Institutions Acts respectively, business transactions were hampered by out-dated legislations. Similarly, the creation of the Securities and Exchange Commission helped to boost the development of the Nigerian capital market. Conversely, business transactions continue to be hampered in Nigeria by the Land Use Act.

4. *Technological Advancement:* knowledge capital is the edge for value creation in the quest for development, and is what pushes further the country's production possibility frontier. An educational system that guarantees a quality labour force and research and development is essential.

5. *Constitutional Order:* a semblance of political stability with structured, predictable succession arrangements to underpin security of lives and property necessary for people to engage in productive labour; for investments to yield fruits and investors to feel safe enough to commit resources for the long-term.

When the above factors are in place, the business environment is characterized by the following features of industrialization:

1. *Factory organization of production:* production moves from the domestic front to organized, purpose-built factories where the work is stream-lined.

2. *Capitalist ownership*: Separation of ownership of the means of production from the workers. There is a clear distinction between the owners, the managers, and the workers respectively.

3. *Division of labour* in the production process. As much as possible, work is divided into different stages for which respective teams or individuals are responsible. This makes for standardized output on a large scale.

4. *Specialization*: increasing specialization in niche areas is the trend among individuals and businesses. This increases the need for exchange which becomes increasingly monetized.

5. *Manufacture by power-driven machines.* As much as possible, work is mechanized and automated.

6. *Financial system*: a well regulated and trusted financial system to pool savings for investment; a central monetary authority in charge of issuance of currency, the management of the money supply, supervision of banks, etc.

7. *Availability of credit for investment.* There are financial institutions to insure commercial activities and assets as well as avail long-term and short term capital necessary to finance production.

8. *Mass production of goods*: beyond the local market or even national market.

9. *Commercial activities* (banking, insurance, transportation, advertising, etc) that facilitate the completion of the production process i.e. getting what is produced to the final consumer. These ensure, among others, that production can take place in anticipation of demand.

10. *Rule of law:* judicial and law enforcement systems and processes for the protection of property, enforcement of contracts and property rights, and maintenance of law and order.

11. *Political stability:* so that economic agents can plan, invest and settle deals and transactions in a conducive and predictable political environment.

Britain was the first industrialized country following from the *Industrial Revolution*, and the rest of Europe quickly followed.

In more recent times, South-Eastern economies like South Korea, Malaysia, Thailand, China and India in Asia, and Brazil and Chile in Latin America has undergone industrialization to become countries whose output consist more of manufactured or processed goods as opposed to primary output.

Strategies of industrialization include Import Substitution Industrialization and Export Led Industrialization.

Nigeria's level of industrialization is shown in the fact that primary produce (agricultural and mining, quarrying) still account for over 50% of national output. This means that the secondary or industrial sector is still underdeveloped, as the over 90% of export still consist of crude oil, a primary product.

The country's effort at industrialization is has been through a public sector-led import substitution strategy. As mirrored in the four national development plans between 1962 and 1985, this saw the construction of petroleum refineries and petrochemical companies, steel plants, hydropower plants, automobile assembly plants, etc. A good number of these failed and had to be privatized.

Industrial Union: a trade union representing different grades of workers in an industry.

Industry: A group of firms producing similar products for the same market. For example all banks together comprise the banking industry; the telecommunication industry comprises all firms offering telecommunication services.

Inelastic: not responsive; for example, where demand or supply is not responsive to changes in another variable such as price or income.

Inelastic Demand: demand for a commodity is described as inelastic when a material change in its price brings about little change in quantity demanded. Demand for goods with no real substitute such as salt, tend to be perfectly inelastic. This means that quantity demanded does not change no matter the movement in price. Demand is described as fairly inelastic where a change in price brings about a less than proportionate change in quantity demanded. Also, the higher a person's income, the more inelastic his demand tends to be. See price elasticity of demand. Demand may be described as perfectly or infinitely elastic, unit elastic, or perfectly or infinitely inelastic

Inelastic Supply: where supply does not respond to an increase in price.

Infant industry: young and newly established industries that are supposedly not yet strong enough to withstand competition from imported products. The need to shelter infant industries from imports is an argument for protectionism in international trade.

Inferior Goods: a good, like *soda* soap and *akpu*, for example, less of which is consumed as income increases. Inferior goods have a negative income effect.

Inflation: steady or persistent increase in the general price level of goods and services. Inflation may be due to increasing cost of production (cost-push inflation), excessive demand over supply or output of goods and services (demand-pull inflation) or too much money in circulation relative to available goods and services. One of the major factors responsible for inflation in Nigeria is the exchange rate. A fall in the exchange rate of the naira brings about increase in prices of raw materials and finished goods imported. Measures to curb inflation include monetary policy aimed at reducing the amount of money in circulation by raising the bank rate and through open market operations by the central bank. Fiscal policy measures to tackle inflation include increasing taxes and reduction in government expenditure.

Creeping or Persistent inflation: a steady but moderate increase in the general price level. This may be due to excessive demand relative to available goods and services i.e. too much money chasing too few goods, for example, due to increase in the national minimum wage or increase in cost of production. Persistent inflation has become a regular feature of modern economies, and the one of the major functions of the Central Bank is to keep persistent inflation within limits.

Hyperinflation: also referred to as galloping or runaway inflation: this is when prices rise so fast over a short period of time that people loses confidence in money as store of value and medium of exchange. In such instances, e.g. in Germany, after the World War I and Zimbabwe 2008, other items such as cigarettes replace money as a medium of exchange, and a new currency has to be issued to replace the old one. In Germany, the money became so worthless people used it as a wallpaper. One of the worst instances of hyperinflation occurred in Zimbabwe in 2008 with prices doubling daily. The Zimbabwean Dollar was redenominated three times, and at a time 100 trillion banknote was issued.

Stagflation: refers to a situation characterized by high inflation and high unemployment. Stagflation is an anomalous or unusual situation as prices are rising in the midst of a recession (economic stagnation). Ordinarily during a recession, aggregate demand is low with downward pressure (deflation) on prices.

Inflationary Gap: the amount by which aggregate demand *exceeds* the amount required to achieve equilibrium level of national income.

Informal Economy: part of the economy comprising unregistered businesses and self-employed persons for which no records of income, output and expenditure are available. This is usually high in developing countries where a good number of businesses are not registered and markets and settlement systems are underdeveloped so that payments are mostly by cash. This means that national income is under-reported, in some cases by up to 50 per cent.

Infrastructure Concession and Regulatory Commission (ICRC): body set up in 2005 to anchor public-private partnership (PPP) in funding the construction as well as the operation/management of infrastructure facilities. This is a fall-out of deregulation which has meant the separation of regulation

from operations/management of facilities. This reform has seen the Nigerian Ports Authority and Federal Airports Authority of Nigeria become landlords/regulators while the management of ports and airport facilities are concessioned to private operators for specified (long-term) periods.

Initial Allowance: the amount a company may deduct in respect of a new capital asset in the calculation of taxable profit.

Initial Public Offering (IPO): the process of listing the shares of company on a stock exchange for the first time. The company issues or sells its securities to the public, and thereby raises capital. The process is usually handled by an issuing house on behalf of the company. The issuing house may underwrite the shares for a fee. Upon being listed on the stock exchange, the shares of the company may now be openly traded without recourse to the directors of the company. A public listing, facilitated by an IPO, gives a company access to the public for long-term equity funds required for business expansion, working capital or to repay long-term debt such debentures or redeemable preference shares.

Injections: autonomous flows into the circular of income, comprising investments, government expenditure and export sales.

Injunction: a court order restraining a party from acting in specified way.

Input: raw material that are processed to produce output; also used to describe the factors of production.

Insider trading: the act of taking undue advantage of information not yet in the public to trade in a financial security listed on a stock exchange. It is a punishable offense.

Insurable Interest: see under Insurance.

Insurance: a contract under which the risk of a loss is transferred from one party (insured) to another (insurer) in return for a payment (premium). The contract is known as the insurance policy. The insured, or policyholder, agrees to make a small payment, called the premium, to the insurance company, which agrees to compensate him against a specified loss, damage or liability.

The insured pays into a common fund (pool of risks) from which those who actually suffer loss are compensated. The idea is based on the law of large numbers, that only a small fraction is likely to suffer a risk at any particular time, if a large number of people are involved. For example, it is not likely that all who insure themselves against a particular risk will suffer loss at the same time. Thus, out of say, 10,000, who take up an insurance policy against fire, only a few, if any, will experience a fire accident at the same time. Specialists, called actuaries, scientifically calculate future losses based on the law of averages to determine premium payable for given risks. Insurance pertaining to human life is termed Life Assurance.

Insurance, Principles of
The practice of insurance is guided by certain principles:

1. Utmost good faith (*uberrimae fides*)—parties to an insurance contract must disclose all material or important facts whether asked or not. The insured must be must not make a false statement nor fail to disclose all facts that will make the insurer decide to accept and determine the appropriate premium and other conditions. Similarly, the insurer is not expected to leave room for doubt about the terms of the insurance policy. The contract is rendered void if any of the parties is found to less than totally truthful in their declarations;

2. *Insurable interest*—in order to secure a valid insurance contract, the insured must stand to suffer a loss should the insured event occur;

3. *Indemnity*—the insured cannot make a profit from an insurance policy. This means that he can only be compensated to the extent of the loss or restored back to the position he was before a loss was suffered. If has multiple insurance policies from multiple insurers, the insurance companies will only pay a proportionate contribution of the loss;

4. *Subrogation*—once the insurer has indemnified the insured, it may take over the rights of the insured to a recover loss e.g. from a third party. ;

5. *Proximate Cause*—a claim can only be made if the cause of loss arises from the cause insured against. A claim cannot be made for compensation, for example, in respect of an asset that was stolen, if fire was insured against.

See also: Life Assurance; Reinsurance

Insurance Broker: an independent agent who advises clients on their insurance needs and the best insurer that can offer the best terms.

Insurance Policy: a document setting out the terms and conditions of an insurance contract.

Intangible Asset: items such as patents rights, copyrights, trademarks, trade names, franchises, licenses, goodwill, etc. They are not tangible but are real. they are treated as long-term assets and amortized over time.

Interest: the cost of and reward for capital as a factor of production.

Interest Rate: the rate at which borrowed funds are paid back.

Interim Dividend: dividend paid before the end of the financial year at which time a 'final dividend' is paid.

Internal Debt: part of national debt owed to the country's own people and denominated in the local currency. See under National Debt.

Internal Economies of Scale: the advantages of large scale production; large scale operations enable a firm to enjoy certain economies: e.g. marketing: being able to afford advertising; financial: ability to secure bigger credit and loans; managerial: ability to hire better qualified staff, etc.

International Bank for Reconstruction and Development (IBRD): international finance organization founded in 1944 under the Bretton Woods Agreement alongside the International Monetary Fund after World War II. The IBRD is the core of the World Bank Group, and its purpose is to provide loans for infrastructural projects and capital development world-wide. See World Bank.

International Development Association: part of the World Bank Group founded in 1956 to provide assistance to the poorest countries who do not qualify to borrow from the International Bank for Reconstruction and Development. It gives low or no interest loans based on the level of per capita income of the eligible countries. Countries with high incidence of poverty may access IDA facilities even if they are not categorized among the world's poorest, on the basis of their GDP or per capita income.

International Finance Corporation (IFC): private-sector finance arm of the World Bank Group. The IFC augment the activities of the International Bank for Reconstruction and Development by providing long-term loans to private enterprise in developing countries.

International Labour Organization, ILO: Agency of the United Nations concerned with ways to improve labour standards, working as well as living conditions. It seeks to balance the interests of workers, employers and governments in formulating international labour standards, desired minimum rights for workers including freedom of association; the right to organize and engage in collective bargaining; equality of opportunity and treatment; and the abolition of forced and child labour.

The ILO was founded in 1919 under the League of Nations, the forerunner of the United Nations. It became the first specialized organ of the United Nations in 1946.

International Monetary Fund (IMF): An international organization founded, alongside the World Bank, in 1944 under the Bretton Woods Agreement, to oversee the international monetary system. The IMF was founded to administer a flexible international monetary system that would maximize trade after the collapse of the Gold Exchange Standard. At inception this meant supervising the system of fixed exchange rates until its collapse in 1971-73. Since that time the IMF has focused on balance of payment issues, technical advice on sustainable economic, fiscal and money policies. The IMF achieves this by pursuing the following objectives:

1. Lending to member nations experiencing temporary *balance of payments* problems;
2. Facilitating the expansion and balanced growth of international trade among member countries;
3. Ensuring that currencies of member countries are fully convertible (exchangeable) and helping countries establish and maintain stable exchange rates;
4. Promoting international monetary cooperation among nations.
5. Providing financial policy to member countries.

Member countries contribute to a pool of gold and foreign currencies from which it may draw up to 25% of its quota in any one year. The purpose of the fund is to enable a country to have a limited adverse balance of payment for a limited period.

The IMF also creates special drawing rights (SDR's), which provide member nations with a source of additional reserves. Member nations are required to subscribe to a Fund quota, paid mainly in their own currency.

International Trade: The need for trade is the same for within and between countries: greater output is possible where there is specialization, which itself necessitates exchange or trade as opposed to a situation where people decide to be self-sufficient and produce all they need. Just as individuals, firms and different regions within a country specialize in areas of production of goods and services in which they are best suited, so also do countries need to specialize in the production of those things in which they have a *comparative cost advantage* over other countries. This enables consumers enjoy a higher standard of living because of a wider range of choice of products; firms are not limited to the internal market for the marketing of their output; and the economy is afforded an added stimulus for economic growth. International trade is based on the theory of Comparative Cost Advantage credited to David Ricardo.

Why Countries Engage in International Trade

1. *Differences in mineral endowments:* countries are not equally endowed with naturally occurring minerals and precious metals required for production e.g. crude oil, bauxite, limestone, coal, platinum, tin, gold, etc. International trade make it possible for a country to trade what it has for what it does not have.

2. *Differences in climatic conditions:* certain crops are better suited to particular climates. Cereals, like wheat, grow better in temperate regions of the world, for example, while most root crops, like cassava are suited to the tropical regions. International trade makes it possible for residents of countries in different regions with contrasting climatic conditions to enjoy crops grown in other regions.

3. *Technical Knowledge and Expertise:* different countries have superior

technical expertise in the production of certain products. Germany is renowned for superior engineering, Switzerland for watch-making, Italy for fashion, etc. Exchange through trade is therefore necessary.

4. *Differences in level of economic development*: countries are at different level of economic development— developed, developing, and under-developed. In order to grow from one level to another, exchange through trade is inevitable.

5. *Comparative Cost Advantage*: due to differences in factor endowments, technical expertise, and level of economic development, countries have different cost advantages in production. With international trade a country may specialize in the production of goods and services in which it has a comparative advantage and exchange its output for those in which it has a comparative disadvantage.

6. *Capital:* Some countries have abundant capital while others are poor; in order to grow, less developed economies have to rely on the advanced economies for the supply of financial capital as well as capital goods. This is only possible through trade.

International Trade Organization: The still-born forerunner of the World Trade Organization (WTO). The organization could not take-off because the United States withdrew its support. The General Agreement on Tariff and Trade (GATT) later evolved into the WTO.

Investment: Spending by government, firms or individuals on capital goods and/or inventories to increase productive capacity in the future. Investment is an injection into the circular flow of income.

Investment and Securities Tribunal (IST): is an independent specialized judicial body with jurisdiction, original and appellate, to interpret and adjudicate on all capital market and investments civil disputes as specified under the Investments and Securities Act. The Pension Reform Act No. 2 of 2004 also vests on the Tribunal the jurisdiction, original and appellate, to hear and determine pension disputes.

It was originally established under the now repealed Investments and Securities Act, 1999, now the Investments and Securities Act, 2007.

Investment Trusts: a company which specializes in buying and holding shares of companies listed on the stock exchange. Through an investment trust, small investors can indirectly invest in diversified portfolios of listed companies.

Invisible Hand: the mechanism that allocates scarce resources between competing ends or needs in a free market (Capitalist) economy without deliberate or central (or government) intervention. First used by Adam Smith.

Invisibles: international trade term for transactions other than merchandise or goods i.e. services; examples include, transportation (shipping, aviation, etc), banking and insurance, payments of interest, profits and dividend and transfers. See Balance of Payments

Invoice: see under Commercial Documents.

Irredeemable debentures: debentures for which no fixed time was stated at which they may be bought back or redeemed.

Isoquant: or equal product curve; a line connecting the points of combination of inputs required to produce the same level of output. An isoquant shows the degree of substitutability between inputs (e.g. labour and capital) that a firm has in the production of a certain level of output.

Issue: refers to a limited liability company's share or stock issue.

Issued Capital: The part of authorized share capital of a company, which has been allotted to investors subscribing to the company's shares. The whole of the authorized may or may not be totally issued out. The issued capital may not necessarily be wholly paid up; thus paid-up capital may be less than issued share capital.

Issuing House: a company that facilitates the sale of shares of a public company by under-writing a share issue. A public company intending to raise capital by selling its shares may contract an issue house to take up the shares and immediately provide the capital to the company. The issuing house will in turn offer the shares to the public. This process is known as *offer for sale*. In an offer for subscription, the public company approaches the public directly without an issuing house.

J

Job Analysis: An analysis of a piece of work to determine the qualities required by a worker to perform it efficiently.

Jobber: a dealer in securities. They deal on their own account, and make their profit (known as the jobber's turn) from the difference between the prices at which they buy and sell securities. They deal only with stockbrokers who act on behalf of investors. Jobbers tend to specialize in certain securities.

Joint demand: where goods are used together in other to satisfy a want, they are described as compliments or goods in joint demand. Thus an increase in the demand for one would bring about an increase in the demand for its compliment.

Joint Stock Company: a limited liability company whose capital is divided into numerous shares which may be subscribed to by hundreds or thousands as co-owners or shareholders, whose liability is limited to their shareholding. This feature of sub-dividing the capital into units of shares enables the joint-stock company to raise large amount capital to realize economies of scale. Also, unlike a sole proprietorship or partnership, a company is recognized as a legal entity separate from its owners enabling it to sue and be sued.

The joint stock company may be a private or public company.

Joint Supply: goods that are produced together like beef and hides, and kerosene and gasoline are in joint supply as a change in the supply of one brings about a similar change in the supply of the other at the same time. Where two commodities, A and B are in joint supply, an increase in the demand for A will bring about the supply of both commodities, since they are produced together. The supply for B will be higher than the demand for it, and therefore bring about a fall in its price.

Journal: an accounting book in which entries are made daily.

K

Karl Marx: German economist (1818-83), credited with providing the basis of communism in his works *Communist Manifesto* and *Das Kapital*. While Marx acknowledged that capitalism rescued many from rural misery, he asserted that capitalism cannot be sustained and was doomed from within. According to him, it was inevitable that increasing concentration of economic power and wealth in fewer hands would impoverish the proletariat who shall ultimately rise up, overthrow and impose a "dictatorship of the proletariat". Marx's version has not panned out because capitalism has continually found ways to check its excesses e.g. by redistributing wealth and regulating market participants. On the other hand, communism economic system has proven to be idealistic but unsustainable, and has been replaced by capitalism in Russia and other former Soviet republics and China.

L

Labour: human resources, physical and mental, skilled and unskilled, used in the production of goods and services.
- Labour as a factor of production, is mobile geographically and occupationally.
- The supply of labour (quantity and quality of labour available) depends on the population growth rate (birth rate minus death rate plus net migration) and the quality of education and training.
- The demand for labour depends on the level of economic activity. Demand for labour is high during periods of economic boom; where level of business activity is low, for example, during periods of recession or depression, levels of employment of labour will be low.
- Ensuring high level of demand for labour (high employment) is one of the key objectives of macro-economic management.
- The reward for labour in production in wages. See under Factors of Production.

Labour Economics: part of economics concerned with labour related issues e.g. efficiency, productivity, wages, redundancy, etc.

Labour Force: the total number of employable people in the country. This consists of the age bracket between 18 and 70 years old.

Labour Intensive: a method of production with a high proportion of labour relative to other factors of production. Relative prices of factors of production will determine how factors are combined in production. Where labour is abundant relative to capital, more labour will be used. Compare capital intensive.

Labour Market: the framework or environment within which demand for and supply of labour interact to determine wages.

Labour Theory of Value: the view that the value of a commodity depends on the amount of labour required to produce it. Thus a good that took two people to produce should cost two times that which required a person to produce. This assumes that workers are all of the same quality, and that demand for the commodities is the same or is not important in price determination.

Labour Turnover: the rate at which workers enters and leaves the firm. A high labour turnover rate implies a firm does not have the conditions e.g. in terms of remuneration and working conditions to retain its staff, and benefit from their experience. Such a firm will become a training ground for its competitors and this will negatively affect the quality of its output and its effectiveness and efficiency.

Labour Union: same as Trade Union.

Laissez-faire: French term meaning "let it be"; the doctrine, attributed to the physiocrats, which became a central principle of classical economics. According to this view, the State or government should let the economy be i.e. to function without intervention; prices being determined by the market forces. Even during periods of economic depression, the government should not seek to intervene, as the economy will sought itself out and revive again. This doctrine was challenged by Maynard Keynes, following the Great Depression of the 1930s, who advocated government intervention to revive aggregate demand during periods of such periods of the business circle. Laissez-faire doctrine was revived in the 1980s, when government's role in the economy was blamed for inefficiencies and wastages. This culminated in an ideological backlash that revived economic conservatism in leading Western countries, and ultimately the World Bank and the International Monetary Fund as distilled in the Washington Consensus, a set of economic reform propositions which spawned a wave of economic reforms in much of the developing world. It brought about and underlined the wave of economic reforms in the form of Structural Adjustment Programmes in most Latin America and African countries with liberalization, deregulation and privatization of economic activities and state-owned enterprises.

Land: see Factors of Production. Natural resources; all natural or non-man made factors or "gifts of nature" – wind, lakes, rivers, sunlight, etc—which are economically useful in the production of goods and services. Land is fixed in supply and immobile. The reward for land as a factor of production is *rent*.

Large-scale Production: mass or industrial production of huge levels of output for near and distant markets. This is usually made possible by the following factors:

- Mechanization of the production process with the use of machines.
- Factory organization of production as oppose to the domestic system or workshop.
- Division of labour and specialization: instead of one worker making the product, the production process is set up such that workers handle only aspect of it in which they become specialized. Output is increased tremendously as a result.
- Mechanized transportation: initially with the invention of the steam boat, then the rail and airplane enabling distribution to distant markets.
- Concept of the joint-stock company which enables the pooling of capital from thousands of subscribers.

A firm may grow by expansion from within or through merger (horizontal or vertical integration) with other firms.

Advantages of large-scale production:
Large-scale production brings about ***internal economies of scale***. These include reduction in the cost of production per unit of output; managerial economies as the firm is now able to employ professional managers; commercial economies i.e. buying, marketing and advertising advantages from buying or dealing in large quantities; Technical economies i.e. advantages of using machines resulting in greater efficiencies and better quality of output; financial economies i.e. access to capital from being able to borrow from banks or the capital market by listing of shares.

Disadvantages or **_diseconomies of large-scale production:_**
Bureaucracy: the larger the firm, the longer the chain of authority and the more bureaucratic it tends to be, with increased paper-work, documentation, record-keeping, form-filling, etc. Decisions take a long time to be reached and implemented, and response to changing market conditions may be slow. A single mistake or oversight may lead to a great loss.

Loss of personal connection with customers: one-on-one connection with customers is usually lost as the firm grows in size, as operations become formalized and impersonal.

Lateral Integration: this happens when firms at the same stage of production or producing similar goods merge or one is absorbed by the other. Two bottling firms may merge for synergy purposes and to take advantage of economies of scale.

Law of Demand: The inverse relationship between the price and the quantity demanded of a good when all other factors are assumed to be constant; stated as the higher the price, the lower the quantity demanded or the lower the price, the higher the quantity demanded. The law of demanded is illustrated by the downward slope of the demand curve.

Law of Diminishing Marginal Returns: states that if increasing amount of a variable factor, e.g., labour, are combined with a fixed factor, e.g., land, marginal output will increase up to point, and after that point it will decline. The law means that there is a limit to how much output can be increased by varying only one factor of production

while leaving other factors of production fixed.

Law of Large Numbers: the principle that only a small proportion, calculable from past experience. is likely to suffer a risk if a large number is involved. This is the basis of insurance practice: the larger the pool, the lower the proportion of risk likely to occur at any point in time.

Leakages: flow of money out of a country's circular flow of income. Examples are savings and expenditure on imports and tax payments. Leakages are also referred to as withdrawals. Compare _injections_.

Lease: a long-term contract giving possession of a property for a specified period of time in consideration of rent.

Ledger: a book of account into which are posted entries made in the original books of original entry.

Legal tender: medium of exchange acceptance of which, as payment for goods and services and settlement of debt, is backed up by law; and which people are obliged to accept.

Lender of Last Resort: the central bank as the ultimate financial recourse.

Leone: standard unit of currency of Sierra Leone; it is subdivided into 100 cents.

Lessor: the owner of a property who allows another (the lease) the use of it for an agreed period of time.

Letter of Allotment: a letter showing the number shares allotted to an applicant of new shares or a shareholder who has taken up his "rights" under a rights issue.

Letter of Credit: A document authorizing a bank to pay the bearer. The buyer establishes an account in favour of his creditor/supplier at a bank. It is used in international trade, between the respective banks of the buyer and that of the seller.

Liabilities: debts or amounts due or owed to outsiders; the opposite of assets. Liabilities can be long-term or short-term in nature. Long-term liabilities are capital funds such as secured loans, debentures and preference shares which may become redeemable in the future. Short-term liabilities are incurred in the ordinary course of business, such as suppliers' credit and usually are payable within a financial year.

Liberalization: reducing or eliminating the use of administrative controls—such as price controls, fixed interest rates, import licensing, subsidies and subventions, etc. in the economy in order to bring about a more rational allocation of resources through the objective interplay of market forces of demand and supply in price determination.

Countries in need of financial support have often been required by the International Monetary Fund, to reform their by liberalizing their economies in order to be on the course for sustainable growth.

Lien: the right exercised over the property of a person until certain obligations are met. For example, a creditor has a lien over a collateral until a loan is paid.

Life Assurance: life policies of insurance are termed life assurance because there is no uncertainty about a claim being made

as death is a certainty. There are two types of life assurance: Endowment and Whole Life Assurance. Endowment policies are a form of saving for a fixed number of years. If the assured is alive at the end of the period, he receives the sum assured or it is paid to his dependants, if he dies before the end of the period. For Whole Life Policies the premium are paid throughout the lifetime or to an agreed age of the assured. Group life assurance is a policy used by employers to cover employees who die in service.

Limited Liability: in a limited liability company the amount due from the owners is limited to the value of shares they subscribe to. In the event of liquidation, a shareholder may be asked to fully pay for his shares, if there is any amount outstanding on his shares. He cannot be asked for more than this, even if creditors are yet to be fully paid.

Limited Partnership: a partner whose liability is limited to the amount he invested. He is usually not involved in the management of the business. In all partnerships, there must be at least one general partner with unlimited liability.

Line of Credit: amount of credit a supplier is allowed to use for the purchase of goods by a creditor.

Liquid Assets: assets in form of cash or that can easily be converted to cash without loss in value received. Money is the most liquid asset; other examples are stocks, shares, money market securities, and bonds.

Liquid Capital: capital in the form of money as opposed to physical assets.

Liquidity Preference: the extent to which economic agents—businesses and individuals—are willing to hold their assets in the form of money instead of investments.

Lira: the standard unit of currency of Italy.

Listing Requirements: the requirements that a public company is to fulfill for its shares to be quoted or listed for trading on the Stock Exchange. The listing requirements of the first-tier of the Nigeria Stock Exchange include the following:
  a. Company must be registered as a Public Company.
  b. Submit to The Exchange financial statements/business record of last 5 years
  c. Date of last audited accounts must not be more than 9 months.
  d. Annual quotation fees based on market capitalization.
  e. At least 25% of share capital must be offered to the public.
  f. Number of shareholders must not be less than 300.
  g. After listing, company must submit quarterly, half-yearly and annual accounts.
  h. Securities must be fully paid up at time of allotment.
  i. Un-allotted securities must be sold on NSE Trading floors.

Localization of Industry: concentration of companies producing similar goods or services in a particular area. This usually makes it possible for the firms concerned to realize or enjoy external economies. The presence of a bulky raw material may cause firms that use it to be located in particular area.

Location of Industry: several factors affect the situation of a firm. These include the following:

- Nearness to raw material: where the raw material is bulky, the industry will likely be situated near the raw material source. For example, because a fertilizer company requires gas as raw material and source of power, the now-privatized National Fertilizer Company of Nigeria is located in Port Harcourt.
- Nearness to markets: many companies are attracted to set up in Nigeria, because of the huge market it offers compared to other countries which are sparsely populated.
- Availability or supply of labour: the supply of skilled labour in the area is a key consideration otherwise the firm may find it difficult to attract the right quality of workers.
- Infrastructure: The availability of basic infrastructure such as roads and power are essential to attract firms to locate in a locality or region. Thus in setting up Export Processing Zones, and industrial estates, the government the government usually provides these services to attract investors.
- Natural factors: the location of extractive industries—mining, agriculture—depends on environmental and climatic factors.
- Political and economic stability: regions that are peaceful and stable will attract investment to it.

Lome Convention: trade and aid agreement between the European Union and some African, Caribbean and Pacific (ACP) countries first signed in Lome, Togo in 1975. The Convention was renegotiated and signed three times covering the period from 1981 to 2000. The European countries increased their aid and investment pledges to the ACP countries from an initial ECU 3.3billion in 1975 to ECU5.5billion under Lome II (1981-1986), to ECU8.5billion, Lome III (1986-1990), to ECU12 billion, Lome IV (1990-2000). The agreement provided preferential access for agricultural and mineral exports to the European countries from the ACP countries.

These privileges were lost following ruling by the World Trade Organization (WTO), upon a petition from the United States, that the Lome Convention violated the WTO regulations.

London Club: a group of private international creditors, mainly commercial banks in industrialized countries, holding unissued and unguaranteed debts, that first met in London 1976.

Long run: In the context of the theory of the firm, the long run is a period of time long enough for the firm to vary the quantities of all the inputs it is using, including its physical plant. In the long-run all factors of production are variable. The long-run vary from industry to industry. In certain industries, it may take more than a year to increase the capacity of a factory; in others it may take a few months.

Loss Leader: a popular product deliberately priced low in order to attract customer traffic, and possible purchase of other products by large retail stores like a department store or supermarket.

M

M1: narrow money includes currency in circulation and current account deposits with commercial deposits with commercial banks.

M2: broad money; the total volume of money in the economy. Narrow money (M1) plus savings and time deposits including foreign denominated deposits.

Macroeconomics: The branch of economic theory concerned with the economy as a whole. It deals with large aggregates such as national output, aggregate demand and supply, etc, rather than with the behaviour of individual consumers and firms.

The subject area or scope of macro-economics is as follows:

a) Determination of National Income and employment. Macro-economics was born during the Great Depression in the 1930s. Since then it has been used to explain the factors which determine the level of aggregate employment and output in an economy.

b) Determination of general level of prices. Macro-economic analysis answers questions as to how the general price level (inflation/deflation) is determined and the importance of various factors which influence the general price level.

c) Economic growth. Macro-economic models enable the formulation economic policies for achieving long-run economic growth with stability. They explain the causes of poverty in under-developed countries and recommends policies to put them on the path to sustainable development.

d) Business cycles. The fluctuations in the national income are analyzed and fiscal and monetary policies to reduce such fluctuations are formulated.

e) International trade. Another important subject of macro-economics is to analyze the various aspects of international trade in goods, services and balance of payment problems, the effect of exchange rate on balance of payment etc.

f) Unemployment. Macro-economic theory provides a theoretical framework to understand the causes of unemployment, and provides tools to counteract them.

g) Macro-Economic Policies. Fiscal and monetary policies affect the performance of the economy. These two major types' of policies are central in macro-economic analysis of the economy.

h) Global Economic System. In macro-economic analysis, a nation's economy is a seen as part of a global economic system. A good or weak performance of a nation's economy can affect the performance of the world economy as a whole.

Malthus, Thomas (1766-1834). Born the son of an eccentric country gentleman-scholar, Malthus was educated at Cambridge, studying mainly social studies and mathematics. Malthus is often called the first professional economist. He published a general treatise on economic principles, *Political Economy*, in 1820, although it attracted less attention than his first book, *An Essay on the Principle of Population as it Affects the Future Improvement of Society*.

Malthusian Population Theory: gloomy view of the trend of population growth vis-à-vis food production in late eighteenth century Britain by Reverend Malthus in his book an *"Essay on the Principle of Population as it Affects the Future Improvement of Society"* (1798). The theory is based on the law of diminishing returns. Malthus stated that population was growing at a geometric progression (2, 4, 16, 32 etc) whereas food production was increasing at arithmetic progression (1, 2, 3, 4, etc). Population will eventually outstrip food production and food shortage will result. He stated that human population increased every quarter of a century until it was checked by man-made or natural disaster like war, famine, etc. Such checks he termed obvious or positive checks. Malthus advocated "preventive checks": moral restraint (i.e. late marriages and smaller families). Malthus' gloomy view was not borne out by history; there were no food shortages and misery brought by hunger. The standard of living grew even

as the population of Britain increased. This was due to several events which Malthus could not have foreseen: the discovery of the New World (America, Australia and New Zealand) which boosted national income of Britain; the Industrial Revolution and its positive impact on agricultural output and transportation and movement of goods and people, improvement in medicine, etc which together increased the standard of living tremendously.

Managed Currency: where the government intervenes to influence the foreign exchange rate, the currency is said to be a managed currency. This is in contrast with a system where the exchange rate is largely determined by market forces. In reality, all currencies are managed to varying degrees.

In its extreme, it may be in the form of exchange control as was the case in Nigeria before liberalization of the foreign exchange market with the introduction of the Second-tier Foreign Exchange Market under the Structural Adjustment Programme in 1986. In the pre-SAP era the Exchange Control Act of 1962 held sway, under a fixed exchange regime. All foreign exchange mechanisms are managed to some degree in the context of the overall economic management/development strategy, as some level of intervention is usually called for at certain points in time given the state of economy.

Management: the process of using resources (men, material, money) otherwise known as factors of production, to achieve goals of the organization or business. It is the function of the entrepreneur. It involves the performance of certain functions including: planning, co-ordination, controlling, organizing and motivation.

Managerial Economies of Scale: see Economies of Scale

Mandate: details of authority to withdraw from an account, as given by a bank's customer.

Manifest: a form containing details of the cargo and destination of a ship or aircraft. It is completed by the captain of the ship and submitted to customs before departure.

Manpower: the working population or labour force—comprising of men and women-of a country. This may influenced by retirement age and ethnic or religious restrictions on women to work.

Manufacturing: the secondary stage or level of production which entail the processing, i.e. adding of value, to the output of primary products, e.g. agricultural produce, to finished goods. The emergence of this sector characterizes industrialization of an economy.

Marginal Analysis: An analytical technique which focuses attention on incremental changes in total values. This approach was introduced by the neo-classical school of economics.

Marginal Cost (MC): The increase in total cost consequent upon a one unit increase in the production of a good.

Marginal Firm: the firm that is just breaking even; the first to exit the industry if cost of production increases.

Marginal Product: the addition to total product as a result of increasing output.

Marginal Propensity to Consume (MPC): the change in spending/consumption that result from a change in income; proportion of *change* in *income* that would be spent on additional *consumption*. It is the rate of change (b) of the Consumption function, $C = a + bY$, which defines the relationship between income and consumption.

Ordinarily, the MPC is greater than 0 but less than 1 i.e. $0 < MPC < 1$, except where a person borrows to supplement consumption.

$$MPC = \Delta C/\Delta Y$$
$$= \frac{\text{Change in consumption}}{\text{Change in disposable income}}$$

Where ΔC = change in consumption; ΔY = change in income.

Given the following in respect of a household,

Disposable Income (N)	Consumption (N)
150	120
250	185

ΔC = change in disposable income
$$= 250 - 150 = 100$$

ΔY = change in consumption = $185 - 120 = 65$

$$MPC = \Delta C/\Delta Y = \frac{65}{100} = 0.65$$

This means that 65kobo will be spent out of every N1.00 increase in income.

The significance of the MPC is in the fact that it is the determinant of the **multiplier** i.e. the ultimate impact on national income if the government should increase disposable income, e.g. by reducing taxes, in a bid to stimulate the economy.

$$\text{Multiplier} = \frac{1}{1 - MPC}$$

Given an MPC of 0.65,

$$= \frac{1}{1 - 0.65} = \frac{1}{0.35}$$

Multiplier
Thus, if the government reduces direct taxes by a total of N20m, for example, national income will increase by

$$20\text{million} \quad x \quad \frac{1}{0.35}$$

$$= N57.14\text{million}$$

Marginal Propensity to Save (MPS): proportion of *change* in *income* that is saved, i.e. not consumed.

$$MPS = \frac{\text{Change in saving}}{\text{Change in disposable income}}$$

= 1 – Marginal Propensity to Consume (MPC)

The MPC is the mathematical reciprocal of the multiplier.

See Marginal Propensity to Consume

Marginal Rate of Substitution (MRS$_{xy}$): the rate at which a consumer will exchange or substitute successive units of a commodity for another while maintaining the same level of satisfaction/utility. It is the slope of indifference curves used in the theory of consumer behaviour to explain how a consumer maximizes the satisfaction/ utility he derives from his expenditure between different commodities, assumed for illustrative purposes to be two, X and Y.

In the table below, the consumer may buy different combinations of X and Y denoted by A, B, C, D and E which yield him the same amount of satisfaction. The more of commodity X the consumer has, the less its marginal utility to him, thus the more of it he is willing to exchange for an extra unit of commodity Y. As his supply of commodity X decreases, its marginal utility increases, and he demands successively higher units of commodity Y for an additional unit of X. This explains the convex shape of indifference curves.

Combination	X (Units)	Y (Units)	MRS$_{xy}$
A	20	8	-
B	19	12	1:4
C	18	15	1:3
D	17	17	1:2
E	16	16	1:1

Marginal Rate of Technical Substitution: The rate at which one factor can be substituted for another to produce a certain level of output. In the table below, the same level of output may be produced by various combinations of labour and capital.

Combination	Labour	Capital	MRTS$_{lk}$
A	1	20	
B	2	16	1:4
C	3	13	1:3
D	4	11	1:2
E	5	10	1:1

However, as we move from a capital intensive combination (A) to more labour intensive combinations, more units of capital have to be given up for each unit of labour. This is due to the law of diminishing marginal returns.

It is the slope of the Production Possibility Frontier (PPF).

Marginal Return: the addition to output as a result of increasing inputs; same as Marginal Product.

Marginal Revenue: Addition to total revenue arising from producing one more unit. Marginal revenue (MR) is equal to price (P) for price takers who must accept the single market price and perfect price discriminators who can sell each unit at its reservation price. MR is below P under single-price searchers who must lower the price for all units just to sell one more unit.

Marginal Revenue Product: The change in total revenue that results from employing one more unit of a factor.

Marginal Utility: the extra amount of satisfaction that comes from the consumption of an addition unit of an item. This extra satisfaction decreases as more of a commodity or service is consumed i.e. as total utility increases. Thus, a thirsty man is prepared to pay more for the first cup of water than for the second. Marginal utility is therefore the basis of demand, not total utility.

Marine Insurance: insurance of ships and their cargoes against losses and liabilities arising from perils of the sea such as tempests, storm, collision, theft, fire, etc. Policies may be taken to cover a ship, the cargo, for a specified period or a particular voyage.

Marine losses against which an insurance policy may be include the following:

1. *Total Loss*: a situation where the subject of insurance, i.e. the cargo, is completely destroyed. This may be subdivided into:
   a. Actual Total Loss: where the goods are completely destroyed by fire or where the goods are no longer fit for the purpose intended due to sea water upon collision.
   b. Constructive Total Loss: where the cost of repair is equal to or almost equal to the value of the goods.
2. *Partial Loss*:
   c. General Average Loss: where some or all of the cargo has to be thrown overboard for the safety of the ship. In this case the loss is averaged between the ship owners and the owners of the cargo.
   d. Particular Average Loss: where the is a damage to part of the ship or its cargo i.e. the loss is not suffered for the benefit of all on board the ship. The loss is borne by the owners of the particular item affected i.e. the ship or the cargo. In the case of a collision, for example, the loss will be borne by the owners of the ship.

Market: The institutions and interactions of buyers and sellers of a particular good or service with the purpose of facilitating trade.

Market Capitalization: the market value of the shares of a company; the quoted share price multiplied by the number of shares issued. The higher the market price of a share the higher the market capitalization of the company concerned.

Market Demand: The relationship between the total quantity of a good demanded and its price.

Market Failure: this is a situation where the free interaction of the forces of demand and supply in the market fail to bring about efficient allocation of resources, and leads to unintended and detrimental effects. Market failure could arise out of imperfect market structure whereby some market participants have undue influence which they exploit to the detriment of other participants and the society. Examples are over-pricing by a monopolist and inefficiencies and poor services by public corporations in a regulated market. *Externalities* such as pollution and environmental degradation which result from the actions of market participants are also examples of the failure of the market. Also, the market is inadequate to deal with the nature of certain goods, e.g. public goods. Public goods—such as roads and street lighting—cannot be efficiently provided by market. Market failure necessitates the intervention of the government in the interest of the society.

Market Forces: the forces of demand and supply, which interact together to determine the allocation of resources through the price mechanism.

Market Fundamentalism: term used to describe the belief by some that a free market system is a cure-all for economic and social problems.

Marketing: the overall process of developing a product to fill a demand and moving the product from the producer or port of importation to the final user. It begins with market research to determine consumers' needs and preference to inform product development and ends with the sale of the product to final consumer. Selling is thus a small part of the marketing process. Marketing completes the production process by adding, *time and place utility* to products. The *functions of marketing* involve all it takes to move goods from the producer to the final consumer: *Buying/Selling, Storage/ Warehousing, Transportation, Risk bearing, Financing, Pricing and Market Research.*

Marketing Boards: Commodity marketing boards were bodies established by government to buy agricultural produce from farmers for export and stabilize agricultural produce price. They appoint agents that bought produce from farmers at prices set by the board. They provided a guaranteed market for the farmers at stable prices, and also provided an organized framework for the grading and export of produce. The collection of export duties on such produce was also made easy through the boards. The boards maintained a Stabilization Fund into which surpluses were paid when world commodity prices were high relative to set domestic prices, and from which low world prices were subsidized.

Overtime, revenue from the boards increasingly informed the setting of prices, and the set prices became out of line with world prices. This discouraged agricultural production and ultimately led to smuggling of agricultural produce.

It was against this background that marketing boards were scrapped under the Structural Adjustment Program.

Marketing Mix: the (*four P's of marketing*) variables—product, price, promotion and place—within a firm's control with which it may influence consumers' reaction and behavior. A '*product*' is a collection of features and attributes from which the consumer derives satisfaction. It consists of brand name/trade mark; packaging, variants, etc. '*Price*' is the exchange value of the good or service, and different price strategies include market penetration, market skimming, target return on investment, following the market leader, product-line promotion, etc. '*Promotion*' is the communication of the product's features to consumers. Promotion entails advertising, sales promotion, personal selling and publicity. '*Place*' involves getting the product to the right location at the right time. It involves decision on the appropriate channel of distribution and transportation.

Market Research: the objective study/investigation of the market by a firm to determine consumers' preferences and market trends in order to effectively and efficiently satisfy demand, and thereby increase its market share. Data gathered in the process informs the firm's four marketing mix—product, price, promotion and place: new product line may be introduced; existing ones may be remodeled, repackaged or scrapped; market research may reveal consumers will be better reached with a new form of advertising campaign.

Market Segmentation: the marketing practice of identifying different group of users (segments) of a product or service, and designing products and services to meet the respective needs of viable segments. Instead of producing a product to meet the needs of all users of buyers, a manufacturer may carry out a market research to ascertain the different users of a bag, for example, and produce one for students, another for corporate workers, etc.

- A segment must be economically viable, i.e. profitable.
- A market may be segmented on the following basis: 1. Geographical; 2. Behavioural; 3. Demographic.
- As matter of corporate strategy, an organization may decide to produce exclusively for only a particular segment of the market in order to maximize its corporate strength.

Market Structure: the way a market is organized in terms of number of buyers/sellers, ease of entry, product differentiation, etc. which determine how participants interact and the pricing power of buyers and sellers respectively. Market structures are categorized into perfect and imperfect market structure conditions.

Market structure affects the relationship between market participants (buyers and sellers) and the way price is determined.

Market Schedule: the combined demand schedule of all buyers in a market over a certain range of prices.

Markets, Laws of: the assertion that supply creates its own demand. It was advanced by French economist J.B. Say. This view prevailed until the Great Depression (1929-1935) when John Maynard Keynes demonstrated in his book, *The General Theory of Employment, Interest and Money*, that this does not apply in modern day market conditions.

Mark-up: the amount added to the cost price of a commodity in order to determine the selling price, expressed as a percentage.

For example, if a good bought for N10 is sold for N12, the markup is 20%. That is, difference between cost price (N10) and selling price (N12) expressed as a percentage of the cost price, i.e. 2/10. Contrast with the **profit margin,** which is the difference between the selling price and the cost price expressed as a percentage of the selling price. In the above example, the profit margin will be 2/12 i.e. 16.67%

Markup is related to Gross Profit Margin by the formula:

$$\text{Markup} = \frac{\text{Gross Margin}}{1 - \text{Gross Margin}} \times 100$$

Marine Insurance: see under Insurance, Types of

Marshall Plan: officially the European Recovery Programme; programme of economic assistance by the United States of America to countries of Western Europe to rebuild their economies after the devastation caused by the Second World War. The programme lasted between 1948 and 1952, and was critical in restoring the economic backbone—the chemical, engineering, and steel industries, as well as transport infrastructure—of the seventeen countries that participated, and set the stage for European economic integration. The programme entailed shipments of food, fuel and machinery, etc., estimated at $13billion; over 5% of the Gross Domestic Product of the United States at the time. At the end of the programme, each of the economies of participating countries had surpassed their pre-war national output.

It was named after the United States Secretary of State at the time, the George Marshall.

Mass Production: production on a large scale. This is made possible by the reduction in average cost per unit brought about by mechanization of production.

Mass Unemployment: a situation where qualified and able persons who are willing to work cannot find productive employment especially where this affects all industries in the economy. This occurs during a depression or serious recession as was the situation in Nigeria in the 1982-1986; or in the United States of America during the Great Depression of 1929, that lasted through the 1930s and the Great Recession of 2008.

Mean: an average; the sum of all the numbers in a distribution divided by the number of items in the distribution. The mean can be used to summarize a mass of data as well as make comparison between sets of data. The mean is the most useful measure of central tendency because it makes use of all items in the distribution. It can also be used for further statistical analysis. One of its disadvantages is that it can be affected by extreme values. For example, in the distribution 4, 4.5, 6, 3.5, 5, 5, 6, 6, 5, 5, 4, 90, the mean, 12, is not representative of the distribution because it is unduly affected by the extreme value in the distribution, 90. Thus, if the distribution were to refer to prices of a commodity in different months of the year, the calculated mean would not show that prices were actually between N4.00 and N6.00 for most of the year.

Advantages
a. It is representative of the distribution because every value in the distribution is used to calculate it.

b. It is useful for further statistical analysis. For, example, in the calculation of the standard deviation.

c. Easy to understand

Disadvantages

a. It may be unduly affected by extreme values. Take the following distribution, for example, 50, 45, 55, 50, 51, 500. The mean of the distribution, (751/6), 125.17, does not truly reflect the distribution, because it is unduly affected by the extreme value of 500. (*Which other average would be a better representative of the distribution?*)

b. It may sometimes give a ridiculous figure. For example, the mean number of employees per department may be 3.7 employees.

Mean Deviation (MD): a measure of dispersion; the arithmetic average of all deviations of the various values in the distribution from the mean. While it makes use of all the values in a distribution, it cannot be used for further statistical analysis.

Measures of Central Tendency: averages (mean, median and mode) around which a distribution of set or distribution of numbers tend to cluster. They can be used to summarize the mass of data of which they are a part as well for comparison of different sets of data or distribution. Measures of central tendency are used to analyze or make sense of data in order to interpret and enable us make decisions.

The three measures of central tendency, Mean, Median, and Mode are averages which are representative of a mass of data from which they are taken or calculated.

Uses of Measures of Central Tendency

1. To **summarize** a mass of data: for example, a measure of central tendency gives us the average price of a commodity in various markets or cities nationwide. Thus, instead of having to deal with hundreds of prices a measure of an average gives only one figure that summarizes all the prices.

2. To make **comparison** between different masses of data. The performance of class of students may be summarized in the average. Relative performance may then be made by comparing their averages.

Measures of Dispersion: statistical measures of the spread or variability of a set of data or numbers; includes the range, mean deviation, standard deviation, and variance..

Mechanization: the predominant use of machinery, relative to labour, in production. This often follows from adoption of division of labour and the factory system. It entails the replacement of labour by machines in some stages of production, and results in increased output. In a bottling company, for example, a machine may cock multiples of filled bottles at a time workers instead individual workers carrying out the same task manually. Mechanization makes standardization possible and results in mass production because of reduced average cost of production per unit.

Median: an average or measure of central tendency; the middle number when numbers in a distribution are arranged in ascending or descending order; in an even set of numbers, the mean of the two middle numbers.

Advantages
1. It is not affected by extreme values in the distribution.

Disadvantages
1. It may be difficult to determine in a large distribution.
2. It is not useful for further statistical analysis.
3. It may need to be supplemented by other data, since it does not include all items in the distribution.

Medium Term Expenditure Framework (MTEF): a medium-term rolling plan approach is increasingly preferred in many African countries to the long-term national planning model that has been the practice.
The medium-term expenditure framework is a planning document which outlines government's revenue and expenditure projections for a multi-year period. The MTEF is a holistic process advocated by the World Bank and the International Monetary Fund to enhance efficiency and effectiveness in public expenditure management by enabling better co-ordination in policy making, planning and budgeting. The approach connects resource allocation, which occurs in the annual budgeting process, to policy and planning which are long-term processes. Thus, each year's budget can be seen in context of a three-year plan. The MTEF process is a dynamic system in that national projections and plans are updated annually thereby accommodating changes in the economic and political environment, as opposed to the long-term five-year development plans which can be rendered redundant or obsolete in the reality of fast changing socio-economic environment, or the short-term annual budget system which tend to be reactive.

Under the MTEF model, each year's budget is presented alongside plans for the next two years, though only the immediate year's budget is deliberated on and approved.

Memorandum of Association: document of a limited liability company which governs the external relations of the company. See *Articles of Association*

Mercantile Law: part of law that deals with commercial transactions comprising law of contract, sale of goods, agency, etc.

Mercantilism: the prevalent school of thought in the 17th and 18th century that believed that a country's prosperity and power derives from its reserves of precious metals resulting from excess of exports over imports. It advocated protectionist policies i.e. limiting imports, increased exports, etc to build up of trade surplus and argued against free trade. This view, championed by the likes of John Law, was opposed by Adam Smith and David Ricardo, who argued that a country's wealth comes from how well it employs its factors of production, and that free trade brings about efficiency through specialization in areas of comparative advantage.

Countries such as Japan, South Korea, Taiwan, China and others were distinctly mercantilist with undervalued exchange rates and high tariffs in the early years of their road to emergence as newly developed countries. Perhaps a mercantilist stance to trade is an inevitable passing phase on the road to the realization of comparative advantage, as a decrease in exports and increase in imports will likely see to a fall in exchange rate, contraction of credit and depression of trade. Until a country has become a creditor nation with sufficient overseas assets, an adverse balance of payments position would be cause for concern to its managers and hardly be one to recommend.

Merchant: a major dealer or distributor, often a wholesaler or big retailer.

Merger: the union or coming together of two or more companies for the purpose of one new company. Shareholders in the respective companies are issued shares in the new company in agreed proportion to their previous shareholding in the old companies. Mergers may be horizontal where the firms concerned are at the same stage of production e.g. where two firms engaged in rubber production. Vertical merger refer to union of two or more firms at different stages of production, e.g. where a rubber production firm merges with a tyre or plastic producer. In the latter case, the output of one of the firms serves as input or raw material for the other firm. Conglomerate merger is where the production activities of the merging firms are not related.

Merit Goods: services such as education, public health immunization, health services, subsidized housing, art galleries, etc, which are provided free or subsidized by the government, as they are thought to be required by all and should not be based, unlike normal goods, on the ability to pay.

Microeconomics: the part of economics concerned with decisions of individual economic units (households, firms and government) rather than the economy as a whole.

Middleman: any intermediary between the producer and the consumer such as a wholesaler, merchant, broker, agent, or retailer. Middlemen perform a vital function in the distribution chain, enabling the producer to concentrate his energies and resources in production rather dealing with a multitude of end-users. Middlemen may be by-passed in certain circumstances e.g. in the case of customized goods which are made to the customer's specifications. Also costly capital equipment are often ordered directly from the manufacturers. Aircraft manufacturers, for example, often deal directly with airlines, doing away with middlemen.

Migration: movement of people in and out of a region or country. Net migration is the difference between emigration and immigration and is one of the determinants of the population of a country.

Minimum Rediscount Rate (MRR): the rate at which the Central Bank lend to banks. It is thus the benchmark rate that determines other interest rates, and it is a means of effecting monetary policy; if the central bank anticipates inflation, and wants banks to cut back on lending, and reduce the amount of money in circulation, it can increase the MRR and cause banks to follow suit. High interest rates would discourage or reduce appetite for credit or loans. Similarly, the central bank may reduce the MRR if it thinks credit expansion is necessary to expand the economy and stop downward pressure on the general price level (deflation).

The MRR also serve as the reference rate for floating coupon rates of financial securities—e.g. bonds and debentures. For example the coupon rate of a debt instrument could be put at 2 per cent above the MRR, subject to a specified range say minimum of 15 per cent and a maximum of 25 per cent.

Minimum Wage: the legally stipulated minimum amount that must be paid by employers of labour, including government, to workers. Minimum wage legislation can distort the working of the market mechanism in the labour market if wages need to adjust below it to reach a new equilibrium. This could mean the persistence of unemployment as employers cannot afford to employ more people because as the minimum wage is high given the present economic conditions.

Mint: an organization responsible for the production of coins.

Minor: a person considered less than 18 years of age, and as such lacking legal capacity.

Minutes: a record of the proceedings of a meeting.

Mistake: an erroneous belief by a party or parties entering into a contract. There are three types of mistakes viz. Unilateral mistake, Mutual mistake, and Common mistake. A mistake may or may not void a contract depending on its materiality to the substance and intent of the contract.

Mixed Economy: an economic system with government and private participation in production, i.e. private and public sectors. Nearly all countries of the world presently operate a mixed economic system to varying degrees.

Mobility: ease of movement of a factor of production geographically or occupationally. Labour is the most mobile, being able to move geographically and occupationally. Occupational mobility is a function of the length of time in training and cost. Thus skilled labour is least mobile occupationally but more mobile geographically than unskilled mobile; a highly skilled engineer may be sought after from any part of the world unlike a plumber or cobbler. Land may be put to different uses—a playground, an office complex, a factory, etc.—but is immobile geographically. Certain forms of capital, such as specialized equipment or machines—e.g. X-ray machines, railway lines, furnaces—cannot be used for any other purpose. Capital controls i.e. laws against the movement of capital funds across national boundaries are increasingly a thing of the past in the age of globalization. Thus foreign portfolio investment and foreign portfolio investment are greatly sought after in most countries. See Factor Specificity.

Mode: a statistical measure of central tendency; an average; the number with the highest frequency in a distribution. It is not negatively affected by extreme values in the distribution but it cannot be used for further statistical analysis.

Advantages
1. It is not negatively affected by extreme values in the distribution.
2. It is easy to determine in an ungrouped frequency distribution.

Disadvantages
1. It cannot be used for further statistical analysis.
2. It is difficult to find in an ungrouped frequency distribution.

Model: theoretical frameworks designed to enable intelligent study of real life situations; models deliberately simplify reality but draws on essential conditions in order to study and draw conclusions of real life situations.

Monetary Policy: action by a central bank to regulate the money supply and credit availability in order to achieve certain objectives in the general price level, level of employment and business activity.

Monetary policy management is one the functions of a central bank. In carrying out this function, central banks use monetary policy instruments to indirectly influence the interest rate and the amount of money in circulation, and thereby bring about an expansion or contraction in lending/credit and business activity in the economy. In this way, monetary policy impacts on the general price level, level of business activity, and the level of employment.

Monetary policy instruments include the bank rate, open market operations, cash reserve ratio, Special deposits, and directives

1. Minimum Rediscount Rate/Bank Rate: the bank rate or MRR is the rate at which the central bank discounts treasury bills or the rate at which it lends to banks and other financial institutions. If the central bank thinks there is too much money in circulation, it may decide to reduce bank lending and credit availability by increasing the bank rate. When it increases the bank rate, banks follow suit by increasing the interest rate, which discourage borrowing. Similarly, when if it deem there is not enough money in circulation, it reduces the bank rate, and bank customers are encouraged to borrow.

2. Open Market Operations: this is the regulation of money supply through the sale of treasury bills by the central bank. Sale of treasury bills reduces the money in circulation as value of the treasury bills is withdrawn upon payment. Purchase of treasury bills has the opposite effect.

3. Cash Reserve Ratio: the CRR is the amount of a bank's assets that must be in cash or liquid form. The higher the CRR, the less cash banks have, the less credit or loans they can grant.

4. Special Deposits: apart from CRR, the central bank may require banks to maintain a certain percentage of their deposit with it, and thereby reduce their ability to create credit. For example, the Central Bank of Nigeria, in 2013, required banks to deposit fifty percent of deposits by government agencies with it.

5. Funding: this is the combination of short-term securities (treasury bills) and medium- or long-term securities (bonds) issued by the central bank. In order to reduce the ability of banks to create credit, the central bank will issue more government bonds; where it wants more credit to be available more treasury bills are issued.

6. Directives: the central bank may also get banks to tow a particular monetary policy stance by issuing directives.

Monetary Policy Committee: The committee responsible for formulating monetary and credit policy for the economy at the Central Bank of Nigeria. It is required to meet at least four times in a year. It sets the monetary policy rate, the benchmark interest rate, which is announced in a communiqué at the end of its meetings.

Monetary Union: a union of countries sharing a common currency such as the Euro by some European countries (the Eurozone) and the CFA franc among some former French colonies in West Africa.

The term also describes situations where a number of countries adopt a uniform exchange rate for their respective currencies.

A monetary union necessitates a central monetary authority or central bank to manage a common monetary policy across the union. Fundamental to the purpose of fostering economic integration, is the maintenance of price stability across member states. In order to achieve this member states must ensure that certain economic and monetary fundamentals—interest and inflation rates; balance of payment balances, foreign reserve levels, national debt levels, etc—are within certain limits, and are aligned with the exchange rate. This is exemplified in the convergence requirements of the Maastricht Treaty. These requirements specify acceptable levels for rate of inflation, long-term interest rates, government deficit and debt for member countries.

A full monetary union requires the elimination of individual currencies and the setting up of a supranational authority like the European Central Bank to ensure monetary discipline among members. On the alternative, or as a first step towards a full monetary union, members may decide to peg their respective currencies a hard currency.

The Eurozone is managed by the European Central Bank (ECB) which is responsible for price stability across the member countries.

The CFA zone has been in existence since 1945, while the euro was adopted in 1999. The French Ce ntral Bank is the ultimate anchor of the CFA zone: the currency was pegged at a fixed exchange rate to the French franc (and ultimately to the euro in 1999), and member states are required to maintain a certain proportion of their reserves with the French Central Bank.

There are plans among members of the West African Monetary Zone (WAMZ) of the Economic Community of West African States (ECOWAS) comprising Ghana, Nigeria, Sierra Leone, Gambia, Guinea and Liberia and the CFA franc countries made up of Benin, Togo, Cote d'Ivoire, Niger, Mauritania, Senegal, Burkina Faso, Mali, and Guinea-Bissau to adopt a common currency, the eco. The realization of this goal, in view of preliminary work required, especially against the backdrop of the experience of Eurozone countries, arguably lies in the distant future.

Money: Anything generally accepted in exchange for goods and services and in settlement of debt. For something to become generally acceptable as a means of exchange, it must have certain qualities. These include portability, divisibility, durability, and scarcity. Money serves a number of functions: it is a *medium of exchange*, it is used as a *unit of account, a measure of value* i.e. a basis of valuing goods and services, and it can be used as a *store of value*. Money facilities exchange and specialization by doing away with the disadvantages of barter which include double co-incidence of wants. Cowries, pepper, salt, manila among others have served as money in different times in different communities. In modern times, the government has imposed its official currency as legal tender, which the people are obliged to accept as a means of exchange and for settlement of debt.

Money, Demand for: The *demand for money* is the desire to hold money. This is as opposed to spending it. It is also referred as *liquidity preference*. Unlike other commodities, money is not demanded for its own sake. Its demand *derives* from what it enables us to do; it is therefore said to have a *derived demand*. Lord Maynard Keynes identified three *motives* for the demand for money:

1. *Transactional motive*: this is the desire to hold money to enable us deal with day-to-day transactions such as transport fares, payment of bills, food stuffs, etc.

2. *Precautionary motive:* We also desire money for contingency or unforeseen circumstances. Such circumstances include accidents, major breakdown of one's vehicle, etc.

3. *Speculative motive:* this is the desire to hold money in order to take advantage of emerging investment opportunities. If people speculate that prices are likely to fall in the future, they will not make purchases in order to profit from the fall in prices. Similarly if interest rates are low, the desire to hold money for speculative purposes will be high.

Money Illusion: to think that an increase in nominal money value necessarily increases real values. The failure to take account of the effects of inflation on the *purchasing power* of money, and therefore to believe that an increase in *money income* necessarily increases the amount of goods and services which can be bought.

Money at Call and Short Notice: loans made banks to other banks, corporate organizations or individuals that are repayable on demand or within fourteen days.

Money Market: the market for short-term loans or credit; network of institutions who buy and sell short-term securities such as treasury bills. Money market securities generally are highly liquid securities that mature in less than one year, typically in less than ninety days. Examples of institutions of the money market are commercial banks, discount houses, hire purchases companies.

Money Supply: The amount of money (coins, paper currency, and checking accounts) that is in circulation in the economy. The money supply must be matched by production i.e. goods and services, otherwise there will be inflation, when there is too much money relative to goods and services or deflation, when there is not enough money relative to available goods and services. The management of the money supply is the essence of monetary policy which is one the functions of the central bank.

Monopolistic Competition: an imperfect competition condition: a market situation in which one or more firms may be capable of influencing the price of the product because of their relative position in the industry. It is characterized by product differentiation, often established through advertising and branding. Differentiation may also be in the form of extent of services rendered, location, or general disposition of the producer. Due to differentiation, a seller can increase the price of its product without losing all its customers because it enjoys a level of "monopoly" because of brand loyalty. Monopolistic competition is often the case in the real world.

Monopoly: An industry with a single seller selling a unique (or patented) product and with has enough market power to practice effective price discrimination. The term "absolute monopoly" is used to describe a situation where there is only one supplier/ producer of a good for which there is no substitute. This is the counterpart extreme of perfect market. Such situations hardly exist in real life. However, the study of the assumed distinct conditions of monopoly, like those of a perfect market, enables an understanding of the varied imperfect market conditions often encountered in real life.

Monopoly Output: the output of the monopolist is influenced by certain realities and factors. First, he cannot decide the price and the quantity supplied at the same time. The monopolist may fix the price at which he may supply and let the market determine the quantity supplied or he may decide on the quantity to be supplied and let the market determine the price at which the quantity supplied will be bought. Secondly, he stands to sell more at a lower price than at a high price. Then there is the factor of elasticity of demand; the higher the degree of elasticity of demand for his good, the less his ability to increase his profit. As with other producers in different market conditions, the monopolist may increase his output until that point is reached where marginal cost is equal to marginal revenue. If output is increased beyond this point, the addition to cost will be more than addition to revenue, and cause profits to fall.

Monopoly Power, Bases of: monopoly may arise out the following situations 1. Patent rights, which bestow exclusive right to produce a new invention on the inventors for a period of time. 2. Copyrights, effectively give writers and artists, effective monopoly. 3. High tariffs may effectively give a dominant local producer monopoly power in the domestic market. 4. When one firm or a combination of firms controls a

significant percentage of the market supply; 5. High cost of entry into the industry may be prohibitive.

Monopoly Power, Control of

Monopoly Profit: profit in excess of "normal profit" received by a monopolist. Also known as surplus profit.

Monopsony: a market dominated by a single buyer of a good or service. Example, the market for defense goods (guns and ammunition) only has the government as the only buyer in most countries.

Moral Suasions: as part of monetary policy, appeal and recommendations by a central bank to banks regarding their lending policies.

Moratorium: a grace period granted by a creditor to a debtor during which payment obligations are deferred.

Mortgage: a legal instrument or document showing that land or property is used as collateral or security for money borrowed. Mortgage banks (mortgagees) usually advance loans to customers (mortgagors) to develop a property, retaining the title to the property until the loans is fully repaid with interest.

Mortgage Bank: a bank that that provides customers with home loans usually at low interest rates for long tenors. The building financed is held as security i.e. mortgaged until the loan is fully paid. In Nigeria, prospective home owners may access the National Housing Fund, administered by the Federal Mortgage Bank of Nigeria, through a Primary Mortgage Bank for a long-term mortgage loan at low rates of interest.

Mortgage Debentures: debentures secured on the issuers' assets.

Multiplier: the multiple or number of times by which national income will be increased by a change in investment expenditure. A change in aggregate demand, brought about by a change in investment expenditure, for example, will bring about a multiple change in national income. The number of times a given change in investment will affect national income is determined by the multiplier. That is, the multiplier is the number by which a change in aggregate demand must be multiplied to give the total change in national income.

Mathematically, the multiplier is the reciprocal of the marginal propensity to save (1-mpc), where MPC is the marginal propensity to consume. This means the higher the MPC, the higher the multiplier. Given an MPC of 0.6,

The multiplier = 1/1-0.6 = 1/0.4 = 2.5

In this case, if government spending or investment should increase by ₦3, 000.00,

National income would increase by

₦3, 000 x 2.5 = ₦7, 500.00

This is illustrated below; the initial amount spent by the government results in a series of income and expenditure. For example, if the government awards a contract for the construction of a bridge to JB Plc, the contractor will spend or pay 0.6 (the MPC) of ₦3,000 (i.e. ₦1,800.00) to sub-contractors, and save the balance N1, 200.00

(0.4 of N3,000.00). The sub-contractors will in turn spend 0.6 of ₦1, 800 (₦1, 080.) on suppliers and workers. The suppliers and workers will in turn boost national expenditure by 0.6 of ₦1, 080 (N648.00), their expense becoming income to others who initiate another round of income and expenditure, etc.

tage	Increase in income =N=	Increase in consumption =N=	Increase in Savings =N=
1	3,000.00	1,800.00	1,200.00
2	1,800.00	1,080.00	720.00
3	1,080.00	648.00	432.00
4	648.00	388.80	259.20
5	388.80	233.28	155.52
6	233.28	139.97	93.31
7	139.97	83.98	55.99
8	83.98	50.39	33.59
9	50.39	30.23	20.16
10	30.23	18.14	12.09
.	.	.	.
.	.	.	.
.			
Total	7,500.00	4,500.00	3,000.00

Multi-National Corporation (MNC): a company with global operations; a corporation which operates in at least one country other than its country of origin. The balance sheets such MNCs such as Coca-Cola and Exxon Mobil, etc. is often larger than the national income of many small countries. The first MNCs such as the British East India Company and the Dutch East India Company, were extension of their home governments which granted them trade charters or monopoly of trade over colonial territories, and were instruments of imperial interests. Most modern MNCs are from developed countries—American, Japanese, South Korean and Western European, with direct investments in developing countries are the drivers of globalization.

Initially, the search for raw materials for factories in the home country was a major driving force as the host country underwent industrial revolution. However with maturity of the home markets and the achievement of developed economy status has meant increase in labour costs.

Thus the quest for low cost of labour and the search for fresh markets has brought about off-shoring of operations to developing countries. A major objective of economic reforms in capital deficient countries is to attract direct investment from MNCs, and the number of MNCs present in a country is an indicator of its business friendliness.

N

NAFTA: North American Free Trade Area comprising Mexico, United States of America and Canada.

NAIRU, Non-Accelerating-Inflation Rate of Unemployment: lowest unemployment rate compatible with low inflation or the rate of unemployment below which inflation would start to accelerate.

Narrow Money (M1): money in circulation plus current account balances in commercial banks. See Broad Money.

National Debt: the money owed by a government. Governments often have to borrow internally i.e. from its citizens and externally i.e. from foreign governments, individuals, international institutions, etc. to finance a budget deficit, development projects, balance of payment disequilibrium, meet a national emergency, finance a war, etc.

The composition of the national debt in terms of domestic debt (denominated in local currency) versus foreign debt (denominated in hard or foreign currency) is critical: whereas domestic debt may be serviced from tax receipts, foreign debt is serviced in hard currency i.e. from export receipts. This impact on foreign reserves and therefore the exchange rate of the local currency, which affects the interest rate and thus level of economic activity in the economy.

National debt as percentage of the Gross Domestic Product (GDP) is a key measure of the financial health of an economy. Beyond a certain ratio, debt may not be sustainable and economic growth may be impaired. On the basis of the convergence criteria of the Eurozone, debt-to-GDP level should not be above 60%. High level of debt is a sign of fiscal irresponsibility on the part of the government and it negatively impacts a country's credit rating and the exchange rate. According to the International Monetary Fund, a country is said to achieve external debt sustainability if it can meet its current and future service obligations in full without recourse to debt scheduling or accumulation of arrears and without impairing growth. This means that the country's export receipts and/or government revenue should cover its debt servicing obligations.

External Debt can be a valuable source of needed capital to realize the productive capacity of an economy, rich in natural resources but deficient in capital funds. In countries like South Korea, external debt was used judiciously as part of an overall development strategy to boost export capacity. Where external funds are procured to finance productive ventures or infrastructure that enhances productive capacity, the capacity of the economy is enhanced as the proceeds from the financed assets can repay the debt. Problem arises when the debt level become unsustainable because loans are used to finance prestige and unviable projects and/or embezzled as has been the case in many African countries.

Nigeria's Debt

Nigeria's domestic debt arises from sale of:

- FGN Development Stocks
- Nigerian Treasury Bills (NTBs)
- Treasury Bonds (TBs);
- Nigerian Treasury Certificates
- Ways and Means Advances.

These are short- and long-term financial securities issued by the government through the Debt Management Office to raise funds for the government from the public. Investors in these securities include banks, discount houses, pension funds, foreign investors. However, the major holders are banks and discount houses, the non-bank public and the Central Bank of Nigeria (CBN).

Apart from the above include amount payable to contractors and suppliers. Contractors may also be issued **Sovereign Debt Notes**. Domestic debt has increased over the years as the government has resorted to the market for its funding of development projects and to cover its deficits.

Sources of External debt include the following:

- Trade debt: debt in the course of international trade to finance imports. Exporters are often guaranteed payment by the government of the exporting country, when the importer defaults in payment; it becomes a debt between the countries concerned. These belong to the Paris Club of creditors. The bulk of Nigeria's debt falls under this category.
- Bilateral debt: debt owed to another government; governments may finance the execution of a capital project by their nationals for another country. For example, the Chinese government, in agreement with the Nigerian government, may underwrite the construction of a rail by a Chinese firm.
- Multilateral Debt: borrowing from the international finance organizations like the International Monetary Fund, the World Bank, International Development Agency (IDA), African Development Bank (AfDB), etc, by government.
- International Capital Market: borrowing from international commercial banks and other commercial lenders. This is the London Club of international creditors.

Management of Nigeria's National Debt

The Debt Management Office is responsible for the management of Nigeria's debt. It carries out its responsibility in hand-in-hand with the Central Bank (CBN) as the management of the national debt is a key component of monetary policy as the issue, servicing and redemption of securities impact on the money supply and credit availability. On the other hand, external debt servicing negatively impact on reserves, which, in turn, exerts a downward pressure on the exchange rate and ultimately the interest rate.

The country's debt management experience has been characterized by the following:

- First Jumbo Loan: Nigeria prosecuted its civil war without borrowing. Reconstruction after the war and the euphoria of the oil boom between 1973 and 1976 encouraged the government to undertake costly infrastructure projects. In order to sustain its commitments, after the collapse of oil prices, the first major loan was a $1billion taken in 1978.

- Reckless and Inefficient Borrowing: Following the revival of crude oil prices upon the fall of the Shah of Iran in 1979, the civilian Federal and State governments, which had just come to power, went on a seeming frenzy for loans on the international capital market. The austerity measures put in place by the preceding administration were abandoned. From US$5.09 billion in 1978 external debt rose to U$8.855 billion in 1980, and $19billion by 1985.

- Declining Export Receipts: The country's ability to meet its debt obligations worsened when crude prices crashed in 1982, and the world economy went into recession. From $35 per barrel in 1981/1983, crude oil prices averaged $15.87 between 1986 and 1988.

- Overvalued Naira Exchange Rate: the exchange rate of the naira was inappropriate with the productive capacity of the economy, and this fostered a consumerist culture, funding an appetite for imported consumer goods that worsened the balance of payment position as just about everything was imported.

- Depreciation of the United States Dollar in which external debt was denominated against other currencies accounted for a good part of the total debt stock; accounting for over $6 billion increase recorded between 2002 and 2004.

- Adverse Interest Rate Movements: London Inter-Bank Offered Rate (LIBOR) which had averaged between 3 and 4 per cent in the

1970s peaked at 13 per cent in the late 1980s. As a result, the pre-1984 debt of most developing countries, Nigeria inclusive, quadrupled by 1990.

- Poor and Inefficient Loan Utilization: The inward looking import substitution industrialization strategy meant that borrowing was not linked to producing for export, and in the Fourth National Development Plan (1981-1985) with its high import content, no attempt was made to relate loan terms to project gestation periods. Most of the projects turned to be unviable becoming a burden on finances.

- Poor Debt Management Practices: Prior to the establishment of the DMO, the country's debt was managed by diverse sections and departments in the CBN and the Federal Ministry of Finance. This posed a challenge of co-ordination, verification of claims and prompt servicing which often led to delays and defaults in servicing resulting in penalties and accumulation of arrears.

- Accumulation of Arrears and Penalties: due to inadequate cash flow position, the country defaulted on its obligations serially. Capitalization of debt service arrears, penalties and accumulation of interests further worsened the debt position.

- Unilateral Suspension of Payment: In the mid- through the late 1990s, Nigeria's debt ballooned uncontrollably—due to compounding of interests, accumulation of arrears and penalties on late payments, as the Abacha government broke off relations with its creditors. These increased an initial total of $12billion to more than $30billion.

National Debt Management Strategies:

- Debt Rescheduling and Refinancing: the government was able to gain some respite from its creditors by essentially postponing maturity profiles of debt obligations, changing some short term to long-term loans and by issuing promissory notes.
- Debt-for-Equity: in a bid to attract foreign investment and manage scarce foreign exchange, external debtors were invited to exchange their debt for equity in Nigerian companies.
- Debt Buy-Back: Between 1988 and 1993, the Nigerian government, through a third party, bought back some of its debt on the international capital market, at discounted values, in a debt buy-back deal that ultimately reduced the national debt by US$5billion.
- Debt Cancellation: between 1989 and 1990, the governments of the United States and Canada cancelled a total of $107.2million debt. In 2006, 60% of Nigeria's debts amounting to $18 billion owed the Paris Club were cancelled, when the country paid up $12billion (40%),as full and final, following a long negotiation
- Nigeria external debt was substantially reduced even further following the pay-off of $500million owed to the London Clubs of Creditors in the first quarter of 2007. By paying three years before, the country saved $34million. Consequently, the external debt stock outstanding as at December 2007

stood at US$3.63 billion, as against $28,635.80 as at December 2002. See tables below.

External Debt Outstanding (US$ million)	1998	2000	2002
Multilateral	4,237.00	3,460.00	2,959.90
Paris Club	20,829.90	21,180.00	24,178.60
London Club	2,043.00	2,043.20	1,441.80
Promissory Notes	1,597.80	1,446.70	1,153.23
Others	65.80	143.80	55.60
Total	28,773.50	28,273.70	28,635.80
Source: The Central Bank of Nigeria			

NIGERIA'S NATIONAL DEBT as at December 31, 2007	2006		2007	
	₦ billion	US$ billion	₦ billion	US$ billion
Consolidated debt	**2,204.7**	**3.06**	**2,597.7**	**3.6**
Domestic debt	1,753.3	2.43	2,169.6	3.00
External debt	451.4	0.63	428.1	0.60
Source: The Central Bank of Nigeria				

National Economic Reconstruction Fund (NERFUND): NERFUND is development finance institution, established in 1989 to provide medium and long-term finance to Small and Medium Enterprises (SMEs), engaged in the real sector i.e. manufacturing, mining, quarrying, industrial support services, etc.

National Development Plan: Development plans are proposed long-term schemes in which development objectives for a specified period are stated or defined and outlines how resources shall be deployed for the actualization of those development objectives. It usually consists of prioritized capital projects for which projected inflows are allocated.

The economic planning process involve taking an inventory of the country's resources including population, an assessment of the nation's production capacity, a projection of a desired standard of living, and identification of sources of funding, projects, formulation of policies and programs required to achieve the projected level of standard of living. A certain level of growth in national output or Gross Domestic Product (GDP) is targeted during the period.

Formal economic planning is associated more with socialist and communist economies but has been widely used by developing countries as tool of economic growth and development. Economic planning, however, exist is one form or the other, in all economies.

In formal development plans, the basic economic question of *what to produce* is answered in the identified projects. Commercial and trade policies may also be outlined. Such plans have proven useful in environments where markets are not yet developed nor even exist, and therefore cannot be trusted to judiciously allocate scarce resources. In such situations, development plans are a way for the State or government to channel scarce resources to targeted areas as part of an overall scheme to start the economic engine of the country. Overtime, markets mature and evolve, and the need for plans and the regulations they occasion may be relaxed.

The First and Second Five-year Development plans were instrumental in transforming the economies of the Soviet Union between 1928 and 1933 to developed economy status, albeit at great human cost.

This model was successfully followed by South Korea between 1962 and 1982.

Between 1968 and 1982, Nigeria formulated four five-year national development plans. The dire straits of the economy and political instability midway through the fourth development plan meant that the fifth development plan, 1986-1990, could not see the light of day. With chronic balance of payments and fiscal deficits, as well as huge external debts, at this time, the economy was put through a Structural Adjustment Program, as prescribed by the International Monetary Fund (IMF), as a condition for granting financial aid. The Structural Adjustment Program, marked a paradigm shift in the development strategy of the economy from a public-sector driven to a private-sector driven one, which has been sustained, through different administrations, since.

The First National Development Plan, 1962-1970. Originally intended to last to 1968, the plan was extended to 1970 because of the civil war. A total of $2.13billion was proposed, and projected a Gross Domestic Product growth rate of 4% with a focus on agricultural and industrial development, and training of high level and intermediate manpower.

Achievements of the First Development Plan included the construction of the Kainji Dam, which commenced in 1964 and was commissioned in 1969; a petroleum refinery, which began operations in Port Harcourt in 1965 with a capacity of 38,000 barrels per day; the construction of trunk "A" roads, the extension of credit finance for agricultural projects through regional governments. Federal universities were established at Nsukka, Ife and Zaria.

Second National Development Plan 1970-74: A total of N3billion was envisaged under this plan; it focused on reconstruction and replacement of infrastructure after the civil war, and following from the First Plan, to further strengthen agriculture and industrial capacity. It also prioritized the development of middle and high level manpower. The importation of machinery, tools and completely-knocked down (CKD) parts for the vehicle assembly and ultimate manufacture of consumer items, under the import substitution industrialization strategy. The Ajaokuta Steel Company was started under this plan.

The dramatic increase in crude oil prices in 1973 accounted for a growth rate of over 12%, as opposed to the 6% targeted. However, not being accompanied by actual increase in productivity and value-added, but brought about by an external factor—the Yom Kippur war in the Middle East—this growth was not accompanied by development.

In retrospect, this was the beginning of the end of organic growth of the economy as increased petrodollars shifted emphasis from the development of agriculture, and overvaluation of the exchange rate of the naira which opened the floodgates to importation of consumer goods which undermined the growth of the secondary sector of the economy.

Third National Development Plan 1975-1980: was an ambitious plan designed against the backdrop of robust financial conditions with crude oil prices on the rise, as a result of the Yom Kippur war in the Middle East. The plan set to expand agriculture, industry, transport, housing, water supplies, health facilities, education, rural electrification,

and community development, and could be termed a transformation plan.

One of the achievements of the plan was the indigenization programme to which may be ascribed the beginning of the emergence of Nigerian business and capitalist class.

This plan could not however be realized as the implementation of the projects were adversely affected by dwindling government revenues. Crude oil prices trended downwards throughout the late 1970s and 1980s after short-lived increases following the Iranian Revolution and the Iran-Iraq war. Indeed worsening revenues compelled the government to impose austerity measures.

Fourth National Development Plan, 1981-1985. The effect of the precipitous fall in crude oil prices starting from the late 1977/78 virtually rendered this plan inoperable. The financial capacity required to import required machinery and construction materials was simply lacking in the face of falling exports and adverse balance of payment position which persisted through this period.

After Structural Adjustment Program, the country opted for a three-tier planning system comprising a twenty-year (long-term) perspective plan, a three-year (medium-term) rolling plan and an annual (short-term) budget.

Rolling plans were thought more adaptable to the reality of rapid changes and uncertainty, as the experience of the past four plans revealed. The rolling plans and annual budgets derive from the perspective or long-term plan. The component rolling plans and annual budgets could be adjusted and adapted as may be dictated by prevailing conditions while keeping the objective of the perspective plan in view.

The first Perspective Plan covering 1989-2009, was formalized and documented but during this period the economy underwent economic and political reforms of a fundamental nature. These saw efforts to encourage exports and increase foreign direct investment, e.g. the first Free Trade Zone in Calabar; the privatization and commercialization of government enterprises continued, liberalization and deregulation saw a revolution in telecommunications services; drastic reduction of external debts; reformation and strengthening of development finance institutions with the setting of the Bank of Industry, commercial banking reforms, etc.

Rolling plans gave way to medium-term expenditure framework (MTEF) under the civilian administration in 1999.

In 1997, the government revealed a comprehensive document, tagged Vision 2010. This was a Perspective Plan, which replaced the earlier plan.

The National Economic and Development Strategy (NEEDS) was adopted in 2003. In contrast to previous plans, NEEDS focused on strategy and policy directions, instead of projects.

This was later also replaced by the Vision20:2020 the stated objective of which is to translate the economy into one of the top twenty economies by the year 2020.

"By 2020 Nigeria will be one of the 20 largest economies in the world able to consolidate its leadership role in Africa and establish itself as a significant player in the global economic and political arena."

That statement remains no more than a statement of intent.

National Income Accounting: the value of all goods and services produced (output) is the same as the sum of rewards (incomes) paid to owners of factors of production used or costs incurred (expenditure) in producing them. Thus, the national income is the same as the national output or national expenditure. Therefore, the national income figure may be calculated in three different methods: the *income, output* or *expenditure* methods or approach respectively. Thus national income, national output and national expenditure are identical:

National Income (NI) ≡ National Output (NO) ≡ National Expenditure (NE)

In accounting for the National Income, the relevant concepts are:

- The Gross Domestic Product, GDP
  o   Net Domestic Product, NDP

- The Gross National Product, GNP
  o   Net National Product, NNP

- Depreciation, (capital consumption)
  o   GDP-Depreciation = NDP
  o   GNP-Depreciation = NNP

- Net Property Income from Abroad
  GDP + Net Property Income from Abroad = **GNP**

Gross Domestic Product (GDP): this the total value of goods and service produced *within* the country by all residents (i.e. foreigners and nationals). It excludes the earnings of citizens resident abroad but includes the earnings of foreigners and foreign investment within the country. *Net Domestic Product* (NDP) is the Gross Domestic Product *minus* depreciation or capital consumption.

Gross National Product (GNP): the total value of goods and services produced by citizens of a country plus net income from their investments abroad. *Net National Product (NNP)* is Gross National Product *minus* depreciation or capital consumption.

Problems of Measuring the National Income

i. *Changes in the value of money*: changes in the value of money must be adjusted for with the use of price index otherwise real national income may be inflated.

ii. *Inadequate statistics:* records are often not available or inaccurate where available because government institutions are poorly equipped in terms of equipment and personnel to gather required data, and also due to the low literacy level and widespread false declaration of income to evade tax.

iii. *Large informal economy*: a good percentage of production takes place outside of the organized private sector of the economy, for which no records of output, income and expenditure are available. There are a lot of unregistered businesses and self-employed persons for whom there are no records. Estimates can only be made for such, leading to underestimation of the national income.

Measuring the National Income

There are three ways of measuring the national income:

1. *Output or net product method*: the monetary value of the all the goods and service produced within the country during the year. To avoid double-counting, calculation is done on a value-added basis. That is, only the net product of output is taken into account. This means that the value of inputs is subtracted from the value of outputs. All exports are included while imports are excluded. The value of all goods and services produced during the year are included. Thus goods consumed by the producers and the value of owner-occupied homes are included by imputing rent Similarly, the value of health, defence, security as well as voluntary organizations, house-helps and housewives are also included.

Problems of the Output Approach

i. *Production not marketed but consumed by the producer*: estimation of the amount of output that is consumed by the producers is a difficult task especially in West Africa where many people are engaged in subsistent production.

ii. *Double-counting*: the value of output must be done on a value-added basis

iii. Subtracting the value of inputs from the value of output. The value of flour, sugar, etc used in the making of bread must be subtracted from the value of bread in order to determine the contribution of bakeries to national output.

iv. *Government services used by the general public*: the value of social services provided by the government such as policing, defense, health, etc is hard to estimate for inclusion.

v. *Monetization* of value of work carried out on one's own house, services of housewives, house-helps, voluntary and other non-profit organizations. Statistics for such services are hard to come by leading to under-estimation.

2. *Income approach:* using this approach we sum up all the earnings or incomes by factors of production (rent, wages/salaries, interest and profit) for their participation in production. Only incomes which are received for production are included. Thus gifts, donations, bursary awards, pensions, social security benefits, etc, also known as *transfer payments,* are not included since they are not earned in the course of production. To include transfer payments would amount to double-counting.

Problems of the Income Method
i. Valuation of rent of owner-occupied houses.
ii. Income not paid to as dividend to factors of production by business.
iii. Estimation of incomes of self-employed people and others who are employed in the informal sectors of the economy.
iv. Payments In kind: not all productive efforts are paid for in cash. Especially in rural areas, payments may be made in kind. Estimation of such is difficult.

Expenditure approach: using this method, national income is computed by summing up the expenditures incurred on goods and services at market prices or basic prices. Indirect taxes are deducted and subsidies are added, where market prices are used.

The expenditure approach is given by the following formula:

$$Y = C + I + G + (X - M)$$

Where,
- **Y = Gross Domestic Product**
- C = *private consumption expenditure,*
- I = *private investment expenditure,*
- G = *Government expenditure on consumption and investment,*
- $X - M$ = *Net Exports (X, export less M, imports).*

Nigeria's National Product, Income and Expenditure, 2011	
National Product	N
Agriculture, fishing and forestry	11,593,434.13
Manufacturing	598,330.90
Crude Petroleum & Natural Gas	15,285,004.21
Financial & Business Services	759,464.75
Public Administration	253,332.33
Telecommunication	292,539.10
Real Estate, Building, Construction	1,880,349.79
Wholesale & Retail trade	5,385,815.10
Road Transport	529,193.39
Others	1,439,507.18
GDP at Market Prices	**38,016,970.88**
National Income	
Wages and Salaries	9,360,985.66
Profit and Interest	1,8261,724.02
Rent and other property income	9,132,713.85
Unclassified income	654,437.09
GDP at Basic prices	37,409,860.62
Less: Indirect taxes	(649,621.64)
Add: Subsides	42,511.17
GDP at Market Prices	**38,016,970.88**
National Expenditure	
Government	4,979,904.24
Private	22,840,832.69
Investment	3,910,589.13
Export	19,961,271.38
Import	(13,675,626.56)
GDP at Market Prices	**38,016,970.88**
Source: National Bureau of Statistics	

Problems of the Expenditure Method

1. Double-counting: The table below shows how a shirt would be included in the national income accounts at N7, 200.00 instead of its right value of N3, 600.00.

	Input	Output	Cost (N)	Value-added (N)
Farm		Cotton	800	800.00
Cotton Gin	Cotton	Yarn	1,000	200.00
Textile Mill	Yarn	Cloth	1,800	800.00
Tailor	Cloth	Shirt	3,600	1,800.00
TOTAL			7,200	3,600.00

2. Estimation of depreciation or capital consumption.
3. Transfer payments: care always has to be taken not to include payments that are made not for engagement in production e.g. bursary awards, gifts, pensions, social security payment, etc.
4. Services not paid for.
5. Payments in Kind

National Income Distribution: the way rewards for participating in production (rent, interest, wage/salary and profit) are distributed. National income distribution is one of the basic questions faced by all societies, i.e. for whom to produce, and which must be addressed by its economic system. In a capitalist economic system, the market, through the price system, determines how national income is distributed. Due to market failures, this may sometimes result in inequitable distribution of national income, resulting in such anomalies where the rich man's (owner of capital) dog has better medical attention and food than owners of labour. In such instance, the government may use fiscal policy to re-distribute national income by taxing the rich and using proceeds to provide public facilities that benefits all.

National Income Equilibrium: the level of national income at which there is balance in the consumption and expenditure of the major sectors of the economy viz. households, businesses, the government and international trade. In the short-term there is a limit to the level of economic activity that can be sustained. Beyond this limit, the economy will be over-heated, resulting in an inflationary gap; below this limit, the level of economic activity will be at sub-optimal level, reflected in a deflationary gap. At national income equilibrium, there is full employment level of output with optimum utilization of resources with neither inflation nor deflation. At equilibrium, aggregate demand is equal to aggregate supply; total leakages (savings, taxes, and imports) from, are equal to injections (investments, government expenditure, and exports) into, the circular flow of income. National Income Equilibrium is the essence of economic management through the use of monetary and fiscal policies to remove inflationary or deflationary gaps.

Graphically, national income is at equilibrium at the point where the aggregate demand intersects the 45^0 line. In the diagram below, there are three points at which the 45^0 line is intersected. However, at Y2, there is an inflationary gap (the difference between AD2 and AD); at Y1, there is a deflationary gap (the difference between AD and AD^1).

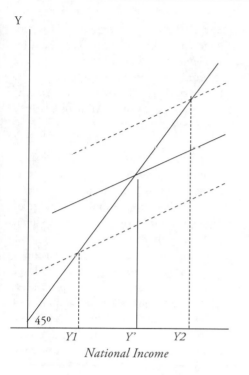

National Income

At Y1, Expenditure exceeds Income, there is deflationary gap.

At Y', Expenditure is equal to Income, there is equilibrium.

At Y2, Income exceeds Expenditure, there is inflationary gap.

Nationalization: taking over of a private business by the government. In Britain the Labour Party government, led by Clement Attlee nationalized the Bank of England in 1946. Coal, steel, electricity, telecommunications, rail and other industries were to follow, so that they will be managed 'in the public interest', as part of its policy of 'putting people before profit'.

Reason for nationalization may be ideological i.e. socialist ideology, as in the case of Britain cited above. In this case,

nationalized industries are a feature of mixed economies where a public sector exists side-by-side with a private sector. This was common in most economies up to the 1970s, when the implication of government ownership on operations of these enterprises prove to be an unsustainable burden, by undermining efficient resource use. As a result, beginning from Thatcher's Britain, in the 1980s, privatization of state-owned enterprises became popular, as governments reduced its role in the economy to that of regulator as opposed to being an economic agent of player.

In unstable developing countries, military governments nationalization often target foreign investments, in what amount to expropriation. Therefore a key concern of foreign investors is a guarantee of appropriate compensation should their investment be nationalized.

The Ashanti Goldfields Corporation was nationalized by the Ghanaian government in 1972.

In Nigeria, government took over British Petroleum and Barclays Bank and renamed them African Petroleum and Union Bank of Nigeria respectively in 1978. This was done to spite the British government for its foreign policy in then-apartheid South Africa.

National Plan: see National Development Plan.

National Product: same as National Income.

Natural Monopoly: A situation where the market can only sustain one firm; arising where optimum efficiency can only be achieved in the industry if there is only one firm. The cost of operating a competing network of pipes, for example, would make a single franchise for the supply of water sensible.

Near Money: an asset that may be regarded or used as money in view of the ease of converting them cash. An example is a short-term bill e.g. a Treasury bill may easily be discounted to realize cash compared to a building which might take some time to market.

NEEDS: The National Economic Empowerment and Development Strategy (NEEDS) grew out of the World Bank's Poverty Reduction Strategy Process (PRSP) which the Obasanjo administration adopted in pursuit of achieving the Millennium Development Goals. However, it became a distinctly home-grown, holistic development strategy/plan that emerged from a highly participatory process, to consolidate the administration's programme between 1999

This was followed by the State version, the State Economic Empowerment and Development Strategy (SEEDS). For the local government level, the Local Government Economic Empowerment and Development Strategy (LEEDS) was developed in 2006.

In contrast to the three-year annual rolling plans before it, that were project-based, NEEDS focused on strategy and policy directions.

It has four goals: Wealth Creation, Employment Generation, Poverty Reduction and Value-Reorientation. The strategy to achieve these is organized on three pillars:

1: Social Charter—Investing In the Nigerian People; Poverty Reduction by implementing socially-oriented policy reforms; Integrated Rural Development; Empowering Women and Youth; Liberalizing Sports Administration. Pension Reforms

2: Creating a Competitive Private Sector: redefine the role of the government as a facilitator and promoter to position the private-sector to take advantage of opportunities in the domestic, regional and global markets by:
- Reducing the cost of doing business: streamline incorporation, land use access and transfer processes, eliminate multiple taxation and fiscal harassment, rationalize port clearance of goods, consolidate immigration matters including visas, work permits, etc.
- Finance: restructure, strengthen, and rationalize the regulatory and supervisory framework in the financial sector; address low capitalization, the poor governance practices of financial intermediaries.
- Improving infrastructure: Transport: provide a legal framework for private sector participation in infrastructure provision through Build-Operate Transfer (BOT), Build-Own-Operate-Transfer (BOOT); Rehabilitate-Operate-Transfer (ROT) and concessioning.
  - Upgrade the country's seaports:
  - Upgrade the railways; privatize or concession the Nigeria Railway Corporation
  - Achieve total radar coverage of the country's airspace.

Power: Unbundle NEPA and privatize the new units; Set-up a regulatory agency for the power sector; Set-up a fund to improve access to electric power in the rural areas.

Promoting Industry: establish one science and technology park in each of the seven geo-political zones and Abuja; encourage linkage between research and industry.

Provide an enabling environment to attract greater inflow of Foreign Direct Investment (FDI) with emphasis on wealthy Nigerians and Africans in the Diaspora.

Trade, Regional Integration

3: Changing the Way Government Works:

Enforcing anti-corruption laws; Reforming Public Procurement; Reforming the Bureaucracy; Increasing Information and Transparency; Increasing Transparency in Privatization and Market Liberalization Processes; Promoting Public-Private Partnership; Monetizing Fringe Benefits in the Federal Public Service

The following may be counted among the successes of NEEDS: Poverty reduction interventions by the National Poverty Eradication Programme (NAPEP) e.g. Keke NAPEP and Micro-credit schemes; The Civil Service Compact (SERVICOM) initiative and the Monetization of fringe benefits (2003); Pension Reforms (2004); reformation of the public procurement process with the setting of the Bureau of Public Procurement (2007); Bank industry consolidation (2004) and corporate governance regime (2009); the founding of the Infrastructure Concession and Regulatory Commission and Airport (Murtala Mohammed International) and

Port management concessioning (2006), Power sector reforms which has seen the unbundling of NEPA and privatization of the emergent units (2013).

Negotiable Instrument: a document, which may be transferred from one person to another, endorsed or signed by a party, promising to pay another party, a certain amount of money at a future date or on demand. Examples are cheques, promissory notes and bills of exchange. In contrast, a non-negotiable instrument is a document (e.g. a waybill) or financial instrument (e.g. a crossed cheque) that cannot be transferred from one party to the other.

Neo-Classical School of Economics: today's orthodox economic theory which introduced mathematical methods of analysis to explain economic issues. Neo-classical economics use marginal analysis and the concept of the equilibrium to explain actions and decisions by economic agents.

It assumes that individuals act to maximize satisfaction or utility from the use of their resources and firms act to maximize profit or minimize costs.

According to neoclassical economic theory, the individual makes his decisions based on his estimation of marginal utility while the firm decides based on marginal revenue.

NEPAD: New Partnership for Africa's Development is a programme of the African Union (AU) adopted in Lusaka, Zambia in 2001, following submissions made by Algeria, Egypt, Nigeria, South Africa and Senegal. NEPAD's main objectives are to reduce poverty, put Africa on a sustainable development path, halt the marginalization of Africa, and empower women. It is the latest programme by the AU aimed at economic development of the African continent. Earlier initiatives with similar objectives include the Lagos Plan of Action (1980) and the African Alternative Framework to Structural Adjustment Programme (1989).

Net Exports (X-M): Exports *minus* Imports; The total value of goods and services exported during the accounting period minus the total value of goods and services imported. A component of the national income equation y = C + I + G +(X-M). Net Exports is added in using the output method in calculating national income.

Net Indirect Taxes: indirect taxes minus subsidies; when using the expenditure method to compute national income at factor cost/prices, indirect taxes must be subtracted, and subsidies must be added back. This is because an indirect tax would raise the price of a product above the factor cost while a subsidy would reduce the price below factor cost.

Net Investment: investment during a period less depreciation i.e. wear and tear or capital consumption.

Net Migration: The total number of people leaving the country to take up permanent residence abroad minus the number of people entering the country for the purpose of taking up permanent residence

Net National Product: Gross National Product less Depreciation.

Net Profit: profit from the operations of a business during the financial year. It is arrived at in the Profit and Loss Account by deducting operating expenses such as rent, rates, taxes, wages and salaries, insurance, maintenance expenses, depreciation, interest on loans, etc from Gross Profit brought forward from The Trading Account.

Net Property Income from Abroad; total of *incomes from investments or assets held abroad* less total *payments to foreigners on assets held in the country* in the course of the year; in national income accounting, it accounts for the difference between Gross Domestic Product (GDP) and Gross National Product (GNP). GNP plus Net Property Income from Abroad = GNP. GDP is greater than GNP if *Net Property Income from Abroad* is negative.

New International Economic Order, The: The New international Economic Order (NIEO). The concern by developing countries that the present order of international trade and finance, exemplified by the Bretton Woods system, put in place after the Second World War in 1945 by the developed countries led by the United States, is structured to suit their interests at the expense of the developing countries led to proposals to bring about a new order. Thus, the developing countries put forward proposals through the United Nations Conference on Trade and Development (UNCTAD) to promote their interests. In 1974, the General Assembly of the United Nations passed a resolution calling for a New International Economic Order (NIEO) aimed at reducing the widening gap between the developed and the developing countries by improving terms of trade, increasing development assistance, freer trade, etc.

The following are some of the issues:

1. Stable and equitable prices for raw materials (the foreign exchange earner for developing countries).
2. Non-discriminatory tariffs to exports of developing countries: developing countries should have easy access to the markets of developed countries.
3. Reform of the International Monetary System: a review of the present system such that like developed countries, developing countries should be able to borrow from the IMF without stringent conditions.
4. Transfer of technology to developing countries:
5. Provision of economic and technical assistance without any strings attached.
6. Regulation and control of multinational organizations (MNC) by developing countries
7. Nationalization and expropriation of foreign property by developing countries.
8. Recognition of the rights of developing countries to set up associations of producers of primary products similar to OPEC

New Issues Market: The primary market of the capital market where new securities are issued to fresh raise funds. New issues may be brought to the market in any of the following ways:

1. Initial Public Offer: the company applies to the stock exchange for a listing or quotation of its shares for trading on the floor of the stock exchange for the first time.
2. Offer for Sale: a sponsoring intermediary e.g. an investment bank or issuing house on behalf of the company for re-sale to the public.
3. Offer for Subscription: this is a direct offer by the company to the public of its shares.
4. Rights Issue: a company already listed on the stock exchange offers its shareholders to take up new shares in a specified proportion to their present holding.

NEXIM: the Nigeria Export-Import Bank set up as an Export Credit Agency to replace the Nigerian Export Credit Guarantee & Insurance Corporation in 1991. The Nigerian Export Credit Guarantee and Insurance Corporation was established in 1988 as part of efforts, under the Structural Adjustment Programme, to promote the development of the export sector.

The Bank's broad mandate is essentially to promote the diversification of the Nigerian economy and develop the external sector through the provision of the following services in support of the non-oil export sector:

1. Credit facilities in both local and foreign currencies;
2. Risk-bearing facilities—export credit guarantee & export credit insurance, i.e. short-term guarantees for loans granted by Nigerian Banks to exporters as well as credit insurance against risks in the event of default by foreign buyers;
3. Business development and
4. Financial advisory services and trade and market information.

The Bank is equally owned by the Central Bank of Nigeria (CBN) and the Federal Ministry of Finance Incorporated (MOFI).

NIBOR: see Nigerian Inter-bank Offered Rate

Niger Basin Authority: organization founded in 1964 to promote the exploitation, development and effective utilization of resources of the (River) Niger Basin. Members: Benin Republic, Burkina Faso, Cameroon, Chad, Guinea, Cote d'Ivoire, Liberia, Mali, Niger, Nigeria, Sierra Leone, and Togo. It is headquartered in Niamey, Niger Republic.

Nigerian Deposit Insurance Corporation (NDIC): the deposit insurer of Nigerian banks. The banks are obligated to pay a certain percentage of their total deposit liabilities as insurance premium to the NDIC. This insures depositor's funds in the event of bank failure. Maximum claim is presently limited to fifty thousand Naira. It is empowered to examine the books and affairs of banks and other deposit taking institutions. The body's role complements that of the Central Bank. It is under the federal ministry of finance.

Nigerian Enterprise Promotion Decree: towards the indigenization of the control of the Nigerian economy, this law promulgated first in 1972 and amended in 1977 to ensure that Nigerians are not marginalized in the running of the economy of their country by reserving ownership of certain lines of business for Nigerians and limiting foreign ownership of others. Certain business, grouped under Schedule I, such as bottling of drinks, assembly of electrical appliances, haulage, advertising, retail trading, municipal bus transportation, etc. were reserved exclusively for Nigerians. Foreign owners of businesses listed were required to transfer ownership to Nigerians by March 1974.

Minimum share or equity ownership of 40% was reserved for Nigerians in businesses listed under Schedule II of the decree.

Widespread fronting and generally lax implementation of the 1972 decree, and protestation over the fact that residents of Lagos and its environs were unduly favoured led to the second decree in 1977.

The second NEPD further restricted foreign ownership in three ways: a) Expanded the list of activities exclusively reserved for Nigerian investors to included bus services, travel agencies, wholesale of home products, film distribution, newspapers, radio and television and hairdressing;

(b) Restricted foreign participation from 60 to 40 per cent and added new businesses such as fish-trawling and processing, plastic and chemicals manufacturing, banking and insurance to the list of businesses in which foreign was limited to 40 per cent.

(c) Created a new list of activities including manufacturing of drugs, some metals, glass, hotels and oil services companies in which foreign investment was reduced from 100 to 60 per cent ownership.

The decrees enabled the transfer of shares to Nigerians on a massive scale over a relatively short period, boosting the development of the Nigerian capital market and the local capital accumulation with the emergence of a Nigerian middle class.

A number of multinational corporations divested from the Nigerian economy as a result.

In the drive to encourage inflow of foreign capital, under the Structural Adjustment

Programme, the decree was amended in 1989 to allow for 100% foreign ownership except in banking, insurance, and mining. The law was repealed in 1995, the Nigerian Investment Promotion Commission Act allowing foreigners to own shares in any Nigerian company.

Nigerian Inter-Bank Offered Rate (NIBOR): the rate of interest charged for short-term loans at the Nigerian inter-bank market. NIBOR is an average of rates quoted by contributing institutions—Banks and Discount Houses selected/appointed quarterly by the NIBOR committee. NIBOR is published daily. It was created in April 1998, and modeled after London Inter-Bank Offer Rate (LIBOR) to provide a credible basis on which pricing and acceptance of coupon on long-tenured instruments could be anchored.

Banks borrow and lend between themselves in their effort to manage liquidity and meet maturing obligations.

Nigerian National Petroleum Corporation (NNPC): The NNPC is Nigeria's national oil company (NOC), formed in 1977 with the responsibility for the development and management of petroleum resources in Nigeria.

The organization was restructured into a holding company with 11 subsidiary companies in 1988 in a bid to improve operational efficiency. These subsidiaries span the Upstream and Downstream sectors of the industry. Upstream activities are exploration and oil & gas production. Downstream activities include petroleum refining and retail services i.e. marketing and distribution.

The government has stated intention to position the NNPC to compete internationally in the NEEDS document.. Unlike other NOCs like the Sinopec and China National Petroleum Corporation (CNPC), for example, whose shares are listed and which raise funds for their operations by issuing bonds, the NNPC does not publish its accounts, and has not been known for its corporate governance and the transparency of its operations.

Exploration and Production
The NNPC does not directly carry out oil exploration. Oil explorations are undertaken by international oil companies (IOCs) in partnership with the corporation's upstream subsidiary, Nigerian Petroleum Development Company, (NPDC). The international oil companies are granted concessionary rights under which they are obliged to pay Petroleum Profit Tax and Royalties into the Federation Account through the NNPC.
Oil exploration companies carry out exploration under the terms of Joint Operating Agreement (JOA) with the NPDC with the IOCs as operators. However, Production Sharing Contracts and Service Contracts are increasingly the norm due to challenges of JOA.

Gas Development
The corporation is the arrowhead of government's gas policy which is to explore natural gas reserves to serve the country's energy needs as well as for export. A subsidiary, the Nigeria Gas Company, supplies gas via a network of pipelines to industrial clients across the country and to the West African region under the West Africa Gas Pipeline project.

Refining

Crude oil is refined into respective petroleum products at four refineries, under different subsidiary companies. They are the Warri Refinery and Petroleum Company and Kaduna Refinery and Petroleum Company and the Port Harcourt Refinery and Petrochemical Company connected by a network of pipelines. Installed capacity is 445,000 barrels per day.

Marketing and Distribution

Marketing and distribution is carried out by the Pipelines and Product Marketing Company (PPMC), via its network of depots and jetties, and the NNPC Retail which operates a network of service stations nationwide.

International oil Trading

The NNPC engages in international crude oil trading through a subsidiary, Duke Oil.

Shipping

The NNPC operates an international oil shipping operations jointly with Daewoo Ship Building and Engineering, the Nigeria-Daewoo Shipping Company (NIDAS).

Nigeria Ports Authority (NPA): The NPA is the government body charged with the responsibility of regulating Nigeria's seaports, harbours, docks and waterways. As the landlord, the NPA has responsibility for the development and maintenance of Nigerian seaport systems which include ports at Onne, Port Harcourt, Calabar, Warri and Lagos.

Until reforms which began in 2000 with the passage of the NPA Act 1999, which deregulated the sector, the NPA was in the regulator and operator of ports in Nigeria. Deregulation meant that private port operations was provided for, and separated port regulation from port operations.

High levels of inefficiency and cargo theft among others, at Nigerian ports, prompted a diagnosis which determined that the NPA could not be expected to deliver world-class terminal service with the-then structure of the industry. This saw a reform process which restructured the industry by redefining the role of the NPA, and brought about the concession of port operations to private operators for the management of the ports which were required to pay royalties and levies to the NPA.

Functions of the NPA
1. Ownership and leasing of port land and infrastructure
2. Port planning and development;
3. Safety, and environmental vigilance within ports
4. Nautical management of the channels and waterways like lighting and dredging activities
5. Provide port security services; maintenance of law and order in collaboration with security agencies.

Nigerian Stock Exchange: the Nigerian bourse was established in 1960 as the Lagos Stock Exchange, as an association limited by shares but became limited by guarantee in 1990. It was promoted by the Central Bank of Nigeria, the Investment Company of Nigeria (later the Nigeria Industrial Development Bank) and members of the Nigerian business community, and received annual subvention from the CBN. It commenced operations in 1961 with 9 securities listed for trading. In 1977, it opened trading floors in other cities and became known as the Nigerian Stock Exchange. It presently has electronic trading floors in Lagos, Abuja, Kaduna, Kano, Onisha, Port Harcourt, Benin, Ibadan, Ilorin, Abeokuta, Bauchi, Owerri and Yola.

The NSE comprises two tiers: the Mainboard and the Alternative Securities Market, for small and medium enterprises, with less stringent listing requirements.

The objectives of the NSE may be summarized as 1) serve as a platform for quotation of new and trading of old issues; 2) Enabling Liquidity as a central market for the trading of securities 3) Financial Intermediation: machinery for the mobilization of savings and the availment of same for investment in financial securities; 4) Platform for sourcing of capital development funds by the three tiers of government.

At inception, the trading system used was the call-over method but an Automated Trading System (ATS) was introduced in 1999 consisting of a network of computers that enable on-line dealing. In 1992, the Central Securities Clearance System (CSCS) was incorporated as a subsidiary of the NSE. The CSCS has succeeded in reducing the clearing and settlement process of trading in securities from months to a matter of days.

The NSE's sources of funds include quotation fees, and Subscription fees from listed companies, annual fees from dealing members as well as investments.

The Listing Requirements (Mainboard) of the NSE include registration as a public limited company, submission of financial statements of the last five years, issuance of at least 25 percent of the share capital to the public, a minimum of 500 shareholders, and submission of audited accounts of the last nine months.

The market indicators of the NSE are the All-Share Index, and the NSE-30, made up of the 30 most capitalized stocks. There are also specialized indices for the Banking, Insurance, Consumer Goods and Oil & Gas Sectors respectively. The Market Capitalization of quoted securities stood at N10.28trrillion as at December 2011. As at December 2011, total number of listed equities was 201, while Bonds, made up of Corporate, Federal, State and Local Governments issues, was 48.

Conspicuous from the list of listed companies on the NSE are upstream petroleum and telecommunications companies as well as utility companies.

Nigerian Stock Exchange At a Glance		
	2011	2012
Total Market Capitalization	N10.33 trillion .... $69.65 billion	N10.28 trillion .... $67.71 billion
Market Capitalization (Equities)	N7.92 trillion ...... $53.40 billion	N6.54 trillion .... $43.06 billion
NSE All Share Index	24,770.52	20,730.63
Total Volume (units)	93.34 billion	89.58billion
Total Value	N797.55 billion .... $5.38 billion	N634.92 billion .... $4.18 billion
Average Daily Volume (units)	377.87 million	364.15 million
Average Daily Value	N3.23 billion .... $21.78 million	N2.58 billion .... $16.99 million
Turnover Ratio	12.51	8.36
No. of New Issues (Approved)	31	34
Value of New Issues (Approved)	N2.44 trillion .... $16.45 billion	N2.03 trillion .... $13.37 billion
No. of Listed Companies	217	198
No. of Listed Equities	220	201
No. of Listed Bonds	44	48
Source: NSE Annual Report 2012		

Normal Good: a good more of which is bought as income increases; a good with a positive *income elasticity of demand*. Contrast *inferior* and *giffen* goods.

Neutral Budget: A budget that does not have any effect on the level of economic activity.

NDP: Net Domestic Product i.e. Gross Domestic Product *less* Depreciation.

NNP: Net National Product—Gross National Product *less* Depreciation.

Nominal cost: the money cost or price of something. If a man chooses to buy a house worth N2million instead of a car, the N2million is the nominal or *money cost*; the car he forgoes is the *opportunity cost* or *real cost*.

Nominal GDP/GNP: GDP or GNP figures for which account has not taken been taken of changes in the value of money or inflation; the GDP or GNP deflator is used to deflate nominal GDP or GNP figures to arrive at real GDP or GNP figures. This is necessary because increase in national income figures (GDP or GNP) may be due to changes in the value of money rather than change in the actual output of goods and services. Nominal GDP or GNP figures are given at money values prevailing at the time. Real GDP or GNP figures are calculated at constant prices; the values prevailing at a chosen base year.

Normal Profit: the return to enterprise necessary to just sustain production. Profit earned by firms in a competitive market in the long run. When an industry is at equilibrium, all firms are earning normal profit. Supernormal profit will attract new entrants into the industry until all firms are earning normal profit. Compare supernormal profit.

Normative Economics: Economics that goes beyond theory and logic to proffer opinion and prescriptions on issues e.g. towards maximization of social welfare. This is opposed to the view of Economics as a Positive science that restricts itself to logic and theory.

O

Occupations: any productive activity engaged in for the purpose of earning a living. A person's occupation is determined by various factors including environmental or climatic conditions, skill and aptitude, education and training, etc. Occupations are classified into three as follows: Industrial, Commercial and Services.

Industrial Occupations are concerned changing the state of natural resources. There are three subdivisions:

Extractive occupations: categorized into agriculture, mining and quarrying, and fishing are concerned with extracting natural resources from the earth for further use or consumption.

Manufacturing occupations: work in factories and workshops to convert raw materials from extractive industry into intermediate or finished goods;

Construction occupations assemble intermediate, finished or manufactured products into other usable forms such as houses, roads, bridges, vehicles, factories, etc.

Commercial Occupations comprises those engaged in trading and activities that facilitate trade such as insurance, banking and finance, advertising, transportation and communication, warehousing, etc.

Service or Tertiary Occupations: enhance production by providing direct and indirect services. Direct services administer personal services e.g. lawyers, doctors, teachers, barbers, entertainers, chefs, cooks. Indirect service occupations render services to the public. These include civil servants, policemen, soldiers and other government workers.

Occupational Mobility: the ease with which a factor of production can move from one type of employment to another. Skilled labour often lacks occupational mobility because of the length and cost of training whereas a person may commercially engage as a gardener and plumber at the same time. See Factor Specificity.

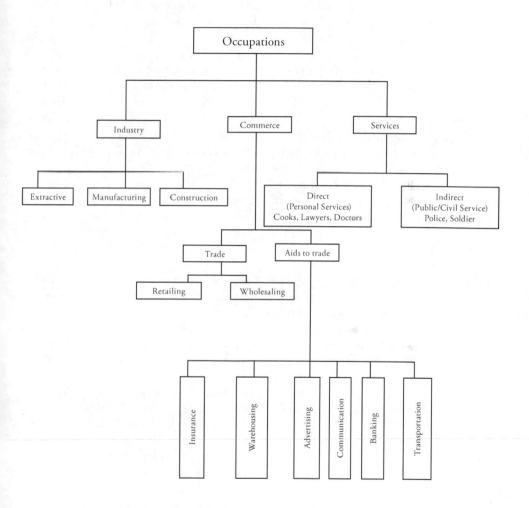

OECD: see **Organization for Economic Co-operation and Development.**

Offer: a statement of the terms on which a person is willing to be bound in a relationship of contractual obligations with another person. The statement or offer must be accepted explicitly or implicitly by the other party for a contract to exist between the parties. See under Contract.

Offer for Sale: an invitation from an issuing house to buy new or existing shares of a company. The issuing house is a sponsoring intermediary which has brought the shares from the company concerned for sale to individual subscribers. It is distinct from an offer for subscription where the company approaches the market without a sponsoring intermediary.

Official Rate: in foreign exchange market, the rate fixed a country's authorities at which its currency will be traded/bought and sold. This bound to give rise to a parallel market where dealers exploit the difference between the official rate and market rate reflecting the forces of demand and supply. The differential will depend on the extent of exchange control or intervention by the monetary authorities.

Oligopoly: A market dominated by a few suppliers or firms. An oligopoly can be brought about by the creation of a cartel.

Oligopsony: a market situation where a few buyers dominate and can influence price and output of firms.

OPEC: see Organization of Petroleum Exporting Countries

Open Market Operations (OMO): a tool of monetary policy which involves purchases and sales of government securities and certain other securities in the open market, carried out by the central bank, to influence the volume of money and credit in the economy. Bank balances with the Central Bank are increased or decreased and thereby the amount of money in circulation and banks' ability to create credit is impacted. For example if the CBN sells a total of N150billion worth of Treasury Bills, buyers of these securities will issue cheques and their banks will pay the amount to the central bank. The cash balances at the CBN are reduced by the amount. Thus, N150billion is withdrawn from circulation. In this way total purchasing power is reduced, and a downward pressure is brought to bear on the general price level: the amount of money chasing available goods and services is reduced and inflation in checked. Similarly when the level of business activity is low and there seem not to be enough credit in the economy, the central bank may decide to encourage banks to lend i.e. give loans to their customers. The reverse of the above will happen by the purchase of treasury bills. For example, a purchase of a total of N50billion worth of treasury bills will increase bank cash reserves by that amount. Increase in cash reserves will encourage banks to lend; they will relax their credit policies e.g. by reducing interest rates and other lending conditions, and the purchasing power is thereby increased. Thus, deflationary tendencies will be checked. See Monetary Policy.

Operation Feed the Nation (OFN): This programme was started by the Obasanjo military administration in 1976; the objective was to bring about self-sufficiency in food production by encouraging subsistent farming. Simple farm implements were supplied at subsidized rates.

Opportunity Cost: The good/service that must be given up (forgone) in order to purchase or produce or get another thing.

To purchase or produce a product (or service) means we have to forgo another product (or service). Opportunity cost is a way of expressing the cost of product (or service) in terms of the product (or service) we have to forgo in order to obtain that product or service.

Scarcity of resources or the fact that resources can be put to alternative uses means individuals, households, firms and the government are always have to make a choice to forgo one in order to satisfy another want.

For example, if Tega has N100, and chooses to purchase a notebook instead of ice-cream, the opportunity cost of the notebook is the ice-cream she did not buy.

Similarly, if a farmer decides to grow cash crops instead of food crops, the real cost (or opportunity cost) of growing cash crops is the food crops forgone.

Executives hire personal cooks and chauffeurs, even if they can do these tasks very well because of they know the real (opportunity) cost of not hiring help is more than the monetary or nominal cost.

Contrast *nominal cost* or *money cost*.

Optimum Firm: a firm operating at its most efficient size where it neither desires to expand nor reduce its scale of production, as costs of production are at a minimum.

Optimum Output: the output at which average total cost is at a minimum (and hence marginal cost equals average total costs), indicating maximum technical efficiency.

Optimum Population: Optimum population is the size of the population that matches available resources and technology to produce the maximum output per worker. The population that provides the labour force that produces the highest output per head, when combined with other factors of production (available resources and present technology). Over-population or under-population is relative to the optimum population i.e. over population is a situation where the optimum population is exceeded while under population is situation where the population is below the optimum population.

Option: a contract or agreement between a which gives one the right (option), in return for a fee, to buy or not to buy an asset—real or financial—at an agreed price during a certain period, if the buyer so wishes. Options are of three kinds namely, put, call or double.

Ordinary Shares: risk capital or equity share capital held by the members of a limited liability company. Ordinary shareholders bear the risk of the business as they are only paid after preference shareholders and holders of debentures have been paid. They do not receive a fixed rate of dividend.

Organization Chart: a diagrammatic representation of the line and functional relationships in a firm.

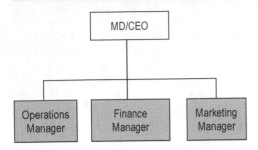

Organization of Petroleum Exporting Countries: (OPEC): a cartel of oil suppliers formed in 1960, with the objective of managing output and stabilization prices of crude oil in the interest of member states. OPEC influences world supply of crude oil by regulating the output of member states through allocation of quotas.

Organization for Economic Co-Operation and Development (OECD): an international economic organization of the mostly developed economies, based in Paris, France. Its purpose is "to promote policies that will improve the economic and social well-being of people around the world," by acting as a forum for the discussion, exchange and co-ordination of economic, environmental and social issues as they affect domestic and international policies of member countries. It engages and cooperates with businesses, trade unions and civil society groups. It produces empirical analysis and publishes books, reports and statistics on the economic performance of countries. Among its successes is successfully anchoring the signing of bi-lateral tax treaties among some countries.

Also the OECD Anti-Bribery Convention aimed at reducing by sanctioning corruption in international business transactions, has been well received and adopted by some non-member countries.

The OECD was formed in 1961, as successor to the Organization for European Economic Co-operation (OEEC), which had been established under the European Recovery Program (Marshall Plan). From the initial 20 membership has risen to 34 countries by 2013; Chile and Israel joined in 2010.

OPEC was formed to take control of the market for crude oil from the international oil companies exemplified by the oil producing corporations—exemplified by the so-called 'Seven Sisters'—which carried out exploration and production of crude oil world-wide. Together these corporations formed an informal cartel controlling over ninety per cent of world oil production and determined crude oil prices from the 1920S. Dissatisfaction with this state of affairs led to the Baghdad Conference of the five founding members—Iran, Iraq, Kuwait, Saudi Arabia and Venezuela—in September 1960. The formation of OPEC was therefore to enable them exercise sovereignty over their natural resources. OPEC became a platform for members to collectively engage with the Seven Sisters to demand higher export prices, higher tax rates, and greater equity in their local subsidiaries.

OPEC's influence reached its peak in the 1970s, when its Arab member countries imposed an oil embargo, in October 1973, on allies of Israel during the Yom Kippur War, resulting in increase in crude oil prices from USD$3 to stabilize at US$12 per barrel at the end of the crisis in 1974, resulting in high inflation in most industrial countries, inducing an economic recession.

The crisis exposed the near total dependence on oil and led to increased exploration, use of alternatives (such as coal, gas and nuclear energy by utilities) energy conservation/ efficiency and research into alternative energy among industrial countries. Increased exploration and production by non-OPEC members like the United States, Canada, Mexico, the United Kingdom, Russia, Uzbekistan and Kazakhstan has led to substantial increase in non-OPEC output of global crude oil. This led to a glut supplies in the 1980s resulting low prices that reached the bottom in 1986.

Nigeria became a member of OPEC in 1971. Other members are: Gabon, Algeria, Angola, Iraq, Iran, Kuwait, Libya, Qatar, Saudi Arabia, United Arab Emirates, and Venezuela. Former members include Indonesia, Ecuador and Gabon. The organization's Secretariat is in Vienna, Austria.

Organized markets: markets such as the stock exchange where business is carried on under a prescribed set of rules and regulations.

Orientation: the process of acquainting a new employee with the work environment— who is who and what is what, in the company, his place in it, etc.—in order to enable him adjust as fast as possible.

Original Entry: in book keeping, subsidiary books such as the Purchases Book, Sales Book and Journal are termed books of original entry because entries are initially entered in them before being posted to the Ledger.

Output: quantity produced by the process of production. Whether a firm is operating under perfect or imperfect market conditions, profit is at a maximum where marginal revenue is equal to marginal cost.

Output Method or approach: see under *National Income Accounting.*

Over-capitalization: a company the value of whose real assets—buildings, machinery, vehicles—is less than the value of its issued capital.

Overdraft: amount by which a bank allows a customer to over draw his balance. For example, a customer with a balance of N100,000.00, may be allowed to withdraw N170,000.00 i.e. an overdraft of N70,000.00. Overdrafts are allowed only on current accounts, and usually attract a lower rate of interest compared to normal loans.

Overhead: costs such as rent, and salary of administrative staff, that do not vary with output.

Over-population: a country or region is said to be over-populated if its population is more than its optimum population. This is a situation where population is more than available resources can adequately support the population.

Over-trading: where a company increases its business operations beyond the level its capital can comfortably accommodate leading to unsustainably high level of account receivables (trade debts). This negatively impacts on working capital to meet its operating expenses. This is indicated where current liabilities exceed current assets (cash, trade debts and stock-in-trade), and may arise where credit sales are granted beyond a level that the business can comfortably accommodate.

P

Packaging: see under Marketing Mix

Paid-up Capital: see under Share Capital

Par Value: nominal or face value. Financial assets—shares, stocks, bonds, bills—may be traded at their face value i.e. at par or below par (discount) or above par (premium) reflecting the state of the underlying asset.

Paradox of Thrift or Saving: where over-saving leads to under-consumption and negatively impact aggregate demand; the rather strange situation that increase in personal savings tend to be harmful to the economy by reducing aggregate demand. Keynes popularized the Parable of Thrift: the higher the marginal propensity to save (MPS), the lower will be the marginal propensity to consume (MPC), and thus if people generally where to save more they consume, business revenues would fall, as demand for their products and services fall.

Paradox of Value: Adam Smith noted that the *value-in-use* of certain commodities differed from their *value-in-exchange* giving rise to a "paradox of value". Water has a high value in use but commands a low price whereas diamonds are a non-essential but are priced high (high value in exchange). This shows that the price of something is determined by its scarcity (supply relative to demand) rather than its usefulness. Diamonds are scarcer relative to demand for them than water ordinarily is. Also, the price of a commodity is determined not by total utility but by marginal utility of the commodity.

Paris Club: The Paris Club is an informal group of creditor governments comprising Austria, Belgium, Denmark, Finland, France, Germany, Italy, Japan, the Netherlands, the Russian Federation, Spain, Switzerland, the United Kingdom and the United States of America. It meets in Paris with debtor countries over government guaranteed export trade loans. The governments take over loans from their nationals in cases of default by the recipient country. In contrast, the London Club consists of international creditor banks, mostly from the Paris Club countries.

Partial Loss: one of the several kinds of marine loss against which an insurance policy may be taken by an exporter. This is where goods are partly damaged or there is a loss to part of a cargo. A marine policy with such a cover is referred to as *With Particular Average* (WPA) while one that excludes such cover is known as Free of Particular Average (FPA).

Participating Preference Shares: see under Preference Shares.

Partnership: Partnership is an unincorporated business owned by an association of 2 to 20 persons who decide to combine their capital, knowledge, experience together in a business venture to make profit. Partnerships are common among professional firms like accountants, lawyers, architects, etc.

Features of Partnership
1. Profits and losses are shared according to the capital and the work each partner contributes.
2. Relationship among partners is governed by the *Deed of Partnership*.
3. The management of the partnership is in the hands of partners; there is no board of directors.
4. The business is not a separate legal personality from the individual partners; it cannot sue and be sued in its own name.
5. The liability of members is not limited to the amount they invest in the business.

Types of Partnerships
Ordinary Partners: an active partner who is involved in the management of the business and has with unlimited liability

Limited Partnership: a sleeping or dormant partner who mainly contributes capital, his liability is limited to the amount invested, and he does not take an active part in the business

Deed of Partnership/Articles of Partnership
This is an agreement among the partners. It contains the rules and regulations of the partnership. Its contents include:
1. Name of the business/partnership.
2. Names of the partners.
3. Amount of capital contributed by each partner.
4. The profit and loss sharing ratio.
5. How new partners are to be admitted
6. How the partnership is to be brought to an end.

7. The role of each member in the partnership.

Advantages
1. More capital compared to a sole proprietorship. Multiple personal savings and it is easier to obtain loans together as a group than a sole proprietor can. This means the business has more capital to run its operations and it easier for it to expand compared to a sole proprietor.
2. *Specialization in management;* partners may have different experience and background. A member may be a marketer, another may be an engineer, etc and together they use their knowledge and expertise for the business. This leads to greater efficiency
3. *A partnership is a team:* a partnership is a team comprising of two to twenty persons. It is stronger than an individual as it can make better decisions, manage and conduct its operations more effectively as two goods heads are better than one, *ceteris paribus.*
4. *Privacy:* A partnership does not have to publish its accounts and balance sheet. Thus there is privacy in managing its affairs.
5. *Continuity:* the death or resignation of a single partner need not affect the business as the remaining partners can carry on the business and admit another partner, if they want.
6. *Spread of business risks and liabilities:* the probability of business failure is reduced and the liability of individual partner is reduced in the event of business failure.

Disadvantages
1. Liability of the business is unlimited
2. The business is not a separate legal entity.
3. Limited capital compared to a joint stock company.
4. Disagreements among partners may hamper progress or even end the business.
5. Exit of a partner may end the business.

Pass Book: a book, issued by a bank to a savings account holder, in which entries of deposits and withdrawals are made.

Payee: the person or persons to be paid. The person to whom a cheque is payable i.e. whose name is written on a cheque.

Paying-in Slip: a bank deposit slip; a document, filled by a bank depositor, showing details of cash or cheque being paid in into an account. The customer usually retains a copy as evidence of deposit or receipt by a teller of the bank, who stamps and signs it.

P/E Ratio: see Price/Earnings Ratio.

Per Capita Income: The income per head of a country. It is calculated by dividing national income (Gross National Product) by the population. It is an indicator or measure of the standard of living in a country over a period of time, and it is used to compare the standard of living between countries.

Per capita Income 2010			
	Country	Nominal GDP $'Millions	Per Capita Income
1.	USA	13,843,825	37,500
2.	Japan	4,383,762	28,620
3.	Germany	3,322,147	27,460
4.	China	3,250,827	
5.	UK	2,772,570	27,650
6.	France	2,560,255	27,460
7.	Italy	2,404,666	26,760
8.	Spain	1,438,959	22,020
9.	Canada	1,432,440	29,740
10.	Brazil	1,313,590	7,480
11.	S. Africa		10,270

It must be noted that PCI figures are based on National Income figures which are largely under-reported or under estimated in poor countries because of the high level of subsistent production and the inadequacy of statistics collection. Also these figures are only averages: the more equitable the national income distribution, the more representative these figures are.

Perfect Competition: A market situation in which no one buyer or seller can influence the market price by its own action. All participants in such markets are "price takers", there is no price leader. A perfect market is characterized by perfect flow of information, large number of sellers and buyers, homogeneity of the product and freedom of entry and exit. The capital market and commodities market approximate perfect market condition.

Perfect Market: a theoretical market situation characterized by the following:
1. Large number of buyers and sellers such that no one buyer and seller

buys or sells a quantity large enough to influence the price of the product; there are no price leaders: all market participants are price-takers.

2. Homogeneity of product: i.e. there is no differentiation in the product. Thus customers have no preference for the product of any particular seller.

3. No Discrimination or Preferential Treatment: there must not be any form of preferential treatment or discrimination against any customer. Thus, quotas, tariffs or subsidies against or for certain products are not allowed in a perfect market.

4. Portability of product: it must be easy to carry about any product traded in a perfect market.

Perfect Monopoly: same as Absolute Monopoly.

Perfect Oligopoly: a form of imperfect market situation where the product is homogenous and there are only a few suppliers of the product. There is dominant supplier, a price leader, who is able to influence the quantity supplied to the market and thereby dictate the price and others are bound to follow.

Personal Income Tax: a form of direct tax imposed on wages, salaries, interest income and investment income. In assessing a person's tax liability, certain allowances e.g. for personal, marriage and children are deducted from *gross income* to arrive at a person's *taxable income* against which the personal income tax rate is applied. Personal Income Tax is a progressive tax.

Personal Selling: one-on-one or face-to-face selling. The salesperson meets with the buyer for the purpose of the sale.

Perspective Plan: a long-term development plan ranging from 15 to 20 years. A Perspective Plan usually comprises medium term plan and short term plan (annual budgets). Nigeria adopted the Perspective Planning to replace the fixed four year plan after the Structural Adjustment Programme.

Petty Cash: amount of money set aside for small cash expenses. usually recorded in a petty cash book under an imprest system.

Phillips Curve: a curve showing the inverse relationship between unemployment and inflation. This is an empirical observation, first made by Professor A. W. Phillips in 1958, based on historical data of the British economy between 1861 and 1957 which suggested that the *lower* the rate of unemployment, the *higher* the rate of inflation. This meant that a level of unemployment has to be tolerated in order to keep inflation in check. One has to be traded off for the other; low unemployment and low inflation do not seem to go together.

One theory put forward to explain this situation is that low unemployment raises workers' bargaining power to push for higher wages, which is ultimately passed onto consumers in the form higher prices, (inflation). However, Milton Friedman and Edmund Phelps pointed out, in 1968, that the trade-off between inflation and unemployment was only in the short-term. They argued that inflation cannot be kept permanently low; that below a certain level of unemployment—a 'natural rate of unemployment'—inflation rises. Thus the natural rate is also known as the Non-Accelerating-Inflation Rate of Unemployment, or NAIRU.

Physical Controls: the direct control or regulation of economic activities through the use of administrative measures such as setting of interest rates, foreign exchange controls, import license/permits, price controls as opposed to market-based instruments such as monetary and fiscal policies. Such measures may be adequate in an environment where markets, legal, institutional and macroeconomic frameworks are not yet mature.

Beyond a point they become a drag on development leading to inefficient allocation of resources, through distortion of prices resulting in economic stagnation. Thus market reforms often target their removal and replacement through deregulation and liberalization.

For example, economic management in Nigeria before the Structural Adjustment Program in 1986 was characterized by administered interest and exchange rates, credit ceilings, selective credit controls; prescribed cash reserve requirements, special deposits, etc. With reforms, open-market-operations is now the major monetary policy tool supplemented by reserve requirements, discount window operations. Similarly the exchange and interest rates are now subject to market forces.

Physiocracy: an 18th-century school of economic thought, consisting mainly of Frenchmen, which preceded and influenced Adam Smith and classical economics. They advocated free competition and laissez-faire or minimal government interference in business activities, and celebrated agriculture as the only productive economic activity.

They opposed the mercantilists' proposition that a nation's wealth lies in its accumulation of gold, and thus the need to always have a favourable balance of trade. Instead, the Physiocrats advanced the argument of free trade between nations. Prominent physiocrats include Francois Quesnay,

Planning: a management function concerned with anticipating the future in terms of positioning and resource requirements, and decisions for possible courses of action in pursuit of the organization's goals and objectives.

Poll Tax: a tax of a certain amount imposed per head of the population. This mean everybody is required to pay a certain amount, e.g. N5,000.00, each. It is an example n everybody is require of a regressive tax, as all are required to pay the same amount irrespective of income levels.

Pooling of Risks: the idea of contributing to a common pool, by people who wish to insure themselves against a risk. Those who actually suffer a loss from the risk are compensated from the common pool.

Population: Population refers to the total number of people living within a geographical area or country at a particular time. Knowledge of the population is important because they provide the labour (*working population*), the market for goods and services (consumers). The number of *dependants*, the *rate of growth* of the population; the composition and structure of the population in terms of *age, sex, occupation* and *geographical* distributions are also of importance because of their implication for economy.

The population of a country depends on three factors; the birth rate, death rate and migration.

Thus, the _rate of growth_ of the population of a country is expressed in the formula:
Birth rate—Death rate + Net migration.
where:

1. _Birth Rate:_ this is the number of birth per thousand of the population in a year.
2. _Death Rate:_ this is the number of death per thousand of the population in a year.

Note: _Natural growth rate of the population_ = Birth rate _less_ Death rate.

3. _Migration:_ this is the movement of people from one place to another in order to settle there. Migration has two parts: emigration and immigration.

Emigration refers to the movement of people out of a place or country.

Immigration refers to the movement of people into a place or country.

The difference between immigration and emigration is _net migration_.

Population Density: the total number of people living per square mile or square kilometre. It is a measure of the concentration of people living in a given area. Note that the population of a place may be high but its population density may be low relative to another. For example, Russia with a higher population has a far lower population density than Nigeria as can be seen from the table below. This is because the population of Russia is spread over a much larger area.

Country	Area in sq. kilometre	Population (2007)	Density per sq. km
Russia	17,075,200	141,377,750	8.3 persons
Nigeria	923,768	135,031,160	146 persons

Population Distribution: Population may be distributed in the following ways
I. Age distribution: 0-15; 16-30; 31-45; 46-60; .60
II. Geographical distribution: urban and rural
III. Sex distribution: male and female
IV. Occupational distribution: primary, secondary and tertiary

Age Distribution: refers to the way in which the population is spread among the different age groups or brackets: 0-19, 20-64, 65 and above. The age distribution varies from country to country. In most developing countries, children are more than adults as compared to developed countries. In most developed countries, the population consists of people aged 65 and above. The 20-64 age group or age bracket constitute the working population or labour force. The 0-19 and 65 and above age groups are the dependant population. People in this age group are not economically or productively active.

Importance of Age Distribution
1. _It determines the size of the labour force._ If the number of people between the 20-64 age-groups is higher than the dependant population, it means that the supply of the labour force is high. If the number of children is high, it means the size of supply of labour will be high in the future.
2. _It affects the standard of living:_ If the size of the dependant population is

high, it means that income per head (per capita income) will be low. Low capita income mean low standard of living. This is because there are more dependants than productively active people.

3. *It determines the natural growth rate of the population.* If there are more people in the 20-64 age-group, birth rate will be high because this group is the child-bearing group. On the other hand, if there are more people in the 65-above age-group, death rate will be high.

4. *Production pattern:* what will be produced depends on what is in demand; what is in demand depends on the age group in majority i.e. the age distribution. If there are more children and teenagers, producers will produce goods demanded by this group, for example.

5. *Dependency Ratio:* this is the ratio of dependants to workers. The more people there are in the dependent age-groups, the higher the dependency ratio.

6. *National Income:* national income depends on the productively active population. High labour force means more people are available for production. More production means higher national income. On the other hand, if there are more dependant people, the labour force will be low. Low labour force means low productivity.

7. *Government Planning and Budgetary provisions.* Government spending would be influenced by the dominant age group. A large number of children would mean the government has to build more schools. If there are aged people, the government would build more old people homes, etc.

II. Occupational Distribution of Population
Occupational distribution of labour refers to the division of the working population into the different types of jobs or occupations they do.

Occupations can be divided into three major categories:

a) *Primary occupations:* These are extractive occupations. They deal directly with the nature. Examples are farming, fishing, mining, quarrying, forestry, etc. Majority of workers in West African countries are in this group.

b) *Secondary occupations:* these are occupations concerned with the transformation of resources provided by the primary occupations (or industries)

c) *Tertiary Occupations:* these are service occupations Examples are transportation, teaching, legal services, banking, insurance, etc.

The structure of the occupation distribution depends on the level of development of the economy. An undeveloped economy would be dominated by primary occupations. A developing economy would be dominated by secondary occupations. Finally, tertiary occupations would be dominant in a developed economy.

III. Sex Distribution of Population:
Sex occupation refers to the classification of the population according to sex i.e. male and female. It indicates the *sex ratio of the population.*

The sex ratio is the defined as the number of males in the population per 1,000 females.

The sex distribution is important because it enables the government to know what the growth rate of the population. If the number of females is high compared or relative to males, there is likely to be a rapid growth of the population in the future. It also gives an indication of the size of the labour force. This is because the higher the number of males in the population the higher will be the labour force, other things being equal.

V. Geographical Distribution of Population

This is the break down or analysis of the population of a country into the different areas where they live. The population of a country cannot be evenly distributed; some areas are thinly populated while some areas are densely population. The geographical distribution of the population depends on physical, historical and economic factors.

1. *Physical Factors:* where the soil and weather and topography of place are amenable and favourable to habitation the more people will settle and live there. The remote desert regions and the swampy rain forest areas of Nigeria for example are thinly populated. On the other hand, areas with arable land and conducive weather conditions attract and retain large population.

2. *Economic factors:* areas endowed with mineral deposits (Warri, Port Harcourt) and those with concentration of commercial and industrial (Lagos, Onitsha) activities attracts people in search of greener opportunities. The fewer these are in any place, the lower the population will be.

3. *Historical factors:* some places are populated because they have been traditional administrative headquarters or commercial centres.

Population, Theories of

1. The Malthusian Theory of Population

In 1798, an English clergyman and economist, Reverend Thomas Malthus, published an essay titled Essay *on the Principle of Population.*

Malthus argued that while population was increasing at a geometric progression (2,4,8,16,32,64, etc), food production was increasing at an arithmetic progression (2,3,4,5,6,7, etc). As a result, a time will come when there will not enough food to feed the population. Malthus' theory *was based on the law of diminishing returns.* There will be food shortages leading to a fall in the standard of living. Malthus argued that population would continue to grow until it was reduced by disasters like war, famine or epidemics. In order to ensure that population does not outgrow the means of subsistence, Malthus suggested *preventive checks.* These preventive checks include birth control and moral restraint i.e. late marriages and restraint by couples from procreation.

Malthus' prediction that population would increase more than food supply leading to a fall in the standard of living of the people did not happen in Britain and other advanced countries. The standard of living did not fall, as Malthus predicted. What was the reason for this?

Why Malthus was proved wrong

a. *Agrarian Revolution.* The first reason was that increase in population was accompanied by increase in food production due to the agrarian revolution that brought about improvements in farming techniques. During the industrial revolution improvement in technology ensured that food production increased faster than increase in population.

POPULATION OF NIGERIA BY STATE AND SEX, 1991 AND 2006					
	1991			2006		
	Male	Female	Total	Male	Female	Total
Abia	1,125,999	1,212,488	2,338,487	1,430,298	1,415,082	2,845,380
Adamawa	1,050,791	1,051,262	2,102,053	1,607,270	1,571,680	3,178,950
Akwa Ibom	1,167,829	1,241,784	2,409,613	1,983,202	1,918,849	3,902,051
Anambra	1,374,671	1,421,804	2,796,475	2,117,984	2,059,844	4,177,828
Bauchi	2,192,423	2,158,584	4,351,007	2,369,266	2,283,800	4,653,066
Bayelsa	-	-	-	874,083	830,432	1,704,515
Benue	1,368,965	1,384,112	2,753,077	2,144,043	2,109,598	4,253,641
Borno	1,296,111	1,239,892	2,536,003	2,163,358	2,007,746	4,171,104
Cross River	956,136	955,161	1,911,297	1,471,967	1,421,021	2,892,988
Delta	1,271,932	1,318,559	2,590,491	2,069,309	2,043,136	4,112,445
Ebonyi	-	-		1,064,156	1,112,791	2,176,947
Edo	1,085,156	1,086,849	2,172,005	1,633,946	1,599,420	3,233,366
Ekiti	-	-	-	1,215,487	1,183,470	2,398,957
Enugu	1,475,648	1,678,732	3,154,380	1,596,042	1,671,795	3,267,837
Gombe	-	-	-	1,244,228	1,120,812	2,365,040
Imo	1,166,448	1,319,187	2,485,635	1,976,471	1,951,092	3,927,563
Jigawa	1,455,780	1,419,745	2,875,525	2,198,076	2,162,926	4,361,002
Kaduna	2,041,141	1,894,477	3,935,618	3,090,438	3,023,065	6,113,503
Kano	2,958,736	2,851,734	5,810,470	4,947,952	4,453,336	9,401,288
Katsina	1,860,658	1,892,475	3,753,133	2,948,279	2,853,305	5,801,584
Kebbi	1,035,723	1,032,767	2,068,490	1,631,629	1,624,912	3,256,541
Kogi	1,039,484	1,108,272	2,147,756	1,672,903	1,641,140	3,314,043
Kwara	773,182	775,230	1,548,412	1,193,783	1,171,570	2,365,353
Lagos	3,010,604	2,714,512	5,725,116	4,719,125	4,394,480	9,113,605
Nassarawa	-	-	-	943,801	925,576	1,869,377
Niger	1,252,466	1,169,115	2,421,581	2,004,350	1,950,422	3,954,772
Ogun	1,147,746	1,185,980	2,333,726	1,864,907	1,886,233	3,751,140
Ondo	1,881,884	1,903,454	3,785,338	1,745,057	1,715,820	3,460,877
Osun	1,043,126	1,115,017	2,158,143	1,734,149	1,682,810	3,416,959
Oyo	1,711,428	1,741,292	3,452,720	2,802,432	2,778,462	5,580,894
Plateau	1,657,209	1,655,203	3,312,412	1,598,998	1,607,533	3,206,531
Rivers	2,239,558	2,069,999	4,309,557	2,673,026	2,525,690	5,198,716
Sokoto	2,208,874	2,261,302	4,470,176	1,863,713	1,838,963	3,702,676
Taraba	759,872	752,291	1,512,163	1,171,931	1,122,869	2,294,800
Yobe	714,729	684,958	1,399,687	1,205,034	1,116,305	2,321,339
Zamfara	-	-	-	1,641,623	1,637,250	3,278,873
FCT Abuja	205,299	166,375	371,674	733,172	673,067	1,406,239
TOTAL	44,529,608	44,462,612	88,992,220	71,345,488	69,086,302	140,431,790

b.   *Discovery of the New World.* The second reason was that new land like America, Africa, New Zealand and Australia were opened up to Europe. The discovery of these areas boosted *international trade* to a new level, leading to increase in the national income of Britain.

c.   *Improvement in transportation.* During the period of industrial revolution gave birth to the steamship and railway system of transportation. This made it possible for movement of produce from the New World.

d.   *Acceptance of smaller families.* The majority chose to have smaller families and use birth control measure without government pressure.

2.   *The Demographic Transition Theory of Population*
According to the demographic transition theory of population, countries go through three stages of demographic patterns based on population changes. This "theory" is *based on the history of Western European countries.* See Demographic Transition Theory.

Portfolio: a collection of investments especially in financial securities.

Portfolio Investment: investment in financial securities such as shares, stocks, bonds and money market instruments by foreign investors primarily for financial returns as opposed to ownership and control of factors of production. Foreign portfolio investors are attracted to countries with low interest and tax rates as well as strong exchange rates.

Positive Economics: non-prescriptive Economics which is concerned only with the facts as opposed to Normative Economics which is involved with value judgement of good or bad and right or wrong.

Power of Attorney: the right of one person to act in the place of another person as specified in a deed.

Precautionary Motive: the desire to hold money for contingency or unforeseen circumstances. Such circumstances include accidents, major breakdown of one's vehicle, etc. see Demand for Money

Preference Shares: shares whose holders have a prior or preferred claim to share of profits before ordinary shareholders. Preference share are paid a fixed rate (e.g. 5% of the value of the shares) of dividend after debenture holders, if any are issued. In the event of winding, they are also paid before ordinary shareholders. However, they are not entitled to vote at ordinary meetings of the company.

Types:

1.   *Cumulative Preference Share:* where a company is unable to make dividend payment, dividend of cumulative preference shareholders accrue and are carried forward till they are paid.

2.   *Participating Preference Shares:* this type participate with ordinary shareholders in sharing of dividend after receiving their fixed dividend.

3.   *Redeemable Preference Shares:* these shares are subject to be redeemed or bought back at a specified future time.

Premium: 1. the payment made in respect of an insurance or assurance policy. 2.

Financial securities—shares, stocks, certificates, etc—may be issued or traded below (discount) or above (premium) their par value at stock exchange.

Preventive Checks: moral restraint i.e. late marriages and smaller families to control the growth of population as advocated by Rev. Thomas Malthus.

Price: the amount which must be paid for the exchange of a commodity; the amount agreed by the buyer and seller as the value of commodity in competitive market situation. Classical economists held a labour theory of value, which based the value of a commodity on labour cost expended in its production. This gave rise to the concepts of value-in-use and value-in-exchange. This view was modified by the neoclassical economics' concept of price as being determined by marginal utility of the commodity to the consumer.

Price Control: official intervention in the market to control inflation by imposing a ceiling on price movements. If the price imposed is below the equilibrium price a shortage will arise.

Price Determination: how the value of commodity is established. In a free market system this is through the interaction of the forces of demand and supply in the market. otherwise, the price may be imposed by a central planning authority.

Price Discrimination: where a firm sells the same good at different prices in different markets for reasons which are not associated with cost. Price discrimination is used in order to increase profit by decreasing consumers' surplus.

Price Effect: the effect of a change in price. This may result in a Substitution Effect (i.e. commodity A being substituted for commodity B due to a rise in the price of B), and an Income Effect (i.e. increase in real income due to a fall in price of a good).

Price Elasticity of Demand (PED): a measure of the responsiveness of demand to changes in price; that is how demand is affected when price rise or fall. Mathematically, PED is expressed as percentage change in demand/parentage change in price. PED is categorized as follows:

Price System, The: in a market economy, the interaction of the forces of demand and supply to determine prices; obtains in a capitalist economic system in which the basic economic decisions (what, how, and for whom to produce) are determined by the free interaction of buyers and sellers.

Primary Industry: extractive industry e.g. mining, forestry, agriculture, etc. the higher the level of development of an economy, the lower the value of primary production as a percentage of national output. Compare Secondary and Tertiary Industries

Prime Costs: all costs of production which varies with output. It is the total of direct labour, direct material and direct material costs.

Private Company: private enterprise; a limited liability company which subjects transfer of its shares to approval by other shareholders or its directors. It is thus referred to as a closed company. 1. A minimum of two members can form a private company with a maximum of fifty; 2. Shares of a private company cannot be freely transferred or sold without consulting the other shareholders; 3. A private company may not publish its accounts; 4. Its shares cannot be listed of the Stock Exchange; 5. Its name ends with Limited (Ltd). Compare *public company* and *public corporation.*

Private Placement: this is when a company raises capital by offering its shares to a group of investors e.g. merchant banks, insurance companies, mutual funds/unit trust, pension funds, etc. A private placement contrasts with a public issue, which may be carried out through an initial public offer, offer for sale, or offer for subscription

Privatization: The selling-off of government-owned enterprises to private owners. This is usually as part of economic reforms seeking to reduce the role of government in direct business activities. The intention is to bring about efficiency of resource use.

Privatization, which became a dominant feature of economic reforms worldwide in the 1980s, is one of the legacies of Margaret Thatcher, Prime Minister of Great Britain, between 1979 and 1991. Many industries were nationalized—Telecoms, Iron & Steel, Coal, Railway, Aerospace, Ship-building, etc—by the Labour Party after WWII. By the late 1970s, however, the British economy was under-performing and many these industries were making and depending on government subvention. Margaret Thatcher divested government interest from these businesses in order to make them more accountable and profitable. It was part of an overall effort to improve the performance of the economy by greater reliance on market forces. According to her ". . . to create a genuine market in a state you have to take the state out of the market."

Privatization in Nigeria
Privatization was a key feature of the Structural Adjustment Program initiated in 1986. Inefficiency of government owned enterprises have resulted in waste of scarce resources as they have not been able to sustain themselves but rather have become dependent on government subvention and subsidies for survival. The austere economic situation in the 1980s forced a re-think of development strategy from a government or public-sector led to a private sector-led development strategy. Lean government finances meant that the government could no longer continue to sustain its enterprises. Government therefore decided to sell off to private investors. Consequently, privatization, along with commercialization, was introduced as part of the Structural Adjustment Programme in 1986. The Technical Committee on Privatization and Commercialization, TCPC (later renamed the Bureau of Public Enterprises, BPE) undertook the first phase of the programme. The government divested all its interest from enterprises in competitive markets such as banks, insurance, vehicle assembly, oil marketing, cement manufacturing, steel, etc.

Beginning in 1989, the following three phases of the privatization program can be identified:

Phase I—divestment of government interest in privatization of banks, oil marketing and cement companies;

Phase II—divestment of government interest in hotels, insurance companies, vehicle assembly and parts, etc.; and

Phase III—divesture from electric power, telecommunications, ports and rails, oil and gas.

Flour Mills of Nigeria became the first government-owned enterprise to be privatized by the Federal Government of Nigeria in 1989.

The objectives of Privatization include the following:

1. *To strengthen the role of the private sector* in the economy through job creation and economic development. The private sector is a critical partner in the development of the economy. Privatizing public corporation helps to increase the capacity of the private sector.

2. *To improve the public sector's financial health* through stoppage of payment of subventions. The financial position of the government is improved with the stoppage of payment of subventions to the privatized organizations.

3. *To make more resources available for infrastructural development and social services:* for allocation to other important sectors activity such as education, health, housing, transportation, and other infrastructure development initiatives. More money is now available to the government for it to use for infrastructural development and social services.

4. *Improved service delivery:* Under private management, the customer is king, and the private business owner knows the consumer has a choice, he therefore continuously innovate to stay ahead of the competition.

5. *Efficient utilization of scarce resources*: under private ownership, management is more purposeful and discipline is strictly enforced among staff. A private business man knows

he has competition in the market; he therefore strives to minimize his losses and maximize his profit by efficiently managing the other inputs of production.

While privatization turned some loss making parastatals into profit making organizations, the same cannot be said for all.

Product Differentiation: acts like advertising and branding purpose of which is to make buyers believe that a product is superior to that being offered by competitors. Product differentiation is a feature of an imperfect market structure e.g. monopolistic competition.

Production: the creation of utility. Any economic activity with the aim of satisfying human want; the transformation of inputs into output of goods and services. The process of production is not complete until the good reaches the final consumer.

Producer's Surplus: a producer's gain from being able to sell at a price above his reservation price. There is a producer's surplus when the equilibrium price is above the least price the producer is willing to accept (reservation price).

Production Possibilities: Levels of output which a country/firm can produce given the level of technology and resources at its disposal at a given point time.

Production Possibility Curve (Frontier): Also known as *transformation curve*; is the curve which shows the best possible combinations of output which can be produced at any point in time given available *resources and technology*.

Features of the PPC
—It is drawn on a graph, with a commodity each on the x – and y-axes respectively.
—The boundary of the curve is defined by the amount of resources and technology available.

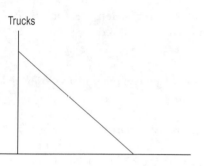

Trucks

Cars

Production Possibilities	Cars	Trucks
K	35	30
L	20	45
M	5	50

Cars

The more resources and technology available, the more production possibilities there will be (i.e. the more the country will be able to

produce), shifting the boundary or curve outward. If, on the other hand, resources and/or technology are reduced, production possibilities will be reduced, shifting the curve inward.

—Three sets of points can be identified: points within the curve, points on the curve and points outside the curve.

—*Points within the curve* (e.g. P and Q) denote *inefficient* combination of resources and technology; production is at sub-optimal or inefficient level.

—*Points on the curve* (e.g., R) denote the best possible combination of resources and technology. These are *efficient* points; production is at optimal level.

—*Points outside the curve* (e.g., T) denote *desirable but not feasible points*, given the resources and technology available *today*. The country might be able to produce at those points when more resources and/or technology become available sometime in the future

Production Possibilities	Cars	Trucks
K	35	30
L	20	45
M	5	50

The slope of the PPC is known as the *marginal rate of transformation, (MRT)*. The PPC slopes downward, from left to right; it has a negative slope. This is because opportunity cost is involved in moving from one combination to another: the more of one commodity that is produced, the less of the other is produced. If we want to produce more cash crops, we have to sacrifice some food crops, and vice versa. The slope of the PPC may be a straight line indicating a constant slope. In this case, the opportunity cost of moving from one production possibility to another is the same. However, it is usually *concave,* indicating increasing opportunity or marginal cost. This is because as more of a good is produced, its opportunity cost *rises* as shown in the table below.

In order to produce 15 more cars at point L, 5 trucks must be given up. That is, the opportunity cost of 15 more cars is 5 trucks. But to.produce at point K, 15 trucks must be given up in order to produce 15 more cars, due to *increasing marginal cost.*

Production Sharing Contract (PSC): an oil exploration contract—first used in Indonesia—designed to transfer exploration risks and funding of exploration and development efforts on new acreage to interested oil companies. Under a PSC, the Nigerian National Petroleum Corporation (NNPC) engages a competent contractor, such as Chevron, to carry out petroleum operations on NNPC's wholly held acreage. The contractor undertakes the initial exploration risks and recovers its costs if and when oil is discovered and extracted. The PSC was introduced in Nigeria in 1993, in view of challenges of government meeting its funding obligations (cash calls) in the Joint Operating Agreement (JOA) with international oil companies; and has been credited with the attraction of foreign investment into the sector.

Profit and Loss Account: an account in which is drawn up to determine the profit or loss made by a business during a period. Sales are credited while and expenses are debited. A debit balance means profit and a credit balance means loss.

Profiteer: a business person only concerned with profits; a person who takes undue advantage of market situation to exploit consumers by charging exorbitant prices.

Profits: return to the factor which bear the risk of production i.e. enterprise/ entrepreneur. The excess of total (TR) revenue over total cost (TC).

Pro-Forma Invoice: see under commercial Documents

Progressive Tax System: a tax whose rate increases as the size of income increases. For example, the rate of tax is 10% for an income of N10, 000.00 but 20% for an income of N20, 000.00. See table below—

Tax Payers	Income ₦	Progressive Tax (Tax rate)	Tax paid ₦
A	30,000.00	15%	4,500.00
B	20,000.00	10%	2,000.00
C	10,000.00	5%	500.00

Promissory Note: an unconditional promise made by one person to another in writing to a pay certain sum on demand or at certain future date a certain sum in money to or to the order of a specified person or bearer. See Bill of Exchange.

Promoter: the person who does the preliminary work necessary to form or finance a company.

Proportional Tax System: a tax which takes the same percentage or proportion of a tax payer income irrespective of the size of income. See example below—

Tax Payers	Income =N=	Proportional Tax (Tax rate)	Tax paid =N=
A	30,000.00	10%	3,000.00
B	20,000.00	10%	2,000.00
C	10,000.00	10%	1,000.00

Propensity to Consume: see Marginal Propensity to Consume (MPC).

Prospectus: A document prepared by a company for circulation to prospective investors. It details the company's history, its business and finances in the present and its prospects in the years ahead. It must be prepared in conformity with provisions of the Companies and Allied Matters Act and legislations and regulations relating to the Stock Exchange.

Proposal Form: A form in which an interested person (proposer) applies for an insurance policy fills out required information.

Proxy: someone who is nominated by a shareholder to represent and vote on his behalf at a meeting of shareholders e.g. an Annual General Meeting.

Public Company: a private enterprise; a limited liability company which can invite the public to subscribe to its shares. Its features include 1. It can be formed by a minimum of two shareholders without an upper limit; 2. Shares can be listed on the Stock Exchange, 3. Shares can be traded without notice to other shareholders.4. It must publish its annual accounts. 5. Its name ends with PLC.

Public Enterprise or Corporation: government-owned places of production. They are set-up to maximize welfare of the people not to make profit. Examples are Nigerian Television Authority, NTA; Nigerian National Petroleum Corporation, NNPC; Federal Radio Corporation of Nigeria, FRCN.

Features
1. Establishment: They are established by a law or statute. Thus, they are also known as statutory corporations.
2. Ownership: The government provides the capital for the business. Thus they are sometimes referred to as parastatals.
3. Aim: the aim of setting up a public corporation is to maximize public welfare by providing essential services.
4. Control: The business is controlled by a *board of directors* appointed by the government.
5. *Capital:* The government provides start-up capital for the operation of a public corporation.
6. *Legal Entity:* A public corporation is a person in law, with rights and responsibilities. It is separate from its owners and workers. It can sue and be sued in its own name.
7. *Risks:* The risks of the business are borne by the government and tax-payers.

Reason for Government Ownership of Public Corporations
1. *Huge Capital:* public services require a huge amount of capital that is beyond what private business can afford.
2. *Non-Profit Motive:* private business cannot provide public services at affordable rates. Only the government can provide these services at subsidized rates that majority of the populace can afford.

3. *Economic Development:* Public services are critical to economic development, thus the government need to provide them so that economic development and industrialization can be promoted.

4. *Sensitive and Strategic Services:* services rendered are of strategic importance to the society and the government. The society cannot afford to have private business people handle airports and seaports, for example lest they fall into foreign or criminal and unpatriotic hands.

5. *Avoidance of Duplication:* certain services are better handled by a monopoly otherwise wastage of scarce resources may result through unneeded duplication.

6. *To Raise the Standard of Living:* the more people who enjoy pipe borne water, electricity and telephone services provided by public corporations, the higher the standard of living of society.

Advantage of Public Corporations

1. *Higher Standard of living:* the people enjoy a higher standard of living with the provision of essential services like electricity, telecommunications, pipe-borne water, etc.

2. *Economic Development:* Public corporations provide infrastructure and social capital that are essential for economic development because they make it easier for private businesses to operate. Without public corporations, private business will find it more expensive to operate.

3. *Affordable Rates:* The generality of the people can enjoy essential services because they are provided by public corporations.

4. *Avoidance of private monopoly:* private monopolies might result if essential services are not provided by public corporations.

5. *Avoidance of foreign domination of strategic* services e.g. power supply, telecommunications, etc is avoided as the government exercise control through public corporations.

6. *Avoidance of waste of capital resources.* Duplication of scarce capital resources by several private businesses is avoided as essential services are provided by a public corporation.

Disadvantages of Public Corporations

1. Political interference: people are appointed to the board of directors because of their political connections not because of their qualifications. Also, most employees get their positions because they are relatives of board members rather than on their qualifications. Contracts may be awarded based on political considerations. All this lead to inefficiencies and waste of resources.

2. *Lack of Competition:* Public corporations are monopolies because they have no competition or rival companies providing the same service. This causes poor attitude to work by workers and managers which gives rise to wrong attitude to work, nonchalance and indiscipline which further leads to waste of resources.

3. *Corruption and Misappropriation of funds:* most time managers and workers use their positions to enrich themselves through stealing and misappropriation of public funds.

4. *Bureaucracy:* public corporations have to work with government ministries. This mean they have to follow civil

rules and regulations often leading to costly delays in decision making and necessary action.

Problems of Public Corporations

Public corporations have become places where scarce resources are inefficiently utilized and wasted, due to the following reasons:

1. *Political influences:* political considerations and factors most times influence decisions and actions of public corporations instead of the market or demands of the customer. For example, projects are justified by political factors rather than economic considerations; there is usually overstaffing due to political patronage, etc.

2. *Corruption and embezzlement of funds:* people who are appointed to head public enterprises often see their appointment as an opportunity to enrich themselves by stealing funds meant for the corporations.

3. *Parasitism*: Almost all public corporations in Nigeria, before commercialization of their operations, failed to sustain themselves by generating funds for their operations. Instead they depend on government subventions even to pay their salaries and other running expenses. Public corporations thereby become parasites of government.

4. *Poor services*, arrogance/insensitivity to customers by managers and staff. Almost without exception the quality of service of public corporations is deplorable, leaving a lot to be desired. The workers do not feel the need to improve the quality of their work by responding to customers' needs as they receive their salary no matter what.

5. *Nepotism/Ethnicism* in hiring, discipline and reward system: public corporations are managed by political appointees who most times are not qualified for their positions. These people in turn appoint their relatives and friends as staff and contractors. This leads to poor work ethics in the work place as workers careless about their job responsibilities.

6. *Diseconomies of scale* due to bureaucracy and red-tape: business processes and actions are slowed down by long delays in decision-taking. This is because series of approval is required to do almost everything. For example, public corporations often have to get approval from their supervising ministries before they can make any move. This causes failure to do the right thing at the right time leading to corporate ineffectiveness.

Public Limited Liability Company	Private Limited Liability Company
Minimum of 7 shareholders	Minimum of 2 shareholders
No maximum of shareholders	Maximum of 50 shareholders
Name ends with Public liability Company (PLC)	Name ends with Limited (LTD)
Can raise capital by issuing or selling shares and debentures to members of the public	Can raise capital by issuing or selling shares and debentures only to members of the company
Its shares can be transferred or sold freely from one person to another	Its shares cannot by transferred without consent or approval of the members of the company

It must publish its accounts	It is not required to publish its accounts
Its shares may be listed for trading on the Stock Exchange	Its shares cannot be listed for trading on the Stock Exchange

Public Corporation	Public Company
Government ownership	Ownership by private individuals
Set-up to maximize public welfare	Set-up to make profit
Established by statute or Act of Parliament	Registered by the Corporate Affairs Commission
Capital is provided by the government	Capital is provided by members.
Ownership not open to the public	Ownership open to any member of the public

Public Issue: offer of shares by a company to the public for subscription in order to raise capital. Only a public company can make a public issue. Public issue may byway of Offer for Subscription or Offer for Sale. A private company can raise capital by Private Placement.

Public Relations: the task of ensuring that an organization is perceived or seen in the most favourable terms by its stakeholders—customers, shareholders, creditors, debtors, government and its agencies, and the general public. The aim of public relations is the branding or image making and favourable positioning of the organization in the minds of the public. The essence is to ensure that customers and others see the company as responsible, trustworthy, reliable, ethical, professional etc and associate these attributes with the company's products and services.

Media of Public Relations: the entrenchment of favourable impression in the mind of the public is carried out using various media

1. Trade Fairs: participation in trade fairs at which the public is enlightened and informed on the activities of the company in a relaxed atmosphere.

2. Exhibitions: these are organized special events used by organizations to display their products and enlighten the public about its services. It affords the company an opportunity to interact with customers from whom they may obtain valuable feedback. Exhibitions are usually organized for particular line of products e.g. agricultural equipment, motor vehicle spare parts, etc.

3. Sponsorship of social programs: some corporate organizations sponsor 'talent hunt', such as Project Fame, 'Nigeria Got Talent' as a way of portraying the organization in good light.

4. Gifts: companies often distribute items such as cups, note pads, pens, key holders, T-shirts branded in the companies' colours and logo to the customers and others. These items serve to entrench the image of a company in the in the mind of the public positively.

5. Corporate Social Responsibility projects: a company may decide to tar a road, build a hostel in a school, renovate and decorate roundabout.

Purchase Day Book: in book-keeping a book where purchases are entered. It is not part of the double entry.

Purchasing Power Parity: the exchange rate at which prices in two countries are equal. For example, if a basket of goods which costs $1.00 in the United States of America are bought for N450.00, then the exchange rate between the two currencies is $1.00 = N450.00.

The PPP is often different from the current exchange rate. It is useful in expressing incomes and prices in a common currency for the purpose of comparing living standards in different countries

Q

Qualified Acceptance: a person to whom a contract offer is made, i.e. an offeree, may vary the terms of an offer e.g. by inserting a condition.

Qualitative Controls: in addition to measures that seek to control credit availability generally, the government may use qualitative measures to direct credit to particular sectors or industries.

Quantity Theory Of Money: The theory that there is a direct relationship between the supply of money in the economy and the price level. Any increase in the quantity of money in the economy (money supply), will bring about an equal increase in the price of goods and services, if it is not accompanied by an increase in the quantity of goods and services. Denoted by the formula, $MV=PT$; where $M=$ supply of money; $V=$ velocity of circulation; Price$=$ price level; quantity of goods. Propounded by Professor Irving Fisher.

Quasi-Rent: economic rent as it applies to a factor of production other than land i.e. the amount

Quesnay Francois (1694-1774): French economist, whose book *"Tableau Economique"* published 1758, was the first to explain the economic system analytically, and provided the foundational basis for the Physiocrats school of thought. Quesnay was a proponent of free private enterprise with minimal state interference or regulations i.e.

laissez-faire, a term he originated. He is also credited with the notion of the equilibrium, the distinction between fixed and working capital and the subsistence theory of wages.

Questionnaire: a document, containing questions, used to gather information in survey or research.

Quick Assets: highly liquid assets or those that can quickly be converted to cash.

Quorum: the minimum number of members that must be present before a meeting can validly hold. The quorum is stated in the Articles of Association for a company or Partnership Deed in the case of a partnership.

Quotation: 1. a statement of the price for a supply of goods.
2. A public company may apply to the Stock Exchange for the listing of its shares for trading on the floor of the Stock Exchange. If the company fulfills the Listing Requirement, it will be able raise capital from general public.

Quoted Company: a public company whose shares are listed for trading on the Stock Exchange.

Quotas: 1. a quantitative limit imposed by a country on the amount of a commodity that can be imported into a country in a time period. Quotas are an alternative to tariffs, and may be imposed to reduce imports in order to correct an adverse balance of trade position or to protect local industries. 2. In an imperfect market, cartels, like the Organization for Petroleum Exporting Country (OPEC), often try influence price in their favour by limiting market supply by imposing a maximum amount of output that a member may produce or supply.

Quoted Company: a company whose shares are listed for trading on the stock exchange.

Only the shares of a public company can be listed. A private company must first convert to a public company before it can apply for listing on the stock exchange.

Quotation: a statement of price for a particular order. A buyer may request a quotation from a seller prior to making a firm order.

R

Range: a measure of dispersion; the difference between the highest and lowest scores in a distribution. It is highly affected by extreme values. Given a distribution/set of values, e.g. 7, 8, 20, 11, 15, 3, 17, the range is the range is the difference between 3, the lowest, and 20, the highest, i. e, 20 − 3 = 17.

Rand: monetary unit of the Republic of South Africa. It is subdivided into 100 cents.

Rate of Return: income on investment expressed as a percentage.

Real Cost: cost expressed in terms of what is forgone in order to have or produce something. If a man decides to buy a house instead of a car, the real cost of the house is the car, not the monetary cost or price of the house. Also referred to as *opportunity cost.*

Real Income: the actual goods and services that money/nominal income can buy. If a person's money (or nominal) income increase by 20% but the prices of goods and services by increase by 25%, his real income has actually fallen by 5%.

Real Estate: freehold land with buildings on it.

Real Investment: the actual production of an of capital—buildings, machinery, fixtures and fittings, trucks—as opposed to investment in a financial asset such as shares, stocks, bonds, etc.

Real Terms: the expression of an economic concept in actual as opposed to nominal or monetary terms. The value of an amount of money in real terms is the amount of goods and services it can buy. Thus an increase in monetary value may only be nominal not real, if the same or less goods and services due to fall in the value of money i.e. inflation.

Real Wages: wages expressed in terms of actual purchasing power i.e. goods and services the money or nominal wages can buy. Money or nominal wages may increase while real wages decrease due to inflation.

Rebate: a quantity discount or reduction in price given, for example, in order to encourage purchase of a large quantity. Contrast *cash discount* given as an incentive for prompt payment.

Receipt: evidence of payment; a written acknowledgement of something received.

Recession: a decline or fall in economic activity. It is characterized by low aggregate demand, low investment, fall in national output, negative economic growth resulting in unemployment. Fiscal and monetary policies may be used to stimulate or reflate the economy at such times but this may be at the risk of inflation.

Reciprocity: principle of *quid pro quo* or doing-as-you-are-done-by which usually underline international trade agreements between countries.

Reconciliation Statement, Bank: the Cash Book and Bank Statement balances may be different, at times. This may be due to cheques which have been entered in the cash book but not yet presented at the bank for payment; cheques that paid into the bank account but not yet entered in the Cash Book; bank Standing Orders not yet entered in the Cash Book; Bank charges not yet entered in the Cash Book, etc. A Reconciliation Statement is made out to agree or reconcile balances in the Cash Book and Bank Account statement.

Reconstruction of a Company: restructuring of the long-term capital base of a company carried out for the purpose of (a) increasing the capital of the company; (b) as part of plans for merger with another company or (c) to avoid liquidation and continue as a going concern. It may entail capitalization of reserves, necessitating the issue of bonus shares to shareholders; conversion of long-term debt capital (debentures) into ordinary shares; writing off accumulated losses; consolidation of the share capital into smaller quantity of greater unit value (e.g. from 100,000 units of 0.50k each to 50,000 units of N1.00 each) or splits into larger quantity of lesser unit value.

Redeemable Preference Shares: a class of shares having prior claim to dividend over ordinary shares, and which may be bought back or redeemed at a fixed date in the future.

Re-distribution of Income: where government thinks there is a high degree of income inequality, taxation is designed to be progressive i.e. higher income groups pay more tax than lower income groups, and the proceeds are used to provide services that benefit lower income groups.

Re-exports: (also known as entrepot trade): Goods imported into a country and exported to other countries without further processing. A member of a free trade area, with lower tariff than other members of the free trade area, may find it profitable to engage in re-exportation to other members of the free trade area. Re-export are not counted as part of a country's exports in international trade.

Reflation: the easing of credit restrictions in order to expand production and/or stimulating aggregate demand which may be carried out using fiscal or monetary policies. This may be necessary during a period of economic recession. Increasing government expenditure and reducing interest rates are steps to boost purchasing power and investment. The downside is a risk of inflation.

Regional Unemployment: the number of people within an area who are willing and able to work but who are cannot find one.

Regressive Tax: a tax whose rate decreases for higher levels of income. The higher the income, the lower the tax rate.

Tax Payer	Income N	Regressive Tax (Tax rate)	Tax paid N
A	30,000.00	5%	1,500.00
B	20,000.00	15%	3,000.00
C	10,000.00	20%	2,000.00

Regulations: administrative rules, restrictions and guidelines that moderate the behaviour of economic agents. They impact on the degree of competition, ownership structure in certain industry, and prices charged, etc. Examples are minimum wages, utility tariff rates, licensing, output quotas, standards prescriptions, safety standards, disclosure requirements, specifications prescription, etc.

Rationale for regulations include the market failure e.g. in specification of emission standards; the need to avoid duplication of resources, for example, as the basis for natural monopolies; check potential power, as the basis for anti-trust legislations, which limits the amount of market share one supplier can have; protection of public/consumers/investors e.g. in disclosure requirements for prospectuses, financial statements and labeling of drugs, etc.; economic development strategy e.g. foreign ownership was restricted in certain industries under the indigenization decrees in Nigeria.

The nature of an industry may necessitate a high level of regulation. Financial services, e.g. banking, is highly regulated e.g. a license is required for entry, disclosure requirements are specified, they are subject to inspections by the monetary authorities and appointment of key officers is subject to oversight approval. Broadcasting, telecommunications, port services, aviation, and power are example of industries with high level regulation usually with a government having regulatory oversight over market participants.

Regulations may stiffen competition and innovation and unduly empower officials with discretionary powers over economic agents. Economic reforms have often translated to mean deregulation i.e. the reduction of regulations in order to promote competition.

Reinsurance: the transfer of a risk by an insurer to another insurer in order to reduce the weight of a loss. An insurance company shares the liability of large risks such as an aircraft or ocean vessel by re-insuring it with another insurance company, a reinsurance company. Reinsurance companies are big insurance companies in which insurance companies insure their risks. In Nigeria, insurance companies were required by law to reinsure 20 per cent of their policies with the Nigeria Reinsurance Corporation before it was privatized.

Remittances: money sent back home to country of origin by foreign workers. Remittances have proven increasingly significant in the national accounts of developing countries. Increasing remittances reflect high emigration and the impact of currency devaluation.. Remittances from the diaspora have become increasingly important source of foreign exchange, in some cases surpassing development aid in developing countries, helping to reduce the severity of poverty by impacting on entrepreneurship and small business investment, health and education expenditures, etc. According to World Bank data, Nigeria rank among the top ten recipients of remittances in 2012 with formal remittances amounting to 7.7 per cent of Gross Domestic Product and 50 per cent of Central Bank of Nigeria's foreign reserves.

Renminbi: an alternative term for the Chinese currency, the yuan.

Rent: the return to land as a factor of production. Contrast *Economic Rent*.

Reserve Currency: a foreign currency held by a government or its central bank as part of its reserve. Currencies of dominant economic powers have widely been used by many countries from the British sterling to the United States dollar, the Euro and increasingly, the Chinese yuan.

Reserve Price: price below which a seller is not ready to sell.

Reserve Ratio: the fraction of a bank's deposit it is required to hold as reserve. The central bank may vary this ratio according to its monetary policy objectives at any point in time.

Reserve Requirement: Regulations set by the Central Bank governing the minimum amount of reserve banks must hold against deposits.

Reserves: a country's accumulation of foreign exchange; part of a company's profits not distributed to shareholders. A company may build up its reserves to finance expansion or it may ultimately be capitalized and issued to shareholders as bonus shares.

Residual Payment: payment received by the entrepreneur for his contribution to production after meeting all payments to other factors of production.

Residual Unemployment: unemployment due the physical or mental challenges.

Resources: inputs used in production or factors of production. These are categorized into land, labour, capital and enterprise. They are also referred to as inputs.

Retail Trade: the final link of the distribution of goods that deals directly with the final consumer; the business carried out by the retailer, who connects the wholesaler to the consumer. He buys from the wholesaler and sells in smaller quantities to the consumer.

Characteristics of the Retail Trade:

Small capital requirement: the retail trade has the lowest capital requirement to start as a business.

Direct contact with the final customer: The retailer deal directly with the final user of the product and this puts him in a position to provide valuable feedback to the manufacturer through the wholesaler.

Stocking of a Variety of Brands: The retailer hardly specializes in the sale of one brand. Instead, in the retailer's shop are a wide variety of brands under one roof.

Classification of Retailers:

1. Large-scale retailers:
    a. Multiple or Chain Stores: These are regional or national network of megastores or chain stores under a central management. They are able to avoid the wholesaler by directly importing and/or buy directly from local manufacturers, and thereby able to offer very low discount prices to the consumer. They have large warehouses of their own. Most outlets are hypermarkets with large expanses of land, offering a multitude of brands— from electronics, furniture, kitchenware, to apparel/ fashion—under one roof in distinct sections or departments, located in central part of a city. A self-service system is used. Examples are Wal-mart, Game, Shoprite, and Spar.

2. Mail order/Online Retailers: mail order retailers receive orders through the telephone and postal systems and deliver on cash-on-delivery (C.O.D) terms to customers who make orders from catalogues. Mail order retailing have become increasingly dominated and influenced by the internet and electronic commerce systems such as online advertising and electronic payments. Orders are now almost entirely placed via websites on the internet.

3. Specialty Stores: These retailers specialize on one or few brands. For example, Wrangler brand of jeans

4. Middle-scale retailers: These are stand-alone supermarkets that typically occupy a whole floor of a building, a fraction of the floor area of a chain store, and offer a limited variety of brands. They are usually owner operated.

5. Small-scale retailers: micro-retail neighbourhood stores, Road-side traders, Hawkers etc.

Functions of the Retailers: see under Distributive Trade:

Returns: profit; reward for production.

Revealed Preference: The idea that a person's choices are revealed by his actual decisions or actions, not his words or thoughts. Revealed preference is one of the concepts used to explain consumer demand, alongside the ordinal and cardinal approaches. According to this approach, in order to determine a consumer's demand, it is sufficient to compare his decisions under situations with different prices and/ or incomes, assuming consistency in his decisions.

Revenue Allocation in Nigeria: Receipts into the Federation Account are shared among the three tiers of government according to a formula set by the Revenue Mobilization Allocation and Fiscal Commission (RMAFC). The Federal Government has always received the lion share of allocation varying between 55% (1981) and 52.68% (1992). In the same period, the States' share has fallen from 30.5% to 26.72%. Local governments' share rose from 10% in 1981 to 20.60% in 1992.

The States' share is divided among the states on the basis of certain factors. These include:

1. *Population*: the higher the population of a state the higher its share of the federation account.

2. *Equality/Minimum Responsibility of Government/National Interest*: All states receive a certain equal amount on the basis that all governments have a minimum responsibility to her citizens.

3. *Federal Presence*: the higher the level of Federal government presence in a state in the form of industry, agriculture, infrastructure, etc, the lower the allocation to a state.

4. *Social Development*: social development is measured on the basis of primary school enrolment: the higher the number of children enrolled in primary school, the higher the revenue.

5. *Even Development*: on the basis of this factor, revenue is shared to encourage even development of states.

6. *Derivation*: the higher the revenue derived from a state, the higher its share of allocation.

7. *Fiscal Effort*: the higher the ratio of internally generated revenue to total

revenue to total recurrent revenue, the higher its share.

The balance on the Federation Account after allocation to the three tiers of government is shared among Federal Capital Territory Development Fund, Ecology Fund, National Reserve Fund and Agriculture, Solid Minerals Development/Technical Research Fund.

RMAFC: Revenue Mobilization, Allocation and Fiscal Commission

Ricardo, David (1772-1823). Born in London, Ricardo had a successful financial career. Ricardo wrote several influential pamphlets on economic issues of his day, particularly on taxation and commercial policy, (developing the theory of comparative advantage as a basis for international trade). In 1817 he published his major work, *Principles of Political Economy and Taxation*. Smith, Malthus and Ricardo are generally regarded as the main members of the classical school of economics.

Rights Issue: new shares offered to existing shareholders of a company in proportion to their existing shareholding at a discount to the current share price. Shareholders need not take up their rights to the new shares, and may sell all or part to a willing buyer, in which case their shareholding is diluted proportionately.

S

Saving(s): forgone consumption; the part of income set aside for the future. It is the act of setting aside of a part of present income for future use. The level of saving is determined by size of income, interest rates, custom, and stability of the general price level among others. Savings are pooled by financial intermediaries (banks, insurance companies, etc) to make funds available for investment; thus the higher the rate of savings, the higher the amount of money available for investment.

A low level of saving means low level of long-term funds required for investment and development and greater reliance on foreign capital.

A high level of saving is therefore a key objective for long-term economic sustainable growth and development. Pension and insurance are major sources of pooling and availing savings for investment. Insurance and pension companies are institutional investors active in the capital markets.

Saving Function: The relationship between saving and income. It gives savings for every level of income.

Given by the expression, consumption function, $C = a + bY$

Then, saving function is $S = - a + (1 - b)Y$;

where a refers to autonomous consumption; b refers to marginal propensity to consume (MPC) and Y, income.

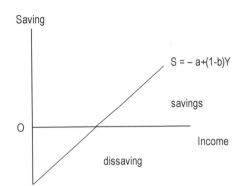

Say's Laws of Markets: principle of classical economics popularized and named after French economist Jean-Baptiste Say (1767-1832). The principle states that every product creates its own demand as the expenses incurred in its production are incomes by workers to be used for purchases. This notion was unchallenged until Keynesian economics after the Great Depression in the 1930s, when John Maynard Keynes forced a re-think with publication of the *General Theory of Employment, Interest and Money* in 1936.

Scale of Preference: an ordered list of wants arranged in the order of importance or preference. It is necessitated by the scarcity of resources relative to wants. A scale of preference is used by households, firms and governments to effectively allocate resources between alternatives uses.

Scarcity: limited in supply. The fact that resources or means of production are not enough relative to the wants or ends that they are used to satisfy is the central problem in Economics. Scarcity of resources necessitates the need to make a choice of the wants to satisfy.

Second-Tier Foreign Exchange Market (SFEM): a mechanism for market determination of the exchange rate of the Naira under the Structural Adjustment Program in Nigeria in established September 1986. The SFEM-determined rate was applied to all transactions except a few such as the rate used in external debt repayment/servicing and obligations to international organizations. The rate for such transactions was administratively determined at the first-tier Foreign Exchange Market. The objectives of SFEM were to (i) enable the Naira to find its true value (ii) to achieve a more optimal allocation of foreign exchange (iii) gradually eliminate the parallel market, and (iv) attract inflow of foreign capital including funds held abroad by Nigerians; eliminate the vices associated with the import license regime.

SFEM comprised of a tender session organized under the CBN, an inter-bank foreign exchange market and over-the-counter between banks and their customers.

The SFEM was a weekly session at which authorized dealers—mainly banks—bid for foreign exchange under guidelines set by the CBN. At the end of the session a market-clearing rate is arrived at. This market clearing rate becomes the exchange rate to be used by the banks in buying and selling foreign exchange from and to their customers until the next bidding session.

Under SFEM, the naira depreciated 66 percent to ₦1.56 = US$1, and the slide has continued since. In 1987, the first and second-tier were merged in a reconstituted Foreign Exchange Market, (FEM) at ₦3.74: $1.00.

The essence of the SFEM mechanism was the determination of a realistic value of the naira which has been deemed over-valued vis-à-vis the underlying economy. This was partly in response to the fundamental balance of payment disequilibrium at the time as well as the long-term objective of encouraging the development of the export and non-oil sector.

The SFEM became the beginning of an evolving process in pursuit of the objective of a market—determined exchange rate for the naira. This process has seen the transition from SFEM to FEM (1987), the Autonomous Foreign Exchange Market, AFEM (1995) and Inter-Bank Foreign Exchange Market, IFEM (1999), the Wholesale Dutch Auction System, WDAS and Retail Dutch Auction System, RDAS, as the CBN fine-tuned the process in response to emerging challenges of implementation, curtailment of excesses of operators, reduction of the differential between the official rate and the black market, minimization of volatility, etc.

Schedule: A table or list of values.

Seasonal Unemployment: Unemployment which occurs regularly because of seasonal changes in the demand for certain kinds of labour. For example, civil construction works generally takes place in the dry season. Thus in the rainy season, construction workers may be out of work or unemployed.

Securities and Exchange Commission (SEC): the apex regulatory organ of the Nigerian capital market. It oversees the activities of Stock Exchanges, stock brokers, issuing houses, unit trusts etc. It also approves and regulates mergers and acquisitions of companies. Its overriding objective is to entrench confidence in the capital market by ensuring orderly and equitable dealings in the capital market; that investors are protected and that there exists a level playing field for operators.

The Securities and Exchange Commission was established in 1979 to replace the Capital Issues Commission which itself emerged from the Capital Issues Committee in 1973, in the wake of the Nigerian Enterprises Promotion Decree which witnessed increased activities in the Nigerian capital market. The enabling legislature was overhauled in 1988, and in 2007, the Investment and Securities Act, from which the Commission presently derives its powers, was passed.

Functions of the SEC

1. Protection of Investors: The Securities and Exchange Commission, Nigeria, broadly has a responsibility to regulate the capital market and ensure that investors are protected. That means working to ensure and improve that processes are transparent and that market participants play by the rules.

2. Regulatory Oversight: the SEC scrutinizes applications from issuing houses, securities dealers/stockbrokers, sub-brokers, registrars, trustees, capital market consultants, reporting accountants, solicitors and investment advisers etc. to operate in the capital market. It can may grant a license or withdraw same. It may also sanction or penalize operators, where they flout the rules or regulations.

3. Surveillance of the Capital Market: SEC has a monitoring role over the capital market to ensure fair practices and reduce the incidence of insider trading or abuses. It also ensures that there exist good corporate governance within quoted companies and that quoted companies deliver on their responsibility for timely and reliable reporting to the investing public.

4. Approval and Registration of Issues: Any party intending to issue securities must apply to and secure approval from the SEC. Securities for issue to the investing public such as equities/shares, debentures/industrial loans, government bonds and investment schemes must be scrutinized before they can be offered to the public.

5. Approval of Trading Floors: Any party or company wishing to operate floors and exchanges, e.g. Stock Exchanges, Commodities Exchanges, Clearing and Settlement agencies must apply to and secure a license from the SEC before it can commence operations.

6. Approval of Major financial transactions like mergers, acquisitions, takeovers and similar forms of business combinations must be approved by Securities and Exchange Commission. This is to ensure that the interest of shareholders are protected and that such transactions follow laid down rules and regulations

7. Adjudication of transaction Disputes: the SEC is the administrator of the Investment and Securities Act

which creates the Investment and Securities Tribunal. The IST fast tracks resolution of disputes arising from investment and securities transactions. An investor or operator who is aggrieved over market transactions by any capital market operator may take its case to the IST. Defaulting operators may be fined or their licenses revoked.

8. Development of the Capital Market: It is a core responsibility of the SEC to see to the orderly and rapid development of the capital market. By looking out to formulate and update comprehensive and practicable legal framework exist that compare favourably with global standards and developed markets; adoption of an efficient trading system that is transparent and effective; working to broaden the number of financial securities available for trading e.g. to include financial derivatives such as options, futures and warrants; education and enlightenment of the general public to be aware of the opportunities and the processes in the capital market.

SEEDS: State Economic Empowerment and Development Strategy, a component of the National Economic Empowerment and Development Strategy.

"Seven Sisters": the *de facto* cartel United States and European international oil companies (IOCs)—Exxon, Shell, BP, Mobil, Texaco, Gulf and Chevron—which dominated and controlled the exploration, production, export and shipping of crude oil worldwide (and much else) until the formation of Organization of Petroleum Exporting Countries (OPEC) in 1960 and the emergence of national oil companies (NOCs) in the 1970s. On the basis of oil reserves, the industry is now increasingly dominated by national oil companies such as Aramco of Saudi Arabia, NIOC of Iran, Petroleos of Venezuela, Petrobras of Brazil, Gazprom of Russia and CNPC of China and other national oil companies now account for over 75% of world oil production.

Sex Ratio: the number of males in the population per 1,000 females. It indicates the likely birth rate.

SFEM: see Second-Tier Foreign Exchange Market.

Share Capital: unit of capital of a business enterprise. In a limited liability company, the capital is that sum subscribed to by the shareholders for the carrying on of the business. The sum authorized to be raised by the Memorandum of Association is called the "nominal" or "authorized" capital. The "called-up capital" is the actual amount that shareholders have been asked to pay up.

A share capital of N10million may comprise of 10,000,000 units of N1.00 each or 5,000,000 units of N2.00 each. Shares may be sold at par, premium or at a discount.

Par: Shares are sold at par when selling price is the same as the nominal unit price. For example, N1.00 and N2.00 per share for N10m share capital divided into 10,000,000 in the first case or 5,000,000 units in the second case, in the example above.

Premium: value above the par value. When a share is sold at above the nominal price, it is said to sell at a premium. For example, the above share of N1.00 each may be sold for N2.50k i.e. at N1.50k premium.

Discount: value of the share below the par value. A share with a par value of N1.00 may be sold for 60k; a discount of 40kobo. This may be due to the financial state of the company at the time.

Types of shares in include *ordinary shares, preference shares, cumulative preference shares, founders' shares,* and *deferred shares.* Ordinary shares constitute owners' interest in a company. It must be present in any shareholding structure whereas the others need not be.

Authorized share capital: the maximum amount a company may issue as specified in its memorandum of association.

Issued share: that part of the authorized share capital that has been issued out to subscribers. With authorized share capital of N10m, only N7m may have been issued out.

Called-up shares: that part of issued shares that subscribers has been asked to pay-up. The company may request subscribers to pay 75k in first call and at another date make a second call of 25k per share for N1.00 share.

Paid-up share: there may be a difference between the amount of share capital called up and the amount actually paid-up by shareholders. Some shareholders may not have paid fully for the amount of shares they subscribed for.

Un-issued share: part of the authorized share capital which has not been issued out to subscribers.

Share Certificate: a document issued to a shareholder by the company's Registrar stating the number, and class of shares subscribed to the shareholder.

Shareholder, Rights of: a shareholder of a limited liability company has certain rights, as specified under the Companies and Allied Matters Act, 1990 as amended. These rights are:

1. Right to vote at meetings.
2. Right to receive dividend.
3. Right to attend annual and extra-ordinary general meetings.
4. Right to appoint a proxy to represent them at meetings.
5. Right to participate in the distribution of assets in the event of liquidation or winding up of the company.

Shock therapy: an approach of administering economic reforms which advocated that for reforms—trade liberalization, deregulation, privatization, etc.—to be effective, the old system—communism, for example, must be done without and dismantled in very rapid sequence and replaced immediately. Former communist countries in which shock therapy reforms e.g. Poland were administered have not been as successful as China which has taken a gradual, evolutionary approach to market reforms. Notable proponents of shock therapy are American economists Jeffrey Sachs and David Lipton.

Short run: a period of time which too short for changes to be made in all inputs or factors of production. For example, periods not long enough to permit the size of the physical plant to be altered. The short run period vary from industry to industry. A furniture workshop can easily be expanded say, in weeks; on the other hand it may take more than a year to expand the capacity of a refinery or steel rolling mill.

Shut-Down Point: that level of production where the firm's Average Cost of output is higher than its Marginal Revenue. Where a firm cannot cover its average cost of production, the firm is better off stopping production until market conditions improve.

Sleeping Partner: a member of a partnership business who invests his capital but is not involved in the management of the business

SMEDAN: The Small and Medium Enterprises Development Agency of Nigeria (SMEDAN) was established in 2003 to promote the development of a structured and efficient micro, small and medium enterprises (MSME) sector of the Nigerian economy.

SMEEIS, Small and Medium Enterprises Equity Investment Scheme: a voluntary initiative of the Nigerian Bankers' Committee, in 1999, to set aside 10% of profit after tax (PAT) of banks as a contribution to a pool of funds for equity investment and promotion of small and medium enterprises. The Scheme was later restructured into a microfinance scheme, in 2008, to involve state governments, percentage of contribution by banks PAT was reduced to 5%, and instead of equity, funding was changed to credit facilities at concessionary interest rate of less than 10%.

Social capital: social infrastructure; the stock of goods which are collectively owned, e.g. roads, hospitals, schools. Social capital is provided by the government and contributes indirectly to production. The more social capital a country has the lower the cost of production and living, the greater the standard of living.

Socialism: an economic system in which the means of production are owned and controlled by the government and the major economic problems of what to produce, how to produce and for whom to produce are determined by the state or government. Income inequality is minimized in a socialist system but scarce production resources may not be efficiently allocated leading to widespread wastage and shortages.

Sole Proprietorship: one-man business. A form of private enterprise in which there is only one owner. Advantages are independence of the owner, quick decision making as he is not obliged to consult anyone. He has personal contact with his staff and customers; the business is easy to set up as no formation formalities are required; sources of capital are personal savings, and loans. The business is, however, unincorporated which means that the liability of the owner is not limited to the amount he invested in the business. This means that he stands to lose his personal property if the business should fail. Another disadvantage is that the business is not a separate legal entity, i.e. the business is not recognized as a person in law; it cannot sue and sue and be sued in its name. The ability to raise capital is limited which means it cannot operate on a large scale and enjoy economies of scale of large scale production

Special Drawing Rights (SDR's): A type of international money created by the International Monetary Fund (IMF) and allocated to its member nations to enable member countries draw beyond their quota, where necessary. SDRs are an international reserve asset, although they are only accounting entries (not actual coin or paper, and not backed by precious metal). Subject to certain conditions of the IMF, a nation that has a balance of payments deficit can use SDRs to settle debts due another nation or to the IMF.

Specialization: the concentration of skill or effort in one area of productive activity. An individual, a company (business firm) or region can engage in specialization. For example, an individual may decide to specialize in an aspect of law e.g. criminal or corporate law; a doctor can decide to specialize in treating the teeth (dentistry) or eye (ophthalmology). Specialization makes it possible for *surplus* to be produced, compared to a situation of *subsistent production* where people are jack-of-all-trades (no specialization) producing all their needs by themselves. Subsistent production is characterizes a backward or underdeveloped economy. As the economy grows and develops, there is increasing specialization, and this ultimately leads to exchange as people specialize in one area and *exchange* their product for goods and services of others. Specialization leads to commercial production as the economy develops. A developed economy is characterized by commercial production which results in mass production as production becomes more specialized with production carried out in factory system with *division of labour*.

Specific Tax: an absolute levy imposed as tax irrespective of the value of the subject of taxation. A specific tax of N2, 000 for every car imported mean that the same amount of tax will be paid irrespective of the value of any car imported. Compare *ad valorem* tax.

Value of item taxed	Tax levy
10, 000.00	2, 000.00
50, 000.00	2, 000.00

Standard Deviation (SD): a statistical measure of dispersion of a set of data; it shows the extent to which data in a distribution deviate from the mean (average) of the distribution. Given a set of data, (45, 60, 75, 80, 90), the standard deviation is calculated as follows:

Step 1, Calculate the mean, $\bar{X}$

$$\frac{45+60+75+80+90}{5} = 70$$

Step 2, Calculate the deviation from the mean

Scores	Mean	Deviation
45	70	-25
60	70	-10
75	70	5
80	70	10
90	70	20

Step 3, Square and sum the deviations

Deviation	Deviation squared
-25	625
-10	100
5	25
10	100
20	400
Sum of deviations =	1250

Step 4, Calculate the **variance** by dividing the sum of deviations by 5 (number of items in distribution)

$$\frac{1250}{5} = 250$$

Step 5, Calculate the Standard Deviation, σ, by taking the square root of the variance:

$\sigma = \sqrt{250} = 15.8113883$

Uses of the Standard Deviation

1. Interpretation of data: The average or mean and standard deviation are essential to fully understand the nature of a distribution of set of data. The higher the standard deviation, the higher the variation of data from the mean. Two countries, for example, with identical average income i.e. per capita income, may have different standard deviations. While both countries may have the same average income, the standard deviation will give insight as to whether income is equitably distributed among the population or not. A high standard deviation in one of the countries will indicate, for example, that ninety per cent of the income is earned by a small fraction of the population, while a low standard deviation will indicate an equitable distribution of income.

2. The standard deviation is also used in financial analysis to assess the level of investment risk between companies or financial assets. Assets or investments with comparable returns may have varying degrees of risk or uncertainty. Degree of risk is indicated by the standard deviation. The higher the standard deviation the higher the investment risk which should be compensated for by commensurate returns of the investment.

3. Standard deviation is used to estimate the characteristics of the parent population from which it is drawn. A normal distribution is specified once the standard deviation and the mean are known.

One standard deviation away from the mean in either direction $(\bar{X} + \sigma)$ and $(\bar{X} - \sigma)$ on the horizontal axis of the normal curve accounts for 68 percent of population; two standard deviations $(\bar{X} + 2\sigma)$ and $(\bar{X} - 2\sigma)$ away from the mean account for 95 percent of the population; and three standard deviations $(\bar{X} + 3\sigma)$ and $(\bar{X} - 3\sigma)$ account for 99 percent of the population.

4. The standard deviation makes it possible for confidence intervals to be established. Confidence levels are used as tolerance limits to test products in industries; products which do not fall within the limits are rejected.

Standards Organization of Nigeria (SON): formerly known as the Nigeria Standards Organization is responsible for ensuring that goods produced or imported into Nigeria comply with specifications and standards. In carrying out its functions it may inspect facilities, materials and products. It is empowered to seize and destroy sub-standard and fake goods.

Stock Brokers: members of a stock exchange through who shares may be bought and sold by the investing public.

Functions of stockbrokers

1. Advice and Research: collect, analyze and interpret quantitative and qualitative information to base investment decisions to clients.

2. Judgment and Valuation: the stockbroker is always called upon to make decision whether to buy or sell a security. As such, he often has to exercise and evaluate situations and make judgements in the context

of company, industry and macro-economic variables.

3. Provision of liquidity: through his activities, which include warehousing securities and providing margin loans to investors, liquidity is provided to the capital market.

4. Others functions including investment management and counseling, portfolio management, corporate financing, consultancy, etc.

Stock Exchange: a highly organized market where stock and shares are traded through authorized dealers, according to a set of rules and regulations. The stock exchange is the centre of the capital market. Anybody interested in buying or selling shares or stocks must do so through the authorized dealers i.e. stockbrokers and jobbers. Only the shares of public companies can be listed or quoted for trading on the stock exchange. A private company desirous of listing its shares on the stock exchange must first convert to a public company. After that it must fulfill the Listing Requirements and subscribe to the rules of the stock exchange, otherwise it could get de-listed. Listing may by way of an Initial Public Offer, Offer for Sale or Offer for Subscription in the Primary Market. Thereafter, the shares become available for trading in the Secondary Market of the stock market.

Once listed a company's shares become a subject of the market's assessment of its prospects; the market scrutinizes all information regarding the company, new contracts and products, management performance, etc. combine to determine the relative strength of demand and supply for its shares. This means that a share with a nominal value of N1.00 per share could trade for multiples of that, say N100.00, or a fraction of it, say, N0.30 per share. The market capitalization is the market price multiplied by the number of shares on issue. The market price therefore is a summary of all that is publicly knowable about the company. The issue of information about quoted companies is therefore critical, and quoted companies are obliged to make any information that is likely to influence their share price e.g. a new or cancelled contract, a judgement in its favour or against it, etc. public. Taking undue advantage of information that is not yet in the public domain to trade in a company's shares is termed insider trading, and is a punishable offense.

The trading system in a stock exchange could vary from the rudimentary manual call-over system to a sophisticated automated auction system. In a call-over system, stock brokers meet on the floor of the stock exchange at appointed times, and listed shares are read out aloud (called out) one by one by an official of the exchange. Stockbrokers then indicate the price they are willing to deal, and the price at which the highest bid and sell orders match becomes the ruling price of the security.

In an advanced market, with thousands of securities listed, an automated system, where orders are routed through a network of computers, is used.

Activities on the stock exchange are characterized by *bulls*, *bears* and *stags*.

Bulls are speculators who expect a rise in the price of shares and therefore eagerly buy up shares with a view to selling at a higher future price.

Bears expect shares prices to fall, and therefore seek to sell their shares, so that they may later buy the back at a lower price.

Stags speculate on newly issued shares; he expects that prices of the shares will rise as soon on trading commences on them on the floor of the stock exchange, at which time he hopes to sell at a profit.

Functions of the Stock Exchange
1. Enabling companies to raise capital.
2. Market for the trading of securities.
3. Investment avenue
4. Mobilization of savings for investment
5. Enabling government to raise funds for development.

Role of the Stock Exchange in Economic Development
1. Mobilization of savings for investment
2. Raising Capital for firms
3. Raising capital funds for government projects.
4. Marketability of Securities

The *Security and Exchange Commission* (SEC) regulates the capital market of which the Nigerian Stock Exchange is a part.

See the Nigerian Stock Exchange.

Stock Market Crash: the ultimate destination of a market bubble. When the prices of securities on the stock market begin to have little bearing on the value of the underlying assets, e.g. due to intense speculation, they are bound to come crashing down sooner than later with telling impact on the macro-economy.

The Stock Market crash of October 1929 sparked a chain of events that culminated in the Great Depression. It came against a backdrop of euphoria of the high growth of the 1920s which saw high expansion of credit including margin debts. Speculative frenzy was such that people were ". . . borrowing at 10 percent, to buy stocks, which, if dividends, on the basis of earnings were paid, could produce only 2 per cent on the purchase price." (S.B Clough and C.W. Cole, D.C. Heath and Co, 1952). In the twenty months to September 1929, market capitalization on the NYSE rose by $51,000,000,000. However, between September 3 and November 13, 1929, there was a reversal of $30,000,000,000 as prices fell. European exchanges took up the downwards plunge. High margin debts meant that the banks bore the brunt. A credit crisis ensued, production went downwards, unemployment spiked across Europe as in the United States.

There was also a crash in October 1987 but quick intervention by the Federal Reserve ensured it was contained.

Structural Adjustment Programme: set of monetary, fiscal and structural policies and reforms that a country may implement to bring about sustainable economic development; often required as a pre-condition to receive financial assistance from the International Monetary Fund (IMF).

Structural reforms aim to enable more efficient allocation of scarce resources and foster competition between economic agents by removing administrative controls that hinder the interaction of market forces as well as institute fiscal discipline. These have entail liberalization/deregulation of the economy, i. e., removal of administrative and bureaucratic controls; privatization of public corporations, currency devaluation, etc. According to the IMF, this is to ensure that its loans are not used to fund recklessness that brought the countries to distress in the first place. Therefore the reforms are supposedly intended to put the economies of the countries on the right footing, i.e. on the path to sustainable economic growth and development. Implementation of these reforms often entailed austerity measures—spending cuts in social services, like education and health and general infrastructure. Given that most of the affected countries are import dependent with low or non-existent industrial base, the immediate effect of these reforms has meant untold economic hardship as government cuts subsidies to social services and hyperinflation results due to high production costs occasioned by devaluation and high taxes. Successful implementation of these measures therefore requires committed leadership that can elicit the necessary buy-in from the general populace, if possible. Where the political leadership has failed to do this, it has resorted to repressive measures to administer the bitter pill. This has been the case in Pinochet's Chile and Rawlings' Ghana. Nigeria implemented a SAP Program between 1986 and 1992 with limited success; the success of the programme was compromised by parallel political reforms that counteracted the aims of the economic reforms. The government's commitment to the programme became half-hearted with the rise in crude oil prices and the attendant improvement in government finances with advent of the Gulf War.

Structural Adjustment in Ghana: see **Economic Reform Program**

Structural Adjustment Programme in Nigeria:
The background:
A combination of factors working together helped to weaken the country's finances from the mid-1970s.

The Nigerian economy was jolted severally by external shocks due to its total dependence on oil. These shocks negatively impacted on the production and consumption patterns, and on the cultivation of the required discipline in planning and administration on the part of government as well as in the conduct of economic agents.

The first shock was the Yom Kippur (Arab-Israeli) War in 1973, the Iranian Revolution and the Iran-Iraq war followed in 1979 and 1980 respectively. These brought about dramatic increase in government revenue.

The effect of these were
- an over-valued exchange rate;
- increase in import bill as imports became effectively subsidized,
- Decline in agriculture.
- Increased rural-to-urban migration.
- Decrease in competitiveness of Nigerian manufactures, against imports and internationally.
- Importation and distribution of finished goods became more profitable than manufacturing.
- bloating of the public service with the establishment of more public corporations,
- Public wage increases, exemplified by the Udoji Awards.

Increasingly, the economic environment became characterized by:
- Dominance of the public sector

- Controls and regulations:
- Restrictive and unfriendly to foreign investment.

As a result, what economic growth there was to speak of lacked the value creation and linkages of the various sectors of the economy that should normally accompany real development.

The Iran-Iraq war of 1980 was followed by glut in the crude oil supply in the international market, and prices reaching a trough in 1986. Low oil prices during the glut years meant the government could not continue with the expenditure pattern it has become used to during the preceding boom years. In order to sustain its spending rate, Federal and State governments of the Second Republic started incurring debt at an alarming rate.

With reduced foreign exchange receipts against a backdrop of a strong and over-valued naira, the government faced a worsening fiscal position and looming balance of payment crisis.

Against this backdrop, the government was forced to request financial assistance from the International Monetary Fund. The IMF prescribed a set of measures as part of an economic reform programme as a pre-condition for its support. The government objected to three of these proposals, namely:

1. Devaluation of the naira by 60%;
2. Removal of subsidy for petroleum products and fertilizer;
3. International trade liberalization.

The Shagari administration, instead, adopted an **Economic Stabilization** programme in 1982. This was a furtherance of the austerity measures initially adopted by the preceding administration, but which had been put in abeyance by the civilian administration when crude oil prices revived.

The stabilization measures consisted of the use of administrative controls including imports controls, exchange controls/restrictions, increases in customs tariffs, wage freezes and capital expenditure, restriction of external borrowing on state governments. Interest rates were administratively raised and ceilings on bank lending were reduced.

These measures did not bring about any meaningful changes, and the increasingly dire economic situation led to the overthrow of the Shagari government on December 31, 1983. The succeeding government also rejected IMF conditions, and introduced even more stringent controls. The government imported and directly distributed essential commodities through the Nigerian National Supply Corporation (NNSC) to ease the shortage of basic essentials. Major suppliers were accused of hoarding and causing artificial shortage; stores were seized, broken into and content distributed.

Lacking foreign exchange needed for importation of inputs required for production, major companies shut down and laid off staff; unemployment soared. To tackle this situation the government resorted to counter-trade: exchanging crude oil for required imports. To ameliorate the unemployment situation, the government expelled "illegal aliens" mainly from neighbouring West African countries.

The government's efforts appeared to yield some level of success in reining in inflation to tolerable levels as the current account position moved from deficit to balance for the first time in years while Gross Domestic Product recorded a seemingly impressive growth. All this were however, attributable to increase in OPEC crude oil quota, not due to any real change in the functioning of the economy.

The measures essentially addressed the effects rather than the causes why the economy was not working and failed to address the chronic problems of the structure of the Nigerian economy: an unsustainable reliance on oil, neglect of the agricultural sector, inward-looking industrial/development strategy, an over-valued exchange rate, pervasive direct controls exemplified by the administered interest rates, import license system and commodity boards which suppressed market signals, thereby leading to misallocation of resources, suppression of initiatives, as well as an unsustainable reliance on the public sector as the engine of the economy instead of the private sector.

The rejection of the IMF plan had meant the cessation of new credit lines and the refusal of the country's creditors to the rescheduling of outstanding servicing obligations. The country was effectively faced a no-choice situation.

It became clear that what was needed was a re-structuring of the Nigerian economy necessitating a re-setting of its fundamentals as well as a paradigm shift in the country's development strategy.

The alternative route having been exhausted by preceding administrations, the Babangida administration, which came to power in August 1985, while publicly rejecting the IMF plan, put forth an economic reform programme—the Structural Adjustment Programme—that tacitly coincided with the IMF's proposals.

Objective of SAP

Essentially, the aim of the Structural Adjustment Programme was to put the Nigerian economy on a path of sustainable growth by making it a market-driven one. This meant changing the role of government from that of a player to one of a referee or regulator; and reliance on market forces (as opposed to direct administrative controls) as levers of regulation in order to create an enabling environment for economic agents to thrive and create value.

In specific terms, the objectives were:
- restructure and diversify the productive base of the economy so as to reduce dependency on the oil sector and imports;
- achieve fiscal and balance of payments viability over the medium term; and
- Promote non-inflationary economic growth.

The key policies designed to achieve these objective were:
- The setting up of a Second-Tier Foreign Exchange Market (SFEM) as a mechanism for market determination of exchange rate and consequently, the alteration of relative prices to enhance efficiency in resource allocation, and to promote domestic-based production and non-oil exports, reduce capital flight and attract foreign capital.
- Exchange Rate Reform: to improve the country's competitiveness, improve terms of trade and balance of

payments, a proximate true exchange rate for the naira was critical. In September 1986, a dual exchange rate system was introduced; an administratively determined official rate, used for Federal Government transactions such as external debt service payments, and an auction rate, determined via the mechanism of a second-tier foreign exchange market (SFEM), where authorized dealer banks bought foreign exchange at weekly sessions from the Central Bank. The naira was devalued by 22 percent in the official or first tier market at N1.538 and by 66 percent on the SFEM at N4.20 to the United States dollar. Both rates were merged in July 1987.

- Further rationalization and restructuring of tariffs in order to aid industrial diversification;
- The liberalization of the external trade and payments system-dismantling of price, trade and exchange controls;
- The elimination of price controls and commodity boards; coupled with the devaluation of the exchange rate of the naira, agricultural exports rose significantly.
- Removal of subsidies for petroleum products. This brought about an increase in price of between 24 and 725 percent. Gasoline price increased by 200%; only the price of kerosene was spared.
- Financial System Reform: in order to bring about a more efficient financial system, the government sought to improve the allocative efficiency of the financial system until then characterized by controlled interest rates, sectoral allocation of credit,

high reserve requirements, and credit ceilings among other factors that hampered financial intermediation. Toward this end, the government deregulated interest rates and began to rely on market based levers such as open market operations to regulate the administration of credit. These measures led to an increase in the number of Nigerian banks from 40 in 1986 to 120 in 1992. Discount Houses and Bureaux de Change were established for the first time as financial services deepened in terms of service and reach. This brought about major regulatory challenges, so that by 1998, over 30 banks had been declared distressed and liquidated. The Nigerian Deposit Insurance Corporation was established and minimum capital requirement was revised upwards.

- Trimming the size of the public sector: Commercialization and Privatization of public enterprises. In order to stop the unsustainable financing of loss making public enterprises, the Technical Committee on Privatization and Commercialization (TCPC) was established in 1988. An initial 110 public enterprises were listed in the enabling law.
- To promote **foreign direct investment** (FDI), the Nigerian Enterprises Decree was amended to allow for 100% foreign ownership of any industry except banking, insurance and mining. This law was repealed in 1995 to allow for foreigners to own shares in any Nigerian company.
- Reducing the **National Debt**: the programme enabled the country

to re-established relations with its international creditors. In order to reduce the external loan stock which stood at $18.6billion in 1986, the government engaged the country's creditors in the following ways:

o Debt Rescheduling and Refinancing: the government was able to gain some temporary relief from its creditors by reducing the debt-servicing ratio to less than 30percent between 1986 and 1990. However, the government could not secure concessional terms.

o Debt-conversion: in a bid to attract foreign investment and manage scarce foreign exchange, external debtors were invited to exchange their debt for equity in Nigerian companies. This use of this approach was minimized because of its inflationary tendency. Though this approach was credited with only about 5% reduction in the external debt stock, this understates the impact of the related foreign management and new technology that accompanied the new foreign direct investment.

• Debt Buy-Back: the country bought back some of its debts at discounted rates on the international capital market through third parties.

• Debt Cancellation: the governments of the United States and Canada cancelled a total of $107.2million.

• A debt reduction operation agreement reached in January 1992, partly involving the purchase of $3.4billion London Club (commercial) debt at 60% discount, reduced London

Club debt by almost $4billion to $2.2billion.

Conclusion

Nigeria's SAP was typical of IMF's 'one size fits all' prescription for struggling economies. Nowhere have these measures been a tale of total success.

As everywhere else where these measures have been implemented, they were met with stiff resistance from the populace who bore the pain of decades of economic mismanagement which strangulated enterprise and business initiatives.

Economic activities were revived as the country regained the confidence of its international trading partners. Production resumed across different sectors as business firms now could easily gain access to foreign exchange to import inputs through their banks. Essential commodities became readily available though at rather high prices with the devalued rate of the naira. While employment picked up, the government had to grapple with the issue of inflation.

The government appeared on course with its reform agenda until after 1990 when it appears to veer off the road. This is attributable to three factors. First, improved government finances as the price of crude oil rose on the international market on the advent of the first Gulf War in 1990 reduced the reformist zeal. Second, a failed but violent putsch against the government in 1991 shook the government to its roots. From then on, survival seemed to be the theme of government activities as it sought to secure its power base. Third, the government embarked on an ambitious political transition programme which contradicted the thrust of the economic reforms. The spending patterns that these factors gave rise to, in government, practically undid the gains of the success of the initial years of reforms.

The limits to the success of the structural adjustment program could be said to have been set to the extent that no significant attention was given to the substructure of the economy—power generation, transportation, communications, technical education, heavy industry, etc.—which constitute the basis of an industrial economy. Structural reforms were necessary but without infrastructure were insufficient to awaken the economy to its potential. The government certainly had the funds to invest in infrastructure with the windfall of the first Gulf War. Such investment for, example, in improving electric power supply and modernizing the railway system, would have been engine for the growth of the economy in the near-term while laying the foundation for the future by significantly increasing marginal productivity of capital.

In the absence such investment, the industrial sector was not able to take advantage of the structural reforms.

Also structural reforms to attract foreign direct investment were stymied in the face of the obvious long-term potential of the economy as a result.

These continue to be the bane of the Nigerian economy, seriously limiting the creative and entrepreneurial energies and the untold potentials of its material and human endowments.

In all, the reform programme did succeed in the following:

1. Freeing the economy from the stranglehold of decades of administrative controls.
2. Begin the process of building a modern economy in terms of institutional and legislative infrastructure
3. Setting the agenda for succeeding governments in the management of the economy, which has been sustained since. The reforms did set the agenda, for succeeding governments.

Structural Unemployment: Long-term joblessness caused by changes in technology in industries. For example, where a production process is being mechanized, workers have to learn new skills, resulting in some unemployment depending how quickly workers can make the transition i.e. occupational mobility. Relocation of an industry may also result in structural unemployment depending on the geographical mobility of the workers.

Subvention: amount paid by government to public corporations to sustain them. "Appropriate pricing" under economic reforms often necessitated the reduction or withdrawal of these payments in the face of lean government finances.

Subsidy: A payment made by the government either to producers in order to keep prices low. One of the features of deregulation which began with the Structural Adjustment Programme in 1986 has been the removal of subsidies. This has seen to increase in social services such as education with increases in tuition and other school fees. Removal of petroleum subsidies has been phases as the government has been restrained from completely deregulation of the downstream sector because of the inflationary implications.

Substitution Effect: a rise in the price of a good will bring about other good(s) being substituted in its place. An income effect may also be brought about as the real income of the consumer may increase or decrease due to price changes.

Supernormal profit: the return or profit to enterprise in excess of normal profit i.e. the positive difference between total revenue and total costs.

Supply: the amount of goods producers are willing and able to offer for sale over a period of time.

Supply (Law of): The higher the price the higher the quantity supplied; the lower the price the lower the quantity supplied.

Supply-side Economics: school of thought that economic growth is best sustained by reducing constraints on producers/suppliers. It advocates low tax rates, reduced regulation.

Surety: same as a guarantor

Surplus: the excess of quantity supplied over quantity demanded. A surplus occurs at any point above the equilibrium price.

Surrender Value: amount payable by an assurance compnay to a holder of an endowment life assurance policy, if he wants to terminate the policy before the policy is mature.

Suspense Account: a ledger account to which entries may be temporarily posted.

Sustainable Debt: the level of national debt that a country can owe and service without resorting to debt rescheduling, accumulation of service arrears, and thereby impairing economic growth. Relevant factors to consider in a country's debt sustainability analysis (DSA) include the level of external debt, external reserves, total export receipts and/or government revenue as well as the debt-to-Gross Domestic Product (GDP) ratio. Together, these factors give an indication of the country's investment risk quotient, impacting on a country's exchange rate, interest rate and its attractiveness to trading partners and foreign investors. The level of financial support and advice a country can obtain from the international capital market and from the likes of the International Monetary Fund and World Bank is based on an assessment of its capacity to service its maturing debt obligations.

T

Tariff: A tax levied on imports.

Terms of trade: the rate at which a country's exports exchanges for its imports. The higher the prices of exports compared to the price of imports, the better the terms of trade. If, for example, the price of crude oil (Nigeria's export) rises from $50 to $70 per barrel while the price of machinery, which Nigeria imports, remain the same, Nigeria's terms of trade has improved. Conversely, if the prices of imports should rise relative to exports, the terms of trade has deteriorated. Overall, the price of commodities such as rubber, cocoa, cotton, palm produce etc has fallen relative to the prices of computer equipment and machinery imported by Nigeria, and this worsened the terms of trade as the country gets less imports from a unit of export. In calculating the terms of trade, the index prices of exports are compared with the index prices of imports to show the changes in terms of trade over a period of time.

Year	Index of average prices of exports	Index of average prices of imports	Terms of trade
1999	100	100	100
2000	109	120	91
2001	119	130	92
2002	110	205	54

Using 1999 as base year, from the above table, terms of trade deteriorated by 54% between 1999 and 2002.

$$\text{Terms of trade} = \frac{\text{Index of export prices}}{\text{Index of export prices}} \times 100$$

Technical Economies of Scale: see Economies of Scale

Tertiary Production: Production in the form of provision of services e.g. transportation, banking, legal services, medical services, education, retail services, consulting, etc. Primary production consists of agriculture and mining, while secondary production consists of manufacturing. The more developed a country's economy, the bigger its tertiary sector. The size of the tertiary sector as a percentage of national output is an indication of the level of development of an economy, as opposed to mere growth.

Theory of the firm: division of economic theory concerned with determining the equilibrium price and output of firms under different market conditions.

Tiger Economies: term used describe the rapid economic growth rate of the Newly Industrialized Countries (NIC) of East Asia namely South Korea, Taiwan, and Hong Kong, Singapore in the 1980s which transformed these economies to developed status. The pattern has been replicated by their neighbours, Malaysia, Indonesia and Thailand. These countries pursued an export-driven development strategy, like

Japan, with a mixture of state planning/ intervention and free market enterprise that defied liberal development economics which emphasize reliance on market forces to efficiently allocate resources. The experiences of these countries show a reliance on market forces and market intervention in the pursuit of defined development goals. The success of these countries has been attributed to a variety of factors as outlined hereunder:

1. Stable Political Environment: in these countries, economic development goals preceded political openness; the right to a job was prioritized over the right to vote; clearly defined national development objectives were pursued against a backdrop of a stable political environment. In South Korea, General Park Chung Hee, who has been credited with overseeing the transformation of his country, was in power for 18 years between 1961 and 1979.

2. Financial Repression: interest rates were maintained at low levels rather than allowed to be determined by market forces. Given the high propensity to save, this effectively meant that savers—i.e. households-subsidized industry and development.

3. High Domestic Savings: these countries were characterized by a high **propensity to save** as opposed to wanton consumerism and instant gratification. This made a pool of cheap investible funds from domestic savings available minimizing the need for reliance on foreign capital for development.

4. Discrete Market Intervention in the implementation of Industrial Policy: market forces did not reign supreme. While a competitive free market system was the norm, the governments of these countries actively provided support to certain strategic industries in the form subsidized loans or tax incentives.

5. Protectionism: these countries did not practice a liberal trade policy. Industries producing for the domestic market were protected against foreign competition.

6. A Skilled Labour Force: South Korea, Taiwan, Singapore and Hong Kong are not particularly endowed with natural resources. They made up for this by paying special attention to the development of their human capital resources. This gave them the edge in taking advantage of the New International Division of Labour. Multinational Corporations (MNC) found a pool of cheap but skilled labour force, and encouraged to relocate their factories to these countries.

7. Confucian Ethic: the people of these countries were greatly influenced by the teachings of the Chinese philosopher, Confucius, which stresses frugality and thriftiness; learning and love of self-application, prudence, diligence and a work ethic, the primacy of the group over the individual, etc, values which pervades their outlook, behaviour and the general conduct, bringing about the evolution of an ethos that positively impacted on the societies socio-politically to underpin economic development. The influence of these values is parallel in much the same way as the "Protectant Ethic", as pointed out by Max Weber, foreran the Industrial Revolution in Western Europe.

8. Managed Exchange Rate: these countries managed their currency

exchange rates to align with the overall objective of export promotion and domestic industry protection. The exchange rate was deliberately undervalued relative to major international currencies in order to ensure exports are competitive in foreign markets and imports are expensive compared to locally made substitutes.

9. Export Promotion: while businesses were protected from foreign competition in the home market, they were often given export targets, and encouraged to meet them by government support.

10. Value-based growth: the basis of growth of these economies was based on value creation as opposed to export earnings from a primary resource such crude oil. Thus these economies benefited from the vital concomitant linkages, in terms of structures and production and consumption patterns, which arise from this process, and invariably result in lasting development.

11. Pro-business Government: the governments worked actively to ensure the smooth flow to facilitate the private sector by providing infrastructure, reducing red tape, excessive taxation as well as provide subsidies, where necessary.

12. Competent Public Administration: the governments' ability to effectively implement industrial policy and pursue set goals is attributable to the existence of competent and honest civil servants.

Token money: money, the face (extrinsic) value, i.e. amount marked or printed on them, is greater than the intrinsic value,

i.e. value of the material (metal or paper) of which they are made. All notes and coins now in circulation are of this nature, as distinct from *standard money*, which was backed up by reserves of gold, for which they can be exchanged.

Total Cost: fixed costs plus variable costs of production.

Total Revenue: quantity sold multiplied by price.

Trade: the exchange of goods and services for other goods and services or for money. The higher the level of specialization and division of labour, the greater the volume of trade. Trade is the essence of all commercial activity, and is divided into Home Trade (Wholesale and Retail Trade) and Foreign Trade (Import and Export)

Trade Association: a voluntary association of individuals, businesses, etc engaged in similar lines of trade, formed for the purposes of advancing their interests. They ensure uniform charges among members; disseminate information among members; act as pressure group in order to influence government policies to favour their members; defend and advance their interests e.g. to secure micro-finance for members; avenue or platform for arbitration and settlement of disputes among members; education and enlightenment of members on trade activities or government policies. Trade Associations are different from Chambers of Commerce as the latter comprise of business and business people from diverse trades and industries.

Trade Cycle: also known as economic cycle or business cycle: the tendency of aggregate economic activity to alternate between boom and bust (recession/depression). The fluctuation follows no predictable or fixed pattern, phases lasting months or years.

Phases of the Trade Cycle

1. Expansion: this is when business confidence is high and economic activity revs up. Demand picks up, prices are increasing, investment increases and businesses are hiring workers.
2. Peak: this the height of the expansion phase; unemployment is practically non-existent and prices are beginning to stabilize.
3. Contraction: slowdown in business activity. Demand for goods and services is low, investment slows down, businesses are not hiring workers.
4. Trough: business activity at the lowest level, unemployment is high and there is deflation as prices of goods and services falls. This may be a recession or depression, depending on the severity of the slowdown.

Until the Great Depression in 1930s, and the publication of John M. Keynes *General Theory*, in 1936, the classical economists' view that prices (interest rates, wages, rent) will automatically adjust at any phase of the trade cycle to move the economy towards equilibrium, was generally accepted. Keynes pointed out that prices do not easily adjustment especially downwards due to rigidities and market imperfections such as trade union actions and labour legislations, and therefore it is possible for the economy to be stuck in a depression, for example. Keynes therefore proposed that the use of monetary and fiscal measures may be necessary to stimulate the aggregate demand at such times.

Trade Deficit: Balance of trade deficit: The amount by which merchandise (visible goods) imports exceed merchandise exports.

Trade Union: an association of workers in the same trade/profession or industry formed for the purpose of securing better working conditions and remuneration through collective engagement/action with employers. Trade basically of two types: union: craft union, which comprises workers engaged in a particular skill or training/profession e.g. Nigeria Union of Teachers (NUT) and industrial unions which comprises all workers, skilled and unskilled employed in the same or related industry e.g. National Union of Petroleum and Natural Gas Workers (NUPENG). In Nigeria all unions are affiliated either to the Nigeria Labour Congress or the Trade Union Congress.

Weapons of Trade Unions

Bargaining: discussion with management to work out a mutually satisfactory position.

Picketing: drawing attention to their cause by disrupting business activities and causing negative publicity to a firm by protesting at its premises.

Work-to-rule: workers doing the very minimum of their work contracts in order to slow down work and productivity. Ridiculous attention is paid to all rules and regulations; not arriving earlier than the opening hours and leaving business premises at official closing hours.

Strike: downing of tools or refusal to work. This is usually the last resort to press home their demands.

Trading Account: A statement drawn up to calculate the gross profit of a business during a period. It may take the vertical format or traditional 'T' format:

CORAL CO. LTD			
Trading Account			
for the year ended 31 December 2012			
Opening Stock	50,000.00	Sales	200,000.00
Purchases	100,000.00	Closing Stock	40,000.00
	150,000.00		
	150,000.00		
Gross Profit	90,000.00		
	240,000.00		240,000.00

Trading Credit Risk Insurance: an insurance policy and a risk management product that is offered by insurance companies and governmental export credit agencies (such as the Nigerian Export-Import Bank) to business entities wishing to protect their accounts receivable from loss due to credit risks, such as protracted default, insolvency, bankruptcy, etc. It is, therefore, a protection against unusually large losses from unpaid accounts receivable.

Transaction Motive: the desire to hold money to enable us deal with day-to-day transactions such as transport fares, payment of bills, food stuffs, etc.

Transfer Earnings: the amount a factor of production would receive in its next best employment.

Transfer Payments: incomes or receipts which do not represent payments for factors services or productive efforts. Examples are bursary awards, gifts, social security payments. In calculating national income, transfer payments are not included because they are mere transfers not earnings from production activities.

Transportation: the movement of freight and passengers. It is one of the ancillaries or aids of trade. It is part of the critical infrastructure that determines the level of economic growth and development. The level of effectiveness and efficiency with which goods and people can be moved impacts on overall economic development.

It is not enough for goods to be produced; they must be moved to where there is demand for them, and the further they can be moved geographically, the greater the market. Thus transportation extends the market, so that a radio made in China, is transported by the means of a container on a cargo ship, and made available to consumer in Nigeria or Brazil, a world away. In the same way, Nigerian crude oil is made available to power cars in New York, in the United States of America, by ocean tankers.

Urbanization and the continued existence and proper functioning of cities depend on good transport systems; foreign trade would not be possible without them.

The existence of an organized and effective transportation system boosts trading activities by ease of movement of people and goods, leading to higher national output, lower prices and enhanced living standards.

The following are some of the effects of transportation systems:

1. Large scale production has been made possible.
2. Boosts international trade.
3. Availability of a variety of goods in the local market.
4. Increase in the volume of trade.
5. Reduced capital investment in inventory as output is quickly dispatched to markets.
6. Increased specialization by regions/countries based on comparative costs.
7. Reduction in the amount of local surplus ending up un-used or waste.

MODES OF TRANSPORTATION
1. Land—Road and Rail
2. Water
3. Air
4. Pipeline

The essence of well-integrated transport system is the development of a transport sector in which the different transport modes move the goods and passengers for which they are best suited.

Intermodal transport involve the use of more than one mode of transport in order to reach the final destination, such as when goods are loaded from a ship onto a truck or train for onward transportation.

Land
Road: The bulk of home trade is conducted by the transport of goods and persons by vehicles – bicycles, motor-cycles, tri-cycles, cars, buses, trucks, trailers, tankers, etc. They are particularly efficient and effective over short distances.

Advantages of Road Transport
1. Cheap: road transport fares are low, relative to air or ship.
2. Door-to-door: goods can be taken from their source, e.g. a warehouse, to where required, a customer's premises, without need of being transferred into another means of transport.
3. Flexibility: road transport does not have to follow a laid down schedule like an aircraft or train.
4. Ideal for short journeys e.g. intra-city shuttles.
5. Adaptable: no special routes required nor fixed terminals, runways nor tracks.
6. Low cost: the cost of acquiring and maintaining a car, or truck is low compared to that of an aircraft, train or ship.

Disadvantages of Road Transport
1. Limited Capacity: motor vehicles cannot carry as much as train, ships nor aircraft in a single trip. As such road transport is not suitable for the transportation of bulky materials like pre-packaged cement, sugar, machinery, etc.
2. Slow for Long journeys. Cross-country journeys are cheaper and faster with trains, where available.
3. Subject to traffic congestions: unlike other modes of transport, road journeys are subject to traffic jams and congestions.

ROAD TRANSPOTATION IN NIGERIA
According to the Federal Ministry of Works, 95% of both passenger and freight traffic are by road in Nigeria because other forms of transport remain under-developed.

Nigeria's road network consist of

Category	Distances (km)	%
Federal (Trunk A)	33,000	16.5
State (Trunk B)	50,000	25
Local (Trunk C)	117,000	58.5
Total	200,000	100
Federal roads account for more than 80 per cent of passenger and freight traffic.		
Source: Federal Ministry of Works.		

Trunk A connects State capitals, cutting across states/regions. These roads are designed and constructed under the supervision of the Ministry of Works and maintained by the Federal Road Maintenance Agency.

Trunk B roads links State capitals to other towns within states. They are under the State ministries of Works.

Truck C roads are mainly feeder roads linking villages and communities, and in many instances may be unpaved. These roads are under the Local Government.

Federal roads account for more than 80 per cent of passenger and freight traffic

Major Trunk A roads
Trunk A roads can be described as the frame of the national road network traversing regions

- Abuja-Kaduna-Kano: a lifeline for trade and commerce facilitating the transportation of agricultural produce from the agricultural belt of the North-West and North-south to the teeming population of the Federal Capital Territory
- Shagamu-Benin-Asaba: trade and commerce between western and eastern part of Nigeria. This road cuts across four states—Ogun, Ondo, Edo and Delta states, leading to the Niger Bridge.
- Niger Bridge: the vital link connecting the west to the east of the country. The bridge was commissioned in 1964, and is no longer adequate to accommodate growth in traffic, which it funnels through Asaba and Onitsha. Thus, government has commenced the construction of a second Niger Bridge.
- Enugu-Port Harcourt Road: a part of the four routes of the Trans-African Highway network that are part of the national road network. It is the key route for most trucks.
- Third Mainland Bridge—at almost 12km, the longest bridge in Africa; a vital link in the country's economic capital, it enables business worth millions of naira as well as the movement as many passengers on a daily basis. Completed in 1990, it is one of the three bridges connecting the mainland to Lagos Island, '*Eko*', a major commercial hub; and Victoria Island, where most banks have their headquarters, and Lekki Peninsula.

Problems of Road Transport in Nigeria
Road Over-use

Nigeria's roads are in deplorable state generally. Part of the problem is the concentration of transportation on the roads. Heavy weight cargos that are better moved by rail, for example, are hauled on the roads.

A percentage of cargo that should borne by the rail system are transported by road as there is no real alternative. Also, the absence of weight bridges to detect excess loads on the roads contributes to road improper road use.

Inadequate Road Network
With a total road network of 200,000km against a land area of 923,768 square kilometers, Nigeria's road density does not compare favourably even with other African countries.

Road network access is put at 100km/100,000 people. Budgetary allocation has proven inadequate vis-à-vis road funding requirements, giving rise to a deficit of about 23 per cent. In addition, the annual budgetary process is fraught with delays and bureaucracy which usually translate to non-implementation and implementation failures.

In order to attract the required level of funding for road construction, government has been exploring the following:
1. Public-Private Partnership
2. Borrowing from Multilateral bodies such as World Bank and African Development Bank
3. Floatation of Highways bonds

Inadequate Funding for Road Maintenance
The country's roads are in deplorable state and an estimated 2.5 per cent of Gross Domestic Product is lost annually as a result.

Depending on budgetary allocations most times means non-release of funds or untimely release of funds for road rehabilitation and maintenance.

In order to bring a about a more responsive road maintenance mechanism , the setting up of a dedicated Road Fund, into which a road user charges—tolls, parking fees, etc.—will be paid was advocated. This led to the passing of a law enabling 5 per cent fuel surcharge in 2007. This law, which awaits implementation, obliges State Governments to set up road maintenance agencies in order to access the 60 percent of the fund, while FERMA utilizes 40 per cent for Federal Roads.

Concession
The government has resorted to Public-Private Partnership as a way around this challenge. This led to the establishment of the Infrastructure Concession and Regulatory Commission by the Federal Government in 2005. Also, the Lagos State Government granted the Lekki Concession Company a 30-year concession to Build-Operate—Transfer the Lekki Expressway in Lagos.

Need for a Federal Road Development Agency
It has been suggested that the Federal Ministry of Works should be freed from the direct responsibility of roads design and construction. Instead, a specialized body, like the Federal Airports Authority of Nigeria, under the Ministry of Aviation, should be established under the Ministry of Works. Such a body will be free from the bureaucratic shackles of the Civil Service, and is expected to be more proactive in its processes.

Un-Organized Transport Operations
The organization of the business of transportation is still largely informal and un-organized. Virtually no formal process exists to be followed in entering the transportation business. As a result, there is a serious lack of professionalism—in fleet management, road manners and ethics, etc. Thus most of the vehicles—especially for

intra-city – are in deplorable state of repairs and/or unkempt for the most part.

Un-organized Parks: Motor-Parks nation-wide, are almost always outside the control of law enforcement agents. Transport operators are levied daily by a host of groups, ranging from local governments and 'area chairmen' accountable only to themselves, who claim to manage the motor-parks, which are hardly known for their cleanliness.

No Vehicle Specifications: there is practically any specification of vehicle types, seating arrangement, minimum leg space, etc., for public transport operations. Existing rules e.g. the maximum number of passengers, are hardly enforced. For example, it is common for a two-seater or to be converted to a three-seater bus, with implications for leg-space and exposure to injury any moment.

RAIL TRANSPORT
Rail transport is the movement of passengers and goods on vehicles running on steel tracks. Rail transport is particularly cost effective in moving mass of heavy cargo over land where there are no waterways, and is the most efficient and safest modes of transport.

Advantage of Rail Transport
1. Economical and Efficient: a single train consists up to tens of trucks making train most economical and efficient in terms of load per trip.
2. Ideal for haulage of bulky materials like pre-packaged cement, iron ore, coal, machinery, etc.
3. Safety: rail transport has recorded the least number of accidents overtime.
4. Speed: modern trains are the fastest means of travel on land capable of reaching 300km per hour.

5. Comfort: train offer coach services on board.
6. Inexpensive: train routes are direct and because number of passenger per trip higher offer the cheapest fares.

Disadvantages
1. Capital intensive to install and maintain: This means government subsidies may be required, at least to take off.
2. Expensive for short journeys.
3. Fixed tracks and terminals means that trains cannot take deliveries direct from nor to warehouses. Therefore other means of transport may be necessary to make the final delivery.
4. Scheduled Services: train services operate on fixed schedule.

Rail Transport in Nigeria
The Nigeria Railway Corporation is the regulator and operator of the Nigeria railway system which consists of 3,505km of narrow gauge tracks and 276km of standard gauge tracks..

The main track of Nigeria's rail system consists of the following:

Western track
Lagos-Ibadan—Kaduna-Kano-Nguru: currently the most active due to recent efforts by the government which has made it possible for the railway's haulage services to resume. The corporation's 20-container wagons takes heavy goods such as cement, sugar, salt, and diesel off-loaded from ships at the Apapa wharf in Lagos to Kaduna/Kano in the north.

Central track:
• Kafanchan-Kaduna

Eastern track
- Port-Harcourt--Enugu--Kafanchan--Maiduguri
- Ajaokuta-Aladja (standard gauge tracks): haulage of iron ore and related products between the steel plants at the two locations.

In Africa, Nigeria's rail network is only behind to those of South Africa (20,041) and Egypt (5,145) in length. Due to sustained neglect over the years, however, it is highly under-utilized, and lags behind most, including those of Ghana and Kenya, on most performance indices, accounting for less than 2% per cent of total freight traffic.

The government's plans towards resuscitating the system include reforms to attract private investors by deregulation of the industry. This will entail separating regulation from operations as well as concession arrangements.

Air Transport
The use of aircraft—mainly aero plane, helicopters—in the movement of freight and passengers. Airport facilities include towers, aprons, hangars, tarmac, runways, lounges, shopping malls, motels, etc.

Advantages of Air Transport
1. Fast: aircraft are the fastest mode of travel.
2. Comfort
3. Ideal for long and urgent distances: cross-continental journeys that are time-sensitive are best by air.
4. Ideal for Perishable Goods:

Disadvantage of Air Transport
1. Capital intensive: aircraft are expensive to procure and maintain. This means a minimum level of traffic is necessary.

2. Expensive: fares are costly.
3. Subject to weather conditions: weather changes can cause havoc to airborne aircraft.
4. Requires additional means of transport to the final destination.

AIR TRANSPORT IN NIGERIA
The Federal Airports Authority of Nigeria, (FAAN) is the landlord/regulator of airport operations in Nigeria, and may grant concession of the management of any particular airport to a private operator for a specified period of time.

There are five international airports in Nigeria viz. Murtala Mohammed, Lagos; Nnamdi Azikiwe, Abuja, Akanu Ibiam, Enugu, Aminu Kano, Kano; and Port Harcourt.

WATER TRANSPORT
Around 90% of global merchandise is transported by sea. For many countries sea transport represents the most important mode of transport for trade.

Ocean going ships are categorized into two types:
i) Cargo liners: these run scheduled regular routes from which they hardly deviate.
ii) Tramp steamers: may pick up a shipment and deliver as required.

Water transport is particularly cost effective in haulage of bulky cargo in circumstances where speed is not a critical factor. A single barge can take the equivalent of over 200 railcars or over 800 trailer-trucks.

Water borne transport involve the use of Ocean liners, ships, boats, canoes of diverse types making use of Ports, Harbours, Docks, Containers, Cranes, etc.

WATER TRANSPORT IN NIGERIA

Nigerian waterways consist of a 7,000km coastline from Badagry in the west through Warri, in the Niger Delta, to Calabar in the east, and an inland waterway system that practically covers the hinterland: the Niger-Benue river system—the River Niger and its tributaries—over 3,000km of navigable watercourses.

Major ports in Nigeria are Apapa Port, Tin can Island, Delta Port (Warri, Burutu, Sapele, Escravos, Forcados), Rivers Port (Port Harcourt and Onne), and Calabar Port.

Nigerian ports were notorious for inefficiency, long turn-around time; congestion; dilapidated cargo handling equipment, cargo theft, and poor and disused port facilities until a reforms process which started 1999. Until this time, the Nigerian Ports Authority was coterminous with the sector as regulator and operator. Under the reforms, the sector was deregulated and restructured: the role of the NPA was re-defined to be that of a landlord/regulator overseeing port operations which was conceded to private operators.

This has brought about a huge increase in private investment in port infrastructure and tremendous improvement in port operations.

The Nigeria Inland Waterway Authority was established in 1997 to oversee the inland waterways as manager and regulator.

Major constraints to inland waterway transport include:

1. Inadequate water depth of the rivers during the dry season making passage difficult for large barges.

2. Existence of bends and meanders.
3. Inadequate facilities for intermodal transport i.e. transfers of cargo between barges and truck/railway.

The government has responded to these challenges by awarding contracts for the dredging Niger and Benue rivers respectively as well as the encouragement of private investment in inland port infrastructure.

Advantage of Water Transport

1. God-given routes: no additional cost is incurred to make out rivers, canals and sea routes unlike roads and rail way tracks.
2. Inexpensive: fares are usually cheap.
3. Capacity for bulky and heavy luggage.
4. Safe: water transport is not prone to accidents.
5. Ideal for perishable and fragile goods.

Disadvantage of Water Transport

1. Capital intensive: the cost of acquiring and maintaining a ship is expensive.
2. Limited Availability: limited only to where waterways are available.
3. Slow: sea travel is known for being slow, taking months to make a cross-continental journey, that will take an aircraft hours to make. Thus it not suitable for perishable goods or when deliveries are to be within a short time.
4. Subject to Weather Conditions: sea storms and tempests can cause delays and even damages.

PIPELINES

Gases and liquids are transported through pressurized pipes over long distances. In Nigeria, pipelines are used to supply crude oil from Warri, in the South to the Kaduna refinery in the north. The Nigeria Gas Company also supplies some of its customers through a network of pipelines in the Lagos metropolis.

Advantages of Pipelines
1. Little or no operating cost after installation.
2. No accidents: unlike other modes of transportation, pipelines are not prone to collision, derailment or shipwreck..
3. Changes in the weather conditions do not make much difference to the continuous flow of the pipeline as issues of visibility, slippery surfaces or wind are irrelevant.

Disadvantages of Pipeline
1. The initial cost of installation is usually very high or capital intensive.
2. Pipelines are vulnerable to tampering, and this may necessitate monitoring.

Treasury Bills: a short-term security issued by the central bank to raise money for the government; they mature between 91-364 days. They are a safe form of investment since they are issued by the government.

Features of Treasury Bills
1. They are issued by the Central Bank of Nigeria on behalf of the Federal Government.
2. They are used by the CBN to manage liquidity in the economy through open-market operations.
3. Tenors: duration before maturity is usually 91, 184 and 364 days.
4. Holders can use them as collateral.
5. They are re-discountable through licensed money market dealers. Thus a holder can sell before maturity.

6. They are actively traded in the secondary market.
7. Yield of between 10 to 13 per cent.
8. Minimum amount: Banks usually insist on investment of a minimum amount of N100, 000.00.
9. They are safe and risk-free being backed by the full faith and credit of the Federal Government.
10. Upfront interest payment: interest are paid up-front, thus a buyer of N100,000 treasury bill of 10 per cent will pay only N90,000.00 i.e. the N10,000 interest is paid up-front.

Trial Balance: a summary of the balances of the books of account of a business usually extracted at the end of an accounting period. The trial balance is drawn up to show the totals of the ledger accounts agree prior to the preparation of the Trading, Profit and Loss and the Balance Sheet. If the totals of the respective (debit) Dr and (credit) Cr columns in the Trial Balance agree it means there are no errors in the accounts, unless such errors cancel themselves out.

	DR	CR
Capital		100,000.00
Stock	5,500.00	
Purchases	10,000.00	
Sales		50,000.00
Motor Van	2,000.00	
Building	111,000.00	
Rent	750.00	
Wages	500.00	
Bank	15,250.00	
Creditors		10,000.00
Debtors	15,000.00	
Total	160,000.00	160,000.00

Trust: assets-money or property-held on behalf of another. A bank, individual or group of persons (trustees) may be the administrators of a trust.

Turnover: the value of trade or sales by a firm or business during a period.

U

Uberrima fides: see Utmost Good Faith.

UEMOA: the French acronym for West African Economic and Monetary Union, a customs and monetary union created in 1994 comprising of Benin, Burkina Faso, Cote d'Ivoire, Mali, Niger, Senegal, Togo and Guinea-Bissau. The member countries use a common currency—the CFA franc, whose exchange rate is linked to the Euro and managed by the French Central Bank. They have adopted a common external tariff. The UEMOA has been acknowledged by the IMF as the furthest evolved of the economic groupings in Africa.

Uncalled Capital: capital subscribed and issued but not yet paid for.

Underdevelopment, economic: economic under-development is a situation where a country's is operating below its economic potential. Such an economy is characterized by high unemployment, low infrastructural development, low per capita income, among others. The economy is usually under-monetized and subsistent; national output and production comprises mostly of primary produce which are largely exported as the secondary or manufacturing/industrial sector is practically non-existent.

Underemployment: refers to a situation where a worker is employed in a job for which he is over-qualified.

Under-Population: sub-optimal population; a situation where the human resources (labour) of a country or region, is less than what is required to adequately exploit a country's natural (land) and material (capital) resources. Under-populated countries usually encourage immigration.

Underwriter: a person or firm who undertakes to accept a risk on behalf of others for a fee. This may be in regard of insurance policy or a share issue. An issuing house may underwrite a new share issue by agreeing to take up any shares not subscribed by the public, in return for a commission. A marine insurance company may agree to pay a certain sum should a loss occur in return for the payment of a premium.

Un-discharged Bankrupt: a bankrupt who has been legally allowed to resume business dealings. He is not allowed to resume business under another name and cannot be made a company director.

Unemployment: involuntary un-application or un-engagement of factors of production, usually labour, in productive activities. The part of the labour force that are willing and ready to work but cannot find work are said to be unemployed. This phenomenon is a fall-out of industrialization which occasioned increasing specialization of labour and complexity of structure and organization of production activities. Industrialized economies, with higher output per man and higher standard of living, are more prone to unemployment than those with primitive production arrangements where available hands may be engaged in doing simple, subsistent tasks.

Types of Unemployment

1. *Structural*: refers unemployment brought about by changes in the pattern of production.
2. *Cyclical* or mass unemployment cuts across most sectors of the economy, and is brought about by low aggregate demand for goods and services due to recession or depression. During a recession or depression, producers lay-off or retrench workers due to low demand for their goods and services.
3. *Seasonal*: some industries witness boom or relatively higher production during certain seasons and low. Seasonal unemployment is unemployment brought about reduced employment during the off season. For example, in agriculture more people are employed during the planting and harvest seasons. The construction industry retrenches some workers during the rainy season as work is usually less. Seasonal unemployment is common with or unskilled labour.
4. *Technological* or frictional unemployment: this refers to unemployment due to changes in the technology or method or producing or rendering a service; the introduction of the computer and GSM telephony made some workers redundant and had to be laid off by their employers.
5. *Voluntary* unemployment: This type of unemployment is due to refusal to work. It refers to a situation

when where people who are fit and qualified to work refuse to take up existing employment opportunities e.g. because such people want to continue to be dependants to their relatives or the state.

6. *Disguised* unemployment or under-employment. Under-employment is a situation when people are employed doing jobs for which they are over qualified because they could not find the job for which they are qualified. For example, when an unemployed engineer converts his vehicle into a taxi in order to makes ends meet. It is described as disguised because it is not obvious, he is actually unemployed.
7. *Residual* unemployment refers to unemployment due to all other causes including those who cannot work due to disabilities or handicap.

Unemployment Rate: the total of those who are able and willing to work without current employment as percentage of the total labour force.

Unfavourable Balance: refers to an adverse or debit balance (imports are greater than exports) in a country's Balance of Payment or Balance of Trade.

Unit Elasticity: the elasticity of demand is said to be unitary or equal to unity if a change in price brings about a proportionate change in demand. For example, a five per cent change in price brings about a five per cent change in demand.

Unit of Account: one of the functions of money is that it serves as a unit of account i.e. accounts can be kept and expressed in terms of money. As a unit of account, relative prices can be assigned to goods and services, and there facilitate exchange. This overcomes one of the problems of barter. Households, businesses and government can show how much they spend, earn and have in terms of money.

Unit Trust: a form of collective investment trust under which thousands of small investors pool their resources to purchase shares of quoted companies under the management of a fund manager. Fund managers minimize risk by diversifying or spreading risk among different companies and sectors while maximizing returns and liquidity. Unit trusts make it possible for the smallest of investors to participate in the capital market, and help to pool capital funds for investment from diverse sources. Unit trust are regulated and overseen by the Securities and Exchange Commission, the apex body of the capital market. Contrast Investment Trusts.

United Nations Conference on Trade and Tariffs, (UNCTAD): United Nations forum for discussing international trade problems of developing countries. The conference was first convened in 1964, in Geneva, Switzerland. The conference has recorded limited success because of the disadvantaged position of developing countries in international trade.

Universal Bank: a bank that provides a commercial and investment banking services.

Unsecured Creditor: a creditor without a collateral security.

Utility: the amount of satisfaction a consumer derives from a commodity at a particular time. Utility, like satisfaction, is not usefulness; it has no ethical significance; utility, like satisfaction, is related to time as what is satisfactory now may not be at another time; utility, like satisfaction, is a subjective idea, in that it varies between individuals.

Utility Function: an algebraic expression that shows the level of satisfaction a consumer derives from levels of consumption of a commodity.

Utmost Good Faith or *'Uberrima fides'*: the principle that parties to a contract must disclose all relevant particulars and details likely to influence a decision to enter into the contract. This is one of the principles of insurance. A person entering into an insurance contract must not make a false statement and must disclose all material facts e.g. any health issues, in the case of a life assurance. Also the insurer must make clear the terms of the cover being offered.

V

Value-Added Tax (VAT): an indirect tax levied on the difference in value between a firm's input cost and output price.

Value judgement: an assessment of the rightness or wrongness of a decision or course of action. This is a question of ethics

Value of Money: the value of money is reflected in changes in prices of the goods and services that money can buy.

Venture capital: start-up capital provided to businesses with perceived long-term potential.

Variable Cost (VC): costs that change as output changes. For example, cost of raw materials. All costs are variable in the long-run.

Variance: a statistical measure of dispersion of a set of data from the mean. The variance of a given set of numbers, 1,2,3,4,5,6,7,8,9,10 is calculated thus:

x	X-X	Mean Deviation (MD)	MD²
1	1-5.5	-4.5	20.25
2	2-5.5	-3.5	12.25
3	3-5.5	-2.5	6.25
4	4-5.5	-1.5	2.25
5	5-5.5	-0.5	0.25
6	6-5.5	0.5	0.25
7	7-5.5	1.5	2.25
8	8-5.5	2.5	6.25
9	9-5.5	3.5	12.25
10	10-5.5	4.5	20.25
$\mathcal{X}$=55			82.5

Variance = 82.5/10 = 8.25

Velocity of Circulation: the rate at which money circulates; the number of times, on the average, that a unit of money changes hands during a given period. For example, a single N200 note may be used for 5 different transactions in a week e.g. between the news vendor, barber, taxi cab driver, mechanic, seamstress, and launderer, in effect doing N1000 worth of work. Thus, it may be derived by dividing the total spending by the amount of money.

Velocity of Circulation =
$$\frac{\text{Total Spending}}{\text{Amount of Money}}$$

It affects the value of money as it brings about the same effect as changes in the quantity of money. It is a measure of the level of business activity in the economy, and a determinant of the value of money; The variable, V, in the equation of exchange, MV=PT, of the Quantity *Theory Of Money*,

Vertical Integration: merger of firms at different stages of production. For example, when a cocoa farming enterprise merges with or absorbs a beverage making enterprise. The output of the farming enterprise becomes the input of the beverage maker. Firms integrate or merge in in order to reap economies of scale from larger operations.

Vicious Circle of Poverty or Under-development: the self-reinforcing circumstances and conditions that characterize developing countries or individuals that perpetuate under-development or poverty; low income gives rise to low savings and investment which give rise to low capital which give rise to low production which give rise to low income, etc. In order to break from this circle, intervention from the outside may be imperative. Such intervention may be in the form of imported or borrowed capital/and or expertise/education.

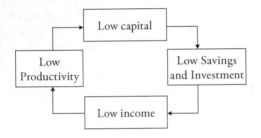

Visible trade: (international trade) part of the current account of the balance of payment concerned with exports and imports of merchandise (goods).

Visible balance: the balance of trade: the difference between exports and in the imports of merchandise, as opposed to services, into a country. Invisible balance is used to refer to the difference in export and import of services such as banking, insurance, aviation, shipping, tourism, etc.

Visible Items: goods or merchandise e.g. equipment and machines as opposed to services, in the Balance of Payments.

Vital Statistics: the birth and death rate statistics of a country.

Voluntary liquidation: winding up of a company by resolution of its shareholders as opposed to winding up or liquidation brought about by a court order.

Voucher: a document stating the fact a payment has been made.

W

Wages: the price of labour; the general term applied to the earnings of labour for its role or contribution in production i.e. as a factor of production.

The following points are worth noting: Wage vs Salary: Wage is a variable cost whereas salary is fixed cost, in the short-run, as it does not vary with changes in output. Thus, wages is treated in the Trading account in the calculation of Cost of Goods Sold and Gross Profit, while salary is treated in the Profit and Loss Account in the calculation of Net Profit. However, the term 'wage' is used in economic to include salary.

Nominal wage vs Real Wages: Nominal wages refers to payments in terms of cash or money. It does not account for changes in the value of money overtime i.e. inflation / deflation; nor changes in income tax. Thus in comparing the amount received by a worker at different times, it is necessary to avoid 'money illusion' by considering the goods and services the income/wages can buy. Real wages is wages in terms of the goods and services money wages can afford.

In comparing nominal wages received by workers in different occupations, it is necessary to account for benefits and payments in kind which may be inseparable from a job such as free air tickets for airline workers, free barrack accommodation for soldiers, etc.

Wages: Theories of Determination:
Wage Fund Theory of Wages: this the classical economists view of wage determination. The theory holds that the amount available to pay wages is related to the amount of capital available. Thus the amount available to pay wages is a definite sum, i.e. a wage fund. This means, according to this theory, that there is fixed number of workers that may be employed; to employ more means that less wages will be payable.

Subsistent Theory of Wages: This theory holds that wages should be equal to the level necessary to maintain the minimum level of subsistence. It asserts that if wages rise above the subsistence level, workers will marry early, increase the birth rate and the supply of labour and wages will fall back to the level of subsistence.

- Criticism
  1. Higher wages leads to Higher Aspirations: It is wrong to suppose that increase in income leads to early marriage; increase in income leads to increase in standard of living and aspirations. A well paid worker will dare to dream to improve his status in life e.g. run a business, improve his level of education, etc.; he will in fact set certain goals to attain before considering marriage.
  2. Demand Side Ignored: The theory excludes the demand side and considers only the supply side (birth rate). Even if there is an increase in

the supply of labour due to early marriage, it is also possible there will be corresponding increase in demand for labour.

3. Trade Unions Ignored: the fact that trade unions often affect the setting wages is ignored by the theory of subsistent wages.

4. Occupational factors: the fact that people, in different occupations, but with the comparable level of education and training differ in earnings, is also ignored by the theory of subsistent wages.

Market Theory of Wages: wages is the price of labour, and like other prices is determined by the interaction of market forces in the factor market, in this case, the labour market. In this sense, wage is a function of the interaction of the demand for and the supply of labour in free market system. Thus wages should rise so long as demand for labour is higher than supply e.g. during periods of economic boom; when a point of stability is reached in the business cycle, and business firms are cutting back on production, demand for labour will reduce and wages will tend to fall. The wage rate, therefore, will be determined at that point where the demand for and the supply of labour are equal.

However, labour legislations e.g. laws on minimum wage, which stipulates the minimum payable to labour; stipulation of retirement age and maximum working hours, as well as the bargaining power of labour unions, can only be ignored in theory.

Marginal Productivity Theory of Wages: This theory derives from the marginal theory of distribution, which holds that the amount payable for any factor of production is equal to the marginal product of that factor. To pay more than the marginal product, is to increase cost more the increase in revenue derivable from employing it.

The wage payable is therefore that amount that equates the income received from employing a worker to the wages paid to him. Thus a firm may continue to employ so long as the revenue receivable by employing a worker is more than the wages payable until marginal revenue is equal wage payable. Beyond this point, addition to revenue will be less than addition to cost.

Criticism

1. Perfect Competition Assumed: Marginal productivity theory is applicable only under conditions of perfect completion which is wholly theoretical concept. The theory assumes that units of labour are homogenous i.e. exactly the same, so that their marginal products can be mathematically determined.

2. Marginal Analysis not Applicable: In fact, while the employment of a particular worker may be surplus to requirements, the non-employment of another individual may seriously disrupt the operations of a business.

3. Impractical: while the theory is sound its reasoning, calculating the marginal product of any factor of production, including labour, is generally impossible.

4. In reality, business prospects and sentiments determine decisions to employ.

5. The productivity of a worker does not depend on his own efforts and efficiency but as much on the quality of other factors especially tools/capital.

Bargaining Theory of Wages: this theory holds that wage payable is the outcome of the process of bargaining between labour union and management in the context of the prevailing economic conditions, i.e. boom or depression/recession. The bargaining power of labour union is function of several factors including the possible impact on the economy; for example a strike by petrol tanker drivers or airline pilots is bound to be more severe than a strike by grocers. However, the prevailing economic situation cannot be ignored. For example, in a period of depression, with high level of unemployment, trade unions will be a weak position to exert their demands.

Wall Street: the financial district of New York, United States of America., where the New York Stock Exchange is located. The term is often used to represent America's financial sector as a whole.

Wants: The desires or wishes people have for goods or services. Wants are the basis of production, and the higher the quantity of wants backed by purchasing power, the higher the level of production. The fact that resources required for production are limited or scarce is the reason for the study of economics.

Warehousing: the act of storing goods until they are needed, performed partly by the manufacturer but mainly by the wholesaler, which makes it possible for goods to be produced in anticipation of demand. Warehousing make it possible for the manufacturer to concentrate his efforts and resources in production without having to worry about storage or immediate sale. In this way, production is not affected by the upswings and downswings in demand. Warehousing also make 'buffer' stock

available which may be vital in cushioning a sudden increase in demand, caused, for example, by change in weather. The cost of warehousing is ultimately borne by the final consumer, but the absence of this service will result in higher price.

Warranty: a promise that in case there is a failure there is a failure to perform any of the terms of a contract, the party injured by such a failure shall be entitled to compensation. The breach of warranty entitles the party injured to damages but does not entitle it to repudiate the contract.

Washington Consensus: term first used by John Williamson of the Institute of International Economics to describe a set of ten economic reform propositions advocated by the International Monetary Fund, the World Bank, the Inter-American Development Bank and the United States Treasury Department, all based in Washington D.C., for Latin American countries in 1989.

The ten reform proposals are as follows:
Fiscal Discipline: the need to maintain government expenditure within limits and avoid budget deficits.

Rationalization of Public Expenditure: re-ordering public expenditure in favour of pro-poor and pro-growth such as basic health care, education and infrastructure and away from subsidies.

Liberalization of Interest Rates: interest rates should be determined by the market not administratively imposed.

Competitive Exchange Rate: the exchange rate should be determined by the demand and supply of foreign exchange, reflecting the country's trading strength/balance of payment position, rather than fixed.

Trade Liberalization: reduce barriers to international trade as much possible.

Liberalization of Inward Foreign Direct Investment: removal of impediments to inflow of foreign direct capital needed for investments.

Privatization: selling of government-owned enterprises.

Deregulation: removal of restrictions on entry into certain industries.

Property Rights: enabling the private sector to gain property rights at reasonable costs.

Tax Reform: combining a broad the tax base with moderate marginal tax rates.

These were later generalized as pre-conditions for other developing countries to implement in order to secure financial assistance. The term captures the shift towards free market reforms that characterized the 1980s, mirroring the thinking in influential western capitals at the time viz. Reaganomics (after President Ronald Reagan) and Thatcherism (after Prime Minister Margaret Thatcher). It marked a paradigm shift from the 1970s, characterized by Keynesianism, which ascribed a major role to government in the economy.

While the term has become largely discredited in the popular press and among politicians and activists, its content and essence still dictate the reform agenda, though the seeming market fundamentalism and fervour that initially accompanied their

initial implementation has been tempered by the apparent dislocation that was experienced in the economies on which they were first tried.

Waybill: a document detailing and accompanying goods in transit.

Wealth: a stock of goods that has the following features: 1. transferable from one person to another; 2. possesses utility, that is capable of giving satisfaction; 3. can be valued in monetary terms; 4. scarce or limited in supply, and 4. owned by someone, company or community (social capital such as library, hospitals, schools, etc).

Welfare Economics: the branch of economics that studies how economic policies impact or affect the overall welfare of the community or society.

Welfare Economies of Scale: See Economies of Scale

West African Clearing House (WACH): clearing house of West African (ECOWAS) central banks formed in 1975 and based in Freetown, Sierra Leone. It settles payments between member countries in local currency as much as possible, and thereby helps them conserve foreign exchange.

West African Currency Board (WACB): the central monetary authority in British West Africa before central banks was set up in respectively in Nigeria, Ghana, Sierra Leone and The Gambia. It was established in 1912. It issued the West African pound in Ghana, Gambia, and Sierra Leone. It essentially functioned as a money changer, exchanging the sterling for the West African pound and vice versa.

West African Economic and Monetary Union (UEMOA): see UEMOA

West African Monetary Zone (WAMZ): a group of six West African countries—Gambia, Ghana, Guinea, Nigeria and Sierra Leone—created in year 2000 for the purpose of creating a monetary union and adoption of a common currency—the *ECO*—by 2015. It is envisaged that the ECO shall eventually merge with the CFA Franc so that members of both groupings shall have a single currency between them. See also Monetary Union.

Whole Life Policy: an assurance policy which lasts the entire life time of the assured; premium is paid until the death of the assured, whether the full amount assured has been paid or not; the sum assured is payable only at death of the assured. Compare Endowment Assurance.

Wholesaler: trader who buys in whole or bulk units and normally links the manufacturer with the retailer. He may sometimes deal directly with consumer, especially consumers who desire to buy in large or wholesale quantities. The following types of wholesalers may be identified; *national wholesaler*: this may be the manufacturer's national representative authorized to deal on his behalf nationally; *Regional wholesaler*, who may cover a state or states; *local wholesaler*, who may cover a town or locality; *importers* who buy directly from producers abroad for onward sale to local wholesalers.

Functions of the wholesaler to the manufacturer

1. *Buying in bulk from the producer:* The wholesaler can afford to buy in bulk from the manufacturer because he has the capital. This enables the manufacturer to concentrate on his primary task of production. Without the wholesaler the manufacturer will have to deal with a large number of retailers buying small quantities or a multitude of consumers buying even smaller quantities. This will be a huge distraction.

2. *Market information:* Keeping manufacturers informed of the state of the market. This enables the manufacturer to respond effectively to the market situation as production is done in anticipation of demand.

3. *Buying in bulk:* by buying in bulk, the wholesaler relieves the manufacturer of the time and expense of dealing with thousands of orders from retailers.

4. *Warehousing:* by warehousing the goods, the factory is free of produced goods so that production can continue ahead of demand.

5. *Financing:* by paying the manufacturer in cash in advance, the manufacturer has needed to cash to finance operations. Even when he does not pay in advance, the manufacturer can use confirmed orders from the wholesaler to secure short-term loans from his bank.

6. *Completion of production:* the wholesaler sometimes completes production of certain goods by blending, sorting, packaging, etc.

7. *Transportation:* the goods are often conveyed from the factory or plant to warehouse by the wholesaler's trucks and vans. This saves the manufacturer transport and logistics expenses and problems.

8. *Branding*: the wholesaler sometimes collects goods from numerous small

producers and markets them in his own trade name or brand.

9. *Advertising:* the wholesaler most times undertakes advertisement of goods in his area.

10. *Trade Promotion and Exhibitions:* sometimes the wholesaler joins with manufacturer to hold trade promotions and exhibitions.

11. Risk bearing: By buying and paying the manufacturer in advance, the wholesaler bears the risk of fall in prices

Functions of the Wholesaler to the Retailer

1. *Breaking the bulk for the retailer:* The wholesaler sells in smaller quantities the retailer can afford. This makes it possible for the retailer to stock the different varieties consumers require

2. Convenient Location: the wholesaler is usually closer to the retailer in terms of physical location.

3. Convenient Quantities: the wholesaler makes it possible for the retailer in smaller quantities that he can afford.

4. Credit facilities: the retailer often buys on credit terms from the wholesaler; allowing the retailer to pay after making sales. In this way, the wholesaler finances the business of the retailer.

5. *Stabilization of prices:* By holding stock of goods and allowing a regular supply in to the market, the wholesaler prevents fluctuation in prices.

6. *Preparation:* the goods are prepared for selling by the grading, pre-packing, and sorting carried out by the wholesaler. The retailer is not equipped to handle this function.

7. *Ready stocks:* by stocks of goods held by the wholesaler assures the retailer of ready stocks and supplies.

Winding Up: the legal process of liquidating or by which the business of a limited liability company, as a going concern, is brought to an end. This process may be involuntary, brought about by a court order, following action brought by a creditor on an insolvent company. Winding up may also be voluntary i.e. the decision of the members.

Working Capital: same as circulating capital.

Working Partner: a member of a partnership who takes an active part in the management of the business. Compare sleeping partner.

Working Population: the labour force of a country, generally of the 18-70 age-bracket.

World Bank, The: The World Bank Group consist of the International Bank for Reconstruction and Development; the International Development Association, and the International Finance Corporation. The organization was set up alongside the IMF at the Bretton Woods Conference in 1944, to help rebuild the European economies after the end of the Second World War. Today, the IBRD assists developing countries with loans for infrastructural development as well as technical assistance in areas of economic planning and project management among others. The International Development Association (IDA) provides concessionary finance assistance i.e. low interest loans and grants to under-developed or very poor countries which do not qualify for IBRD loans from funds provided by donor countries. The International Finance

Corporation (IFC) supports private sector projects. The IBRD derives its income by activities on the international capital market where it issues bonds, and from lending from its reserves.

World Trade Organization: organization founded to promote free trade among countries by ensuring adherence to international trade agreements and serving as platform for trade negotiations and settlement of trade disputes. The organization emerged from the General Agreement for Tariffs and Trade (GATT) which was one the many international organizations, along with the World Bank and IMF, formed after the World War II.

The GATT took the place of the still-born International Trade Organization (ITO) which failed to get the support and approval of the United States of America and other key players. GATT evolved through seven rounds of trade negotiations between 1947 and the 1994.

Each of the rounds of trade negotiations under GATT resulted in major trade concessions and reductions between members; the Kennedy Round in 1964 saw the signing of anti-dumping agreement after over three years of negotiations.

The WTO was one of the outcomes of the Uruguay Round in January 1995, which also gave rise to the General Agreement on Trade in Services (GATS) and the Trade Related aspects of Intellectual Property Rights (TRIPS). Thus GATT became one the three major trade agreements making up the WTO.

The WTO has evolved five principles to serve as the ground rules of international trade:
1. Non-discrimination:
    - No Most Favoured Nation (MFN) treatment: grant a trading partner a special favour and you will have to do the same to all WTO members.
    - No special national treatment: foreigners and citizens must be treated the same.
2. Freer Trade
3. Predictability: certainty in business by promising not to raise tariffs
4. Promoting Fair Competition
5. Encouraging Development and Economic Reforms.

Y

Yield: The annual rate of return from a financial security, expressed as a percentage of the current market price of the security.

Appendices

BASIC TOOLS FOR ECONOMIC ANALYSIS

Tables, Charts, and Graphs are used in Economics to present data (units of information) in an orderly manner, which helps to make sense of the information contained.

Tables: A table consists of properly-titled rows and columns. It summarizes, helps to understand and makes for easy comparison of the facts or data presented.

The following relates to government expenditure in a three-year period:

2000: military defence: N24million, External relations N39m, roads N80; transportation and communication N478m; Housing N 131m; internal affairs 521m; Sports 1979; rural development 854m. Education N240m

2001: military defence: N52million, External relations N67m, roads N150; transportation and communication N157m; Housing N2,115m; internal affairs 1380m; Sports 1600; rural development N1,450; Education N380m

2002: military defence: N95million, External relations N90m, roads N250; transportation and communication N668m; Housing N3, 009m; internal affairs 1,765m; Sports 2811m; rural development N2,345m; Education N454m.

The above information could be orderly and more meaningfully presented in a table:

Charts and Graphs

Graphs are used to show the relationship between two variables e.g. price and quantity demanded. The variables are represented on the horizontal and vertical axes respectively. A curve may be traced on the graph. The shape of the curve shows on the type of relationship that exists between the variables. Relationship may be direct or inverse as illustrated in the two graphs below:

Pie Charts: are circular diagrams in which information is presented in sectors.

Exercise:

The table below shows the budgetary allocation of Delta State to selected sectors in a particular year. Present the information in the table in the form of pie chart. Show your workings clearly

Sectors	Amount (N million)
Education	6250
Mining	2150
Agriculture	4300
Infrastructure	2400
Health	2900

Solution:
Workings:

Sectors	Amount		
Education	6,250	$\frac{6250}{18,000} \times 360$	125
Mining	2,150	$\frac{2150}{18,000} \times 360$	43
Agriculture	4,300	$\frac{4300}{18,000} \times 360$	86
Infrastructure	2,400	$\frac{2400}{18,000} \times 360$	48
Health	2,900	$\frac{2900}{18,000} \times 360$	58
	18,000		360

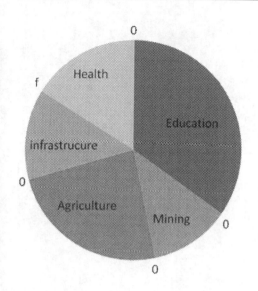

Bar charts

A bar chart makes for easy comparison and contrast of data or facts presented. At a glance we are able to see how one variable compares with another.

- **Simple bar chart**
  Illustrative example
  SSCE 1996: The daily sales of department store for one week are as follows:

	Monday	Tuesday	Wednesday	Thursday	Friday	Saturday
Sales	1750	1000	3500	2250	1000	2500

a) Present the above data in a bar graph
b) Calculate the average sales for the week

Solution:

a)

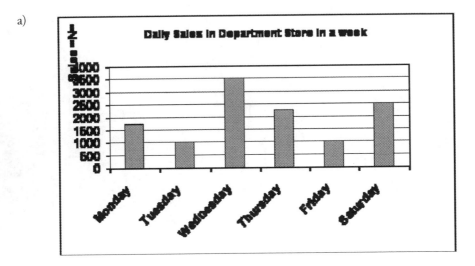

b)
Average sales per week = total sales/6 days = 1750 +1000+3500+2250+1000+2500 = 12,000/6 days = =N=2,000.

- **Component Bar Chart**
Illustrative example
- **SSCE June 1992**
The values of different types of accounts held in Nigerian banks for the period 1984 to 1988 are as follows (in =N= million)

Year	1984	1985	1986	1987	1988
Savings	100	120	120	180	200
Current	65	75	70	100	130
Fixed Deposit	40	45	60	145	50

Present the data above in the form of a component bar chart.
Solution:

—Multiple bar charts
The following table shows the sales of three brands of drinks of a retail shop during the first quarter of 2006.

Present the information in a multiple bar chart.

	January	Feb	March
Maltina	25	15	15
Malta	30	12	18
Amstel	15	8	6

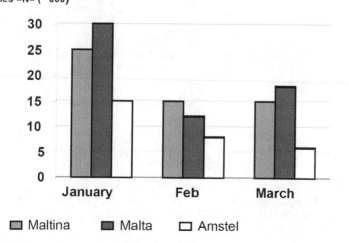

Sales for 1st Quarter 2006

Sales =N= (' 000)

Pictograms: in a pictogram pictures or drawings are used represent data. Pictograms are not complicated and information conveyed can easily be interpreted by almost anybody. For example, given the table below, showing
Imports of *BlueBird* buses into Nigeria

Year	Number of buses (millions)
2005	4
2004	2
2003	3

The same information may be represented in a pictogram as shown below:

Where a bus-like drawing represent 1million buses.

Histograms may be described as special bar charts in which variables in distribution are presented against their respective frequencies. The variables are scaled on the x-axis while the frequencies are scaled on the y-axis. There are no gaps between bars except were the frequency is zero.

Cardinal Utility Theory
According to this theory, the utility can be measured in specific units called 'utils'.

Assumptions
1. The consumer is a rational being; he aims to maximize the satisfaction (utility) he derives from his income or expenditure.
2. The consumer derives a definite amount of satisfaction from each unit of the commodity consumed.
3. Utility is cardinal
4. The marginal utility of money is constant at any point in time.
5. The consumer has full knowledge of the different commodities, their prices and amount of utility that can be derived from them.
6. Diminishing Marginal utility
7. Total utility derivable from the consumption of a commodity depends on the number of units consumed.

Equilibrium of the Consumer

1. **Single commodity**: where only one commodity is involved, the consumer will maximize his utility at the point where the marginal utility of the commodity is equal to the price of the commodity, i.e. $MU_{X} = P_{X}$

2. **Combination of commodities**:

   1st Criterion: Utility is maximized when the MU per last kobo spent on one commodity is equal to the MU per last kobo spent on any other commodity. Thus, $MU_{A}/P_{A} = MU_{B}/P_{B} = MU_{C}/P_{C} \ldots MU_{n}/P_{n}$

2nd Criterion: Total expenditure must not exceed the consumer's total income. This means that the consumer's ability to maximize his utility is subject to his income constraint.

Exercise: In the table below, the price of commodity y is N2 and that of x is N1 while the individual has an income of N12. Determine the combination of the two commodities the individual should consume to maximize his utility.

Q	1	2	3	4	5	6	7	8
MU_Y	16	14	12	10	8	8	4	2
MU_X	11	10	9	8	7	6	5	4

Solution

Qx	Px	MUx	MUx/Px	Qy	Py	MUy	MUy/Py
1	1	11	11	1	2	16	8
2	1	10	10	2	2	14	7
3	1	9	9	3	2	12	6
4	1	8	8	4	2	10	5
5	1	7	7	5	2	8	4
6	1	6	6	6	2	8	4
7	1	5	5	7	2	4	2
8	1	4	4	8	2	2	1

If he buys 4 units of x and 1 unit of y, his will spend a total of $4(1) + 8(2) = 4 + 16 = N20$. This is not feasible or possible as he only has N12.

The second condition or criteria is met when,
$MUx/ Px = MUy/ Py = 6$;
At this point, the second condition gives, $6x + 3y = 6(1) + 3(2) = N12.00$

1st condition: $MU_x/P_x = MU_y/P_y$

MUx/Px = MUy/Py in the range of purchases high-lighted.

2nd Condition: the consumer can only maximize his utility within the constraint of his income.

Criticism of the Cardinal Theory

1. Utility is a personal psychological phenomenon which cannot be precisely measured or calculated
2. The utility of money cannot be constant because as income rises, the marginal utility of money changes.
3. Utility cannot be measured in terms of money.

Worked Example

Orange	Total utility	Mangoes	Total utility
1	100	1	50
2	190	2	95
3	270	3	135
4	340	4	170
5	400	5	200
6	450	6	225
7	490	7	245
8	520	8	260

The table above shows Mr. Y's total utility schedule for oranges and mangoes. The prices of oranges and mangoes are $1.00 each. Mr. Y has $10.00 to spend on the goods. Use the information contained in the table to answer the questions that follow.

a) Calculate the marginal utility for all the levels of consumption for the goods.
b) At equilibrium, how many oranges and mangoes will the consumer buy?
c) i) State the law of diminishing marginal utility. ii) State the condition for utility satisfaction

Solution (a)

Oranges		Mangoes	
Total utility	Marginal utility	Total utility	Marginal utility
100	100	50	
190	190 – 100 = 90	95	
270	270–190 = 80	135	
340	340 – 270 =70	170	
400	400-340 = 60	200	
450	450-400 = 50	225	
490	490-450 = 40	245	
520	520 – 490 = 30	260	

(b)

Q_r	P_r	MU_r	$MUrPr$	Q_m	P_m	MU_m	$MUmP_m$
1	1	100	100	1	1	50	50
2	1	90	90	2	1	45	45
3	1	80	80	3	1	40	40
4	1	70	70	4	1	35	35
5	1	60	60	5	1	30	30
6	1	50	50	6	1	25	25
7	1	40	40	7	1	20	20
8	1	30	30	8	1	15	15

Utility is maximized when

$$MU_R/P_R = MU_M/P_M$$

This condition is satisfied at the following combinations or bundles

6 oranges, 5 mangoes
7 oranges, 3 mangoes
8 oranges, 5 mangoes

However since the consumer has only $10.00 to spend, he must settle for 7 oranges and 3 mangoes, because he cannot afford the order combinations.

WORKED EXAMPLES

The following is the summary of the books of MMM Ltd during the year:

Sales	200,000.00

Purchases	100,000.00
Creditors	60,000.00
Overdraft	35,000.00
Sales Returns	12,000.00
Return Inwards	15,000.00
Prepayments	15,250.00
Premises	80,000.00
Machinery	20,000.00
Cash	50,750.00
Debtors	30,000.00
Stock	50,000.00
Motor Vehicle	50,000.00
Office Furniture	30,000.00
Rent	13,500.00
Wages	5,000.00
Transport	1,000.00
Electricity	2,500.00

At the end of the year Stock was valued at N40, 000.00

Calculate:

1. Fixed assets
2. Current Assets
3. Current Liabilities
4. Capital Employed
5. Working capital
6. Cost of goods sold
7. Gross profit
8. Net profit
9. Gross profit percentage
10. Net profit percentage
11. Average Stock
12. Net Sales

SOLUTION

TOTAL FIXED ASSETS	N
Premises	80,000.00
Machinery	20,000.00
Motor Vehicle	50,000.00
Office Furniture	30,000.00
	180,000.00

2. CURRENT ASSETS

Prepayments	15,250.00
Cash	50,750.00
Debtors	30,000.00
Stock	40,000.00
	136,000.00

3. CURRENT LIABILITIES

Creditors	60,000.00
Overdraft	35,000.00
4. CAPITAL EMPLOYED	**95,000.00**

= Total Assets less Current Liabilities

Total Fixed Assets

Premises	80,000.00	
Machinery	20,000.00	
Motor Vehicle	50,000.00	
Office Furniture	30,000.00	180,000.00
less:		
Current Liabilities		
Creditors	60,000.00	
Overdraft	35,000.00	(95,000.00)
Capital Employed		**85,000.00**

5. WORKING CAPITAL

Current Assets		
Prepayments	15,250.00	
Cash	50,750.00	
Debtors	30,000.00	
Stock	40,000.00	
	136,000.00	136,000.00
less:		
Current Liabilities		
Creditors	60,000.00	
Overdraft	35,000.00	(95,000.00)
Working Capital		41,000.00

6. COST OF GOODS SOLD

Opening Stock	50,000.00
Purchases	100,000.00
	150,000.00
less: Closing Stock	(40,000.00)
Cost of Goods Sold	110,000.00

7. GROSS PROFIT

		N
Sales		200,000.00
less: Return Inwards		(15,000.00)
		185,000.00
Opening Stock	50,000.00	
Purchases	100,000.00	
	150,000.00	
less: Closing Stock	(40,000.00)	(110,000.00)
Gross Profit		75,000.00

8. NET PROFIT

		N
Sales		200,000.00
less: Return Inwards		(15,000.00)
		185,000.00
Opening Stock	50,000.00	

Purchases	100,000.00	
	150,000.00	
less: Closing Stock	(40,000.00)	(110,000.00)
Gross Profit		75,000.00
less: Expenses		
Rent	13,500.00	
Wages	5,000.00	
Transport	1,000.00	
Electricity	2,500.00	(22,000.00)
Net Profit		53,000.00

9. GROSS PROFIT PERCENTAGE

$$\frac{\text{GROSS PROFIT.}}{\text{SALES}} \quad X \quad 100$$

$$\frac{75,000}{200,000} \quad X \quad 100 \quad = \quad \underline{37.5\%}$$

10. NET PROFIT PERCENTAGE

10. $\frac{\text{NET PROFIT}}{\text{SALES}} \quad X \quad 100$

$$\frac{53,000}{200,0000} \quad X \quad 100 \quad = \quad 0.265$$

11. Average Stock

$= \dfrac{\text{opening stock + closing stock}}{2}$

$= \dfrac{50,000 + 40,000}{2}$

= N45,000,00

12. NET SALES

Sales less Return Inwards

= N200,000 – N15,000 = N185,000

3ZEE Ltd has authorized share capital of 5,000,000 ordinary shares of N5.00 each. The company issued 3,000,000 ordinary shares and all shares were subscribed and paid for at N2 a share, except 1,000 shares subscribed by Mr. Tony.

Calculate i) authorized capital ii) issued capital iii) called-up share capital iv) Paid-up capital

i) Authorized capital:
    5,000,000 x N5 = N25, 000,000.00

ii) Issued Share Capital:
    3,000,000 x N2 = N6, 000,000.00

iii) Called-up share capital:
    3,000,000 x N2 = N6, 000,000.00

iv) Paid-up Share Capital:
    (3,000,000 less 1,000) x N2 = N5,998,000

Common Abbreviations in Commerce

A/c   account
Ad val.   Ad valorem, i.e. according to the value
Amt.   Amount
Appro.   Approval
Bal.   Balance
b/d   brought down
B/Dft   Bank Draft
B/E   Bill of Exchange
b/f   brought forward
B/L   Bill of Lading
Bros.   Brothers
B.S.   Bill of Sale

Carr. Fwd   Carriage Forward
Carr. Pd.   Carriage paid
Cat.   Catalogue
c/d   carried down
c. & f.   cost and freight
Cert.   Certificate
c/f   carried forward
chq   cheque
c.i.f.   Cost, insurance and freight
C/N   Credit Note
Co.   Company
C.O.D   Cash on delivery
Cr.   Credit
cum div..   including dividend
C.W.O   Cash With Order

Deb.   Debentures
Del. cred.   Del credere
Dept.   Department
Disc.   Discount
Div.   Dividend
D/N   Debit Note
Doz.   dozen
Dr.   Debit

E.& O. E.   Errors and Omissions Exempted
EFT   Electronic Funds Transfer
E.O.M.   End of Month
E.T.A   Estimated Time of Arrival
E.T.D.   Estimated time of Departure
ex. div.   excluding dividend
E.U.   European Union
Exors.   Executors
Exs.   Expenses

F.O.   Firm Order
f.o.b.   free on board
f.o.r.   Free on rail
FT   Funds Transfer
Fwd   forward

G.A.   General Average
gr.   gross

H.P.   Hire Purchase

id.   the same
i.e.   that is
Inc.   Incorporated
Int.   Interest
Inv.   Invoice
I.P.S   International Paper Sizes
L/C   Letter of Credit
Ltd   Limited

Max.   Maximum
Min.   Minimum
M.O.   Money Order
N.A.   not available
NBV   Net Book Value
n.d.   no date

Ord. Order
O/D Overdraft
O/R Owner's Risk
o/s out of stock

p. (pp.) page (s)
P.A. Particular Average
PAYE Pay As You Earn
Par. Paragraph
P/C Prices Current
Pd. Paid
per pro or **p.p** on behalf of
pkg. Package
P.L. Partial Loss
P/N Promissory Note
P.O. Postal Order

Ppd Pre-paid
Pro. forma taking the form of
PV Par Value

q.v. Which see

Recd received
Ref reference
Regd Registered

Sgd signed
S/N Shipping Note
Std Standard

T.L. Total Loss
x/d excluding dividend

World Currencies

Afghanistan-Afghani = 100 puls
Albania Lek = *100* qindarka
Algeria-Algerian dinar = *100* santeem
Angola-Kwanza = *100* cêntimos
Anguila-East Caribbean dollar = *100* cents
Antigua and Berbuda-East Caribbean dollar = *100* cents
Argentina-Peso = *100* centavos
Armenia-Dram = *100* luma
Aruba-Aruban florin = *100* qindarka
Australia-Australian dollar = *100* cents
Austria-Euro = *100* cents
Azerbaijan-manat = *100* qəpik
Bahamas-Bahamian dollar = *100* cents
Bahrain-Bahraini dinar = *1000* fils
Bangladesh-Taka = *100* poisha
Barbados-Barbados Dollar = *100* cents
Belarus-Ruble = *100* kapeykas
Belgium-Euro
Belize-Belize Dollar
Benin-CFA Franc = *100* centimes
Bermuda-Bermuda Dollar = *100* cents
Bolivia-Boliviano = *100* centavo
Bosnia-Herzegovina-Dinar
Botswana-Pula = *100* thebe
Brazil-Real = *100* centavos
Brunei-Brunei Dollar
Bulgaria-Lev = *100* stotinki
Burkina Faso-CFA Franc
Burundi-Burundian franc
Cambodia-Riel = *100* centimes
Cameroon-CFA Franc
Canada-Canadian Dollar
Canary Island-Euro
Cape Verde-Cape Verde Escudo = *100* centavos

Cayman Islands-Cayman Islands Dollar
Central African Republic-CFA Franc
Chad-CFA Franc
Channel Islands-Pound Sterling
Chile-Chilean Peso = *100* centavos
China-Yuan (Renminbi)
Colombia-Colombian peso = *100* centavos
Comoros, The-Comorian franc
Congo-CFA Franc
Congo, Democratic Republic of-Congolese Franc = *100* makuta
Costa Rica-Colon = *100* centimos
Cote d'Ivoire-CFA Franc
Croatia-Kuna
Cuba-Cuban peso
Cyprus-Cyprus pound
Czech Republic, The-Koruna
Denmark-Danish krone
Djibouti-Djibouti franc
Dominican Republic-Dominican peso
East Timor-US Dollar
Ecuador-Sucre
Egypt-Egyptian Pound
El Salvador-Colon
Equatorial Guinea-CFA franc
Eritrea-Ethiopian birr
Estonia-kroon
Ethiopia-Ethiopian birr
Fiji-Fijian Dollar
Finland-Euro
France-Euro
Gabon-CFA Franc
Gambia, The-Dalasi
Georgia-Lari
Germany-Euro
Ghana-cedi (= 100 pesewa)

Greece-Euro
Greenland-Danish krone
Grenada-East Caribbean Dollar
Guadeloupe-Euro
Guam-US Dollar
Guatemalia-Quetza
Guiana-Euro
Guinea-Guinean franc
Guinea-Bissau-Peso
Guyana-Guyana Dollar
Haiti-Gourde
Honduras-Lempira
Hong Kong-Hong Kong dollar
Hungary-forint
Iceland-Icelandic krona
India-Rupee
Indonesia-Rupiah
Iran-Rial (=100 dinars)
Iraq-Iraqi dinar (
Ireland, Republic of-Euro
Isreal-New Isreali shekel
Italy-Euro
Jamaica-Jamaican Dollar
Japan-Yen
Jordan-Jordanian dinar
Kazakhstan-Tenge
Kenya-Kenyan shilling
Kiribati-Australian dollar
Korea, Democratic Republic of-Won
Korea-Republic of-won
Kuwaiti-Kuwaiti dinar
Kyrgyzatan-Som
Laos-New Kip
Latvia-Lat
Lebanon-Lebanese pound
Lesotho-Loti
Liberia-Liberian dollar
Lithuania-Litas
Luxembourg-Euro
Macao (Macau)-Pataca
Macedonia-Dinar
Madagascar-Franc Magache
Malawi-Kwacha
Malaysia-ringgit or Malaysian dollar

Maldives, Republic of-Rufiyaa
Mali-CFA Franc
Malta-Maltese Pound
Marshall Islands-US Dollar
Martinique-Euro
Mauritania-Ouguiya
Mauritius-Mauritian rupee
Mexico-Mexican peso
Micronesia-US dollar
Moldova-Leu
Monaco-Euro
Mongolia-Tughrik
Morocco-Dirham
Mozambique-Metical
Myanmar, Union of-Kyat
Namibia-Namibian dollar
Nepal-Nepalese rupee
Netherlands, The-Euro
New Zealand-New Zealand dollar
Nicaragua-Cordoba oro
Niger-CFA Franc
Nigeria-Naira
Norway-Norwagian krone
Oman, The Sultanate of-Rial Omani
Pakistan-Pakistan rupee
Palau-US Dollar
Panama-balboa
Papua New Guinea-Kina
Paraguay-Guarani
Peru-sol
Philippines-Philippine peso
Poland-zloty
Portugal-Euro
Puerto Rico-US Dollar
Qatar-Qatar riyal
Romania-Leu
Russia-Rouble
Rwanda-Rwandan franc
Sao Tome and Principe-Dobra
Suadi Arabia-Riyal
Senegal-CFA Franc
Seychelles rupee
Sierra Leone-Leone
Singapore-Singaporean dollar

Slovakia-Slovak koruna
Slovenia-Tolar
Solomon Island-Solomon Island dollar
Somalia-Somali shilling
South Africa-Rand
Spain-Euro
Sri Lanka-Sri Lankan rupee
Sudan-Sudanese dinar
Suriname-Suriname guilder
Swaziland-Lilangeni
Sweden-Krona
Switzerland-Swiss franc
Syria-Syrian pound
Taiwan-New Taiwan dollar
Tajikistan-Tajik rouble
Tanzania-Tanzanian shilling
Thailand-Baht
Togo-CFA franc
Tonga-

Trinidad and Tobago-Trinidad and Tobago
dollar
Tunisia-dinar
Turkey-Turkish Lira
Turkmenistan-Manat
Uganda-Ugandan shilling
Ukraine-Rouble
United Arab Emirates-Dirham
United Kingdom-Pound sterling
United States of America-US dollar
Uruguay-Peso
Uzbekistan-Soum
Vanuatu-Vatu
Vatican City-Euro
Venezuela-Bolivar
Vietnam-New dong
Western Sahara-Moroccan dirham
Yemen-Riyal
Zambia-Kwacha
Zimbabwe-Zimbabwean dollar